Ubuntu

18.04

LTS

Desktop

Applications
and
Administration

To Larisa, Ryan, and ?

Ubuntu 18.04 LTS Desktop: Applications and Administration
Richard Petersen

Surfing Turtle Press

Alameda, CA

www.surfingturtlepress.com

Please send inquiries to: editor@surfingturtlepress.com

ISBN   1-936280-52-3

ISBN-13   978-1-936280-52-0

Preface

This book covers the Ubuntu 18.04 LTS (Bionic Beaver) release, focusing on applications and administrative tools. The emphasis here is on what users will face when using Ubuntu, covering topics like installation, applications, software management, the Ubuntu desktops (GNOME and KDE), shell commands, network connections, and system administration tasks. Ubuntu 18.04 introduces several new features, as well as numerous smaller modifications. It is a long-term support release. The Ubuntu desktop with the GNOME interface is examined in detail. Ubuntu GNOME uses a Dock and a Dash (dashboard) to manage access to applications and devices. Advanced components are also examined such as the GRUB 2 boot loader, PulseAudio sound configuration, and Disk Utility (Udisks).

The Ubuntu desktop uses a Dock and a Dash (dashboard) to manage access to applications and devices. In addition, Ubuntu 18.04 desktop is based on GNOME 3, with several desktop configuration tools and the System Settings dialog. In addition, features such as messaging, the user switcher, desktop menus, and the GNOME Files file manager, are covered. The Kubuntu desktop, which uses KDE, provides a very different interface using plasma containers to support panels, menus, activities, configuration tools, and plasmoids (widgets). Ubuntu MATE is based on the traditional GNOME 2 desktop, with menus and panels.

Part 1 focuses on getting started, covering Ubuntu information and resources, using Ubuntu Live DVD/USB discs, installing and setting up Ubuntu, upgrading Ubuntu, basic use of the desktop interface, and connecting to wired and wireless networks. Repositories and their use are covered in detail. Ubuntu Software and Synaptic Package manager, which provides easy and effective software management, are both discussed.

Part 2 keys in on office, multimedia, mail, Internet, and social media applications such as the Evolution and Thunderbird email applications, the Videos media player, the Rhythmbox music player, and the LibreOffice office suite. The section includes coverage of the PulseAudio sound interface with its volume control support, Firefox Web browser, and VoIP applications like Skype and Ekiga.

Part 3 covers the Ubuntu, Kubuntu, Ubuntu MATE, Ubuntu Cinnamon, Xubuntu, and Lubuntu desktops. as well as the BASH shell. The Ubuntu desktop with the GNOME interface features a Dock, Dash, and system area menu. The Kubuntu desktop is examined which is based on the KDE desktop with features such as plasmoids, activities, panels, menus, KWin desktop effects, and the Discover software manager. Ubuntu MATE provides an older style desktop with the traditional GNOME 2 panels and menusAll the desktops are very different, but all access and install software from the Ubuntu software repositories. All are also official Ubuntu Flavours, different desktops but the same compatible software, most of which can run on any of the flavours.

The BASH shell interface is also explored, with its command editing, directory navigation, and file operations.

Part 4 deals with administration topics, first discussing system tools like the GNOME system monitor, the Disk Usage Analyzer, and Disk Utility (Udisks). Then a detailed chapter on Ubuntu system administration tools is presented, covering tasks such as managing users and file systems, Bluetooth setup, network folder sharing, backups, and printing. The network connections chapter covers a variety of network tasks, including manual configuration of wired and wireless connections, and firewalls (the Gufw and FirewallD).

Overview

Part 3: Desktops

Part 4: Administration

Contents

Part 1: Getting Started

Part 2: Applications

Part 3: Desktops

Part 4: Administration

14. System Administration **431**

Part 1: Getting Started

Introduction
Installation
Usage Basics
Managing Software

1. Ubuntu 18.04 Introduction

Ubuntu Releases

Ubuntu 18.04

Ubuntu Release

Ubuntu Flavours

Ubuntu Live DVD and USB

Ubuntu Software

Ubuntu Help and Documentation

Open Source Software

History of Linux and UNIX

Ubuntu Linux is currently one of the most popular end-user Linux distributions (**https://www.ubuntu.com**). Ubuntu Linux is managed by the Ubuntu foundation, which is sponsored by Canonical, Ltd (**https://www.canonical.com**), a commercial organization that supports and promotes open source projects. Ubuntu is based on Debian Linux, one of the oldest Linux distributions, which is dedicated to incorporating cutting-edge developments and features (**https://www.debian.org**). Mark Shuttleworth, a South African and Debian Linux developer, initiated the Ubuntu project. Debian Linux is primarily a Linux development project, trying out new features. Ubuntu provides a Debian-based Linux distribution that is stable, reliable, and easy to use.

Ubuntu is designed as a Linux operating system that can be used easily by everyone. The name Ubuntu means "humanity to others." As the Ubuntu project describes it: "Ubuntu is an African word meaning 'Humanity to others", or "I am what I am because of who we all are." The Ubuntu distribution brings the spirit of Ubuntu to the software world."

The official Ubuntu philosophy lists the following principles.

1. Every computer user should have the freedom to download, run, copy, distribute study, share, change, and improve their software for any purpose, without paying licensing fees.

2. Every computer user should be able to use their software in the language of their choice.

3. Every computer user should be given every opportunity to use software, even if they work under a disability.

The emphasis on language reflects Ubuntu's international scope. It is meant to be a global distribution that does not focus on any single market. Language support has been integrated into Linux in general by its internationalization projects, denoted by the term i18n.

Making software available to all users involves both full accessibility supports for users with disabilities as well as seamless integration of software access using online repositories, making massive amounts of software available to all users at the touch of a button. Ubuntu also makes full use of Linux's automatic device detection ability, greatly simplifying installation as well as access to removable devices and attached storage.

Ubuntu aims to provide a fully supported and reliable, open source and free, easy to use and modify, Linux operating system. Ubuntu makes the following promises about its distribution.

Ubuntu will always be free of charge, including enterprise releases and security updates.

Ubuntu comes with full commercial support from Canonical and hundreds of companies around the world.

Ubuntu includes the very best translations and accessibility infrastructure that the free software community has to offer.

Ubuntu DVDs contain only free software applications; we encourage you to use free and open source software, improve it and pass it on (Ubuntu repositories contain some proprietary software like vendor graphics drivers that is also free).

Ubuntu 18.04

Ubuntu 18.04 introduces several new features, as well as numerous smaller modifications. It is a long-term support release based on the Linux 4.4 kernel. The Ubuntu repositories support several major desktops, including the Ubuntu Desktop (GNOME), Kubuntu (KDE), MATE Ubuntu, and GNOME Ubuntu (GNOME 3). You can think of Ubuntu as a multi-desktop system, where the same repositories support different desktops. The Ubuntu Desktop features the GNOME user interface with a Dock, dash, and indicator menus. Referred to as simply the Ubuntu desktop, GNOME is the default desktop (see Figure 1-1). It is based on GNOME 3.18.

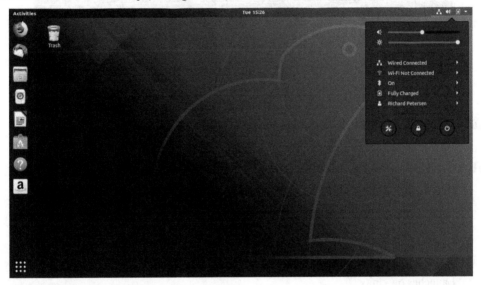

Figure 1-1: Ubuntu 18.04 Ubuntu Desktop

For documentation check:

`https://help.ubuntu.com/`

Check the Ubuntu Release Notes for an explanation of changes.

`https://wiki.ubuntu.com/BionicBeaver/ReleaseNotes`

For basic tutorials of Ubuntu tasks such as installation and setting up Samba, see the Ubuntu tutorials site.

`https://tutorials.ubuntu.com/`

Ubuntu 18.04 also features a minimal install. Only the Web browser and a few utilities are installed, instead of a full set of applications (see Figure 1-2). You can choose the minimal installation options during the Installation processes on the "Updates and other software" screen. Under the heading "What apps would you like to start with?", there are two options: Normal Installation and Minimal Installation. The Normal Instlalation option is selected by default. For minimal, choose the Minimal Installation option.

Figure 1-2: Ubuntu 18.04 Ubuntu Desktop, Minimal Installation

Ubuntu 18.04 Key Changes

Several key changes have been made for the 18.04 release.

The Ubuntu Desktop now uses GNOME instead of Unity. As such there is no longer a GNOME Ubuntu flavor. You can install **gnome-session** for a more recent version of GNOME, and **vanilla-gnome-desktop** for a GNOME only version.

The Ubuntu Desktop implements a Dash to Dock extension that works similar to the Launcher on Unity.

Ubuntu uses netplan.io to manage network devices. The ifdown is no longer installed. There is no longer an ifup and ifdown command. You can install ifdown if you want.

The SMB protocol supported is now 2.1 and higher to conform with Windows changes. This means that desktop network browsing may not work. On the desktop you can use specific host and share access methods with Connect to Server operations instead.

A swap file is now used instead of a swap partition, though you can still use a swap partition if you want. If you are just upgrading from a previous release, your old swap partition is still used.

A minimal install option is now available for the Ubuntu Desktop. The only major applications it installs are the Web browser and standard tools. You can install what you want later.

The new Wayland display server is an option whenever you log in (Ubuntu on Wayland). Be warned though that Wayland is still considered unstable, though in future releases it will become the default. The older Xorg server is currently the default.

Ubuntu no longer provides 32bit versions for Ubuntu, neither server or desktop. But the Ubuntu Flavors still provide 32bit versions, including Kubuntu, Ubuntu-Mate, Xubuntu, and Budgie Ubuntu.

The Ubuntu Sever now uses systemd-networkd for implementing network connections. The Ubuntu Desktop still uses NetworkManager. Either can be used on the other.

Chrony is used instead of ntpd as the network time server.

Canonical provides a live patch service for security updates, so that you would not have to reboot for the update to take effect. This is more of an issue for servers, which have to run constantly, rather than the desktop.

The Snap repository is integrated into Ubuntu Software. You can choose what channel to use.

To change desktop themes and icon styles you have to install GNOME Tweaks and use its Appearance tab.

The future default desktop theme is the community theme. It can now be downloaded on Ubuntu Software as communitheme.

Ubuntu Releases

Ubuntu provides both long-term and short-term support releases. Long-term support releases (LTS), such as Ubuntu 18.04, are released every two years. Short-term releases, such as Ubuntu 17.10, are provided every six months between the LTS versions. They are designed to make available the latest applications and support for the newest hardware. Each has its own nickname, like Bionic Beaver for the 18.04 release. The long-term support releases are supported for three years for desktops and five years for servers, whereas short-term support releases are supported for 18 months. In addition, Canonical provides limited commercial support for companies that purchase it.

Installing Ubuntu is easy to do. A core set of applications are installed, and you can add to them as you wish. Following installation, additional software can be downloaded from online repositories. There are only a few install screens, which move quickly through default partitioning, user setup, and time settings. Hardware components such as graphics cards and network connections are configured and detected automatically. With Ubuntu Software (installed by default), you can find and install additional software with the click of a button.

The Ubuntu distribution of Linux is available online at numerous sites. Ubuntu maintains its own site for the desktop edition at **https://www.ubuntu.com/desktop** You can download the current release of Ubuntu Linux from **https://www.ubuntu.com/download/desktop**.

Ubuntu Flavours

Ubuntu supports several desktops, known as flavours, each designed for a distinct group of users or functions. Flavours install different collections of software such as the Xfce (Xubuntu) or MATE desktops, the KDE desktop (Kubuntu), servers, educational software, and multimedia applications. Table 1-2 lists the websites where you can download ISO images for these flavours. ISO images can be downloaded directly or by using a BitTorrent application like Transmission. Metalink downloads are also supported which make effective use of mirrors. If you have already downloaded a pre-release ISO image, like a beta version, you can use zsync to download just the final changes, greatly reducing download times.

Ubuntu Flavor	Description
Ubuntu Desktop	Live DVD/USB and Install with the GNOME interface, **https://www.ubuntu.com/download/desktop**.
Ubuntu Server	Install server software (no desktop), **https://www.ubuntu.com/download/server**
Kubuntu	Live DVD/USB and Install using the KDE desktop, instead of GNOME, **https://www.kubuntu.org**. Add to Ubuntu desktop with the **kubuntu-desktop** metapackage.
Ubuntu MATE	Uses the MATE desktop, **https://ubuntu-mate.org.** Add to Ubuntu desktop with the **ubuntu-mate-desktop** metapackage.
Xubuntu	Uses the Xfce desktop instead of GNOME, **http://xubuntu.org**. Useful for laptops.
Lubuntu	Lightweight version of Ubuntu based on the LXDE desktop, **https://lubuntu.me/**
Ubuntu Studio	Ubuntu desktop with multimedia and graphics production applications, **https://ubuntustudio.org**. Add to Ubuntu desktop with the **ubuntustudio-desktop** metapackage
Ubuntu Kylin	Ubuntu Desktop for Chinese users, **https://ubuntukylin.com**.
Ubuntu Budgie	The Budgie desktop based on the Ubuntu desktop, **https://ubuntubudgie.org**

Table 1-1: Ubuntu Flavours

The Ubuntu Desktop edition provides desktop functionality for end users. The Ubuntu Desktop release provides a Live DVD/USB using the GNOME desktop. Most users would install this version. You can download the Ubuntu Desktop from the Download page, which you can access from the Ubuntu site (**https://www.ubuntu.com**) by clicking on the Download menu and choosing Desktop. The page address is:

```
https://www.ubuntu.com/download/desktop
```

You can choose either the 32-bit, 64-bit, or 64-bit Mac versions, though 64-bit is the default.

For upgrade instructions, click on the "Software Updater" link in the "From an older version" section.

```
https://tutorials.ubuntu.com/tutorial/tutorial-upgrading-ubuntu-desktop#0
```

To open the Alternative Download page, click on the "Alternative downloads and torrents" link below the Download button.

```
https://www.ubuntu.com/download/alternative-downloads
```

The Alternative Downloads page provides information on BitTorrent files for downloading the Ubuntu 18.04 DVD release.

On the desktop download page, you can click on the "Buy now" link under the title "Buy a 18.04 LTS USB stick", in the "Get the version you need" section to connect to the Ubuntu Shop on the shop canonical site where you can buy Ubuntu usb sticks at a low price. Also, on the Ubuntu Shop page, you can click on the "Bootable USB stick" link at the left.

```
https://shop.canonical.com/
```

Those who want to run Ubuntu as a server, to provide an Internet service such as a website, would use the Ubuntu Server edition. The Server edition provides only a simple command line interface; it does not install the desktop. It is designed primarily to run servers. Keep in mind that you could install the desktop first, and later download server software from the Ubuntu repositories, running them from a system that also has a desktop, though there are overhead costs for a server running a desktop. You do not have to install the Server edition to install and run servers. You can download the Server edition from the Ubuntu Server download page, which you can access from the Ubuntu site (**http://www.ubuntu.com**) by clicking on the Download tab and then the Server sub-tab. The page address is:

```
http://www.ubuntu.com/download/server
```

The releases site provides a DVD download page with download files for BitTorrent, zsync, and metalink, as well as a direct download link.

```
http://releases.ubuntu.com/bionic/
```

Apple powerpc, ARM, and IBM z compatible Ubuntu Desktop DVDs can also be downloaded from cdimages site:

```
http://cdimages.ubuntu.com/releases/bionic/release/
```

Ubuntu Flavours have the same Ubuntu packages but use either a different desktop or a specialized collection of software for certain groups of users. Kubuntu uses the KDE desktop instead of GNOME. Xubuntu is a stripped down and highly efficient desktop using the Xfce desktop, ideal for low power use on laptops and smaller computer. Edubuntu provides educational software that can be used with a specialized Edubuntu server, providing educational software on a school network. Ubuntu Studio provides a collection of multimedia and image production software. Lubuntu is based on the LXDE desktop, providing a very lightweight version of Ubuntu. Ubuntu MATE uses the MATE desktop. Ubuntu Kylin is the Ubuntu Desktop for Chinese users. Table 1-2 lists websites where you can download ISO images for the various flavors.

You can download flavours from their respective websites, or from **http://releases.ubuntu.com**. The links for their sites are available at:

```
https://www.ubuntu.com/download/flavours
```

The versions featuring different desktops are listed here.

https://www.kubuntu.org   KDE desktop version

https://ubuntu-mate.org   MATE desktop version

https://xubuntu.org   Xfce desktop version

https://lubuntu.me/   LXDE desktop version

https://ubuntubudgie.org/   Budgie desktop version

You can find out more about flavours at: **https://www.ubuntu.com/download/flavours**, which you can access from the Ubuntu site (**https://www.ubuntu.com**). Click the Download menu, choosing Ubuntu Flavours. Links to their websites are provided on the Ubuntu flavours page, where you can then download their live/install DVDs. All these flavors can be downloaded from their respective websites, as well as from:

`http://releases.ubuntu.com/`

URL	Internet Site
https://www.ubuntu.com/download/	Primary download site for Desktop and Server DVDs
http://releases.ubuntu.com/bionic/	Download site for Desktop DVD and Server CDs, including alternate install methods like torrent, zsync, and metalink.
http://cdimages.ubuntu.com/releases/bionic/release/	Download site for Ubuntu DVDs for Apple powerpc, arm, and IBM z systems.
http://cdimages.ubuntu.com/	Download site for all Ubuntu flavors, including Kubuntu, Ubuntu Mate, Ubuntu Cinnamon, Xubuntu, and Ubuntu Studio. Check also their respective websites.

Table 1-2: Ubuntu DVD ISO Image locations

The **http://releases.ubuntu.com** and **http://cdimages.ubuntu.com** sites hold both BitTorrent and full image files for the flavours they provide. The **http://releases.ubuntu.com** site also provides downloads from multiple mirrors and zsync files for synchronizing downloads. Keep in mind that most of these flavours are released as Live DVD/USB discs, for which there are two versions, 32-bit x86 and 64-bit x86_64. Older computers and small netbooks may only support a 32-bit version, whereas most desktop computers will support the 64-bit versions. Check your computer hardware specifications to be sure. The 64-bit version should run faster, and most computer software is now available in stable 64-bit packages.

Ubuntu Live DVD/USB

The Ubuntu Desktop DVD/USB can operate as a Live session (the Server edition does not), so you can run Ubuntu from any DVD-ROM drive. You can also install the Ubuntu Desktop DVD image to a USB drive. In effect, you can carry your operating system with you on a DVD-ROM or a USB drive. New users can also use the Live-DVD/USB to try out Ubuntu to see if they like it. The Ubuntu Desktop DVD/USB will run as a Live session automatically using Ubuntu GNOME as the desktop. If you want to use the KDE desktop as your Live session instead, you would use the Kubuntu DVD/USB. To create a Live USB, you install the Ubuntu Desktop DVD image to a USB drive using a USB creator application such as usb-creator or the Fedora Media Writer.

Ubuntu Desktop Live DVD

The Desktop Live DVD/USB provided by Ubuntu includes a basic collection of software packages. You will have a fully operational Ubuntu desktop (see Figure 1-3). You have the full set of administrative tools, with which you can add users, change configuration settings, and even add software, while the Live session is running. When you shut down, the configuration information is lost, including any software you have added. Files and data can be written to removable devices like USB drives and DVD write discs, letting you save your data during a Live session.

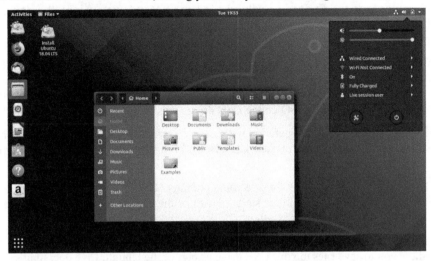

Figure 1-3: Ubuntu Live DVD/USB

When you start up the Ubuntu Desktop DVD/USB, the startup screen is displayed, with the "Try Ubuntu" option selected. This option starts up a Live session, and will start automatically after a few seconds. The Live DVD/USB desktop is then displayed (see Figure 1-2) and you are logged in as the **ubuntu** user. The Dock on the left side displays an install Ubuntu icon, icons for a Web browser (Firefox), Thunderbird mailer, Rhythmbox music player, LibreOffice writer, Ubuntu Software, Ubuntu desktop help, and an Amazon link. On the menu bar to the right the System Status area menu with entries for network connections, which you can configure for wireless access, as well as a power button for shutting down your system.

You can save files to your home directory, but they are temporary and disappear at the end of the session. Copy them to a DVD, USB drive, or another removable device to save them.

All the Live DVD/USB/USBs also function as install discs for Ubuntu, providing a basic collection of software, and installing a full-fledged Ubuntu operating system that can be expanded and updated from Ubuntu online repositories. An Install icon lets you install Ubuntu on your computer, performing a standard installation to your hard drive. From the Live session desktop, double-click the Install icon on the desktop or on the Dock to start the installation.

Ubuntu Live USB drive

On Ubuntu, you can use the USB Startup Disk Creator utility to install any Ubuntu disc image on a USB drive. The USB Live/install drive is generated using the DVD image that you first have to download. Check the Ubuntu tutorial on create a Live USB drive.

https://tutorials.ubuntu.com/tutorial/tutorial-create-a-usb-stick-on-ubuntu#0

Note: Alternatively, you could download and use the Fedora Media Writer to create the USB drive. The Fedora Media Writer can be installed on Windows and Mac operating systems. If you do not already have an Ubuntu system, you could use the Fedora Media Writer to create your Ubuntu USB drives on Windows or Mac. IF you access the Fedora download site from a Windows system, the download button downloads the Fedora Media Writer for Windows, https://getfedora.org/en/workstation/download/.

Click "Startup Disk Creator" icon on the Applications overview to open the Make Startup Disk window with an entry at the top to select an ISO image and an entry below to select the USB drive to use. Click the Other button to locate a specific disk image to use. Then click the "Make Startup Disk" button to install the ISO on the USB drive.

The "Make Startup Disk" operation will not erase any data already on your USB drive. You can still access it, even Windows data. The Ubuntu Live OS will coexist with your current data, occupying available free space.

To boot from the Live USB, be sure your computer (BIOS) is configured to boot from the USB drive. The Live USB drive will then start up just like the Live DVD, displaying the install screen with options to try Ubuntu or install it.

When you create the Live USB drive, you have the option to specify writable memory. This will allow you to save files to your USB drive as part of the Ubuntu Live operating system. You can save files to your Document or Pictures directory and then access them later. You can also create new users, and give those users administrative permission, just as you would on a normally installed OS. With the GNOME Settings' User Accounts tool, you could even have the new user be the automatic login, instead of the **ubuntu** user. In effect, the Ubuntu Live USB drive becomes a portable Ubuntu OS. Even with these changes, the Ubuntu Live USB remains the equivalent of a Live DVD, just one that you can write to. There is no GRUB boot loader. You still use the install start up screen. In addition, you cannot update the kernel.

If you want a truly portable Ubuntu OS, just perform a standard installation to a USB drive, instead of to a hard drive. You will have to create a new clean partition on the USB drive to install to. You would either reduce the size of the current partition, preserving data, or simply delete it, opening up the entire drive for use by the new Ubuntu OS.

Ubuntu Software

All Linux software for Ubuntu is currently available from online repositories. You can download applications for desktops, Internet servers, office suites, and programming packages, among others. Software packages are distributed primarily through the official Ubuntu repository. Downloads and updates are handled automatically by your desktop software manager and updater. Many popular applications are included in separate sections of the repository. During installation, your system is configured to access Ubuntu repositories. You can update to the latest software from the Ubuntu repository using the software updater.

A complete listing of software packages for the Ubuntu distribution, along with a search capability is located at:

```
http://packages.ubuntu.com
```

In addition, you could download from third-party sources software that is in the form of compressed archives or in DEB packages. DEB packages are archived using the Debian Package Manager and have the extension **.deb**. Compressed archives have an extension such as **.tar.gz**. You also can download the source version and compile it directly on your system. This has become a simple process, almost as simple as installing the compiled DEB versions.

Due to licensing restrictions, multimedia support for popular operations like MP3, DVD, and DivX are included with Ubuntu in a separate section of the repository called multiverse. Ubuntu includes on its restricted repository NVIDIA and AMD vendor graphics drivers. Ubuntu also provides as part of its standard installation, the generic X.org drivers that will enable your graphics cards to work.

All software packages in the Ubuntu repositories are accessible directly with Ubuntu Software and the Synaptic Package Manager, which provide easy software installation, removal, and searching. Ubuntu Software is an implementation of GNOME Software.

Ubuntu Help and Documentation

A great deal of help and documentation is available online for Ubuntu, ranging from detailed install procedures to beginner questions (see Table 1-3). The documentation for Ubuntu 18.04 is located at **https://help.ubuntu.com/**. The Firefox Web browser start page displays links for two major help sites: Ubuntu documentation at **https://help.ubuntu.com** and Ubuntu Community at **https://help.ubuntu.com/community**. Check the Ubuntu tutorials site (**https://tutorials.ubuntu.com/**) for basic tutorials on different Ubuntu tasks Tutorials for Ubuntu topics and tasks, such as running the Live DVD/USB, setting up Samba, Install the Ubuntu desktop, and configuring the Apache Web server.

For detailed online support, check the Ubuntu forums at **https://ubuntuforums.org**. In addition, there are blog and news sites as well as the standard Linux documentation. Ubuntu Community features Ubuntu documentation, support, blogs, and news. A Contribute section links to sites where you can contribute in development, artwork, documentation, and support. The Ask Ubuntu site is a question and answer site based on community support, which provides answers to many common questions (**https://askubuntu.com**).

For mailing lists, check **https://lists.ubuntu.com**. There are lists for categories like Ubuntu announcements, community support for specific flavors, and development for areas like the desktop, servers, or mobile implementation. For more specialized tasks like Samba support and LAMP server installation check **http://www.ubuntugeek.com**.

help.ubuntu.com

Ubuntu-specific documentation is available at **https://help.ubuntu.com**. Here, on listed links, you can find specific documentation for different releases. Always check the release help page first for documentation, though it may be sparse and cover mainly changed areas. For 18.04 the Documentation section provides the Ubuntu Desktop Guide (Desktop), the Ubuntu Server Guide, and Ubuntu installation (per architecture). The Ubuntu Desktop Guide covers the GNOME interfaces and is the same guide installed with your desktop, accessible as Help (Applications overview).

```
https://help.ubuntu.com/lts/ubuntu-help/index.html
```

Site	Description
https://help.ubuntu.com/	Help pages and install documentation
https://packages.ubuntu.com	Ubuntu software package list and search
https://ubuntuforums.org	Ubuntu forums
https://askubuntu.com	Ask Ubuntu Q&A site for users and developers (community based)
https://tutorials.ubuntu.com/	Tutorials for Ubuntu topics and tasks
http://fridge.ubuntu.com	News and developments
http://planet.ubuntu.com	Member and developer blogs
https://blog.ubuntu.com/	Latest Ubuntu news
http://www.tldp.org	Linux Documentation Project website
https://help.ubuntu.com/community	Community Documentation
https://lists.ubuntu.com	Ubuntu mailing lists
http://www.ubuntugeek.com	Tutorials and guides for specialized tasks

Table 1-3: Ubuntu help and documentation

One of the more helpful pages is the Community Help page, **https://help.ubuntu.com/community**. Here you will find detailed documentation on the installation of all Ubuntu releases, using the desktop, installing software, and configuring devices. Always check the page for your Ubuntu release first. The page includes these main sections:

Installation: Link to Install page with sections on desktop, server, and alternate installations.

Hardware: Sections on managing hardware. Links to pages on drives and partitions, input devices, wireless configuration, printers, sound, and video.

Further Topics: Links to pages on system administration, security, and troubleshooting, servers, networking, and software development.

Ubuntu Flavours: Links to documentation on different Ubuntu versions such as Lubuntu and Kubuntu.

ubuntuforums.org

Ubuntu forums provide detailed online support and discussion for users (**https://ubuntuforums.org**). A "New to Ubuntu" section provides an area where new users can obtain answers to questions. Sticky threads include both quick and complete guides to installation for the current Ubuntu release. You can use the search feature to find discussions on your topic of interest. The main support categories section covers specific support areas like networking, multimedia, laptops, security, and 64-bit support.

Other community discussions cover ongoing work such as virtualization, art and design, gaming, education and science, Wine, assistive technology, and the Ubuntu cloud. Here you will also find community announcements and news.

The forum community discussion is where you talk about anything else. The Ubuntu Forums site also provides a gallery page for posted screenshots as well as RSS feeds for specific forums.

Ubuntu news and blog sites

Several news and blog sites are accessible from the News page at **https://wiki.ubuntu.com/Home**.

http://fridge.ubuntu.com The Fridge site lists the latest news and developments for Ubuntu. It features the Weekly newsletter, latest announcements, and upcoming events.

http://planet.ubuntu.com Ubuntu blog for members and developers

https://blog.ubuntu.com/ Ubuntu news

Linux documentation

The Linux Documentation Project (LDP) has developed a complete set of Linux manuals. The documentation is available at the LDP home site at **http://www.tldp.org**. The Linux documentation for your installed software will be available in your **/usr/share/doc** directory.

Open Source Software

Linux is developed as a cooperative Open Source effort over the Internet, so no company or institution controls Linux. Software developed for Linux reflects this background. Development often takes place when Linux users decide to work together on a project. Most Linux software is developed as Open Source software. The source code for an application is freely distributed along with the application. Programmers over the Internet can make their own contributions to a software package's development, modifying and correcting the source code. As an open source operating system, the Linux source code is included in all its distributions and is freely available. Many major software development efforts are also open source projects, as are the KDE and GNOME desktops along with most of their applications. You can find more information about the Open Source movement at **https://www.opensource.org**.

Open source software is protected by public licenses that prevent commercial companies from taking control of open source software by adding modifications of their own, copyrighting those changes, and selling the software as their own product. The most popular public license is the GNU General Public License (GPL) provided by the Free Software Foundation. Linux is distributed under this license. The GNU General Public License retains the copyright, freely licensing the software with the requirement that the software and any modifications made to it are always freely available. Other public licenses have been created to support the demands of different kinds of open source projects. The GNU Lesser General Public License (LGPL) lets commercial applications use GNU licensed software libraries. The Qt Public License (QPL) lets open source developers use the Qt libraries essential to the KDE desktop. You can find a complete listing at **https://www.opensource.org**.

Linux is currently copyrighted under a GNU public license provided by the Free Software Foundation (see **http://www.gnu.org/**). GNU software is distributed free, provided it is freely distributed to others. GNU software has proved both reliable and effective. Many of the popular Linux utilities, such as C compilers, shells, and editors, are GNU software applications. In addition, many open source software projects are licensed under the GNU General Public License (GPL). Most of these applications are available on the Ubuntu software repositories. Chapter 4 describes in detail the process of accessing these repositories to download and install software applications from them on your system.

Under the terms of the GNU General Public License, the original author retains the copyright, although anyone can modify the software and redistribute it, provided the source code is included, made public, and provided free. In addition, no restriction exists on selling the software or giving it away free. One distributor could charge for the software, while another could provide it free of charge. Major software companies are also providing Linux versions of their most popular applications. (you can use Wine, the Windows compatibility layer, to run many Microsoft applications on Linux, directly.)

Linux

Linux is a fast, stable, and open source operating system for PCs and workstations that features professional-level Internet services, extensive development tools, fully functional graphical user interfaces (GUIs), and a massive number of applications ranging from office suites to multimedia applications. Linux was developed in the early 1990s by Linus Torvalds, along with other programmers around the world. As an operating system, Linux performs many of the same functions as UNIX, Macintosh, and Windows. However, Linux is distinguished by its power and flexibility, along with being freely available. Most PC operating systems, such as Windows, began their development within the confines of small, restricted personal computers, which have become more versatile and powerful machines. Such operating systems are constantly being upgraded to keep up with the ever-changing capabilities of PC hardware. Linux, on the other hand, was developed in a different context. Linux is a PC version of the UNIX operating system that has been used for decades on mainframes and is currently the system of choice for network servers and workstations.

Technically, Linux consists of the operating system program referred to as the kernel, which is the part originally developed by Linus Torvalds. However, it has always been distributed with a large number of software applications, ranging from network servers and security programs to office applications and development tools. Linux has evolved as part of the open source software movement, in which independent programmers joined to provide free quality software to any user. Linux has become the premier platform for open source software, much of it developed by the Free Software Foundation's GNU project. Most of these applications are also available on the Ubuntu repository, providing packages that are Debian compliant.

Linux operating system capabilities include powerful networking features, including support for Internet, intranets, and Windows networking. As a norm, Linux distributions include fast, efficient, and stable Internet servers, such as the Web, FTP, and DNS servers, along with proxy, news, and mail servers. In other words, Linux has everything you need to set up, support, and maintain a fully functional network.

Linux is distributed freely under a GNU General Public License (GPL) as specified by the Free Software Foundation, making it available to anyone who wants to use it. GNU (which stands for "GNU's Not Unix") is a project initiated and managed by the Free Software Foundation to provide free software to users, programmers, and developers. Linux is copyrighted, not public domain. The GNU General Public License is designed to ensure that Linux remains free and, at the same time, standardized. Linux is technically the operating system kernel—the core operations—

and only one official Linux kernel exists. Its power and stability have made Linux an operating system of choice as a network server.

Originally designed specifically for Intel-based personal computers, Linux started out as a personal project of computer science student Linus Torvalds at the University of Helsinki. At that time, students were making use of a program called Minix, which highlighted different UNIX features. Minix was created by Professor Andrew Tanenbaum and widely distributed over the Internet to students around the world. Torvalds's intention was to create an effective PC version of UNIX for Minix users. It was named Linux, and in 1991, Torvalds released version 0.11. Linux was widely distributed over the Internet, and in the following years, other programmers refined and added to it, incorporating most of the applications and features now found in standard UNIX systems. All the major window managers have been ported to Linux. Linux has all the networking tools, such as FTP file transfer support, Web browsers, and the whole range of network services such as email, the domain name service, and dynamic host configuration, along with FTP, Web, and print servers. It also has a full set of program development utilities, such as C++ compilers and debuggers. Given all its features, the Linux operating system remains small, stable, and fast.

Linux development is overseen by The Linux Foundation (**https://www.linuxfoundation.org**), which is a merger of The Free Standards Group and Open Source Development Labs (OSDL). This is the group with which Linux Torvalds works to develop new Linux versions. Linux kernels are released at **https://www.kernel.org/**.

2. Installing Ubuntu

Installing Ubuntu Linux is a very simple procedure, using just a few screens with default entries for easy installation. A pre-selected collection of software is installed. Most of your devices, like your display and network connection, are detected automatically. The most difficult part would be a manual partitioning of the hard drive, but you can use automatic partitioning for fresh installs, as is usually the case.

Check the Ubuntu documentation for the Installing Ubuntu for complete installation details for PC, PowerPC, and ARM installs.

https://help.ubuntu.com/18.04/installation-guide/index.html

Install Discs

In most cases, installation is performed using an Ubuntu Desktop DVD that will install the Ubuntu desktop, along with a pre-selected set of software packages for multimedia players, office applications, and games. The Ubuntu Desktop DVD is also designed to run from the DVD disc, while providing the option to install Ubuntu on your hard drive. This is the disc image you will download from the Ubuntu download site. The Ubuntu Desktop DVD has only a 64-bit version.

http://www.ubuntu.com/download/desktop

You can also download the Ubuntu Desktop ISO image directly from:

http://releases.ubuntu.com/bionic

Ubuntu releases	Description
Ubuntu Desktop Live/Install DVD/USB	Primary Ubuntu release, Ubuntu desktop, can be burned to either DVD disc or USB drive.
Ubuntu Server CD	Server-only installation, no desktop, command line interface
Ubuntu Cloud	Cloud based install for OpenStack

Table 2-1: Ubuntu releases

The Desktop DVD and Server CD are available at:

http://releases.ubuntu.com/bionic

Installation choices

Ubuntu tailors its installs by providing different install disc for different releases and versions (see Table 2-1). The Desktop DVD disc is not the only Ubuntu installation available. Ubuntu provides two other discs: the Server CD designed for servers and the Mac DVD for Apple desktops.

Desktop DVD Run as a Live DVD/USB or install Ubuntu Linux with the Ubuntu desktop and a standard set of applications.

Desktop USB Run as Live USB or install Ubuntu Linux with the Ubuntu desktop and a standard set of applications, uses the Ubuntu Desktop DVD image installed on a USB drive.

Server install CD   Install Ubuntu with a standard set of servers; this uses the command line interface (no desktop).

Using BitTorrent: Transmission

Most current Linux and Windows systems support BitTorrent for downloading. BitTorrent provides an efficient, safe, and fast method for downloading large files. Various BitTorrent clients are available, including one from the original BitTorrent developer. Transmission is the preferred BitTorrent client for Ubuntu 18.04. When downloading a new release just when it comes out, BitTorrent is often the only practical solution. In addition, it is the preferred download method for the DVD. One exception is if you have a slow Internet connection. BitTorrent relies on making multiple connections that can use up bandwidth quickly. For slow connections, especially just for the Desktop DVD, you may want to download directly from the Ubuntu site.

The BitTorrent files for all versions (Desktop and Server) can be found at the primary download sites, along with direct downloads:

```
http://releases.ubuntu.com/18.04
```

Metalinks

Metalinks are XML files that work like mirror lists, allowing download clients to easily choose a fast mirror and perform a more controlled download. You would need to use a download client that supports metalinks, like KGet, **gget**, or **aria2**. For more information about using metalink with Ubuntu, see:

```
https://wiki.ubuntu.com/MetalinkIsoDownloads
```

For general information see.

```
http://en.wikipedia.org/wiki/Metalink
```

A metalink file will have the extension **.metalink**. Metalink files for the Ubuntu releases are available at:

```
http://releases.ubuntu.com/18.04/
```

Zsync

Ubuntu also provides zsync downloads for its Ubuntu ISO images. The **zsync** program operates like **rsync**, but with very little overhead. It is designed for distributing a single file to many locations. In effect, you are synchronizing your copy to the original. The zsync program is designed to download just those parts of the original file that the downloaded copy needs. It uses a **.zsync** file that has the name of the ISO image you want to download. You can download **.zsync** files for Ubuntu ISO images from the **http://releases.ubuntu.com/bionic/** download page.

The **zsync** program is very useful for users who have already download a pre-release version of an Ubuntu ISO image, such as the beta version. You would rename the beta image file to that of the new release, and then perform a zsync operation on it using the appropriate **.zsync** file provided by the Ubuntu download page. Only those parts of the final version that differ from the beta version would be downloaded, greatly reducing the actual amount of data downloaded.

You can install **zsync** using the Synaptic Package Manager. For more information, see the zsync Man page and the Zsync site: **http://zsync.moria.org.uk/**. For information on how to use zsync with Ubuntu, see:

http://ubuntu-tutorials.com/2009/10/29/use-zsync-to-update-existing-iso-images/

Installing Multiple-Boot Systems

The GRUB boot loader already supports multiple booting. Should you have both Ubuntu and Windows systems installed on your hard disks; GRUB will let you choose to boot either the Ubuntu system or a Windows system. During installation, GRUB will automatically detect any other operating systems installed on your computer and configure your boot loader menu to let you access them. You do not have to perform any configuration yourself.

If you want a Windows system installed on your computer, you should install it first. Windows would overwrite the boot loader installed by a previous Ubuntu system, cutting off access to the Linux system. If you installed Windows after having installed Ubuntu, you will need to re-install the Ubuntu GRUB boot loader. See the section at the end of this Chapter on re-installing the boot loader. There are several ways you can do it, most very simple.

If you have already installed Windows on your hard drive and configured it to take up the entire hard drive, you can select the "Install alongside" option during installation to free up space and set up Ubuntu partitions.

Tip: You can also use the Ubuntu Live DVD/USB to start up Ubuntu and perform any necessary hard disk partitioning using GParted.

Hardware Requirements

Most hardware today meets the requirements for running Ubuntu. Ubuntu can be installed on a wide variety of systems, ranging from the very weak to the very powerful. The install procedure will detect most of your hardware automatically. You will only need to specify your keyboard, though a default is automatically detected for you. Check the Ubuntu installation guide's chapter on System Requirements for details.

https://help.ubuntu.com/18.04/installation-guide/

You can also check the Ubuntu System Requirements page at **http://help.ubuntu.com** for details:

http://help.ubuntu.com/community/Installation/SystemRequirements

Installation Overview

Installing Ubuntu involves several processes, beginning with creating Linux partitions, then loading the Ubuntu software, selecting a time zone, and creating new user accounts. The installation program used for Ubuntu is a screen-based program that takes you through all these processes, step-by-step, as one continuous procedure. You can use either your mouse or the keyboard to make selections. When you finish with a screen, click the Continue button at the bottom to move to the next screen. If you need to move back to the previous screen, click Back. You can also press TAB, the arrow keys, SPACEBAR, and ENTER to make selections.

Installation is a straightforward process. A graphical installation is easy to use, providing full mouse support.

Most systems today already meet hardware requirements and have automatic connections to the Internet.

They also support booting a DVD-ROM disc, though this support may have to be explicitly configured in the system BIOS.

If you are installing on a blank hard drive or on a drive with free space, or if you are performing a simple update that uses the same partitions, installing Ubuntu is a simple process. Ubuntu also features an automatic partitioning function that will perform the partitioning for you.

A preconfigured set of packages are installed, so you will not even have to select packages.

For a quick installation, you can simply start up the installation process by placing your DVD disc in the DVD drive and starting up your system. Graphical installation is a simple matter of following the instructions in each window as you progress. Installation follows a few easy stages:

1. **Welcome**   A default language is chosen for you, like English, so you can usually just click Continue.

2. **Preparing to install**   On the "Preparing to install" screen your system is checked and you can opt to install updates during installation and certain third party software such as the Fluendo MP3 codec.

3. **Installation type**   For automatic partitioning you have different options, depending on what other operating systems may have been installed on your hard drive. For drives that have other operating systems installed, you can install alongside them or, if Ubuntu 16.04 or 17.10 is installed, choose to upgrade, or choose to erase the entire disk. In all cases, you can also choose to partition your disk manually instead. As soon as you click the "Install Now' button, formatting and installation begins.

4. **Installation type: partitioner**   Used for manual partitioning only, in which you set up partitions yourself. Otherwise, this is skipped.

5. **Where are you? Time Zone**   Use the map to choose your time zone or select your city from the drop-down menu.

6. **Keyboard Layout**   A default is chosen for you; you can usually just click Continue.

7. **Who are you?**   Set up a username and hostname for your computer, as well as a password for that user. You can also choose to log in automatically, as well as encrypt your home folder.

After the installation, the DVD disc ejects and you will be asked to remove it and press ENTER. This will reboot your system.

Installation with the Ubuntu Desktop DVD/USB

The Ubuntu Desktop DVD/USB is designed for running Ubuntu from the DVD/USB (Live DVD/USB) and installing Ubuntu. Most users will use the Ubuntu Desktop DVD to install Ubuntu. You can first start up Ubuntu, and then initiate an installation, or install directly. Just place the DVD disc in the DVD-ROM drive before you start your computer. After you turn on or restart your computer, the installation program starts up.

Tip: Most computers are already set up to boot first from the DVD-ROM drive. If your computer cannot boot the DVD disc, then the boot sequence may be set up in the wrong order. You may first have to change the boot sequence setting in your computer's BIOS so that the computer will try to boot first from the DVD-ROM. This requires some technical ability and knowledge of how to set your motherboard's BIOS configuration.

On most screens, a Continue button is displayed on the lower-right corner of an installation dialog. Once finished with a screen, click Continue to move on. In some cases, you will be able to click a Back button to return to a previous screen. As each screen appears in the installation, default entries will be selected, usually by the auto-probing capability of the installation program. If these entries are correct, you can click Continue to accept them and go on to the next screen.

You have two ways to begin the install. You can start the installation directly or you can first start up the Ubuntu Live session. The Advantage to the Live session is that you will be able to configure your Network access and any other devices you have. The Live session is a fully functional Ubuntu system. Configuration options are listed in the System Setting dialog accessible from the Status Area menu (top right side) (see Figure 2-1). Click the System Setting button (wrench icon) at the bottom of the menu. To configure your network, expand the network entry and click Network Setting.

Figure 2-1: Ubuntu Live session System Status Area menu and Network configuration

Most users will not need to perform any configuration. In this case, you can install directly. The Status Area menu is available, but it only allows you to choose a Wi-Fi connection (see Figure 2-2).

Figure 2-2: Ubuntu direct install Network Connection

Welcome and Language

On newer computers with the EUFI BIOS, when the Ubuntu Desktop DVD/USB first boots, a text screen first appears with the following options:

```
Try Ubuntu without installing
Install Ubuntu
OEM install (for manufacturing)
Check disc for defects
```

An asterisk appears before the selected entry. Use the up and down arrows to move between entries, and press ENTER to choose one.

The "Try Ubuntu without installing" wording can be misleading. This entry starts up a Live session, instead of installing directly. But you can still install from the Live session. There will be an install icon you can click to start the installation, should you want to.

On older computers without an EUFI BIOS, the installer displays a Welcome screen (see Figure 2-3) with buttons for two options: Try Ubuntu and Install Ubuntu.

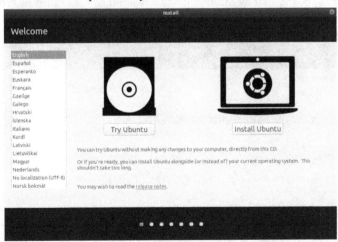

Figure 2-3: Install Welcome screen for Ubuntu Desktop DVD

On the Welcome screen, select the language you want from the list on the left. A default language will already be selected, usually English. Click the "Install Ubuntu" button to start up the installation.

The "Try Ubuntu" button will start Ubuntu as a Live session. Even if you just opt to try Ubuntu, you can still perform an installation from the Live DVD/USB. To install, click the Install icon on the desktop (see Figure 2-4). The Install window opens to the Welcome screen for choosing your language. Click the Continue button to start the installation.

Figure 2-4: Live DVD/USB (Desktop) with Install icon

Keyboard Layout

You are then asked to select a keyboard layout, "Choose your keyboard layout." Keyboard entries are selected first by location in the left scroll box, and then by type on the right scroll box. A default is already selected, such as English (US) (see Figure 2-5). If the selection is not correct, you can choose another keyboard, first by location in the left scroll box, and then by type on the right scroll box.

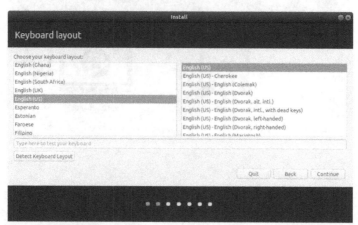

Figure 2-5: Keyboard Layout

To test your keyboard, click on the text box at the bottom of the screen and press keys, "Type here to test your keyboard."

The "Detect Keyboard Layout" button tries to detect the keyboard using your input. A series of dialogs opens, prompting you to press keys and asking you if certain keys are present on your keyboard. When the dialogs finish, the detected keyboard is then selected in the "Choose your keyboard layout" scroll boxes.

Click the Continue button to continue.

Minimal Install, Updates, and Third Party Software

The "Updates and Other Software" dialog appears that lets you choose a normal or minimal installation (see Figure 2-6). You can add software once installed. You can also choose to download current updates while installing, using the latest packages and avoiding an extensive update after the install. This can take longer, though.

You can also install third party applications and codecs (non-open source), such as the licensed Fluendo MP3 playback codec, Adobe Flash, and Gstreamer multimedia codecs (**ubuntu-restricted-addons** package).

Click the Continue button to continue.

Your system detects your hardware, providing any configuration specifications that may be required.

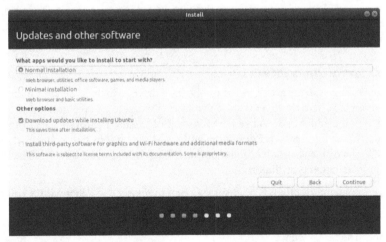

Figure 2-6: Updates and Other Software

Installation type

You are now asked to designate the Linux partitions and hard disk configurations you want to use on your hard drives. Ubuntu provides automatic partitioning that covers most situations, like using a blank or new hard drive and overwriting old partitions on a hard drive. Ubuntu can even repartition a system with an operating system that uses all of the hard drive, but with unused space within it. In this case, the install procedure reduces the space used by the original operating system and installs Ubuntu on the new free space. A default partition layout sets up a swap partition and a root partition of type **ext4** (Linux native) for the kernel and applications.

Alternatively, you can configure your hard disk manually (the "Something else" option). Ubuntu provides a very simple partitioning tool you can use to set up Linux partitions.

For multiple-boot systems using Windows, Ubuntu automatically detects a Windows system.

No partitions will be changed or formatted until you click the "Install Now" button. You can opt out of the installation until then, and your original partitions will remain untouched.

Warning: The "Erase disk and install Ubuntu" option will wipe out any existing partitions on the selected hard drive. If you want to preserve any partitions on that drive, like Windows or other Linux partitions, always choose a different option such as "Install Ubuntu alongside ..." or "Something else".

You are given choices, depending on the state of the hard disk you choose. A hard disk could be blank, have an older Ubuntu operating system on it, or have a different operating system, such as Windows, already installed. If an operating system is already installed, it may take up the entire disk or may only use part of the disk, with the remainder available for the Ubuntu installation.

Tip: Some existing Linux systems may use several Linux partitions. Some of these may be used for just the system software, such as the boot and root partitions. These can be formatted. Others may have extensive user files, such as a /home partition that normally holds user home directories and all the files they have created. You should *not* format such partitions.

No detected operating systems

If no operating systems are detected on the hard drive, which is the case with a drive with only data files or a blank hard drive, you are given four choices: to use the entire disk, to additionally encrypt the entire disk, to use LVM instead of standard partitions, or to specify partitions manually (see Figure 2-7). Encryption and LVM are options that you can choose in addition to the "Erase disk and install Ubuntu option." They have square buttons. The message displayed on the Installation type dialog is:

"This computer currently has no detected operating systems. What would you like to do?"

You are given four choices.

```
Erase disk and install Ubuntu
Encrypt the new Ubuntu installation for security
Use LVM with the new Ubuntu installation
Something else
```

If you choose to install Ubuntu without LVM, your hard drive is automatically partitioned creating two partitions, a primary partition for your entire file system (a root file system, /), and a swap partition.

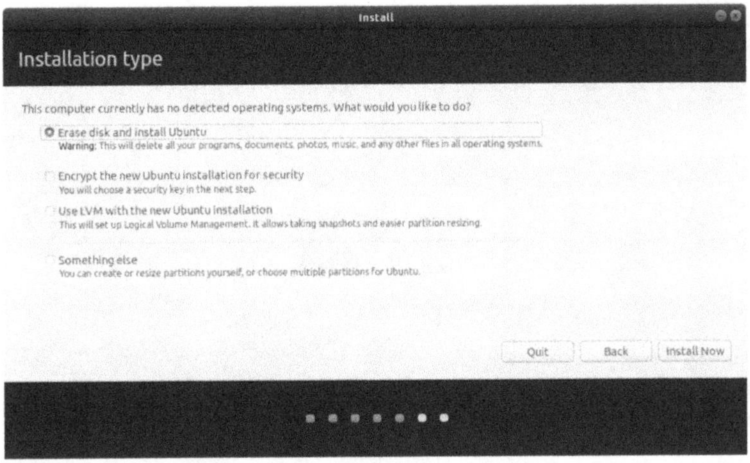

Figure 2-7: No detected operating systems

Use LVM

With the "Use LVM with the new Ubuntu installation" option, LVM partitions are set up using physical and logical volumes, which can be added to and replaced easily. A small standard ext4 partition is set up to hold the boot directory. Then an LVM physical volume is set up, which contains two LVM logical volumes, one for the swap space and one for the root (see Figure 2-8). After you have installed your system, you can manage your LVM partitions using the LVM commands(see Chapter 13). The default LVM partitions are shown here with **pvscan** (physical volumes), **vgscan** (volume group), and **lvscan** (logical volume) operations. There is one volume group, **ubuntu-vg**, with two logical volumes, **root** and **swap_1**. The physical LVM partition is named **lvm2**.

```
$ sudo pvscan
  PV /dev/mapper/sda3_crypt   VG ubuntu-vg        lvm2 [<464.54 GiB / 0    free]
  Total: 1 [<464.54 GiB] / in use: 1 [<464.54 GiB] / in no VG: 0 [0    ]
$ sudo vgscan
  Reading volume groups from cache.
  Found volume group "ubuntu-vg" using metadata type lvm2
$ sudo lvscan
  ACTIVE              '/dev/ubuntu-vg/root' [463.58 GiB] inherit
  ACTIVE              '/dev/ubuntu-vg/swap_1' [980.00 MiB] inherit
```

Three physical paritions are created: an EFI boot partition (for the newer EFI computers only), a standard ext2 partition for the Linux boot folder, and the LVM physical partition.

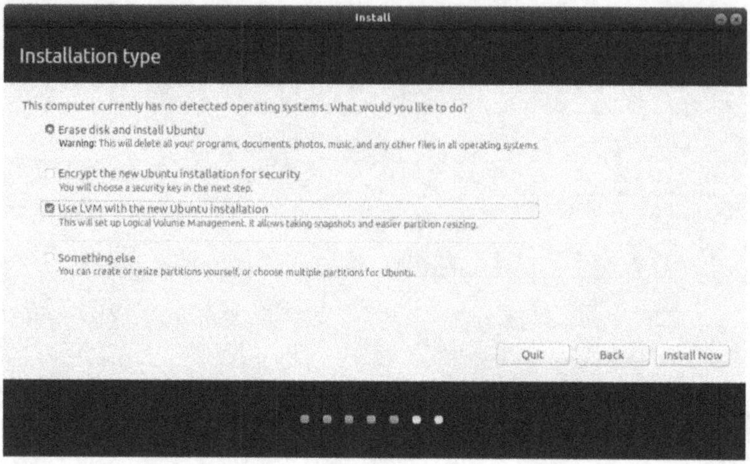

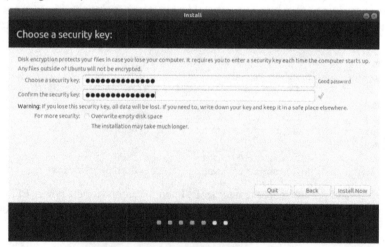

Figure 2-8: LVM install option

Encrypt the disk

The "Encrypt the new Ubuntu installation for security" option lets you encrypt your entire system with a password. You cannot access your system without that password. The encryption option will destroy any existing partitions if there are any, creating new partitions. Your hard drive will then have only your new Ubuntu system on it. On the "Choose a security key" screen that follows you are prompted to enter a security key (password), along with the option to overwrite empty space (see Figure 2-9).

Figure 2-9: Security key for encrypted system

After installation, whenever you start up your system, you are prompted to enter that security key (see Figure 2-10).

Figure 2-10: Security key login

Detected Ubuntu operating system

If you have another Ubuntu operating system on your disk, you will have the option to erase the Ubuntu system and replace it with Ubuntu 18.04. If the installed Ubuntu system is version 17.10, then you are also given the option to upgrade your system, preserving your personal files and installed software. You are also given the option to erase the installed operating system, and install the new system.

If the current system has enough unused space, you are also given an install alongside option, resizing the disk to free up space and installing 18.04 in added partitions on the free space. This will keep your original Linux system, as well as install the new one.

The message displayed on the Installation type dialog is something like this:

"This computer currently has Ubuntu 17.10 on it. What would you like to do?"

You are given three choices. The Upgrade Ubuntu option is selected by default.

If you choose to Erase Ubuntu 17.10 and reinstall, you can also choose the options to encrypt the drive and to use LVM partitions.

```
Upgrade Ubuntu 17.10 to Ubuntu 18.04
Erase Ubuntu 17.10 and reinstall
Something else
```

On systems that also have Windows installed alongside Ubuntu, you are given the same options, but with an added option to erase everything including your Windows system. You are warned that both Windows and Ubuntu are installed on your system. Should you choose to erase Ubuntu and reinstall (the first entry), your Windows system will be preserved.

Detected other operating systems with free space

If you have another operating system on your disk that has been allocated use of part of the disk, you will have an option beginning with "Install Ubuntu alongside" with the name of the installed operating system listed. Keep in mind that LVM installations, like Fedora Linux, are not detected. To preserve an LVM installation you should choose the "Something else" option and enter the disk configuration manually.

In this example, you are given three choices. Should you choose to Replace, then the disk encryption and LVM options become active. However, with the Replace option, your Windows system will be overwritten and erased.

```
Install Ubuntu alongside Microsoft Windows
Replace Microsoft Windows with Ubuntu
Something else
```

Detected another operating system using entire disk (resize)

If you have another operating system on your disk that has been allocated use of the entire disk, you will have an option beginning with "Install Ubuntu alongside" with the name of the installed operating system listed. This option is selected initially. This option is designed for use on hard disks with no unallocated free space but with a large amount of unused space on an existing partition. This is the case for a system where a partition has already been allocated the entire disk. This option will perform a resize of the existing partition, reducing that partition, preserving the data on it, and then creating an Ubuntu partition on that free space. Be warned that this could be a very time-consuming operation. If the original operating system was used heavily, the disk could be fragmented, with files stored all over the hard disk. In this case, the files have to be moved to one area of the hard disk, freeing up continuous space on the remaining area. If the original operating system was used very lightly, then there may be unused continuous space already on the hard drive. In this case, re-partitioning would be quick.

On the "Install alongside" dialog two partitions are displayed, the original showing the new size it will have after the resize, and the new partition for Ubuntu 18.04 formed from the unused space. The size is automatically determined. You can adjust the size if you want by clicking on the space between the partitions to display a space icon, which you can drag left, or right to change the proportional sizes of the partitions.

Upon clicking the Install Now button, a dialog will prompt you with the warning that the resize cannot be undone, and that it may take a long time. Click Continue to perform the resize, or click Go Back to return to the "Installation type" screen. The time it will take depends on the amount of fragmentation on the disk.

Something else

All install situations will include a "Something else" option to let you partition the hard drive manually. The "Something else" option starts up the partitioner, which will let you create, edit, and delete partitions. You can set your own size and type for your partitions. Use this option to preserve or reuse any existing partitions. When you have finished making your changes, click the Install Now button to continue. At this point, your partitions are changed and software is installed, while you continue with the remaining install configuration for time zone and user login.

The partitioner screen displays the partitions on your current hard disk, and lists options for creating your Linux partitions. A graphical bar at the top shows the current state of your hard disk, showing any existing partitions, if any, along with their sizes and labels.

A Boot Loader section at the bottom of the screen provides a drop-down menu of hard drives where you can install the boot loader (see Figure 2-16). Your first hard drive is selected by default. If you have several hard drives on your system, you can choose the one on which to install the boot loader. Systems with only one hard drive, such as laptops, have only one hard drive entry.

The partitioner interface lists any existing partitions (see Figure 2-18). The graphical bar at the top will show the partition on your selected hard drive. The depiction changes as you add, delete, or edit your partitions. Each partition device name and label will be displayed. Unused space will be labeled as free space.

Each hard disk is labeled by its device name, such as **sda** for the first Serial ATA device. Underneath the hard disk graphics bar are labels for the partitions and free space available, along with the partition type and size. The partitions are identified by their colors. At the bottom of the screen are actions you can perform on partitions and free space. To the right are the "New partition table" and Revert buttons for the entire disk. To the left are add, delete, and edit buttons for partitions (+, -, and Change). Your current hard disks and their partitions are listed in the main scrollable pane, with headings for Device, Type, Mount point, Format, Size, and Used space for each partition.

Creating new partitions on a blank hard drive manually

To create partitions on a blank hard drive manually, choose "Something else" (see Figure 2-11). The partitioner interface starts up with the "Installation type" screen, listing any existing partitions (see Figure 2-12). For a blank hard drive, the hard drive only is listed in the main pane.

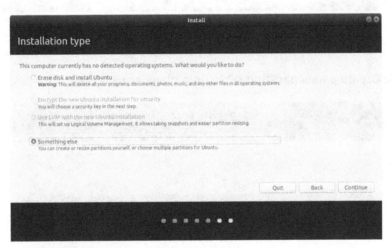

Figure 2-11: Something Else (manual partitioning)

For a new blank hard drive, you first create the partition table by clicking the New Partition Table button (see Figure 2-12). This displays a warning that it will erase any data on the drive. Click Continue (see Figure 2-13). The warning dialog is there in case you accidentally click the New Partition Table button on a drive that has partitions you want to preserve. In this case, you can click Go Back and no new partition table is created.

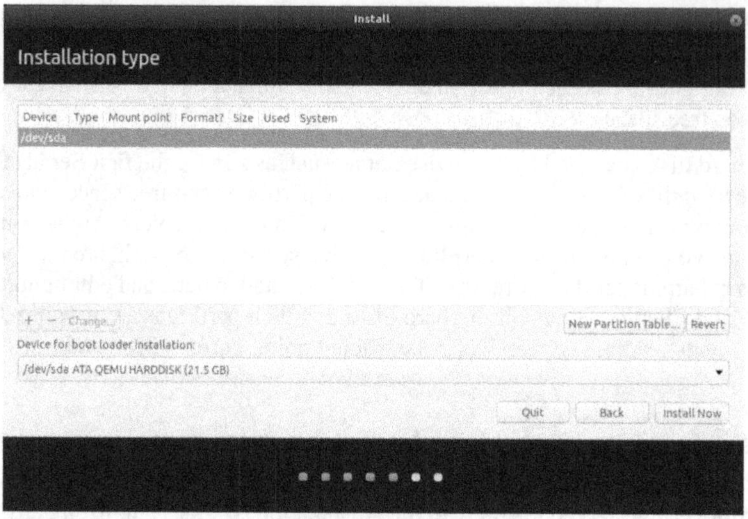

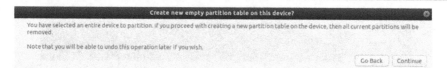

Figure 2-12: Manually partitioning a new hard drive

Figure 2-13: Create a new partition table on a blank hard drive

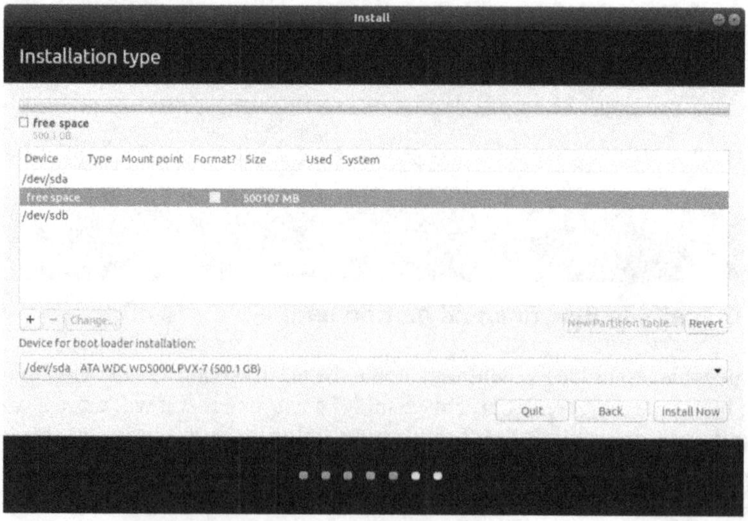

Figure 2-14: Select free space on a blank hard drive

Once the new partition table is set up, the free space entry appears and a graphical bar at the top shows the free space. (see Figure 2-14). If your system already has an operating system installed that takes up only part of the disk, you do not need to create a new partition table. Your free space is already listed (see Figure 2-15).

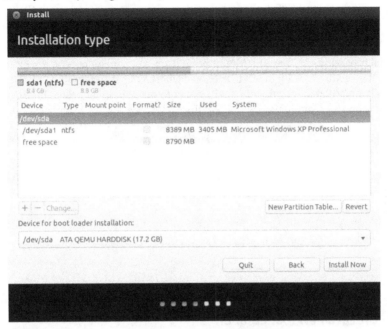

Figure 2-15: Hard drive with windows on part of the drive

For Ubuntu Linux, you will have to create at least one partition, a Linux root partition, where your system will be installed. If your computer also supports EFI boot, as most do, you will also have to add a boot partition of type EFI System Partition. You can create other partitions if you wish. The swap partition is no longer needed. A swap file is used instead. You can, though, if you want, still set up and use a swap partition. To create a new partition, select the free space entry for the hard disk and click the + button. This opens a Create Partition dialog where you can choose the file system type (Use as) and the size of your partition (see Figure 2-16). Do this for each partition. The EFI and swap partitions have no mount point. You only set the size.

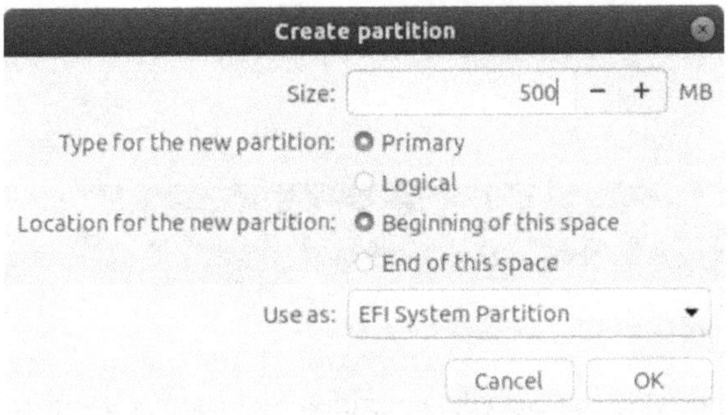

Figure 2-16: Create a new boot partition

The Create Partition dialog displays entries for the partition type (Primary or Logical), the size in megabytes, the location (beginning or end), the file system type (Use as), and the Mount point. For the partition type, the "Do not use" partition entry is initially selected. Choose a partition type from the drop-down menu. Select "Ext4 journaling file system" for the root partition and choose Boot for the boot partition..

For the root partition, from the Mount point drop down menu choose the mount point /, which is the root directory (see Figure 2-17). This is where your system will be installed. The size of the partition is specified in megabytes. It will be set to the remaining space. If you have not already set up the swap partition, reduce the size to allow space for the swap partition.

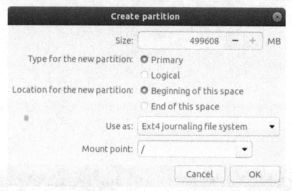

Figure 2-17: Create a new root partition

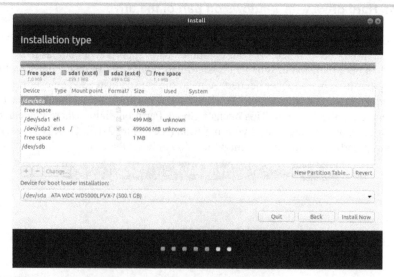

Figure 2-18: Manual partitions

If you make a mistake, you can edit a partition by selecting it and clicking the Change button. This opens an Edit partitions window where you can make changes. You can also delete a partition, returning its space to free space, and then create a new one. Select the partition and click the - button (delete). The partition is not actually deleted at this point. No changes are made at all until you start installing Ubuntu. The "Revert" button is always available to undo all the changes you specified so far, and start over from the original state of the hard disk.

When you have finished setting up your partitions, you will see entries for them displayed. The graphical bar at the top will show their size and location (see Figure 2-18). Click the "Install Now" button to perform the partitioning, formatting, and installation.

Where Are You?

On the "Where are you?" screen, you can set the time zone by using a map to specify your location (see Figure 2-19). The Time Zone tool uses a map feature that displays the entire earth, with sections for each time zone. Click on your general location, and the entire time zone for your part of the world will be highlighted in green. The major city closest to your location will be labeled with its current time. The selected city will appear in the text box located below the map. You can also select your time zone entering the city in the text box. As you type in the city name, a pop-up menu appears showing progressively limited choices. The corresponding time zone will be highlighted on the map.

Click the Continue button to continue.

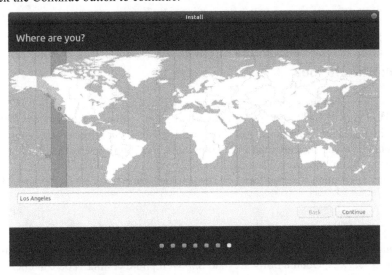

Figure 2-19: Where Are You, Time zone

At the same time as the "Where are you?" dialog appears, Ubuntu begins to format your partitions, copy files to your hard drive, and install the software. A progress bar at the bottom of the dialog shows the progression of the copy process. You can click an expansion arrow next to the progress bar to open a small terminal section that displays the install operations as they occur.

Who Are You?

On the Who are you? screen you enter your name, your user login name, and password (see Figure 2-20). When you enter your name, a username will be generated for you using your first name, and a computer name will be entered using your first name and your computer's make and model name. You can change these names if you want. The name for the computer is the computer's network host name. The user you are creating will have administrative access, allowing you to change your system configuration, add new users and printers, and install new software. When you enter your password a Strength notice is displayed indicating whether it is too short, weak, fair, or good. For a good password include numbers and uppercase characters.

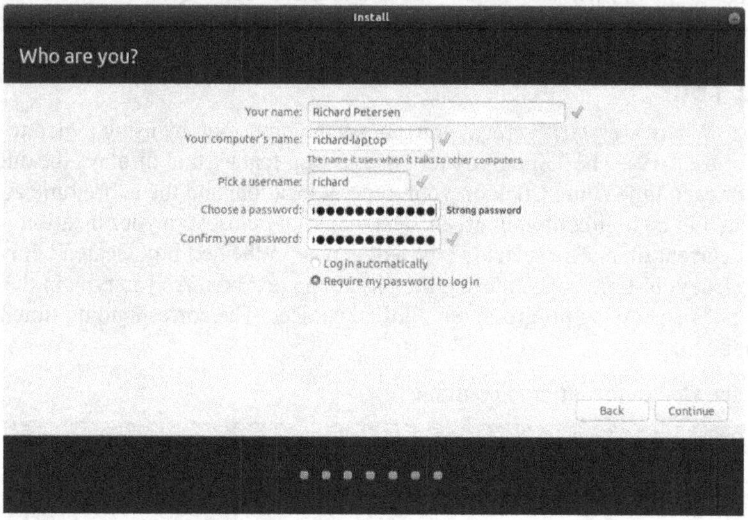

Figure 2-20: Who are you?

At the bottom of the screen, you have the options: "Log in automatically" and "Require my password to log in." The "Require my password to login" option has an additional check box for "Encrypt my home folder." Choose the "Log in automatically" option to have your system login to your account when you start up, instead of stopping at the login screen. The "Require my password to log in" entry provides a standard login screen. If you choose "Encrypt my home folder" private directory encryption is set up for your home folder, encrypting all the home folder files and subfolders.

Install Progress

Your installation continues with a slide show of Ubuntu 18.04 features such as Web browsers, social services, Ubuntu Software, and Shotwell photo editing. You can click on the arrow tabs at either end to move through the slide show manually (see Figure 2-21).

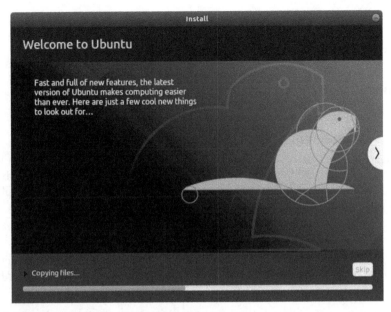

Figure 2-21: Install progress slide show

Once finished, the Installation Complete dialog appears (see Figure 2-22). Click the Restart Now button to restart and reboot to the new installation. Your DVD disc is ejected, and a screen will appear prompting you to remove the disc, and then press ENTER. If you installed from the Live DVD/USB session, you are also given the option to return to that session.

Figure 2-22: Installation completed

Tip: Pressing ESC from the graphics menu places you at the boot prompt for text mode install.

Upgrading

You can upgrade a current Ubuntu system to the next release using the APT package manager or the Ubuntu Desktop DVD. Upgrading is a simple matter of updating software to the new release versions, along with updating your GRUB configuration. Check the following site for upgrade details:

`https://help.ubuntu.com/community/BionicUpgrades`

You can only upgrade to Ubuntu 18.04 from Ubuntu 17.10, and to Ubuntu 18.04.1 (summer, 2016) from 16.04. Be sure you have first performed any needed updates for your Ubuntu system. It must be completely up to date before you perform an upgrade to Ubuntu 18.04.

You cannot upgrade from Ubuntu 17.04, or earlier to 18.04 directly. To upgrade from an earlier release other than 17.10, first, upgrade sequentially up to 17.10. For example, to upgrade from 17.04, you would first upgrade to 17.10, and then you can upgrade from 17.10 to 18.04.

You can upgrade from 16.04, but only to the 18.04.1 version or later, not the 18.04 version initially released. The 18.04.1 version will be released three months after the 18.04 version, and 16.04 users will be notified of the available upgrade at that time.

Upgrade over a network from Ubuntu 16.04 and 17.10

To upgrade your system using your Internet connection, you can use Software Updater. The upgrade will be performed by downloading the latest package versions from the Ubuntu repository, directly. When a new release becomes available, Software Updater will display a message notifying you of the new release (provided it is configured to do so).

Be sure to first enable distribution notification for long term support versions. On the Ubuntu Software Updater dialog, click the Settings button on the lower left to open the Software & Updates dialog at the Updates tab. On the last menu "Notify me of a new Ubuntu version," choose the "For any new versions" for Ubuntu 17.10, and "For long-term support versions" for Ubuntu 16.04.

An Upgrade button will be displayed next to the message should you decide to upgrade your system to that release (see Figure 2-23). If you want to stay with the Ubuntu 17.10 release, for now, you just click the OK button. Should you want to upgrade to the new release, in this case, Ubuntu 18.04, you click the Upgrade button to start the upgrade. A Welcome dialog is displayed with links for information about the release. Click the Upgrade button on this dialog to begin the upgrade. Be sure first to update all your current software. An upgrade should be performed from the most recent versions of your current release's software packages.

Figure 2-23: Upgrade message

You can also start the software updater directly for the distribution upgrade by entering the following on a command line (the **-d** option performs a distribution upgrade). Use either a terminal window or press Alt-F2 to open a Run Application window.

```
sudo update-manager -d
```

A Distribution Upgrade dialog opens showing the progress of the upgrade. The upgrade procedure will first prepare the upgrade, detecting the collection of software packages that have to be downloaded. A dialog will notify you of software packages for which support has ended (older deprecated software). Then a dialog will then open asking if you want to start the upgrade, displaying both a Cancel and Start Upgrade button. You can still cancel the upgrade at this time and nothing will be changed on your system (click the Cancel button). To continue with the Upgrade, click the Start Upgrade button.

The Distribution Upgrade dialog is again displayed (see Figure 2-24). Packages are downloaded (Getting new packages), and then installed on your system (Installing the upgrades). The download process can take some time depending on the speed of your Internet connection.

Figure 2-24: Distribution Upgrade dialog

If the download is taking too long, you can click the Cancel button and run the upgrade later. A dialog is displayed telling you that the download will continue later from where it left off.

To start the upgrade again, first start Software Updater, click the Upgrade button, and proceed through the initial steps again, though this time will be much faster (Release notes, Preparing to upgrade, Setting new software channels). The Getting new packages stage will continue with next package.

Note: Depending on the packages you are upgrading, you may have to enter configuration information through the terminal interface. Click the terminal arrow to open the terminal interface and respond to any prompts that may occur.

Once the upgrade is completed, a completion message is displayed. Reboot to start your system with the new release and its kernel.

Upgrading to a new release with apt-get

You can also use the **apt-get** command in a terminal window or on a command line interface to upgrade your system. To upgrade to an entirely new release, use the **dist-upgrade** option. A **dist-upgrade** would install a new release, preserving your original configuration and data. This option will also remove obsolete software packages.

```
sudo apt-get update
sudo apt-get dist-upgrade
```

Recovery, rescue, and boot loader re-install

Ubuntu provides the means to start up systems that have failed for some reason. A system that may boot but fails to start up, can be started in a recovery mode, already set up for you as an entry on your boot loader menu.

Recovery Mode (Advanced Options menu)

If for some reason your system is not able to start up, it may be due to conflicting configurations, libraries, or applications. On the GRUB menu first, choose the "Advanced options or Ubuntu" to open the advanced options menu. Then select the recovery mode entry, the Ubuntu kernel entry with the (recovery mode) label attached to the end. This starts up a menu where you can use the arrow and ENTER keys to select from several recovery options (see Figure 2-25). These include resume, clean, dpkg, grub, network, and root. Short descriptions for each item are displayed on the menu.

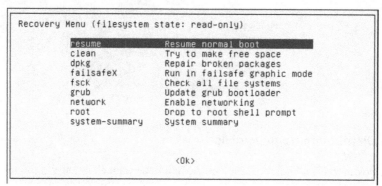

Figure 2-25: Recovery options

The root option starts up Ubuntu as the root user with a command line shell prompt. In this case, you can boot your Linux system in a recovery mode and then edit configuration files with a text editor such as Vi, remove the suspect libraries, or reinstall damaged software with **apt-get**.

The resume entry will start up Ubuntu normally, but into the command line mode.

The **grub** entry will update the grub boot loader. With GRUB2 your hard drive is re-scanned, detecting your installed operating systems and Ubuntu kernels, and implementing any GRUB configuration changes you may have made without updating GRUB.

To rescue a broken system, choose the **root** entry. Your broken system will be mounted and made accessible with a command line interface. You can then use command line operations and editors to fix configuration files.

Re-Installing the Boot Loader

If you have a multiple-boot system, that runs both Windows and Linux on the same machine, you may run into a situation where you have to reinstall your GRUB boot loader. This problem occurs if your Windows system completely crashes beyond repair and you have to install a new version of Windows, if you added Windows to your machine after having installed Linux, or if you upgraded to a new version of Windows. A Windows installation will automatically overwrite your boot loader (alternatively, you could install your boot loader on your Linux partition instead of the master boot record, MBR). You will no longer be able to access your Linux system.

You can reinstall your boot loader manually, using your Ubuntu Desktop DVD live session. The procedure is more complicated, as you have to mount your Ubuntu system. On the

Ubuntu Desktop DVD Live session, you can use GParted to find out what partition your Ubuntu system uses. In a terminal window, create a directory on which to mount the system.

```
sudo mkdir myubuntu
```

Then mount it, making sure you have the correct file system type and partition name (usually **/dev/sda5** on dual boot systems).

```
sudo mount -t ext4 /dev/sda5 myubuntu
```

Then use **grub-install** and the device name of your first partition to install the boot loader, with the **--root-directory** option to specify the directory where you mounted your Ubuntu file system. The **--root-directory** option requires a full path name, which for the Ubuntu Desktop DVD would be **/home/ubuntu** for the home directory. Using the **myubuntu** directory for this example, the full path name of the Ubuntu file system would be **/home/ubuntu/myubuntu**. You would then enter the following **grub-install** command.

```
sudo grub-install --root-directory=/home/ubuntu/myubuntu /dev/sda
```

This will re-install your current GRUB boot loader. You can then reboot, and the GRUB boot loader will start up.

3. Usage Basics: Login, Desktop, Network, and Help

graphical logins and desktop interfaces, including the GNOME interface and Kubuntu (KDE). Even the standard Linux command line interface is user-friendly with editable commands, history lists, and cursor-based tools. To start using Ubuntu, you have to know how to access your system and, once you are on the system, how to execute commands and run applications. Access is supported through a graphical login. A simple screen appears with menus for selecting login options and your username. Once you access your system, you can interact with it using windows, menus, and icons.

Linux is noted for providing easy access to extensive help documentation. It is easy to obtain information quickly about any Linux command and utility while logged into the system. You can access an online manual that describes each command, or obtain help that provides explanations that are more detailed. All the desktops provide help systems with easy access to desktop, system, and application help files.

Accessing Your Ubuntu System

You access your Ubuntu system using the GRUB bootloader to first start Ubuntu, and then use the display manager to log in to your account. Once logged in, you also can switch to other users using the Session menu. You can also log in as a guest user, letting others quickly use your computer without access to your files. From the desktop Session menu (power button, top right) you can shut down, restart, or suspend your system. It is also possible to access Ubuntu using a command line interface only, bypassing the desktop interface and its required graphical support.

Ubuntu now uses the systemd login manager, logind, to manage logins and sessions, replacing consolekit, which is no longer supported.   You can configure login manager options with the **/etc/systemd/logind.conf** file. You can set options such as the number of terminals (default is 6), the idle action, and hardware key operations, such as the power key. Check the **logind.conf** man page for details.

GRUB Boot Loader

When your system restarts, the GRUB boot loader will quickly select your default operating system and start up its login screen. If you have just installed Ubuntu, the default operating system will be Ubuntu.

If you have installed more than one operating system, the GRUB menu is displayed for several seconds at startup, before loading the default operating system automatically. To display the GRUB menu should you have only your Ubuntu system installed, press the ESC key at start up. Once displayed, press any key to have GRUB wait until you have made a selection. Your GRUB menu is displayed as shown in Figure 3-1. The Advanced options entry allows you to start Ubuntu in recovery mode.

The GRUB menu lists Ubuntu along with any other operating systems installed on your hard drive, such as Windows or other versions of Linux. Use the arrow keys to move to the entry you want and press ENTER

For graphical installations, some displays may have difficulty running the graphical startup display. If you have this problem, you can edit your Linux GRUB entry and remove the **splash** term at the end of the **linux** line. Press the **e** key to edit a GRUB entry (see Figure 3-2).

GNU GRUB version 2.02
Advanced options for Linux Mint 19 Cinnamon
Memory test (memtest86+)
Memory test (memtest86+, serial console 115200)
Use the ↑ and ↓ keys to select which entry is highlighted.
Press enter to boot the selected OS, `e' to edit the commands
before booting or `c' for a command-line.

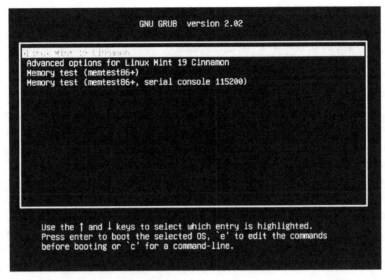

Figure 3-1: Ubuntu GRUB menu

To change a particular line, use the up/down arrow keys to move to the line. You can use the left/right arrow keys to move along the line. The Backspace key will delete characters and typing will insert characters. The editing changes are temporary. Permanent changes can only be made by directly editing the GRUB configuration **/etc/default/grub** file, and then running the following command:

```
sudo update-grub
```

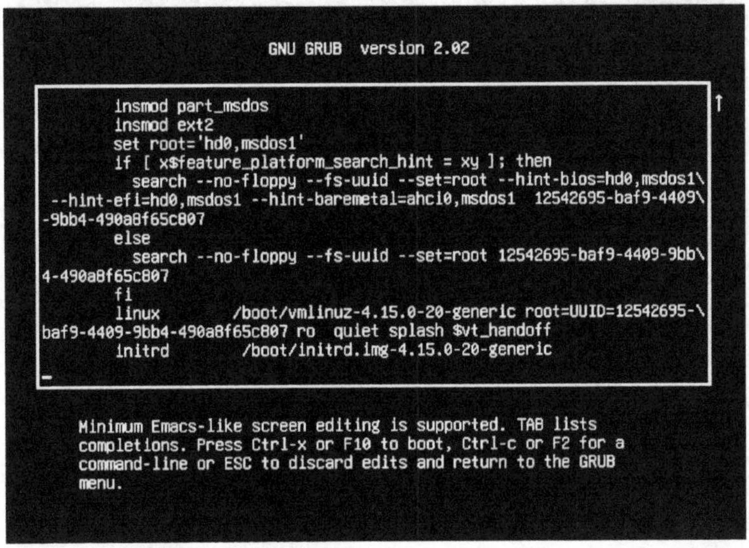

GNU GRUB version 2.02
insmod part_msdos
insmod ext2
set root='hd0,msdos1'
if [x$feature_platform_search_hint = xy]; then
search --no-floppy --fs-uuid --set=root --hint-bios=hd0,msdos1\
--hint-efi=hd0,msdos1 --hint-baremetal=ahci0,msdos1 12542695-baf9-4409\
-9bb4-490a8f65c807
else
search --no-floppy --fs-uuid --set=root 12542695-baf9-4409-9bb\
4-490a8f65c807
fi
linux /boot/vmlinuz-4.15.0-20-generic root=UUID=12542695-\
baf9-4409-9bb4-490a8f65c807 ro quiet splash $vt_handoff
initrd /boot/initrd.img-4.15.0-20-generic
Minimum Emacs-like screen editing is supported. TAB lists
completions. Press Ctrl-x or F10 to boot, Ctrl-c or F2 for a
command-line or ESC to discard edits and return to the GRUB
menu.

Figure 3-2: Editing a GRUB menu item

When your Ubuntu operating system starts up, an Ubuntu logo appears during the startup. You can press the ESC key to see the startup messages instead. Ubuntu uses Plymouth with its kernel modesetting ability to display a startup animation. The Plymouth Ubuntu logo theme is used by default.

The GNOME Display Manager: GDM

The graphical login interface displays a login window with a box listing a menu of usernames. When you click a username, a login box replaces the listing of users, displaying the selected username and a text box in which you then enter your password. Upon clicking the Sign In button or pressing Enter, you log in to the selected account, and your desktop starts up.

Graphical logins are handled by the GNOME Display Manager (GDM). The GDM manages the login interface, in addition to authenticating a user password and username, and then starts up a selected desktop. From the GDM, you can shift to the command-line interface with Ctrl+Alt+F2, and then shift back to the GDM with Ctrl+Alt+F1 (from a desktop, you would use the same keys to shift to a command-line interface and to shift back). The keys F2 through F6 provide different command-line terminals, as in Ctrl+Alt+F3 for the second command-line terminal.

When the GDM starts up, it shows a listing of users (see Figure 3-3). A System Status Area at the top right of the screen displays icons indicating the status of the sound and battery. Clicking the icons displays the System Status Area menu, which shows the entries for sound adjustment, network wireless (if supported), and the battery status (if a laptop), as well as the status your network connections. A power button at the bottom will display a power off dialog with options to Power Off and Restart. To shut down your system, click the Power Off button on the dialog.

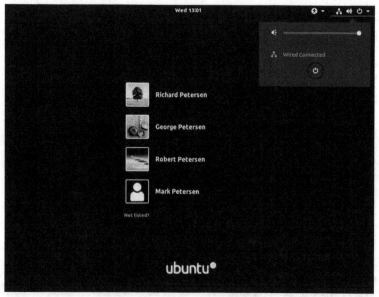

Figure 3-3: The GDM user listing

At the top center of the screen is the date (day of the week) and time. Clicking on the time displays the calendar with the full date specified, and the notifications menu.

Next to the System Status Area icons is a menu for accessibility, which displays a menu of switches that let you turn on accessibility tools and such features as the onscreen keyboard, enhanced contrast, and the screen magnifier.

To log in, click a username from the list of users. You are then prompted to enter the user's password (see Figure 3-4). A new dialog replaces the user list, showing the username you selected and a Password text box in which you can enter the user's password. Once you enter the password, click the Sign In button or press Enter. By default, the GNOME desktop starts up. If the name of a user you want to log in as is not listed, click the "Not Listed" entry at the end, to open a text box, which prompts you for a username, and then the password.

Though GNOME is the primary desktop for Ubuntu, it is possible to install and use other desktops, such as KDE (Kubuntu), Xfce (Xubuntu), and Mate. These are available on the Ubuntu repository. Should you have more than one desktop installed, such as both GNOME and KDE, when you click a username under which to log in, a Session button (gear icon) is displayed below the Password text box next to the "Sign in" button. Click that Session button to open a menu listing the installed desktops, then click the one you want to use (see Figure 3-5).

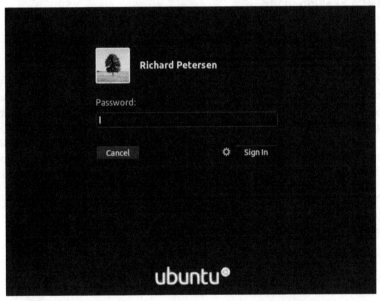

Figure 3-4: GDM login

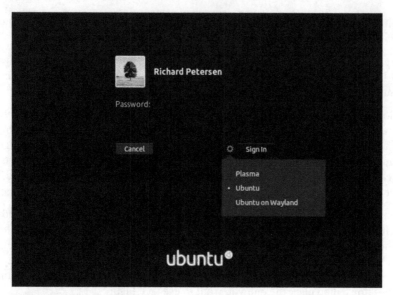

Figure 3-5: GDM Session menu

The System Status Area

Once logged in, the System Status Area is displayed on the right side of the top bar of the desktop (see Figure 3-6) . The area will include status icons for features such as sound and power. Clicking the button showing the sound, power, and down arrow icons displays the System Status Area menu, with items for sound, brightness, wired and wireless connections, the battery, the current user, in addition to buttons at the bottom for opening GNOME Settings, activating the lock screen, and shutting down or rebooting the system. The sound and brightness items feature sliding bars with which you can adjust the volume and brightness. The Wi-Fi, Battery, and current user entries expand to submenus with added entries. The buttons at the bottom open separate dialogs.

On systems that are not laptops, there will be no brightness slider or Battery entry on the System Status Area menu. If the system also has no wireless device, the Wi-Fi entry will also be missing. A system of this kind will only have a sound slider and a user entry.

Figure 3-6: System Status Area menu

Lock Screen

You can choose to lock your screen and suspend your system by click the Lock button, the middle button at the bottom of the System Status Area menu. To start up again, press the spacebar and the Lock Screen dialog appears (see Figure 3-7). This is the same as the login screen, with only a single entry for your username and the password prompt. Enter your password to start up your desktop session again.

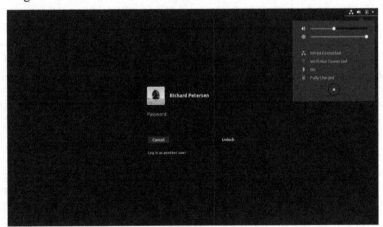

Figure 3-7: Lock Screen

Logging Out and Switching Users

If you want to exit your desktop and return to the GDM login screen, or switch to a different user, you click the user entry in the System Status Area menu to expand to a menu with entries for Switch User, Log Out, and Account Settings (see Figure 3-8). If you have only once user configured for your system, then the Switch User entry does not appear.

Figure 3-8: GNOME Log Out menu entry

Click the Log Out entry to display a dialog that shows buttons for Cancel and Log Out (see Figure 3-9). Click the Log Out button to log out of your account, exiting GNOME and returning to the login screen, where you can log in again as a different user or shut down the system. A countdown will commence in the dialog, showing how much time you have left before it performs the logout automatically.

Figure 3-9: Log Out dialog

The Switch User entry switches out from the current user and runs the GDM to display a list of users you can log in as. Click the name to open a password prompt and display a session button. You can then log in as that user. The sessions of users already logged will continue with the same open windows and applications that were running when the user switched off. You can switch back and forth between logged-in users, with all users retaining their session from where they left off. When you switch off from a user, that user's running programs will continue in the background.

Poweroff

From the login screen, you can poweroff (shut down) the system using the System Status Area menu on either the login screen or the desktop. Click the power button at the bottom right on the System Status Area menu. This displays a power off dialog with options to restart or power off (see Figure 3-10). A countdown will commence in the dialog, showing how much time you have left before it performs the shutdown automatically. You can also simply press the power button on your computer to display the Power Off dialog.

Figure 3-10: Power Off and Restart dialog

Should your display freeze or become corrupted, one safe way to shut down and restart is to press a command line interface key (like CTRL-ALT-F1) to revert to the command line interface, and then press CTRL-ALT-DEL to restart. You can also log in on the command line interface (terminal) and then enter the **sudo poweroff** command.

On the desktop, you can also shut down your system from a terminal window, using the **poweroff** command with the **sudo** command. You will be prompted to enter your password.

```
sudo poweroff
```

To perform a reboot from a terminal window, you can use the **reboot** command.

```
sudo reboot
```

The shutdown process works through systemd using the **systemctl** command. The poweroff, halt, and reboot commands invoke systemd service files activated through corresponding target files. The systemctl command, in turn, uses the **/lib/systemd/system-shutdown** program to perform the actual shut down operation. In the **/lib/systemd/system** directory, the **systemd-poweroff.service** file shows the systemctl poweroff command. The man page for the shutdown service is **systemd-halt-service**. Always use the **poweroff**, **reboot**, and **halt** commands to shut down, not the **systemctl** command. The corresponding systemd target and service files ensure that the shutdown process proceeds safely.

systemd-poweroff.service

```
#   This file is part of systemd.
#
#   systemd is free software; you can redistribute it and/or modify it
#   under the terms of the GNU Lesser General Public License as published by
#   the Free Software Foundation; either version 2.1 of the License, or
#   (at your option) any later version.

[Unit]
Description=Power-Off
Documentation=man:systemd-halt.service(8)
DefaultDependencies=no
Requires=shutdown.target umount.target final.target
After=shutdown.target umount.target final.target

[Service]
Type=oneshot
ExecStart=/bin/systemctl --force poweroff
```

Accessing Linux from the Command Line Interface

You can access the command-line interface by pressing CTRL-ALT-F1 at any time (CTRL-ALT-F7 returns to the graphics interface). For the command line interface, you are initially given a login prompt. The login prompt is preceded by the hostname you gave your system. In this example, the hostname is **richard-desktop**. When you finish using Linux, you log out with the **logout** command. Linux then displays the same login prompt, waiting for you or another user to log in again. This is the equivalent of the login window provided by the GDM display manager. You can then log in to another account.

Once you log in as a user, you can enter and execute commands. To log in, enter your username and your password. If you make a mistake, you can erase characters with the BACKSPACE key. In the next example, the user enters the username **richard** and is then prompted to enter the password:

```
Ubuntu 18.04 LTS richard-desktop tty1

richard-desktop login: richard
Password:
```

When you type in your password, it does not appear on the screen. This is to protect your password from being seen by others. If you enter either the username or the password incorrectly, the system will respond with the error message "Login incorrect" and will ask for your username again, starting the login process over. You can then reenter your username and password.

Once you enter your username and password, you are logged in to the system and the command line prompt is displayed, waiting for you to enter a command. The command line prompt is a dollar sign (**$**). On Ubuntu, your prompt is preceded by the hostname and the directory you are in. The home directory is indicated by a tilde (~).

```
richard@richard-desktop:~$
richard@richard-desktop:~$ cd Pictures
richard@richard-desktop:~/Pictures$
```

To end your session, issue the **logout** or **exit** command. This returns you to the login prompt, and Linux waits for another user to log in.

```
richard@richard-desktop:~$ logout
```

To, instead, shut down your system from the command line, you can use the **poweroff** command with the **sudo** command. You will be prompted to enter your password.

```
sudo poweroff
```

To perform a reboot from the terminal window, you can use the **reboot** command.

```
sudo reboot
```

If you want a time delay on the shutdown, you would use the **shutdown** command with **-h** and the time options with administrative access (**sudo** command). This command will log you out and shut down the system after 5 minutes.

```
richard@richard-desktop:~$ sudo shutdown -h +5
```

The Ubuntu Desktop

Ubuntu 18.04 supports two major different desktop interfaces: Ubuntu and Kubuntu. The Ubuntu Desktop DVD installs Ubuntu. The Ubuntu desktop uses the Ubuntu GNOME interface.

Ubuntu prefers hardware acceleration support provided by the appropriate display driver. If your current graphics driver does not support hardware acceleration, you will be logged in using acceleration simulation with LLVMpipe on OpenGL running on the CPU. This can result in a slower system.

The Kubuntu DVD installs the KDE desktop interface. You can also install KDE on an Ubuntu desktop system using the KDE meta-packages: **kubuntu-desktop** or **kubuntu-full**. Although the GNOME and KDE interfaces appear similar, they are very different desktop interfaces with separate tools for configuring preferences.

Ubuntu uses the Ubuntu Ambiance theme for its interface with the Ubuntu screen background, and menu icons as its default (see Figure 3-11). Another Ubuntu theme is available called Radiance. Ambiance is a darker color theme, while Radiance uses lighter colors. The Ambiance theme is used in the examples in this book. You can change to the Radiance theme using the GNOME Tweaks Appearance tab's Themes | Applications menu.

Keypress	Action
SHIFT	Move a file or directory, default
CTRL	Copy a file or directory
CTRL-SHIFT	Create a link for a file or directory
F2	Rename selected file or directory
CTRL-ALT-Arrow (right, left, up, down)	Move to a different desktop
CTRL-w	Close current window
ALT-spacebar	Open window menu for window operations
ALT-F2	Open Run command box
ALT-F1	Open Applications menu
Ctrl-F	Find file

Table 3-1: Window and File Manager Keyboard shortcuts

The Ambiance and Radiance themes place the window control buttons (close, maximize, and minimize buttons) on the right side of a window title bar, as shown here. There are three window buttons: an x for close, a dash (-) for minimize, and a square for maximize. The close button is highlighted in orange.

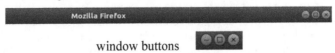

window buttons

To move a window, click and drag its title bar. Each window supports Minimize, Maximize, and Close buttons located on the left side of the title bar. Double-clicking the title bar will maximize the window. Many keyboard operations are also similar as listed in Table 3-1.

Ubuntu GNOME

Ubuntu 18.04 uses the GNOME desktop. It provides easy-to-use overviews and menus, along with a flexible file manager and desktop. GNOME is based on the gnome-shell, which is a compositing window manager. When you first login, a "What's new in Ubuntu" screen displays an image showing the key features of the GNOME desktop such as the System menu, Window switcher, Launcher, and Apps button. These are descriptive names, not the actual names of the elements. The screen is shown here.

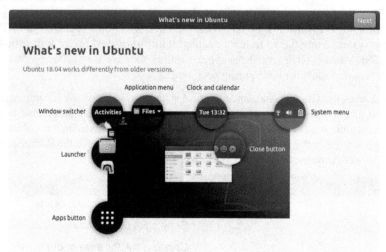

The Ubuntu desktop displays a top bar, through which you access your applications, windows, and settings. Clicking the System Status Area button at the right side of the top bar displays the status user area menu, from which you can access buttons at the bottom to display the system setting dialog, lock the screen, and shut down the system (see Figure 3-11). The dock is a bar on the left side with icons for your favorite applications. Initially, there are icons for the Firefox web browser, Thunerbird mail, Files (the GNOME file manager), Rythymnbox music application, LibreOffice Writer, Ubuntu Software, GNOME help, a link to Amazon, and the Applications overview, as depicted in Figure 3-11. The last icon opens an Applications overview that you can use to start other applications. To open an application from the dock, click its icon or right-click on the icon and choose New Window from the pop-up menu. You can remove any of them except the Applications overview by right-clicking and choosing "Remove from Favorites." Running applications will also be shown in the dock, which you can make part of your Favorites if you want. The Ubuntu dock is a GNOME extension implemented by Ubuntu and is a modified version of the GNOME Dock to Dash extension, which places a GNOME dash on the desktop.

You can also access applications and windows by using the Activities overview mode. Click the Activities button at the left side of the top bar (or move the mouse to the left corner, or press the Windows button). The overview mode consists of a dash listing your favorites and running applications, workspaces, and windows (see Figure 3-12). Large thumbnails of open windows are displayed on the windows overview (the desktop area). You can use the Search box at the top to locate an application quickly. Partially hidden thumbnails of your desktop workspaces are displayed on the right side. Initially, there are two. Moving your mouse to the right side displays the workspace thumbnails.

You can manually leave the overview at any time by pressing the ESC key or by clicking a window thumbnail.

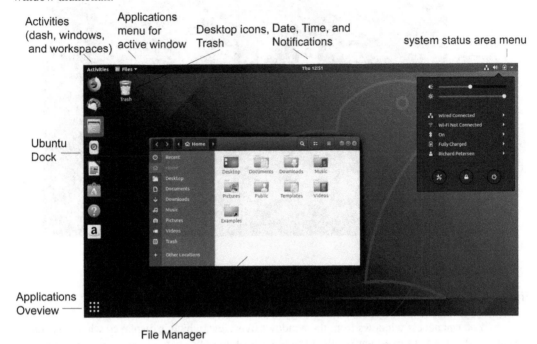

Figure 3-11: The Ubuntu GNOME desktop

The dash is a bar on the left side of the overview with icons for your favorite applications. Initially. It operates the same as the Ubuntu dock, from which it was derived (see Figure 3-12). as on the dock, the last icon opens an Applications overview that you can use to start other applications. To open an application from the dash, click its icon or right-click on the icon and choose New Window from the pop-up menu. You can also click and drag the icon to the windows overview or to a workspace thumbnail on the right side.

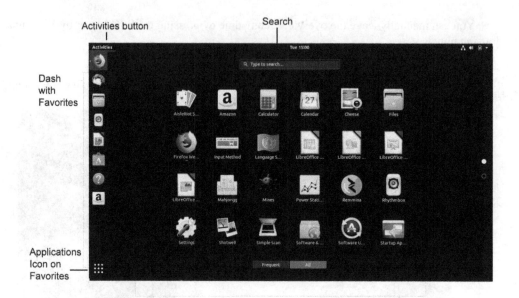

Activities Applications Overview

Figure 3-12: GNOME Activities overview mode for applications

You can access windows from the windows overview, which is displayed when you start Activities. The windows overview displays thumbnails of all your open windows. When you pass your mouse over a window thumbnail, a close box appears, at the upper-right corner, with which you can close the window. You can also move the window on the desktop and to another workspace.

To move a window on the desktop, click and drag its title bar. To maximize a window, double-click its title bar or drag it to the top bar. To minimize, double-click the title bar again or drag it away from the top bar. To close a window, click its close box (upper right).

Two sub-folders are available on the applications overview: Utilities and Sundry. Utilities lists several tools, such as the text editor and system monitor, and Sundry lists older administrative tools, such as system-config-printer and firewall-config. These sub-folders function like a submenu, overlaying the main overview with a sub-folder. You can use the Ubuntu Software Installed tab to create your own sub-folders and place application icons in them.

GNOME File Manager

You can access your home folder from the Files icon on the dash. A file manager window opens, showing your Home folder (see Figure 3-13). Your Home folder will already have default directories created for commonly used files. These include Documents, Downloads, Music, Pictures, and Videos. Your office applications will automatically save files to the Documents folder by default. Image and photo applications place image files in the Pictures directory. The Desktop folder will hold all files and directories saved to your desktop. When you download a file, it is placed in the Downloads directory.

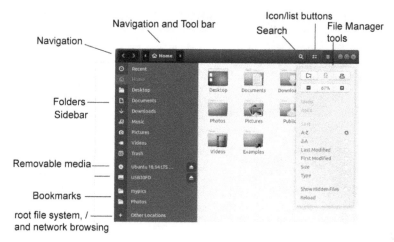

Figure 3-13: File manager for the Home folder

The file manager window displays several components, including a header bar, which combines the title bar and toolbar, and a sidebar. When you open a new directory, the same window is used to display it, and you can use the forward and back arrows to move through previously opened directories. The header bar displays navigation folder buttons that show your current folder and its parent folders. You can click a parent folder to move to it. The GNOME file manager also supports tabs. You can open several folders in the same file manager window. Click on the menu button on the right side of the titlebar to display the file manager tools with buttons to add a new folder, tab, or bookmark, as well as zoom buttons for enlarging or reducing the size of the folder icons. You can also sort files and show hidden files.

GNOME Customization with Tweak Tool: Themes, Icons, Fonts, Startup Applications, and Extensions

You can perform common desktop customizations using the GNOME Tweak Tool. Areas to customize include the desktop icons, fonts, themes, startup applications, workspaces, window behavior, and the time display. You can access Tweak Tool from the Applications overview | Utilities. The GNOME Tweak Tool has tabs for Appearance, Desktop, Extensions, Fonts, Keyboard and Mouse, Power, Startup Applications, Top Bar, Typing, Windows, and Workspaces (see Figure 3-14).

The Appearance tab lets you set the theme for your windows, icons, and cursor. GNOME 3 uses the Adwaita Theme. This theme has a light and dark variant. The Global Light Theme is the default, but you can use the switch on the Appearance tab to enable the Global Dark Theme. The Global Dark Theme shades the background of windows to a dark gray, while text and button images appear in white.

As you add other desktops, such as Cinnamon, the available themes increase. There are many window themes to choose from, including Clearlooks, Mist, and Glider. For icons, you can choose among Oxygen (KDE), Mist (Cinnamon), and GNOME.

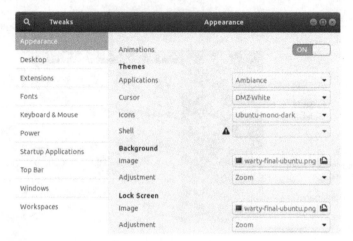

Figure 3-14: GNOME Tweak Tool - Appearance tab (themes)

You may also want to display Home, Trash, and Mounted Volumes like USB drives, on the desktop, as other desktops do. Use the Desktop tab on Tweak Tool to display these icons (see Figure 3-15). Turn on the "Icons on Desktop" switch. Home, Trash, and Mounted Volumes are checked by default. Uncheck them in order not to display the icon. You can also check a Network Servers option to display icons for remotely accessed folders.

Figure 3-15: GNOME Tweak Tool - Desktop tab (desktop icons)

Desktop fonts for window titles, interface (application or dialog text), documents, and monospace (terminal windows or code) can be changed in the Fonts tab (see Figure 3-16). You can adjust the size of the font or change the font style. Clicking the font name opens a "Pick a Font" dialog from which you can choose a different font. The quality of text display can be further adjusted with Hinting and Antialiasing options. To simply increase or decrease the size of all fonts on your desktop interface, you can adjust the Scaling Factor.

Figure 3-16: GNOME Tweak Tool - Fonts tab

At times, there may be certain applications that you want started up when you log in, such as the Gedit text editor, the Firefox web browser, or the Videos movie player. On the Startup Applications tab, you can choose the applications to start up (see Figure 3-17). Click the plus (+) button to open an applications dialog from which you can choose an application to start up. Once added, you can later remove the application by clicking its Remove button.

Figure 3-17: GNOME Tweak Tool - Startup Applications tab

Extensions function much as applets did in GNOME 2. They are third-party programs that enhance or modify the GNOME desktop, such as a system monitor, sensors, and applications menu. Extensions appear on the top bar or the message tray at the bottom of the screen. You can display the message tray with the Super+m keys or by holding the cursor down on the bottom edge for a few seconds. Installed extensions are listed on the Extensions tab of Tweak Tool, where you can turn them on or off.

Network Connections

Network connections will be set up for you by Network Manager, which will detect your network connections automatically, both wired and wireless. Network Manager provides status information for your connection and allows you to switch easily from one configured connection to another, as needed. For initial configuration, it detects as much information as possible about the new connection.

Network Manager is user specific. Wired connections will be started automatically. For wireless connections, when a user logs in, Network Manager selects the connection preferred by that user. From a menu of detected wireless networks, the user can select a wireless connection to use.

Network Manager displays active network connections in the System Status Area: Wired for the wired connection and Wi-Fi for a wireless connection. Each entry will indicate its status, as connected or disconnected. The Network Manager icon for these entries will vary according to the connection status: solid for an active connection and faded for a disconnected connection (see Figure 3-18). On wired systems that have no wireless devices, there is no Wi-Fi network entry in the System Status Area menu.

Figure 3-18: System Status Area Network Connections

Network Manager Wired Connections

For computers connected to a wired network, such as an Ethernet connection, Network Manager automatically detects and establishes the network connection. Most networks use DHCP to provide such network information as an IP address and DNS server. With this kind of connection, Network Manager can connect automatically to your network whenever you start your system.

Network Manager Wireless Connections

With multiple wireless access points for Internet connections, a system could have several network connections to choose from. This is particularly true for notebook computers that access different wireless connections at different locations. Instead of manually configuring a new connection each time one is encountered, the Network Manager tool can configure and select a connection to use automatically. Click the Wired entry in the System Status Area to expand the menu to show entries from which to connect or disconnect to wired networking, and open the GNOME Network Settings dialog at the Wired tab (Wired Settings).

Network Manager will scan for wireless connections, checking for Extended Service Set Identifiers (ESSIDs). If an ESSID identifies a previously used connection, it is selected. If several are found, the recently used one is chosen. If only new connections are available, Network Manager waits for the user to choose one. A connection is selected if the user is logged in.

Click the Wi-Fi entry in the System Status Area to expand the menu to show entries from which to select a network, turn off wireless networking, and open the GNOME Network Settings dialog at the Wi-Fi tab (Wi-Fi Settings). Click the Select Network item to open a dialog that shows a list of all available wireless connections (see Figure 3-19). Entries display the name of the wireless network and a wave graph showing the strength of its signal. To connect to a network, click its entry, then click the Connect button, to activate the connection. If this is the first time you are trying to connect to that network, you will be prompted to enter the password or encryption key (see Figure 3-20).

Figure 3-19: Network Manager connections menu - wireless

Figure 3-20: Network Manager wireless authentication

You can turn off wireless by clicking the Turn Off entry in the expanded Wi-Fi section of the System Status Area (see Figure 3-21). When turned off, the entry label changes to Turn On. entry. To reactivate your wireless connection, click the Turn On entry.

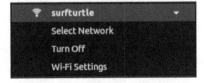

Figure 3-21: Network Manager wireless on and off

Configuring Network Connections with GNOME Settings

On the GNOME Settings dialog there is a Wi-Fi tab for wireless configuration and a Network tab for wired, VPN, and proxy configurations. For Wi-Fi choose the tab in the Choose Wi-Fi Settings from the expanded Wi-Fi entries in the System Status Area, or click the Wi-Fi tab in the Settings dialog, to open the Wi-Fi tab (see Figure 3-22). On the Wi-Fi tab, an Airplane Mode switch and a list of visible wireless connections are listed to the right. The currently active connection will have a checkmark next to its name. On the top right bar is a switch for turning wireless on and off. A menu to the right of the switch list entries for connections to hidden networks, turning your computer's Wi-Fi hotspot capability, and listing previously accessed Wi-Fi Networks.

Figure 3-22: Settings Network wireless connections

Your current active connection will have a checkmark next to it and a gear button to the right. Click the gear button to display a dialog with tabs for managing the connection. The Details tab provides information about the connection (see Figure 3-23). The Security, Identity, IPv4, and IPv6 tabs let you perform a detailed configuration of your connection, as described in Chapter 10. The settings are fixed to automatic by default. Should you make any changes, click the Apply button to have them take effect. The Details tab has options both for connecting automatically and for providing availability to other users. These are set by default. Should you not want to connect to the wireless network automatically, be sure to uncheck this option. To remove a network's connection information, click the Forget button on the Details tab.

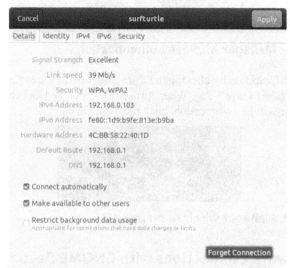

Figure 3-23: Settings Network wireless connection - Details tab

For a wired connection, click the Network tab on GNOME Settings to display lists for Wired, VPN, and Network Proxy. The Wired list shows your current wired connections with on and off switched for each. A plus button at the top right of the Wired list lets you add more wired connections. Next to a connection's switch a gear button is displayed (see Figure 3-24). Clicking the gear button opens a configuration dialog with tabs for Details, Identity, IPv4, IPv6, and Security.

Figure 3-24: Settings Network wired connection

Clicking on the Network proxy gear button opens a Network Proxy dialog menu with Disabled, Manual, and Automatic options (see Figure 3-25). The Manual option lets you enter address and port information. For the Automatic option, you enter a configuration address.

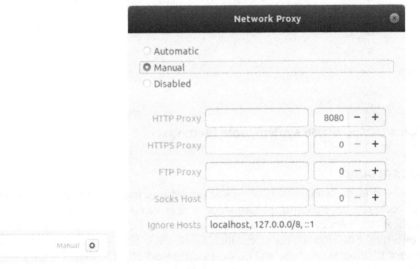

Figure 3-25: Network proxy settings (Settings Network)

To add a vpn connection, click the plus (+) button to the right of the VPN title to open Add Vpn dialog network.

Settings

You can configure desktop settings and perform most administrative tasks using the GNOME configuration tools (see Table 3-2) listed in the GNOME Settings dialog, accessible from the System Status Area dialog (lower left button) . It displays tabs for different desktop and system configurations (see Figure 3-26). There are two subheadings for system administration (Details) and device configuration (Devices). Devices include keyboards, displays, and printers. Details has tabs for users, the date and time, and default applications. A few settings tabs invoke the supported system tools available from previous releases, such as Sound (PulseAudio). Most use the new GNOME 3 configuration and administrative tools such as Background, Privacy, Users, and Power.

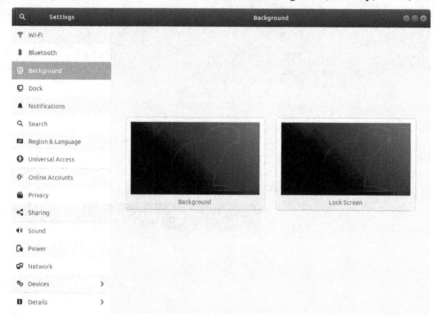

Figure 3-26: GNOME system tools (Settings)

Background

With the Background dialog, you can set your background for both the desktop and screen lock backgrounds: wallpaper, picture, or color. You can access the Background dialog from Applications overview or from the Settings dialog (see Figure 3-27). The current backgrounds are shown for the desktop and the screen lock. Click one to open the Select Background dialog, with tabs for Wallpapers, Pictures, and Colors (see Figure 3-28). The dialog is the same for both desktop and screen lock backgrounds. If you choose Wallpapers, the installed backgrounds are displayed. The Colors tab displays solid color images you can use instead. The Pictures tab displays images in your Pictures folder, which you can scroll through to select one to use for your background. To add your own image, first, add the image to your Pictures folder. Then click the Pictures tab to display all the images in your Pictures folder. Once you make your selection, click the Select button at the upper right. You return to the main Background dialog, showing your new background. The background on your display is updated immediately.

Setting	Description
Personal	
Wi-Fi	Lets you configure and manage wireless networks.
Bluetooth	Sets Bluetooth detection and configuration
Background	Sets desktop and screen lock backgrounds (wallpaper, color, and image)
Notifications	Turns on notifications for different applications
Search	Specifies the resources and locations searched by the GNOME overview search box
Region & Language	Chooses a language, region (formats), and keyboard layout
Universal Access	Enables features such as accessible login and keyboard screen
Online Accounts	Configures online accounts for use by e-mail and browser applications
Privacy	Turns on privacy features, such as screen lock and purging trash
Sharing	Turns on sharing for media, remote login, and screen access
Sound	Configures sound effects, output volume, input volume, and sound application settings
Power	Sets the power options for laptop inactivity
Network	Lets you turn wired networks on or off. Allows access to an available wired network. Also specifies proxy configuration, if needed.
Devices	
Displays	Changes your screen resolution, refresh rate, and screen orientation
Keyboard	Configures repeat key sensitivity and shortcut keys for special tasks, such as multimedia operations
Mouse & Touchpad	Sets mouse and touchpad configuration; selects hand orientation, speed, and accessibility
Printers	Turns printers on or off and accesses their print queues
Removable Media	Default applications for removeable media
Wacom Tablet	Provides tablet options

Color	Sets the color profile for a device
Details	
About	Sets the hostname of your computer, displays hardware information, and assigns default applications for certain basic tasks
Date & Time	Sets the date, time, time zone, and network time
Users	Manages accounts
Default Applications	Default applications for different for user files

Table 3-2: Settings

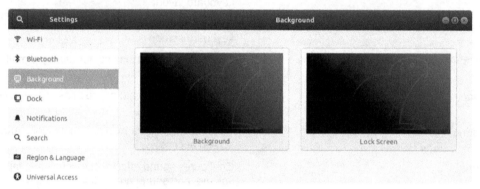

Figure 3-27: Background

Figure 3-28: Select Background

Install the gnome-background package to add a collection of GNOME backgrounds. You can download more GNOME backgrounds (wallpapers) from **http://gnome-look.org/**.

Date & Time

The Date & Time calendar and menu are located on the top bar at the center (see Figure 3-29) . The dialog displays the current time and day of the week but can be modified to display 24-hour or AM/PM time. The calendar shows the current date, but you can move to different months and years using the month scroll arrows at the top of the calendar. The right side of the Date & Time dialog shows your Evolution calendar events for the current and next days. Click the Open

Calendar entry at the bottom to open the Evolution mail calendar application, with which you can enter events. The Clocks link opens the GNOME Clocks tool for selecting world clocks.

Figure 3-29: Date & Time dialog

You can further adjust the top bar time display using the GNOME Tweak Tool's Top Bar tab (see Figure 3-30). In the Clock section, there are options to show the date and seconds. For the Calendar, you can show week numbers.

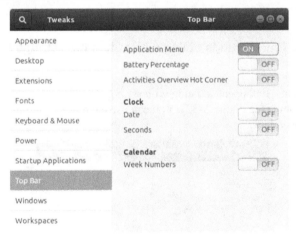

Figure 3-30: GNOME Tweak Tool - Top Bar (clock options)

Date & Time options are set using the Date & Time tab in the Settings Details tab. The Date & Time tab lets you set the time zone and time. Both are configured for automatic settings using Internet time servers (see Figure 3-31). The time zone or the time and date can be set manually by turning off the Automatic switches. Once turned off, the Date & Time and the Time Zone links become active.

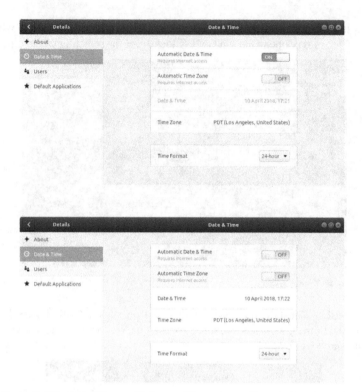

Figure 3-31: Date & Time Settings dialog with automatic settings turned on (top) and off (bottom)

The Date & Time link opens a dialog with settings for the hour, minutes, day, and year, with a menu for the month (see Figure 3-32). You can use the plus (+) and minus (-) buttons to sequentially change the values.

Figure 3-32: Date & Time manual settings

The Time Zone link opens a dialog with a map of the time zones and the current one selected (see Figure 3-33). Click a new time zone to change the zone.

Figure 3-33: Time Zone dialog

You can also set the system time manually using the **date** command. The **date** command has several options for adjusting both displaying and setting the date and time. Check the date man page for a detailed list, **man date**. You can set the time with the **--set** option and a string specifying the date. You use human readable terms for the time string, such as Mon or Monday for the day and Jul or July for the month. Hour, minute, and second can be represented by numbers separated by colons. The following sets the date to July 9, 8:15 AM 2018.

```
sudo date --set='Monday July 9 08:15 2018'
```

To just set the time you would enter something like:

```
sudo date --set='12:15:43'
```

Notifications

The Notifications dialog lets you configure notifications for different applications. You can also have the options show pop-up banners at the bottom of the screen or show notices on the lock screen. Both are turned on by default. A listing of supported applications for notifications is displayed (see Figure 3-34).

Figure 3-34: Notifications dialog

Click an application to display a dialog from which you can turn notifications for the application on or off, as well as set options such as sound alerts, pop-up notifications, and lock screen notification (see Figure 3-35).

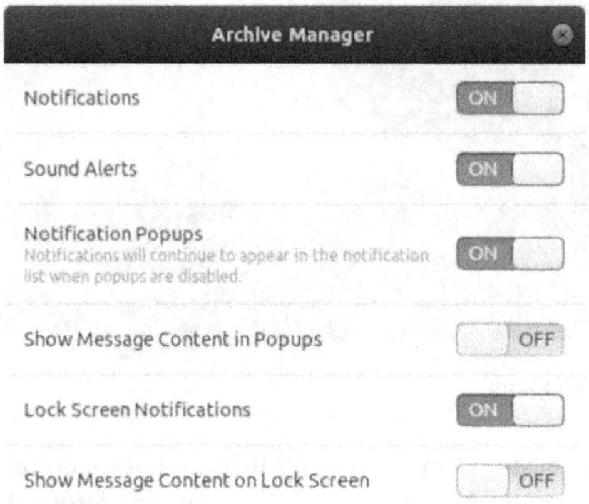

Figure 3-35: Notification settings for an application

Privacy

The Privacy dialog allows you to turn privacy features, such as the screen lock, usage and history logs, and the purging of trash and temporary files, on or off (see Figure 3-35) . Screen Lock and Usage & History are turned on by default. The "Purge Trash & Temporary Files" and Location Services are turned off. Location Services allows your geographical location to be determined.

Figure 3-36: Privacy

Clicking the Screen Lock entry opens the Screen Lock configuration dialog, from which you can turn Screen Lock on or off or set it to turn on after a period of idle time and allow or deny notifications on the Screen Lock screen (see Figure 3-37).

Figure 3-37: Privacy - Screen Lock configuration

Click the Usage & History entry to open a dialog from which you can turn usage history on or off and set how long to keep it. The entry also has a button that allows you to clear recent history (see Figure 3-38).

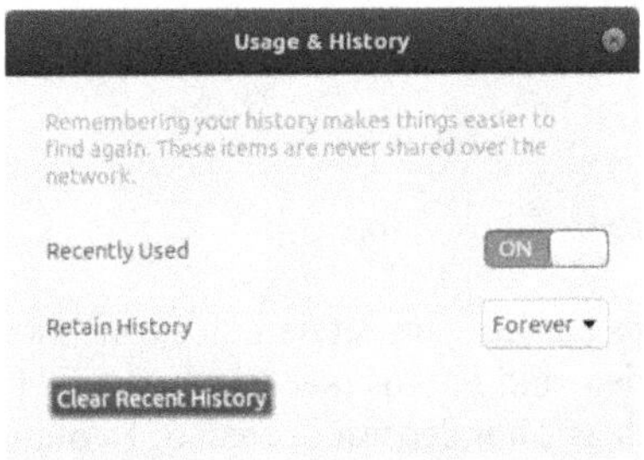

Figure 3-38: Privacy - Usage & History configuration

The Purge Trash & Temporary Files entry has options to automatically empty trash and remove temporary files (see Figure 3-39). You can also set a time limit for purging files. These options are turned off by default. The link also has buttons that allow you to empty trash and purge temporary files immediately.

Figure 3-39: Privacy - Purge Trash & Temporary Files configuration

Details (System Information)

The Details dialog shows system information, using the following three tabs: Overview, Default Applications, and Removable Media. The Overview tab shows your hardware specifications (memory, CPU, graphics card chip, and free disk space), in addition to the hostname (Device name) and the OS type (64- or 33-bit system) (see Figure 3-40). You can change the hostname here if you wish. When you open the dialog, updates are checked, and, if found, an Install Update button is displayed, which opens Software Updates, allowing you to update your system (see Chapter 4).

Figure 3-40: Details - Overview

The Default Applications tab lets you set default applications for basic types of files: Web, Mail, Calendar, Music, Video, and Photos (see Figure 3-41). Use the drop-down menus to choose installed alternatives, such as Thunderbird instead of Evolution for Mail or Image Viewer instead of Shotwell for Photos.

Figure 3-41: Details - Default Applications

Using Removable Devices and Media

Ubuntu supports removable devices and media, such as digital cameras, PDAs, card readers, and USB printers. These devices are handled automatically with device interfaces set up for them when needed. Removable media, such as CD and DVD discs, USB storage disks, and digital cameras, will be displayed as entries in the message tray Removable Devices menu. On the Overview screen, when you click on the message number notice at the bottom of the screen, the Removable Devices icon is displayed. Clicking this icon displays a menu of all your removable devices, with an Eject button next to each entry. Click an entry to open the device in its associated applications, such as a file manager window for a USB drive. Be sure always to click the Eject button for device entry before removing a drive, such as a USB drive or removable disk drive. Removing the drive before clicking eject can result in incomplete write operations on the disk.

Removable storage devices and media will also appear in the file manager Devices sidebar with eject buttons that you can use instead of the message menu to eject the devices. For example, when you connect a USB drive to your system, it will be detected and can be displayed as a storage device with its own file system by the file manager.

Removable devices and media, such as USB drives and DVD/CD discs, can be ejected using Eject buttons in the Devices section of the file manager sidebar. The sidebar lists all your storage devices, including removable media. Removable devices and media will have an Eject button to the right. Just click the Eject button, and the media is ejected or unmounted. You can right-click the Device entry and, from a pop-up menu, choose the Eject entry.

The Settings Devices Removable Media tab lets you specify default actions for CD Audio, DVD Video, Music Player, Photos, and Software media (see Figure 3-42). You can select from drop-down menus the application to use for the different media. These menus also include options for Ask What To Do, Do Nothing, and Open Folder. The Open Folder option will open a window displaying the files on the disc. A button labeled "Other Media" opens a dialog that lets you set up an association for less used media such as Blu-Ray discs and Audio DVD. Initially, the Ask What To Do option is set for all entries. Possible options are listed for the appropriate media, such as Rhythmbox Media Player for CD Audio discs and Videos (Totem) for DVD-Video. Photos can be opened with the Shotwell photo manager.

Figure 3-42: Details - Removable Media defaults

When you insert removable media, such as a CD audio disc, its associated application is automatically started, unless you change that preference. If you want to turn off this feature for a particular kind of media, you can select the Do Nothing entry from its application drop-down menu. If you want to be prompted for options, use the Ask What To Do entry. Then, when you insert a disc, a dialog with a drop-down menu for possible actions is displayed. From this menu, you can select another application or select the Do Nothing or Open Folder options.

You can turn the automatic startup off for all media by checking the box labeled "Never prompt or start programs on media insertion," at the bottom of the Removable Media tab.

Sharing

On the Sharing dialog, you can allow access to your account and your screen. A switch lets you turn all sharing on or off (see Figure 3-43). You can also choose what network device to you if you have more than one.

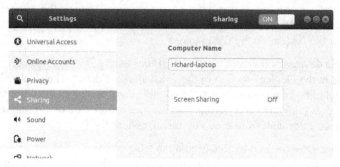

Figure 3-43: Sharing

Clicking the Screen Sharing entry opens a dialog from which you can allow a remote user to see or control your screen. You can also require and set a password (see Figure 3-44).

Figure 3-44: Sharing - File and Media access by other users

Power Management

For laptops and systems with remote battery devices such as mice, a power icon is displayed in the System Status Area (right side of the top bar) . The System Status Area menu shows the current strength of the battery (see Figure 3-45). The entry expands to show a Power Settings entry, which you can use to open the Settings Power dialog.

Figure 3-45: GNOME Power Manager menu

The GNOME Power manager is configured with the Power dialog, accessible as Power from Settings (see Figure 3-46). The dialog is organized into four sections: Battery, Devices, Power Saving, and Suspend & Power Off. On laptops, the Battery section shows the battery charge. The Devices section shows the strength of any remote devices, such as a wireless mouse. In the Power Saving section, you can set power saving features for your monitor, wireless devices, and network connections. When inactive for a period of time, you can choose to turn off the screen, as well as dim it whenever it is inactive. For laptops, you can also set the screen brightness. You can also choose to turn off Bluetooth, Wi-Fi, and Mobile broadband. In the Suspend & Power Off section, you can turn on the automatic suspend for when a system remains inactive and, for laptops, hibernate or turn off when the battery is critically low.

Using the GNOME Tweak Tool's Power tab, you can further specify the action to take, such as suspend or shut down, when the Power button is pressed, or to suspend when the laptop lid is closed.

Figure 3-46: GNOME Power manager

powertop, tuned, and BLTK

For more refined power management you can use the powertop and tuned tools. The **powertop** tool runs in a terminal window as the root user. It will detect and display information about the use of the CPU by running applications and connected devices. Recommendations are listed on how to configure the power usage. To display a listing of the powertop results including recommendations, add the **-d** option.

```
su
powertop -d
```

For automatic tuning of hard disk and network devices you can use tuned (**tuned** and **tuned** utils packages). The tuned daemon monitors your system and tunes the settings dynamically. You can use tuned's **diskdevstat** and **netdevstat** tools to monitor your hard disk and network devices.

For laptops, you can use the Battery Life Tool Kit (BLTK) to test and analyze battery performance. Options specify different types of workloads, such as **-O** for office suite use and **-P** for multimedia usage. Depending on the option you specified different applications would be opened and run during the test such as Libreoffice Writer or the Totem multimedia player.

```
bltk -O
```

You can also run the test on desktop systems using an **-a** option.

```
bltk -a -O
```

Mouse and Touchpad

The Mouse & Touchpad dialog is the primary tool for configuring your mouse and touchpad (see Figure 3-47) . Mouse preferences allow you to choose the mouse's speed, hand orientation, and double-click times. A "Test Your Settings" button lets you check clicks, double-clicks, and scrolling. For laptops, you can configure your touchpad, enabling touchpad clicks and disabling them when typing. You can turn the touchpad on or off.

The GNOME Tweak Tool's Keyboard and Mouse tab has options to enable a middle-click paste for the mouse and to show the location of the pointer on the screen.

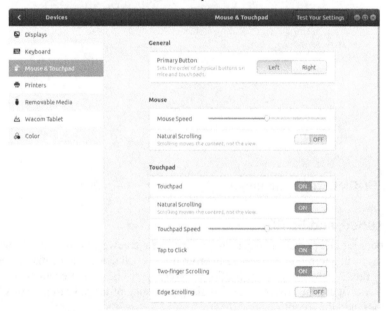

Figure 3-47: GNOME system tools - mouse and touchpad

Display (Resolution and Rotation)

The display drivers for Linux used on Ubuntu support user-level resolution and orientation changes. Any user can specify a resolution or orientation, without affecting the settings of other users. The Settings Displays dialog provides a simple interface for setting rotation, resolution, and selecting added monitors, allowing for cloned or extended displays across several connected monitors (see Figure 3-48). The dialog displays icons for connected monitors. Click one to open a dialog, which shows the display's size, aspect ratio, and resolution. From the resolution menu, you can set the resolution. Use the arrow buttons below the display image to set the rotation. After you have made your changes, click Apply. The new resolution is displayed with a dialog with buttons that ask you whether to keep the new resolution or return to the previous one. With multiple displays, you can turn a monitor off or mirror displays.

Figure 3-48: Displays

The graphics interface for your desktop display is implemented by the X Window System. The default version used on Ubuntu is X.org (**x.org**). X.org provides its own drivers for various graphics cards and monitors. You can find out more about X.org at **www.x.org**. X.org will automatically detect most hardware. The **/etc/X11/xorg.conf** file is no longer used for the open source drivers (nv and amd). Information such as the monitor used is determined automatically.

Universal Access

The Universal Access dialog in Settings lets you configure alternative access to your interface for your keyboard and mouse actions. Four sections set the display (Seeing), sound properties (Hearing), typing, and point-and-click features. Seeing lets you adjust the contrast and text size, and whether to allow zooming or use of screen reader (see Figure 3-49). Hearing uses visual cues for alert sounds. Typing displays a screen keyboard and adjusts key presses. Pointing and Clicking lets you use the keyboard for mouse operations.

Figure 3-49: Universal Access

Keyboard and Language

The Settings Keyboard dialog shows tabs for shortcuts (see Figure 3-49). You can assign keys to perform such tasks as starting the web browser. The plus button at the bottom of the screen lets you create custom shortcuts. The Reset All button resets the shortcuts to their default value. Click on an entry to set the shortcut. When the Set Shortcut dialog appears, type the keys for the shortcut, usually three. The keys appear on the next dialog with a Set button in the upper right corner. The changed entry then appears on the Keyboard dialog with a delete box you can click to remove your shortcut setting. The plus button opens an Add Custom Shortcut dialog where you enter the name and command befor setting the shortcut.

On the GNOME Tweak Tool's Typing tab, you can specify the behavior of certain keys, such as the key sequence to stop the X server, the Caps Lock behavior, and the numeric keypad layout.

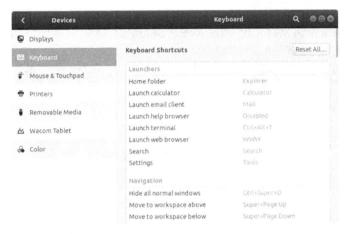

Figure 3-50: Keyboard

The Region & Language dialog lets you set the input source for the keyboard (see Figure 3-51) . The current input language source is listed and selected. You can access the Region & Language dialog directly from Settings. Click the plus (+) button to open a dialog listing other language sources, which you can add. Click the Keyboard button to see the keyboard layout of your currently selected input source.

Figure 3-51: Region & Language with Input Sources

Color Profiles (GNOME Color Manager)

You can manage the color for different devices by using color profiles specified with the Color dialog accessible from Settings. The Color dialog lists devices for which you can set color profiles. Click a device to display buttons at the bottom of the screen to Add profile and Calibrate. Your monitor will have a profile set up automatically. Click the Add Profile button to open a dialog with an Automatic Profiles menu from which you can choose a color profile. Click the Add button to add the profile. Available profiles include Adobe RGB, sRGB, and Kodak ProPhoto RGB. You can also import a profile from an ICC profile file of your own.

When you click on a device entry, its Profiles are listed (see Figure 3-52). Click on a profile to display buttons to Set for all users, Remove profile, and View details. Click the View details button for the color profile information.

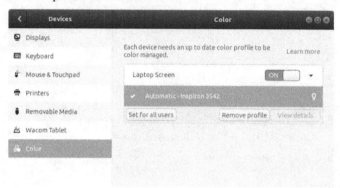

Figure 3-52: Color management dialog

Online Accounts

You can configure your online accounts using the Online Accounts dialog in Settings. Instead of separately configuring mail and chat clients, you can set up access once, using online accounts. Click on an entry to start the sign-in procedure. You are prompted to sign in using your e-mail and password. Access is provided to Google, Facebook, Flickr, Microsoft, Microsoft Exchange, Nextcloud, Foursquare, and Pocket. Once access is granted, you will see an entry for service. Clicking on the service shows the different kinds of applications that it can be used for such as mail, calendar, contacts, chat, and documents (see Figure 3-53). Switches that you can use to turn access on and off are provided.

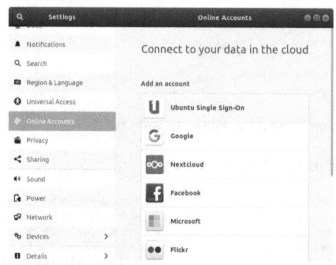

Figure 3-53: Online Accounts

File Manager Search

The file manager provides a search tool, with similar features. You can access the file manager search from any file manager window by clicking the Search button on the toolbar (Looking glass on the right side) to open a Search box. Enter the pattern to search and press ENTER. The results are displayed (see Figure 3-54). Click the menu button to the right (down arrow) to add file-type (What) and date (When) search parameters, or to search file text or just the file name. Selecting the When entry opens a dialog where you can specify the recency of the document's last use or modification, by day, week, month, or year. A calendar button to the right of the text box for the date opens a calendar to let you choose a specific date. The What entry displays a menu with different file categories such as music, Documents, folders, picture, and PDF.

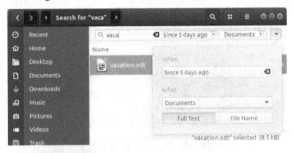

Figure 3-54: Gnome File Manager Search

Accessing File Systems and Devices

When you attach an external storage device such as a USB, CD/DVD-ROM, or ESATA drive, it will be mounted automatically, and you will be prompted to open it in a file manager window. Be sure to unmount (Eject) a drive before removing it, so that data will be written.

Your file systems and removable media appear as entries in the file manager sidebar and as icons on the desktop (see Figure 3-55). External devices such as USB drives are mounted automatically and have Eject buttons next to their entries. Internal hard drive partitions not mounted at boot, such as Windows file systems, are not mounted automatically. Double-click the hard drive partition entry to mount them. An Eject button then appears next to the hard drive entry. You are also prompted to open the drive's file system in a new file manager window.

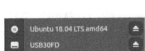

Figure 3-55: Devices sidebar in the file manager window and icons on the desktop

Removable media also appears on the desktop as an icon. Double click on the icon to open it in a file manager window. Right-click on the icon to display options, such as Eject, Properties, and "Open in a New Window".

File systems on removable media will also appear automatically as entries directly on your desktop notifications dialog (see Figure 3-56). A dialog briefly appears that lets you open the media in a file window.

If you have already configured associated applications for video and audio DVD/CDs, or disks with images, sound, or video files, the disk will be opened with the appropriate application; such as Shotwell for images, Rhythmbox for audio, and Movie Player for DVD/video. If you have not yet configured these associations, you will be prompted to specify which application you want to open it with.

Figure 3-56: Removable Devices message tray menu with hard drives mounted

To see network resources, click the Other Locations entry in the file manager sidebar. This network window will list your connected network computers. Opening these networks displays the shares they provide, such as shared directories that you can have access to. Drag-and-drop operations are supported for all shared directories, letting you copy files and folders between a shared directory on another computer with a directory on your system. You first must configure your firewall to accept Samba connections before you can browse Windows systems on GNOME. Opening a network resource may require you to login to access the resource.

Ubuntu automatically mounts media. You can turn this feature on or off using the GNOME Tweaks Desktop tab.

Accessing Archives from GNOME: Archive Mounter

Ubuntu supports the access of archives directly from GNOME using Archive Mounter. You can select the archive file, then right-click and select Archive Mounter to open the archive. The archive contents are listed in a GNOME Files file manager window. You can extract or display the contents.

You can also use Archive Mounter to mount CD/DVD disk ISO image files as archives. You can then browse and extract the contents of the CD/DVD. Right-click on a disk ISO image file (**.iso** extension) and select "Open with Archive Mounter." The image is automatically mounted as an archive. An entry for it appears on the file manager sidebar. It will be read-only. The disc will also appear in the Computer folder as a valid disc. To unmount the disk image as an archive, click the eject button, or right-click on the entry or icon and choose Unmount.

File Manager CD/DVD Creator interface

Using the GNOME file manager to burn data to a DVD or CD is a simple matter of dragging files to an open blank CD or DVD and clicking the Write To Disc button. When you insert and open a blank DVD/CD, a window will open labeled CD/DVD Creator. To burn files, just drag them to that window. Click the Write To Disc button when ready to burn a DVD/CD. A disc burning setup dialog will open, which will perform the actual write operation. Also, click the Properties button to open a dialog with burning options like the burn speed.

The GNOME file manager also supports burning ISO images. Just double-click the ISO image file. This opens the Image Burning Setup dialog, which prompts you to burn the image. Be sure first to insert a blank CD or DVD into your CD/DVD burner.

Note: The older Brasero CD/DVD burner is still available on the Ubuntu repository, though no longer supported. You can perform disc copy, erasing, and checking.

Startup Applications Preferences

On the Startup Applications Preferences dialog, you can select additional programs you want started automatically (accessible from the Applications overview as Startup Applications). Some are selected automatically like the NVidia X Server Settings for the NVidia proprietary server (see Figure 3-57). Uncheck an entry if you no longer want it to start up automatically. To add an application not listed, click the Add button and enter the application name and program (use Browse to select a program, usually in **/usr/bin**).

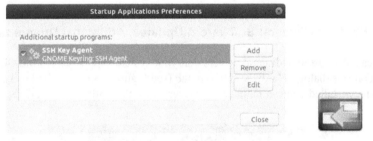

Figure 3-57: Startup Applications Preferences

Display Configuration and Additional Drivers

The graphics interface for your desktop display is implemented by the X Window System. The version used on Ubuntu is X.org (**x.org**). X.org provides its own drivers for various graphics cards and monitors. You can find out more about X.org at **http://www.x.org**.

Your display is detected automatically, configuring both your graphics card and monitor. Normally you should not need to perform any configuration yourself. However, if you have a graphics card that uses Graphics processors from a major Graphics vendor like NVIDIA, you have the option of using their driver, instead of the open source X drivers installed with Ubuntu. Some graphics cards may work better with the vendor driver, and provide access to more of the card's features like 3D support. The open source AMD driver is **xserver-xorg-video-radeon**, and the open source NVidia driver is **xserver-xorg-video-nouveau**.

If available, you can select proprietary drivers to use instead, such as the NVIDIA driver. Open the Software & Updates application (Applications overview) and click on the Additional Drivers tab to list available drivers (see Figure 3-58). Select the driver entry you want and then click on the Apply Changes button to use download and install the driver. The drivers are part of the restricted repository, supported by the vendor but not by Ubuntu. They are not open source, but proprietary.

Once installed, an examination of the Additional Drivers tab on Software & Updates will show the selected driver in use. Should you want to use the original driver, click the Revert button. The open source Xorg driver will be automatically selected and used. For NVIDIA cards, the Nouveau open source drivers are used, which provides some acceleration support. You can switch to another driver by selecting it and clicking the Apply Changes button.

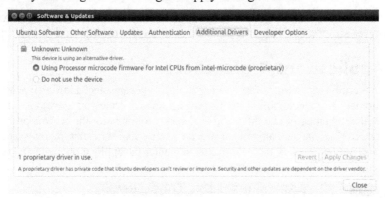

Figure 3-58: Hardware Drivers: Software & Updates, Additional Drivers tab

You can also install additional drivers that your system supports from the Ubuntu Software | Addon-ons dialog's Hardware Drivers tab (see Figure 3-59). Installed drivers will show a checkmark. Once installed you can manage the drivers from the Software & Updates, Additional Drivers tab.

Figure 3-59: Hardware Drivers: Software & Updates, Additional Drivers tab

When you install a new kernel, compatible kernel drivers for your proprietary graphics driver are generated automatically for you by the DKMS (Dynamic Kernel Module Support) utility.

The graphic vendors also have their own Linux-based configuration tools, which are installed with the driver. The NVIDIA configuration tool is in the **nvidia-settings** package. Once installed, you will see NVIDIA Server Settings in the Applications overview. This interface provides NVIDIA vendor access to many of the features of NVIDIA graphics cards like color corrections, video brightness and contrast, and thermal monitoring. You can also set the screen resolution and color depth.

For AMD you would use the open source drivers, amdgpu or Xorg radeon. The fglrx driver (Catalyst proprietary driver) has been deprecated and is no longer supported by Ubuntu. It is no longer available in any form for Ubuntu Linux 18.04. Much of the AMD video drivers have now become open source. For AMD video cards with GCN 1.2 capability and above (series 300 and above), it is recommended that you use the amdgpu AMD open source driver.

If you have problems with the vendor driver, you can always switch back to the original (Revert button). Your original Xorg open source driver will be used instead. The change-over will be automatic.

If the problem is more severe, with the display not working, you can use the GRUB menu on startup to select the recovery kernel. Your system will be started without the vendor graphics driver. You can use the "drop to shell" to enter the command line mode. From there you can use **apt-get** command-line APT tool to remove the graphics driver. The NVIDIA drivers have the prefix **nvidia**. In the following example, the asterisk will match on all the **nvidia** packages.

```
sudo apt-get remove nvidia*
```

Help Resources

A great deal of support documentation is already installed on your system and is accessible from online sources. Table 1-3 lists Help tools and resources accessible on your Ubuntu Linux system. Both the GNOME and KDE desktops feature Help systems that use a browser-like interface to display help files. The Help browsers support the Ubuntu Help Center, which provides Ubuntu specific help.

If you need to ask a question, you can access the Ubuntu help support at **https://answers.launchpad.net**. and at **http://askubuntu.com**. Here you can submit your question, and check answered questions about Ubuntu.

Ubuntu Desktop Guide

To start the Ubuntu Desktop Guide, choose Ubuntu Help from the Session menu. Also, you can click the Help icon (question mark) on the dash. Guide displays several links covering Ubuntu topics (see Figure 3-60). GNOME topics covered include the Dock, the Dash, indicator menus, window management, and workspace access.

You can use the right and left arrows to move through the previous documentation you displayed. You can also search for topics. Click on the search button on the right side of the toolbar to open a search box. As you enter a search term possible results are displayed. You can also add bookmarks for documents and search results by clicking the star button on the right side of the toolbar to open the bookmark menu with an "Add Bookmark" button. You can also quickly access a bookmarked page from the bookmark menu (star button).

Figure 3-60: Ubuntu Desktop Guide

The pages are organized more like frequently asked questions documents, with more detailed headings designed to provide a clearer understanding of what the document is about (see Figure 3-61). The Sound, video, and pictures link opens a page with entries like "Why won't DVDs play" and "My new iPod won't work."

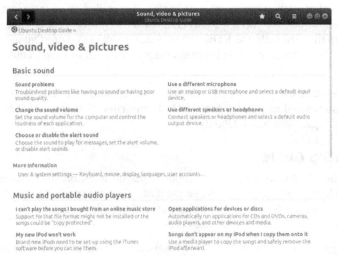

Figure 3-61: Ubuntu Desktop Guide topics

Help documents will include helpful links (see Figure 3-62). At the bottom of most pages, a More Information section will have links for more detailed information.

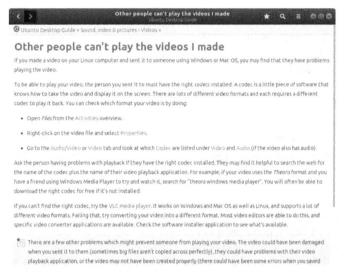

Figure 3-62: Ubuntu Desktop Guide page

If you want to see the application help documents available, choose All Help from the Help application's menu on the right side of its toolbar. You will see application manuals installed applications such as the Shotwell, Synaptic package manager, Videos movie player, Ubuntu Software, and Rhythmbox (see Figure 3-63).

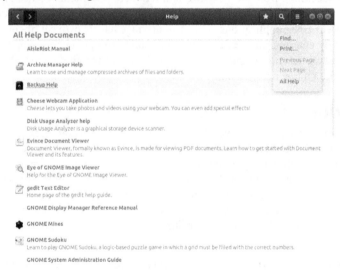

Figure 3-63: Ubuntu Help, All Documents

Context-Sensitive Help

Both GNOME and KDE, along with applications, provide context-sensitive help. Each KDE and GNOME application features detailed manuals that are displayed using their respective Help browsers. In addition, system administrative tools feature detailed explanations for each task.

Application Documentation

On your system, the **/usr/share/doc** directory contains documentation files installed by each application. Within each directory, you can usually find HOW-TO, README, and INSTALL documents for that application.

The Man Pages

You can access the Man pages, which are manuals for Linux commands available either from the command line interface, using the **man** command. In a terminal window, enter **man** along with the command on which you want information. The following example asks for information on the **ls** command:

```
$ man ls
```

Pressing the SPACEBAR key advances, you to the next page. Pressing the **b** key moves you back a page. When you finish, press the **q** key to quit the Man utility and return to the command line. You activate a search by pressing either the slash (/) or question mark (?) keys. The / key searches forward and the ? key searches backward. When you press the / key, a line opens at the bottom of your screen, where you can enter a text to search for. Press ENTER to activate the search. You can repeat the same search by pressing the **n** key. You need not re-enter the pattern.

The Info Pages

Documentation for GNU applications, such as the gcc compiler and the Emacs editor, also exist as info pages accessible from the GNOME and KDE Help Centers. You can also access this documentation by entering the command **info** in a terminal window. This brings up a special screen listing different GNU applications. The info interface has its own set of commands. You can learn more about it by entering **info info** at the command prompt. Typing **m** opens a line at the bottom of the screen where you can enter the first few letters of the application. Pressing ENTER brings up the info file on that application.

Terminal Window

The Terminal window allows you to enter Linux commands on a command line. It also provides you with a shell interface for using shell commands instead of your desktop. The command line is editable, allowing you to use the backspace key to erase characters on the line. Pressing a key will insert that character. You can use the left and right arrow keys to move anywhere on the line, and then press keys to insert characters, or use backspace to delete characters (see Figure 3-64). Folders, files, and executable files are color-coded: black for files, blue for folders, green for executable files, and aqua for links. Shared folders are displayed with a green background.

The terminal window will remember the previous commands you entered. Use the up and down arrows to have those commands displayed in turn on the command line. Press the ENTER key to re-execute the currently displayed command. You can even edit a previous command before running it, allowing you to execute a modified version of a previous command. This can be helpful if you need to re-execute a complex command with a different argument, or if you mistyped a complex command and want to correct it without having to re-type the entire command. The terminal window will display all your previous interactions and commands for that session. Use the scrollbar to see any previous commands you ran and their displayed results.

Figure 3-64: Terminal Window

You can open as many terminal windows as you want, each working in its own shell. Instead of opening a separate window for each new shell, you can open several shells in the same window, using tabs. Use the keys **Shift-Ctrl-t** or click the Open Tab item on the File menu to open a new tab. A tab toolbar opens at the top of the terminal window with the folder name and a close button for each tab. Each tab runs a separate shell, letting you enter different commands in each (see Figure 3-65). You can right-click on the tab's folder name to display a pop-up menu to move to a different tab, or just click on a tab's folder name. You can also use the Tabs menu, or the **Ctrl-PageUp** and **Ctrl-PageDown** keys to move to different tabs. The Tabs menu is displayed if multiple tabs are open.

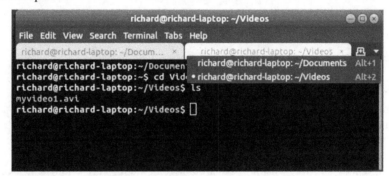

Figure 3-65: Terminal Window with tabs

The terminal window also supports desktop cut/copy and paste operations. You can copy a line from a Web page and then paste it to the terminal window (you can use the Paste entry on the Terminal window's Edit menu or press **Shift-Ctrl-v**). The command will appear and then you can press ENTER to execute the command. This is useful for command line operations displayed on an instructional Web page. Instead of typing in a complex command yourself, just select and copy from the Web page directly, and then paste to the Terminal window. You can also perform any edits on the command, if needed, before executing it. Should you want to copy a command on the terminal window, select the text with your mouse and then use **Shift-Ctrl-c** keys (or the Copy entry on the Terminal window's Edit menu) to copy the command. You can select part of a line or multiple lines, as long as they are shown on the terminal window.

You can customize terminal windows using profiles. A default profile is set up already. To customize your terminal window, select Preferences from the Edit menu. This opens a window for setting your default profile options with option categories on the sidebar for Global and Profiles. IN the Profiles section there will be an "Unnamed" profile, the default. Click on the down menu button to the right to open a menu with the options to copy the profile or change the name. To add another profile, click on the plus button to the right of the "Profiles" heading to open a dialog to create a new profile. For profiles you create you have the added options to delete them and or to set one as the default. A selected profile displays tabs for Text, Colors, Scrolling, Command, and Compatibility (see Figure 3-66). On the Text tab, you can select the default size of a terminal window in text rows and columns.

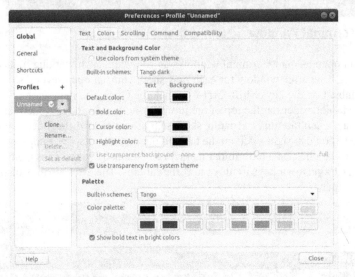

Figure 3-66: Terminal Window Profile configuration

Your terminal window will be set up to use a white background with dark text. To change this, you can edit the profile to change the background and text colors on the Colors tab. De-select the "Use colors from system theme" entry. This enables the "Built-in schemes" menu from which you can select a "Black on white" display. Other color combinations are also listed, such as "Black on light yellow" and "Green on black." The Custom option lets you choose your own text and background colors. The colors on your open terminal window will change according to your selection, allowing you to see how the color choices will look. For a transparent background, choose the "Use transparent background" entry and then set the amount of shading (none is completely transparent and full shows no transparency).

The Scrolling tab specifies the number of command lines your terminal history will keep, as well as other scroll options such as the scroll speed and whether to display the scrollbar. These are the lines you can move back through and select to re-execute. You can de-select the Limit scrollback option to set this to unlimited to keep all the commands.

You can create new profiles with customized preferences. To create a new profile, choose New Profile from the File menu to open the New Profile window where you can enter the profile name and select any profile to base it on. The default profile is chosen initially. Use the Change Profile submenu on the Terminal menu to change profiles.

To edit a particular profile, select Preferences from the Edit menu to open the Preferences window, and then click on the one you want in the Profiles section.

Command Line Interface

When using the command line interface, you are given a simple prompt at which you type in a command. Even when you are using a desktop like GNOME, you sometimes need to execute commands on a command line. You can do so in a terminal window, which is accessed from the Applications overview. You can keep the terminal window icon on the Dock by right-clicking on it and choosing "Add to Favorites"

Linux commands make extensive use of options and arguments. Be careful to place your arguments and options in their correct order on the command line. The format for a Linux command is the command name followed by options, and then by arguments, as shown here:

```
$ command-name options arguments
```

An *option* is a one-letter code preceded by one or two hyphens, which modifies the type of action the command takes. Options and arguments may or may not be optional, depending on the command. For example, the **ls** command can take an option, **-s**. The **ls** command displays a listing of files in your directory, and the **-s** option adds the size of each file in blocks. You enter the command and its option on the command line as follows:

```
$ ls -s
```

If you are uncertain what format and options a command uses, you can check the command syntax quickly by displaying its man page. Most commands have a man page. Just enter the **man** command with the command name as an argument.

An argument is data the command may need to execute its task. In many cases, this is a filename. An argument is entered as a word on the command line that appears after any options. For example, to display the contents of a file, you can use the **more** command with the file's name as its argument. The **less** or **more** command used with the filename **mydata** would be entered on the command line as follows:

```
$ less mydata
```

The command line is actually a buffer of text you can edit. Before you press ENTER to execute the command, you can edit the command on the command line. The editing capabilities provide a way to correct mistakes you may make when typing a command and its options. The **Backspace** key lets you erase the character you just typed (the one to the left of the cursor) and the **Del** key lets you erase the character the cursor is on. With this character-erasing capability, you can backspace over the entire line if you want, erasing what you entered. **Ctrl-u** erases the whole command line and lets you start over again at the prompt.

You can use the **Up Arrow** key to redisplay your last executed command. You can then re-execute that command, or you can edit it and execute the modified command. This is helpful when you have to repeat certain operations, such as editing the same file. It is also helpful when you have already executed a command you entered incorrectly.

4. Installing and Updating Software

Installing Software Packages

Ubuntu Package Management Software

Ubuntu Software Repositories

Updating Ubuntu with Software updater

Managing Packages with Ubuntu (GNOME) Software

Synaptic Package Manager

Source code files

DEB Software Packages

Managing software with apt-get

Command Line Search and Information

Managing non-repository packages with dpkg

Using packages with other software formats

Ubuntu software distribution is implemented using the online Ubuntu software repositories, which contain an extensive collection of Ubuntu-compliant software. With the integration of repository access into your Linux system, you can think of that software as an easily installed extension of your current collection. You can add software to your system by accessing software repositories that support Debian packages (DEB) and the Advanced Package Tool (APT). Software is packaged into DEB software package files. These files are, in turn, installed and managed by APT. Ubuntu Software provides an easy-to-use front end for installing software with just a click, accessible from Ubuntu Software dock icon and from the Applications overview.

The Ubuntu software repository is organized into sections, depending on how the software is supported. Software supported directly is located in the main Ubuntu repository section. Other Linux software that is most likely compatible is placed in the Universe repository section. Many software applications, particularly multimedia applications, have potential licensing conflicts. Such applications are placed in the Multiverse repository section, which is not maintained directly by Ubuntu. Many of the popular multimedia drivers and applications, such as video and digital music, support can be obtained from the Ubuntu Multiverse sections using the same simple APT commands you use for Ubuntu-supported software. Software from the Multiverse and Universe sections are integrated into package managers like Ubuntu Software and the Synaptic Package Manager, and can be installed just as easily as Ubuntu main section software. Some drivers are entirely proprietary and supplied directly by vendors. This is the case with the NVIDIA vendor-provided drivers. These drivers are placed in a restricted section, noting that there is no open source support.

You can also download source code versions of applications, then compile, and install them on your system. Where this process once was complex, it has been streamlined significantly with the use of configure scripts. Most current source code, including GNU software, is distributed with a configure script, which automatically detects your system configuration and creates a binary file that is compatible with your system.

You can download Linux software from many online sources directly, but it is always advised that you use the Ubuntu prepared package versions if available. Most software for GNOME and KDE have corresponding Ubuntu-compliant packages in the Ubuntu Universe and Multiverse sections.

Installing Software Packages

Installing software is an administrative function performed by a user with administrative access. During the Ubuntu installation, only some of the many applications and utilities available for users on Linux were installed on your system. On Ubuntu, you can install or remove software from your system with Ubuntu (GNOME) Software, the Synaptic Package Manager, or the **apt-get** command. Alternatively, you could install software as separate DEB files, or by downloading and compiling its source code.

APT (Advanced Package Tool) is integrated as the primary tool for installing packages. When you install a package with Ubuntu Software or with the Synaptic Package Manager, APT will be invoked and will select and download the package automatically from the appropriate online repository. This will include the entire Ubuntu online repository, including the main, universe, multiverse, and restricted sections.

A DEB software package includes all the files needed for a software application. A Linux software application often consists of several files that must be installed in different directories. The application program itself is placed in a system directory such as **/usr/bin**, online manual files go in another directory, and library files go in yet another directory. When you select an application for installation, APT will install any additional dependent (required) packages. APT also will install all recommended packages by default. Many software applications have additional features that rely on recommended packages.

Ubuntu Package Management Software

Although all Ubuntu software packages have the same DEB format, they can be managed and installed using different package management software tools. The underlying software management tool is APT, though Ubuntu Software also supports Snappy packages.

Ubuntu Software is the primary desktop interface for locating and installing Ubuntu software, repository files at **/var/cache/apt**. Designed as a central software management application for handling Linux packages, it is used on several Linux distributions, including Fedora and Ubuntu. Ubuntu Software is an implementation of GNOME Software. On Ubuntu, it uses the same desktop icon as the deprecated Ubuntu Software Center. The Ubuntu Software also supports Snappy packages, letting you install them as easily as APT packages. Snappy packages are installed to the **/snap** directory.

APT (Advanced Package Tool) performs the actual software management operations for all applications installed from a repository. Ubuntu Software, the Synaptic Package Manager, update-manager, dpkg, and apt-get are all front-ends for APT, repository files at **/var/cache/apt**.

Synaptic Package Manager is a Graphical front end for APT that manages packages; repository files are located at **/var/cache/apt**.

Software updater is the Ubuntu graphical front end for updating installed software using APT.

Discover Package Manager is the KDE software manager base on Ubuntu Software and is a graphical front end for APT.

tasksel is a cursor-based screen for selecting package groups and particular servers (front-end for APT). This tool will work on the command-line interface installed by the Ubuntu Server CD. You can also run it in a terminal window on a desktop (**sudo tasksel**). Use arrow keys to move to an entry, the spacebar to select, the tab key to move to the OK button. Press ENTER on the OK button to perform your installs.

apt-get is the primary command line tool for APT to install, update, and remove software; uses its own database, **/var/lib/apt/**; repository information at **/var/cache/apt**

dpkg is the older command line tool used to install, update, remove, and query software packages; uses its own database, **/var/lib/dpkg**; repository files are kept at **/var/cache/apt**, the same as APT.

aptitude is a cursor based front end for **dpkg** and **apt-get**, which uses its own database, **/var/lib/aptitude**.

snap is the command line interface command for managing Snappy packages. Snappy packages have a different format from deb, and cannot be managed by APT. Snappy is a completely different package management system, though Snappy applications can be installed alongside APT packages, and accessed seamlessly on the Ubuntu desktop.

Ubuntu Software Repositories

Four main components or sections make up the Ubuntu repository: main, restricted, universe, and multiverse. These components are described in detail at:

`https://help.ubuntu.com/community/Repositories/Ubuntu`

To see a listing of all packages in the Ubuntu repository see:

`http://packages.ubuntu.com`

To see available repositories and their sections, open the Ubuntu Software tab on Software & Updates, accessible from the Applications overview.

Repository Components

The following repository components are included in the Ubuntu repository:

main: Officially supported Ubuntu software (canonical), includes GStreamer Good plug-ins.

restricted: Software commonly used and required for many applications, but not open source or freely licensed, like the proprietary graphics card drivers from NVIDIA needed for hardware support. Because they are not open source, they are not guaranteed to work.

universe: All open source Linux software not directly supported by Ubuntu includes GStreamer Bad plug-ins.

multiverse: Linux software that does not meet licensing requirements and is not considered essential. It is not guaranteed to work. For example, the GStreamer ugly package is in this repository. Check **http://www.ubuntu.com/about/about-ubuntu/licensing**.

Repositories

In addition to the Ubuntu repository, Ubuntu maintains several other repositories used primarily for maintenance and support for existing packages. The updates repository holds updated packages for a release. The security updates repository contains critical security package updates every system will need.

Ubuntu repository: Collection of Ubuntu-compliant software packages for releases organized into main, universe, multiverse, and restricted sections.

Updates: Updates for packages in the main repository, both main and restricted sections.

Backports: Software under development for the next Ubuntu release, but packaged for use in the current one. Not guaranteed or fully tested. Backports access is now enabled by default.

Security updates: Critical security fixes for main repository software.

Partners: Third party proprietary software tested to work on Ubuntu. You need to authorize access manually.

The Backports repository provides un-finalized or development versions for new and current software. They are not guaranteed to work, but may provide needed features.

Note: Though it is possible to add the Debian Linux distribution repository, it is not advisable. Packages are designed for specific distributions. Combining them can lead to irresolvable conflicts.

Ubuntu Repository Configuration file: sources.list and sources.list.d

Repository configuration is managed by APT using configuration files in the **/etc/apt** directory. The **/etc/apt/sources.list** file holds repository entries. The main and restricted sections are enabled by default. An entry consists of a single line with the following format:

```
format   URI   release   section
```

The format is normally **deb**, for Debian package format. The URI (universal resource identifier) provides the location of the repository, such as an FTP or Web URL. The release name is the official name of a particular Ubuntu distribution like bionic and trusty. Ubuntu 18.04 has the name **bionic**. The section can be one or more terms that identify a section in that release's repository. There can be more than one term used to specify a section, like **main** and **restricted** to specify the restricted section in the Ubuntu repository. The Multiverse and Universe sections can be specified by single terms: **universe** and **multiverse**. You can also list individual packages if you want. The entry for the Bionic restricted section is shown here.

```
deb http://us.archive.ubuntu.com/ubuntu/  bionic   main restricted
```

Corresponding source code repositories will use a **deb-src** format.

```
deb-src http://us.archive.ubuntu.com/ubuntu/ bionic main restricted
```

The update repository for a section is referenced by the **-updates** suffix, as in **bionic-updates**.

```
deb https://us.archive.ubuntu.com/ubuntu/  bionic-updates  main restricted
```

The security repository for a section is referenced with the suffix **-security**, as **bionic-security**.

```
deb http://security.ubuntu.com/ubuntu/  bionic-security  main restricted
```

Both Universe and Multiverse repositories should already be enabled. Each will have an updates repository as well as corresponding source code repositories, like those shown here for Universe and Multiverse.

```
deb http://us.archive.ubuntu.com/ubuntu/ bionic universe
# deb-src http://us.archive.ubuntu.com/ubuntu/ bionic universe
deb http://us.archive.ubuntu.com/ubuntu/ bionic-updates universe
# deb-src http://us.archive.ubuntu.com/ubuntu/ bionic-updates universe
deb http://us.archive.ubuntu.com/ubuntu/ bionic multiverse
# deb-src http://us.archive.ubuntu.com/ubuntu/ bionic multiverse
deb http://us.archive.ubuntu.com/ubuntu/ bionic-updates multiverse
# deb-src http://us.archive.ubuntu.com/ubuntu/ bionic-updates multiverse
```

Comments begin with a # mark. You can add comments of your own if you wish. Commenting an entry effectively disables that component of a repository. Placing a # mark before a repository entry will effectively disable it.

The Backports and extras repositories are enabled by default. Backports holds applications being developed for future Ubuntu releases and may not work well. Extras includes third party applications.

Commented entries are included for the Canonical partner repository. Partners include companies like Adobe and Skype.

Most entries, including third-party entries for Ubuntu partners, can be managed using Software & Updates. Entries can also be managed by editing the **sources.list** file with the following command.

```
sudo gedit /etc/apt/sources.list
```

Remove the # at the beginning of the line to activate a repository such as partner.

```
# deb http://archive.canonical.com/ubuntu/ bionic partner
```

Repository information does not have to be added to the **sources.list** file directly. It can also be placed in a text file in the **/etc/apt/sources.list.d** directory, which APT will read as if part of the **sources.list** file. This way you do not have to edit the **/etc/apt/sources.list** file. Editing such an important file always includes the risk of incorrectly changing the entries.

Software & Updates managed from Ubuntu Desktop

You can manage your repositories with the Software & Updates dialog, allowing you to enable or disable repository sections, as well as add new entries. This dialog edits the **/etc/apt/sources.list** file directly. You can access Software & Updates from the Applications overview. You can also access it on the Synaptic Package Manager from the Settings menu as the Repositories entry. The Software & Updates dialog displays six tabs: Ubuntu Software, Other Software, Updates, Authentication, Additional Drivers, and Developer Options (see Figure 4-1).

The Ubuntu Software tab lists all the Ubuntu repository section entries. These include the main repository, universe, restricted, and multiverse, as well as source code. Those that are enabled will be checked. Initially, all of them, except the source code, will be enabled. You can enable or disable a repository section by checking or un-checking its entry. You can select the repository server to use from the "Download from" drop-down menu.

Figure 4-1: Software & Updates Ubuntu Software repository sections

On the Other Software tab, you can add repositories for third-party software (see Figure 4-2). The repository for Ubuntu partners will already be listed, but not checked. Check that entry if you want access to software from the Partners repository such as Adobe reader. To add a third-party repository manually, click the Add button. This opens a dialog where you are prompted to enter the complete APT entry, starting with the deb format, followed by the URL, release, and sections or packages. For a Personal Package Archives (PPA) repository, such as those maintained by the Wine project, you would just enter the ppa: entry. This is the line as it will appear in the **/etc/apt/sources.list** file. Once entered, click the Add Source button. The Add Volume button is used for adding a repository residing on a CD/DVD disc.

Figure 4-2: Software & Updates Other Software configuration

The Updates tab lets you configure how updates are managed (see Figure 4-3). The tab specifies both your update repositories and how automatic updates are handled. You have the option to install Important Security Updates (bionic-security), Recommended Updates (bionic-updates), and Unsupported Updates (bionic-backports). The Important Security and Recommended updates will already be selected; these cover updates for the entire Ubuntu repository. Unsupported updates are useful if you have installed any packages from the backports or pre-release repositories.

Your system is already configured to check for updates automatically on a daily basis. You can opt not to check for updates by choosing never from the "Automatically check for updates" menu. You also have options for how updates are handled. You can install any security updates automatically, without confirmation. You can download updates in the background. Or you can just be notified of available updates, and then choose to install them when you want. The options are exclusive. On this tab, you also can choose what releases to be notified of: the LTS releases only, all releases, or none.

The Authentication tab shows the repository software signature keys that are installed on your system (see Figure 4-4). Ubuntu requires a signature key for any package that it installs. Signature keys for all the Ubuntu repositories are installed and are listed on this tab, including your CD/DVD disc.

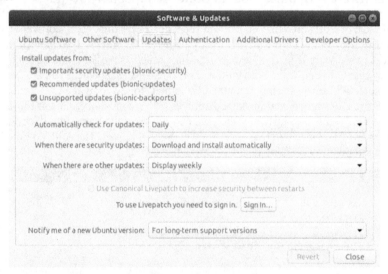

Figure 4-3: Software & Updates Update configuration

Most other third party or customized repositories will provide a signature key file for you to download and import. You can add such keys manually from the Authentication tab. Click the "Import Key File" button to open a file browser where you can select the downloaded key file. This procedure is the same as the **apt-key add** operation. Both add keys that APT then uses to verify DEB software packages downloaded from repositories before it installs them.

Figure 4-4: Software & Updates Authentication, package signature keys

On the Developer Options tab, you can click the Pre-released Updates (bionic-proposed) option to choose to receive development updates (see Figure 4-5). As noted these are for testing and may introduce instability.

Figure 4-5: Software & Updates Developer Options

After you have made changes and click the Close button, the Software & Updates tool will notify you that your software package information is out of date, displaying a Reload button. Click the Reload button to make the new repositories or components available on your package managers like Ubuntu Software and the Synaptic Package Manager. You also can reload your repository configuration by running **apt-get update**, clicking the Reload button on the Synaptic Package Manager, or clicking the Check button on the Software updater.

Updating Ubuntu

New updates are continually being prepared for particular software packages as well as system components. These are posted as updates you can download from software repositories and install on your system. These include new versions of applications, servers, and even the kernel. Such updates may range from single software packages to whole components. When updates become available, a message appears on your desktop.

Updating Ubuntu with Software Updater

Updating your Ubuntu system is a very simple procedure, using Software Updater, which provides a graphical update interface for APT. The Software Updater icon appears on the Dock when updates are available. The Software Updater then displays a simple dialog that shows the amount to be downloaded with "Remind Me Later" and "Install Now" buttons (see Figure 4-6). You can also manually update by starting the Software Update from the Applications overview.

Figure 4-6: Software Updater with selected packages

To see actual packages to be updated, click the "Details of updates" arrow. Packages are organized into application categories such as Ubuntu base for the Linux OS packages, Firefox for Firefox updates, and LibreOffice for office updates. You can expand these to individual packages. The checkboxes for each entry lets you de-select any particular packages you do not want to update (see Figure 4-7). Packages are organized according to importance, beginning with Important security updates and followed by Recommended updates. You should always install the security updates. All the APT-compatible repositories that are configured on your system will be checked for updates.

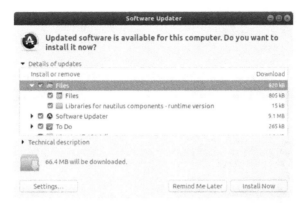

Figure 4-7: Details of updates

Figure 4-8: Details of updates, Technical description

To see a detailed description of a particular update, select the update and then click the "Technical description" arrow (see Figure 4-8). Two tabs are displayed: Changes and Description. The Changes tab lists detailed update information, and Description provides information about the software.

Click the Install Now button to start updating. The packages will be downloaded from their appropriate repository. Once downloaded, the packages are updated.

When downloading and installing, a dialog appears showing the download and install progress (see Figure 4-9). You can choose to show progress for individual files. A window will open up that lists each file and its progress. Once downloaded, the updates are installed. Click the Details arrow to see install messages for particular software packages.

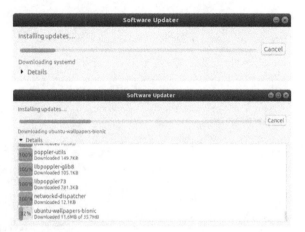

Figure 4-9: Download updates

When the update completes, Software updater will display a message saying that your system is up-to-date. If a critical package was installed such as a new kernel, you will be prompted to restart your system. The power icon will turn red as a warning, and the Session menu will have the added entry "Restart required."

You can configure Software Updater using the dconf editor. The Software Updater keys are located at apps | update-manager. There are keys to auto-close the install window, check for distribution upgrades, show details and versions, and set the window dimensions.

Updating Ubuntu with Ubuntu Software, Update tab

As an alternative to Software Updater, it may be possible to use the Update tab in Ubuntu (GNOME) Software (see Figure 4-10). It is still under development. Software Updater, though, is more reliable and should be used instead. Ubuntu Software may not always display updates, but Software Updater will.

The Updates tab on Ubuntu Software should list the updatesTo perform all the updates, click the Install button on the top toolbar to the right. The label for an update's install button will change to "Installing." To update selectively, click on the update button for the one you want. Clicking an update entry opens a dialog showing information about the update. Some entries, such as OS Updates, will have several packages that have to be updated. When you are ready, click the Restart & Install button on the header bar to shut down your system and install the updates as it restarts.

Figure 4-10: Ubuntu Software: Update tab

Managing Packages with Ubuntu Software

To perform simple installation and removal of software, you can use Ubuntu Software, which is the primary supported package manager for Ubuntu (see Figure 4-12). Ubuntu Software is the Ubuntu implementation of GNOME Software. On the Ubuntu desktop, it has the same icon as the deprecated Ubuntu Software Center used in previous releases. Ubuntu Software is designed to be the centralized utility for managing all your software. It is designed to be a cross-distribution package manager that can be used on supported Linux distribution. Ubuntu Software performs a variety of different software tasks, including installation, removal, updating of software, as well as the management of system-addons such as codecs, fonts, drivers and desktop (shell) extensions.

Figure 4-11: Ubuntu Software

To use the Ubuntu Software, click the Ubuntu Software icon on the dock or on the Applications overview. A window opens with three tabs at the top for All, Installed, and Updates. You can install applications from the All tab, which displays a text box at the top for searching, a collection of category buttons, a list of editor picks, recent releases (see Figure 4-12), and recommended applications for the user (see Figure 4-13).

Figure 4-12: Ubuntu Software, Categories, Picks, and Recent Releases

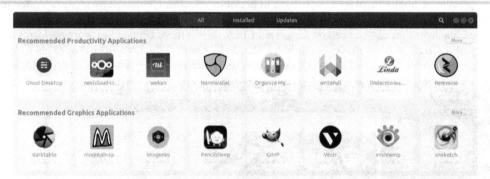

Figure 4-13: Ubuntu Software, Recomendations

The category buttons include Audio & Video, Games, Communication & News, Graphics & Photography, Productivity, and Add-ons. Click on any category button to open a dialog with subcategories. The Add-ons category is a special category that covers enhancements to your desktop, such as codecs, fonts, drivers and desktop (shell) extensions.

Categories may allow you to further filter the selection using a Show menu. The Graphics & Photography category has filters such as Vector Graphics, Scanning, and Photography (Figure 4-14). A Sort menu lets you also sort items by name or rating. The software in each category is listed as icons. A few featured packages are listed at the top. Packages already installed have a checkmark on a packet emblem displayed in the upper right corner of the package icon.

Figure 4-14: Ubuntu Software, Graphics category

Click a software icon to open its description page, which provides a brief description of the software and a link to its related website (see Figure 4-15). Uninstalled software displays an Install button below the software's name, and installed software shows a Remove button. To the right of the name is a star rating with the number of reviews.

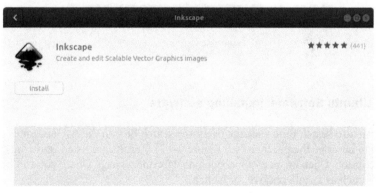

Figure 4-15: Ubuntu Software, software descriptor page

Click the Install button to install the software. As the software is installed, an Installing progress bar appears (see Figure 4-16). When complete, Launch and Remove buttons are displayed below the name. You can use these to start or uninstall the software.

Figure 4-16: Ubuntu Software, installing software

You can also search for a package using the search box on the All tab. Enter part of the name or a term to describe the package (see Figure 4-17). Results are listed, showing an icon, name, and description. Click on an entry to open its description page where you can perform possible actions such as install, remove, or launch.

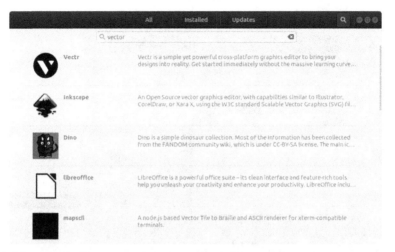

Figure 4-17: Ubuntu Software, using the search box

The Installed tab lists your installed software (see Figure 4-18). If the applications is located on the overview within a folder, that folder name is listed under the application name. To remove an application, click its Remove button. You can also use the installed tab to organize the applications overview, creating new category folders on the overview or moving applications into existing folders. Click on the checkbox at the right on the title bar on the Installed tab. Round checkboxes will appear to the left of each software entry, which you can click to select that application (see Figure 4-19). Three buttons are listed at the bottom of the window labeled "Add to Folder", "Move to Folder", "Remove from Folder". When you select an item, the possible buttons become active. Initially, most applications are not in folders, so when you select and application, only the "Add to Folder" button becomes active. Clicking on it opens an "Add to Applications Folder" dialog, which lists possible folder to move the application to. Clicking on the plus icon below the list opens a dialog where you can create a new folder with a name of your choosing. Click the Cancel button at the top right when you are finished. This feature lets you organize your Applications overview using folders of your choosing.

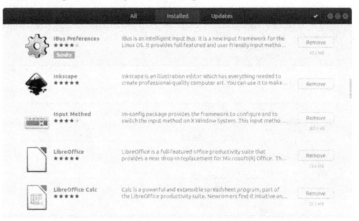

Figure 4-18: Ubuntu Software, installed tab

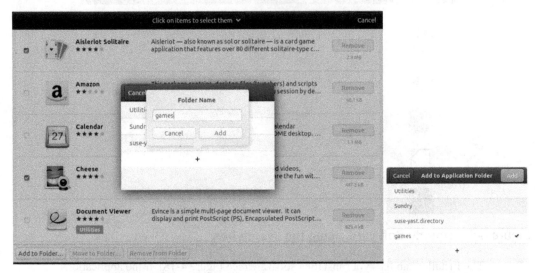

Figure 4-19: Ubuntu Software, installed tab, organize applications overview

Using the Add-ons category, you can easily manage your fonts, graphics drivers, multimedia codecs, and any additional third-party apps or features you want installed on your system. Clicking on the Add-ons category on the All tab opens the Add-ons dialog with tabs for Codecs, Fonts, Hardware Drivers, Input Sources, and Shell Extensions (see Figure 4-20). Installed software will show an emblem with a checkmark in the top right corner of their icons. To install or remove and add-on, click on its icon to open a description dialog. Installed add-ons will show a Remove button, and Uninstalled ones will show an Install button.

Figure 4-20: Ubuntu Software, Add-ons tab

The Shell Extensions tab shows extensions you can add to your desktop, which are not supported by Ubuntu. You are warned to install them at your own risk. Clicking on the Shell Extensions button allows you to turn on support for application indicators on the top bar and for a Gnome dock. The button then becomes an "Extension Settings" button you can use to display the extensions you have installed and turn them on or off (see Figure 4-21). Many of the shell extensions provided are designed to operate as indicators on the top bar.

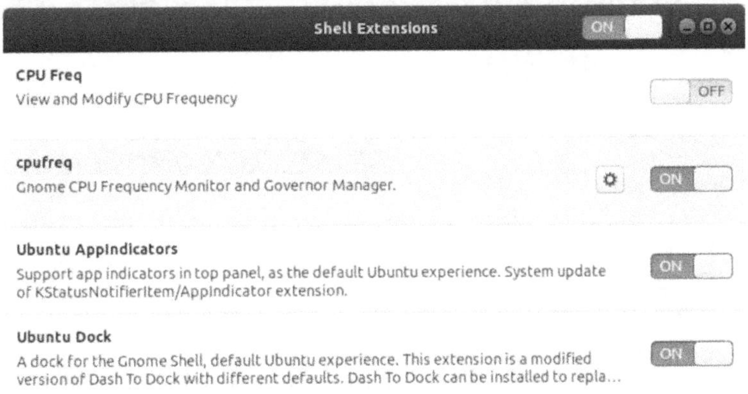

Figure 4-21: Shell Extension (Ubuntu Software), Managing Installed Shell Extensions

Many of the shell extensions provided are designed to operate as indictors on the top bar. Others add features to the desktop. Keep in mind that the extensions are not guaranteed to work. Some of the extensions will have a configuration button you can click to display features you can set such as that for the cpufreq, which lets you set the frequency of the update interval. The two Ubuntu extensions, Ubuntu Dock and Ubuntu Appindicators, though technically extension,are integrated into the desktop and cannot be turned off.

Ubuntu Software is a front end for the APT package manager. When you install a package with the Ubuntu Software, APT is invoked and automatically selects and downloads the package from the appropriate online repository.

The packages listed in the Ubuntu Software are set up using the **app-install-data** packages, accessible through the Synaptic Package Manager. The **app-install-data** and **app-install-data-partner** packages are already installed. These list the commonly used packages on the Ubuntu repository.

Synaptic Package Manager

The Synaptic Package Manager has been replaced by Ubuntu (GNOME) Software as the primary package manager. It is not installed by default. Synaptic is no longer supported by Ubuntu, though support is still provided by the Ubuntu community. Packages are listed by name and include supporting packages like libraries and system critical packages. Once installed, you can access the Synaptic Package Manager on the Applications overview.

The Synaptic Package Manager displays three panes: a side pane for listing software categories and buttons, a top pane for listing software packages, and a bottom pane for displaying a selected package's description. When a package is selected, the description pane also displays a Get Screenshot button. Clicking this button will download and display an image of the application if there is one. Click the Get Changelog button to display a window listing the application changes.

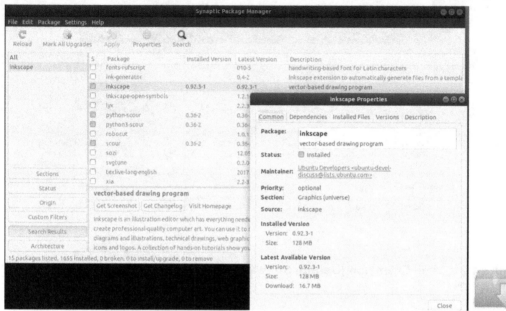

Figure 4-22: Synaptic Package Manager

Buttons at the lower left of the Synaptic Package Manager window provide options for organizing and refining the list of packages shown (see Figure 4-22). Five options are available: Sections, Status, Origin, Custom Filters, Search results, and Architecture. The dialog pane above the buttons changes depending on which option you choose. Clicking the Sections button will list section categories for your software such as Graphics, Communications, and Development. The Status button will list options for installed and not installed software. The Origin button shows entries for different repositories and their sections, as well as those locally installed (manual or disc based installations). Custom filters lets you choose a filter to use for listing packages. You can create your own filter and use it to display selected packages. Search results will list your current and previous searches, letting you move from one to the other.

The Sections option is selected by default (see Figure 4-23). You can choose to list all packages, or refine your listing using categories provided in the pane. The All entry in this pane will list all available packages. Packages are organized into categories such as Cross Platform, Communications, and Editors. Each category is, in turn, subdivided by multiverse, universe, and restricted software.

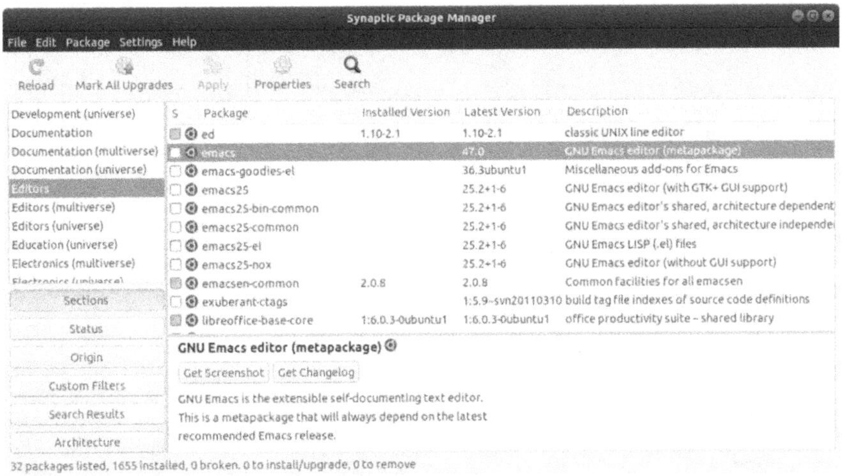

Figure 4-23: Synaptic Package Manager: Sections

To perform a quick search, enter the pattern to be searched for in the "Quick Filter" box and the results will appear. In Figure 4-19 the inkscape pattern is used to locate the Inkscape graphics software. Quick searches will be performed within selected sections. Selecting different sections applies your quick search pattern to the packages in that section. Clicking on the Editors section with an inkscape search pattern would give no results since Inkscape is not an editor package. Should the Quick Filter box not be active or displayed, use the Search tool instead.

To perform more detailed searches, you can use the Search tool. Click the Search button on the toolbar to open a Search dialog with a text box where you can enter search terms. A pop-up menu lets you specify what features of a package to search such as the "Description and Name" feature. You can search other package features like the Name, the maintainer name (Maintainer), the package version (Version), packages it may depend on (Dependencies), or associated packages (Provided Packages). A list of searches will be displayed in Search Results. You can move back and forth between search results by clicking on the search entries in this listing.

Status entries further refine installed software as manual or as upgradeable (see Figure 4-24). Local software consists of packages you download and install manually.

With the Origin options, Ubuntu-compliant repositories may further refine access according to multiverse, universe, and restricted software. A main section selects Ubuntu-supported software. The Architecture options let you select software compatible with a specified architecture, such as 64-bit or 32-bit.

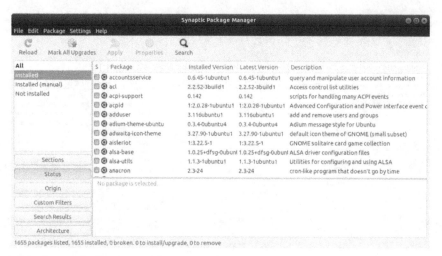

Figure 4-24: Synaptic Package Manager: Status

Properties

To find out information about a package, select the package and click the Properties button. This opens a window with Common, Dependencies, Installed Files, Versions, and Description tabs (see Figure 4-16). The Common tab provides section, versions, and maintainer information. The Installed Files tab show you exactly what files are installed, which is useful for finding the exact location, and names for configuration files, as well as commands. The Description tab displays detailed information about the software. The Dependencies tab shows all dependent software packages needed by this software, usually libraries.

Installing packages

Before installing software, you should press the Reload button to load the most recent package lists from the active repositories

To install a package, right-click on its name to display a pop-up menu and select the Mark for installation entry. Should any dependent packages exist, a dialog opens listing those packages. Click the Mark button in the dialog to mark those packages for installation. The package entry's checkbox will then be marked in the Synaptic Package Manager window.

Once you have selected the packages you want to install, click the Apply button on the toolbar to begin the installation process. A Summary dialog opens showing all the packages to be installed. You have the option to download the package files. The number of packages to be installed is listed, along with the size of the download and the amount of disk space used. Click the Apply button on the Summary dialog to download and install the packages. A download window will then appear showing the progress of your package installations. You can choose to show the progress of individual packages, which opens a terminal window listing each package as it is downloaded and installed.

Once downloaded, the dialog name changes to Installing Software. You can choose to have the dialog close automatically when finished. Sometimes installation requires user input to configure the software. You will be prompted to enter the information if necessary.

When you right-click a package name, you also see options for Mark Suggested for Installation or Mark Recommended for Installation. These will mark applications that can enhance your selected software, though they are not essential. If there are no suggested or recommended packages for that application, then these entries will be grayed out.

Certain software, like desktops or office suites that require a significant number of packages, can be selected all at once using metapackages. A metapackage has configuration files that select, download, and configure the range of packages needed for such complex software. For example, the **kubuntu-desktop** meta package will install the entire Kubuntu desktop (Sections | Meta Packages).

Removing packages

To remove a package, first, locate it. Then right-click it and select the "Mark package for removal" entry. This will leave configuration files untouched. Alternatively, you can mark a package for complete removal, which will also remove any configuration files, "Mark for Complete Removal." Dependent packages will not be removed.

Once you have marked packages for removal, click the Apply button. A summary dialog displays the packages that will be removed. Click Apply to remove them.

The Synaptic Package Manager may not remove dependent packages, especially shared libraries that might be used by other applications. This means that your system could have installed packages that are never being used.

Search filters

You can further refine your search for packages by creating search filters. Select the Settings | Filters menu entry to open the Filters window. The Filters window shows two panes, a filter list on the left, and three tabs on the right: Status, Section, and Properties. To create a new filter, click the New button located just below the filter listing. Click the New Filter 1 entry in the filter list on the left pane. On the Status tab, you can refine your search criteria according to a package's status. You can search only uninstalled packages, include installed packages, include or exclude packages marked for removal, or search or those that are new in the repository. Initially, all criteria are selected. Uncheck those you do not want included in your search. The Section tab lets you include or exclude different repository sections like games, documentation, or administration. If you are looking for a game, you could choose to include just the game section, excluding everything else. On the Properties tab, you can specify patterns to search on package information such as package names, using Boolean operators to refine your search criteria. Package search criteria are entered using the two pop-up menus and the text box at the bottom of the tab, along with AND or OR Boolean operators.

Note: For KDE you can use the Discover Software Center to install and update packages (see Chapter 11).

Ubuntu Software for separate DEB packages

You can also use Ubuntu (GNOME) Software to perform an installation of a single DEB software package. Usually, these packages are downloaded directly from a website and have few or no dependent packages. When you right-click on a deb package, you will see the entry "Open With Software Install." Choose this entry to open Ubuntu Software, listing the package name, description, and details (version number, size, and source), along with a warning that it is installed without repository support, and so will not be automatically updated. Below the package name is an install button, which you click to install the package.

Snappy Packages

Snappy is the new package format that will replace the deb package management system on Ubuntu. The packages are called snaps. With the deb format, as with other Linux pack formats like RPM, the component software files for a software application are installed directly to global system directories such as **/lib**, **/etc**, and **/usr/bin**. In addition, a deb software package usually has several dependent packages, which also have to be installed. These can be extensive. Under this system, shared libraries, used by different applications can be a problem for developers, as changes in software may have to wait for supporting changes in the shared libraries.

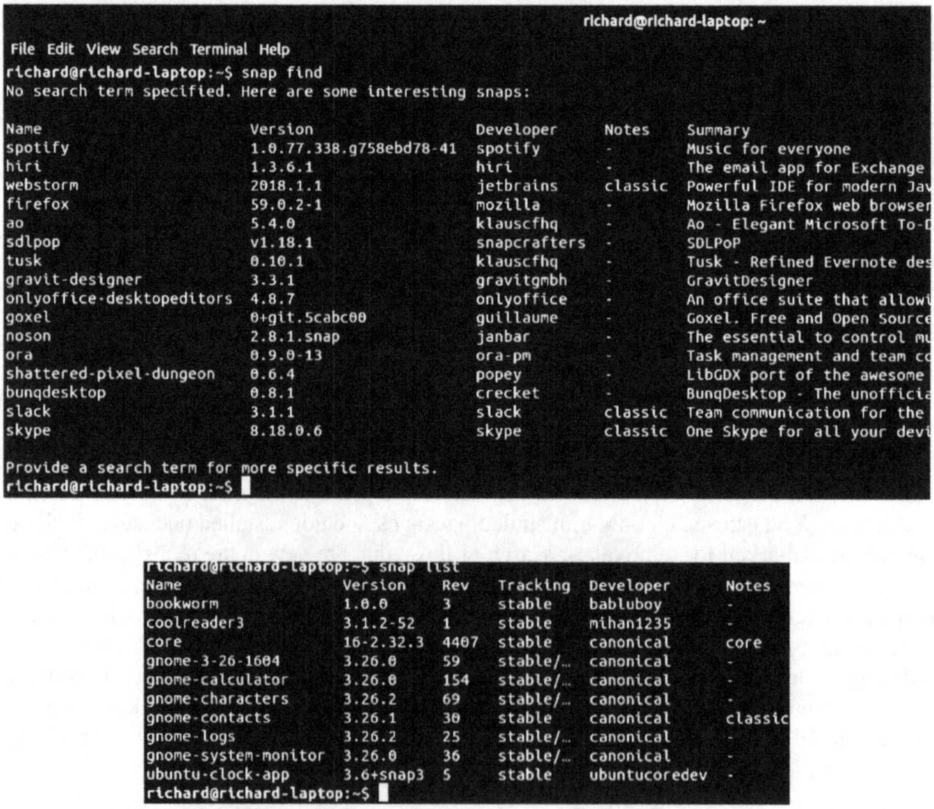

Figure 4-25: Snappy Package listing

With Snappy, the software files for an application are no longer installed in global directories. They are installed in one separate location, and any dependent software and shared libraries are included as part of the snap package. In effect, there are no longer any dependencies, and libraries are no longer shared. This makes for more secure and faster updates, though a larger set of installed files. The problem of a failed update due to broken dependencies is no longer an issue. Applications that used to make use of the same shared library, will now have their own copies of that library. Developers that used to have to wait for changes to be made to a shared library, can now directly just change their own copy. Though logically separate, Snappy plans to avoid duplication of libraries, storing the same exact library in one location.

Ubuntu Software has a snappy backend that integrates snappy packages and allows you to install and remove them. Alternatively, you can simply use the **snap** command in a terminal window.

To find a snap package, use the **snap** command and the **find** option with the search term (see Figure 4-25). Without the search term, a list of popular snap packages is displayed. To see a list of snap packages already installed, use the **list** option.

```
snap find skype
snap find
```

To install a package, use the **snap** command with the **install** option. The following installs the skype snappy application.

```
sudo snap install skype
```

Once installed, the Snappy applications will appear on the Applications overview, just as any other application.

Use the **remove** option to remove a package.

```
sudo snap remove skype
```

Use the **refresh** command to update your snappy packages.

```
sudo snap refresh skype
```

The **list** option displays your installed snappy applications.

```
snap list
```

Snappy applications are stored in the **/snap** directory under the package name. They include the application executables, as well as all configuration and system support files. In effect, each Snappy application has its own **/etc**, **/usr**, **/bin**, **/lib**, and **/var** directory. A script for running the application is held in the **/snap/bin** directoryIn effect, the ubuntu-core system, which is also installed on your system under the **/snap** directory, operates as a kind of shell for the Snappy applications. User data for a Snappy application is held in a **snap** folder in your home folder. Systemd support for Snappy is provided by the systemd **snapd.service** and **snapd.socket** files.

Should you want to create a snap package, you can use **snapcraft**, which you can install with **apt-get** or the Synaptic Package Manager.

Installing and Running Windows Software on Linux: Wine

Wine is a Windows compatibility layer that will allow you to run many Windows applications natively on Linux. The actual Windows operating system is not required. Windows applications will run as if they were Linux applications, able to access the entire Linux file system and use Linux-connected devices. Applications that are heavily driver-dependent, like graphic intensive games, may not run. Others that do not rely on any specialized drivers, may run very well, including Photoshop and Microsoft Office. For some applications, you may also need to copy over specific Windows dynamic link libraries (DLLs) from a working Windows system to your Wine Windows system32 or system directory.

You can install Wine on your system from Ubuntu Software | System | Wine Microsoft Windows Compatibility Layer. The **ttf-mscorefonts-installer** for the Microsoft core fonts will also be installed. You will be prompted to accept the Microsoft end user agreement for using those fonts.

Once installed, you can access Wine applications from the Applications overview, or search on *wine*. The Wine applications include Wine configuration, the Wine software uninstaller, and Wine file browser, as well as Winetricks and notepad.

To set up Wine, start the Wine Configuration tool ("Configure Wine") to open a window with tabs for Applications, Libraries (DLL selection), Audio (sound drivers), Drives, Desktop Integration, and Graphics. On the Applications tab, you can select the version of Windows an application is designed for. The Drives tab lists your detected partitions, as well as your Windows-emulated drives, such as drive C. The C: drive is actually just a directory, **.wine/drive_c**, not a partition of a fixed size. Your actual Linux file system will be listed as the Z drive.

Once configured, Wine will set up a **.wine** directory on the user's home directory (the directory is hidden, enable Show Hidden Files in the file manager View menu to display it). Within that directory will be the **drive_c** directory, which functions as the C: drive that holds your Windows system files and program files in the Windows and Program File subdirectories. The System and System32 directories are located in the Windows directory. This is where you would place any needed DLL files. The Program Files directory holds your installed Windows programs, just as they would be installed on a Windows Program Files directory.

To install a Windows application with Wine, you right-click on the application icon in the file manager window, and then choose "Open With Wine Windows Program Loader." Alternatively, you can open a terminal window and run the **wine** command with a Windows application as an argument.

```
$ wine winprogram.exe
```

Icons for installed Windows software will appear on your desktop. Just double-click an icon to start up an application. It will run normally within a Linux window, as would any Linux application.

Installing Windows fonts on Wine is a simple matter of copying fonts from a Windows font directory to your Wine **.wine/drive_c/Windows/fonts** directory. You can copy any Windows **.ttf** file to this directory to install a font.

Wine should work on both **.exe** and **.msi** files. You may have to make them executable by checking the file's Properties dialog Permissions tab's Execute checkbox. If an **.msi** file cannot be run, you may have to use the **msiexec** command with the **/a** option.

```
msiexec /a winprogram.msi
```

Alternatively, you can use the commercial Windows compatibility layer called Crossover Office. This is a commercial product tested to run certain applications like Microsoft Office. Check **http://www.codeweavers.com** for more details. Crossover Office is based on Wine, which CodeWeavers supports directly.

Source code files

You can install source code files using **apt-get**. Specify the **source** operation with the package name. Packages will be downloaded and extracted.

```
sudo apt-get source mplayer
```

The **--download** option lets you just download the source package without extracting it. The **--compile** option will download, extract, compile, and package the source code into a Debian binary package, ready for installation.

With the **source** operation, no dependent packages will be downloaded. If a software packages requires any dependent packages to run, you would have to download and compile those. To obtain needed dependent files, you use the **build-dep** option. All your dependent files will be located and downloaded for you automatically.

```
sudo apt-get build-dep mplayer
```

Installing from source code requires that supporting development libraries and source code header files be installed. You can do this separately for each major development platform like GNOME, KDE, or the kernel. Alternatively, you can run the APT meta-package **build-essential** for all the Ubuntu development packages. You will have to do this only once.

```
sudo apt-get install build-essential
```

Software Package Types

Ubuntu uses Debian-compliant software packages (DEB) whose filenames have a **.deb** extension. Other packages, such as those in the form of source code that you need to compile, may come in a variety of compressed archives. These commonly have the extension **.tar.gz**, **.tgz**, or **.tar.bz2**. Packages with the **.rpm** extension are Red Hat Package software packages used on Red Hat, Fedora, SuSE and other Linux distributions that use RPM packages. They are not compatible directly with Ubuntu. You can use the **alien** utility to convert most RPM packages to DEB packages that you can then install on Ubuntu. Table 4-1 lists several common file extensions that you will find for the great variety of Linux software packages available. You can download any Ubuntu-compliant deb package as well as the original source code package, as single files, directly from **http://packages.ubuntu.com**.

DEB Software Packages

A Debian package will automatically resolve dependencies, installing any other needed packages instead of simply reporting their absence. Packages are named with the software name, the version number, and the **.deb** extension. Check **https://www.debian.org/doc** for more information. Filename format is as follows:

> **the package name**
>
> **version number**
>
> **distribution label and build number**. Packages created specifically for Ubuntu have the ubuntu label here. Attached to it is the build number, the number of times the package was built for Ubuntu.

architecture   The type of system on which the package runs, like i386 for Intel 32-bit x86 systems, or amd64 for both Intel and AMD 64-bit systems, x86_64.

package format. This is always **deb**

For example, the package name for 3dchess is 3dchess, with a version and build number 0.8.1-20, and an amd64 architecture for a 64-bit system.

```
3dchess_0.8.1-20_amd64.deb
```

The following package has an Ubuntu label, a package specifically created for Ubuntu. The version and build number is 3.22.0-3. The architecture is i386 for a 32-bit system.

```
gnome-mahjongg_3.22.0-3_i386.deb
```

Extension	File
.deb	A Debian/Ubuntu Linux package
.gz	A **gzip**-compressed file (use **gunzip** to decompress)
.bz2	A **bzip2**-compressed file (use **bunzip2** to decompress; also use the **j** option with **tar**, as in **xvjf**)
.tar	A tar archive file (use **tar** with **xvf** to extract)
.tar.gz	A **gzip**-compressed **tar** archive file (use **gunzip** to decompress and **tar** to extract; use the **z** option with **tar**, as in **xvzf**, to both decompress and extract in one step)
.tar.bz2	A **bzip2**-compressed **tar** archive file (extract with **tar -xvzj**)
.tz	A **tar** archive file compressed with the **compress** command
.Z	A file compressed with the **compress** command (use the **decompress** command to decompress)
.bin	A self-extracting software file
.rpm	A software package created with the Red Hat Software Package Manager, used on Fedora, Red Hat, Centos, and SuSE distributions
snap	The snappy packages, replacement for .deb

Table 4-1: Linux Software Package File Extensions

Managing software with apt-get

APT is designed to work with repositories, and will handle any dependencies for you. It uses **dpkg** to install and remove individual packages, but can also determine what dependent packages need to be installed, as well as query and download packages from repositories. Several popular tools for APT let you manage your software easily, like the Synaptic Package Manager, Ubuntu (GNOME) Software, and aptitude. Ubuntu Software and the Synaptic Package Manager rely on a desktop interface like GNOME. If you are using the command line interface, you can use **apt-get** to manage packages. Using the **apt-get** command on the command line you can install, update, and remove packages. Check the **apt-get** man page for a detailed listing of **apt-get** commands (see Table 4-2).

```
apt-get command   package
```

The **apt-get** command takes two arguments: the command to perform and the name of the package. Other APT package tools follow the same format. The command is a term such as **install** for installing packages or **remove** to uninstall a package. Use the **install**, **remove**, or **update** commands respectively. You only need to specify the software name, not the package's full filename. APT will determine that. To install the MPlayer package you would use:

```
sudo apt-get install mplayer
```

To make sure that **apt-get** has current repository information, use the **apt-get update** command.

```
sudo apt-get update
```

To remove packages, you use the **remove** command.

```
sudo apt-get remove mplayer
```

Command	Description
update	Download and resynchronize the package listing of available and updated packages for APT supported repositories. APT repositories updated are those specified in **/etc/apt/sources.list**
upgrade	Update packages, install new versions of installed packages if available.
dist-upgrade	Update (upgrade) all your installed packages to a new release
install	Install a specific package, using its package name, not full package filename.
remove	Remove a software package from your system.
source	Download and extract a source code package
check	Check for broken dependencies
clean	Removes the downloaded packages held in the repository cache on your system. Used to free up disk space.

Table 4-2: apt-get commands

You can use the **-s** option to check the remove or install first, especially to check whether any dependency problems exist. For remove operations, you can use **-s** to find out first what dependent packages will also be removed.

```
sudo apt-get remove -s mplayer
```

The **apt-get** command can be very helpful if your X Windows System server ever fails (your display driver). For example, if you installed a restricted vendor display driver, and then your desktop fails to start, you can start up in the recovery mode, start the root shell, and use **apt-get** to remove the restricted display driver. Your former X open source display drivers would be restored automatically. The following would remove the NVIDIA restricted display driver.

```
sudo apt-get remove nvidia*
```

A complete log of all install, remove, and update operations are kept in the **/var/log/dpkg.log** file. You can consult this file to find out exactly what files were installed or removed.

Configuration for APT is held in the **/etc/apt** directory. Here the **sources.list** file lists the distribution repositories from where packages are installed. Source lists for additional third-party repositories are kept in the **/etc/apt/sources.list.d** directory. GPG (GNU Privacy Guard) database files hold validation keys for those repositories. Specific options for **apt-get** are can be found in an /etc/apt.conf file or in various files located in the **/etc/apt.conf.d** directory.

Updating packages (Upgrading) with apt-get

The **apt-get** tool also lets you easily update your entire system at once. The terms update and upgrade are used differently from other software tools. In **apt-get**, the **update** command just updates your package listing, checking for packages that may need to install newer versions, but not installing those versions. Technically, it updates the package list that APT uses to determine what packages need to be updated. The term upgrade is used to denote the actual update of a software package; a new version is downloaded and installed. What is referred to as updating by **apt-get**, other package managers refer to as obtaining the list of software packages to be updated (the reload operation). In **apt-get**, upgrading is what other package managers refer to as performing updates.

TIP: The terms update and upgrade can be confusing when used with apt-get. The update operation updates the Apt package list only, whereas an upgrade actually downloads and installs updated packages.

Upgrading is a simple matter of using the **upgrade** command. With no package specified, using **apt-get** with the **upgrade** command will upgrade your entire system. Add the –u option to list packages as they are upgraded. First, make sure your repository information (package list) is up to date with the **update** command, then issue the **upgrade** command.

```
sudo apt-get update
sudo apt-get -u upgrade
```

Command Line Search and Information: dpkg-query and apt-cache tools

The **dpkg-query** command lets you list detailed information about your packages. It operates on the command line (terminal window). Use **dpkg-query** with the -l option to list all your packages.

```
dpkg-query -l
```

The **dpkg** command can operate as a front end for **dpkg-query**, detecting its options to perform the appropriate task. The preceding command could also be run as:

```
dpkg -l
```

Listing a particular package requires and exact match on the package name unless you use pattern matching operators. The following command lists the **samba** package (Windows Compatibility Layer).

```
dpkg-query -l samba
```

A pattern matching operator, such as *, placed after a pattern will display any packages beginning with the specified pattern. The pattern with its operators needs to be placed in single quotation marks to prevent an attempt by the shell to use the pattern to match on filenames in your current directory. The following example finds all packages beginning with the pattern "samba". This would include packages with names such as **samba-client** and **samba-common**.

```
dpkg-query -l 'samba*'
```

You can further refine the results by using **grep** to perform an additional search. The following operation first outputs all packages beginning with **samba**, and from those results, the **grep** operations lists only those with the pattern common in their name, such as **samba-common**.

```
dpkg -l 'samba*' | grep 'common'
```

Use the **-L** option to list the files that a package has installed.

```
dpkg-query -L samba
```

To see the status information about a package, including its dependencies and configuration files, use the **-s** option. Fields will include Status, Section, Architecture, Version, Depends (dependent packages), Suggests, Conflicts (conflicting packages), and Conffiles (configuration files).

```
dpkg-query -s samba
```

The status information will also provide suggested dependencies. These are packages not installed, but likely to be used. For the samba package, the **chrony** time server package is suggested.

```
dpkg-query -s samba | grep Suggests
```

Use the **-S** option to determine to which package a particular file belongs to.

```
dpkg-query -S filename
```

You can also obtain information with the **apt-cache** tool. Use the search command with **apt-cache** to perform a search.

```
apt-cache search samba
```

To find dependencies for a particular package, use the **depends** command.

```
apt-cache depends samba
```

To display just the package description, use the **show** command.

```
apt-cache show samba
```

Note: If you have installed Aptitude software manager, you can use the aptitude command with the search and show options to find and display information about packages.

Managing non-repository packages with dpkg

You can use **dpkg** to install a software package you have already downloaded directly, not with an APT enabled software tools like **apt-get**, Ubuntu Software, or the Synaptic Package Manager. In this case, you are not installing from a repository. Instead, you have manually downloaded the package file from a Web or FTP site to a folder on your system. Such a situation would be rare, reserved for software not available on the Ubuntu repository or any APT enabled repository. Keep in mind that most software is already on your Ubuntu or APT enabled repositories. Check there first for the software package before performing a direct download, and install with **dpkg**. The **dpkg** configuration files are located in the **/etc/dpkg** directory. Configuration is held in the **dpkg.cfg** file. See the **dpkg** man page for a detailed listing of options.

One situation, for which you would use **dpkg**, is for packages you have built yourself, like packages you created when converting a package in another format to a Debian package (DEB). This is the case when converting an RPM package (Red Hat Package Manager) to a Debian package format.

For **dpkg**, you use the **-i** option to install a package and **-r** to remove it.

```
sudo dpkg -i package.deb
```

The major failing for **dpkg** is that it provides no dependency support. It will inform you of needed dependencies, but you will have to install them separately. **dpkg** installs only the specified package. It is useful for packages that have no dependencies.

You use the **-I** option to obtain package information directly from the DEB package file.

```
sudo dpkg -I package.deb
```

To remove a package, you use the **-r** option with the package software name. You do not need version or extension information like **.386** or **.deb**. With **dpkg**, when removing a package with dependencies, you first have to remove all its dependencies manually. You will not be able to uninstall the package until you do this. Configuration files are not removed.

```
sudo dpkg -r packagename
```

If you install a package that requires dependencies, and then fail to install these dependencies, your install database will be marked as having broken packages. In this case, APT will not allow new packages to be installed until the broken packages are fixed. You can enter the **apt-get** command with the **-f** and install options to fix all broken packages at once.

```
sudo apt-get -f install
```

Using packages with other software formats

You can convert software packages in other software formats into DEB packages that can then be installed on Ubuntu. To do this you use the **alien** tool, which can convert several different kinds of formats such as RPM and even TGZ (**.tgz**). You use the **--to-deb** option to convert to a DEB package format that Ubuntu can then install. The **--scripts** option attempts also to convert any pre or post install configuration scripts.

```
alien --scripts --to-deb package.rpm
```

Once you have generated the **.deb** package, you can use **dpkg** to install it.

Part 2: Applications

Office Suites, Editors, and E-mail
Multimedia and Graphics
Internet Applications

ubuntu®

5. Office Suites, Editors, and E-mail

LibreOffice

Calligra

GNOME Office Applications

Running Microsoft Office on Linux

Document Viewers (PostScript, PDF, and DVI)

Ebook readers

GNOME Notes, Clocks, and Weather

Editors

Database Management Systems

Mail Clients: Evolution, Thunderbird, Kmail

Command Line Mail Clients

Newsreaders

Several office suites are now available for Ubuntu (see Table 5-1). These include professional-level word processors, presentation managers, drawing tools, and spreadsheets. The freely available versions are described in this chapter. LibreOffice is currently the primary office suite supported by Ubuntu. Calligra is an office suite designed for use with KDE. CodeWeavers CrossOver Office provides reliable support for running Microsoft Office Windows applications directly on Linux, integrating them with KDE and GNOME. You can also download the Apache OpenOffice suite (originally, Oracle/StarOffice).

Web Site	Description
https://www.libreoffice.org	LibreOffice open source office suite
https://www.calligra.org	Calligra Suite, for KDE
https://www.codeweavers.com	CrossOver Office (MICROSOFT Office support)
https://www.openoffice.org	Apache OpenOffice
https://www.scribus.net	Scribus desktop publishing tool

Table 5-1: Linux Office Suites

Several database management systems are also available for Linux, which include high-powered, commercial-level database management systems, such as Oracle and IBM's DB2. Most of the database management systems available for Linux are designed to support large relational databases. Ubuntu includes both MySQL and PostgreSQL open source databases in its distribution, which can support smaller databases. Various database management systems available to run under Linux are listed in Table 5-8 later in this chapter.

Linux also provides several text editors that range from simple text editors for simple notes to editors with more complex features such as spell-checkers, buffers, or complex pattern matching. All generate character text files and can be used to edit any Linux text files. Text editors are often used in system administration tasks to change or add entries in Linux configuration files found in the **/etc** directory or a user's initialization or application configuration files located in a user's home directory (dot files). You can also use a text editor to work on source code files for any of the programming languages or shell program scripts.

Ubuntu also supports several Ebook readers. Some such as Calibre and FBReader run natively on Linux. Some of the Window versions of Ebook readers such as Adobe Digital Editions run under Wine (the Windows compatibility layer for Linux).

LibreOffice

LibreOffice is a fully integrated suite of office applications developed as an open source project and freely distributed to all. It is the primary office suite for Ubuntu. LibreOffice applications are accessible from the Applications overview. There are also default dock items for three commonly used LibreOffice applications (Writer, Calc, and Impress). LibreOffice is the open source and freely available office suite derived originally from OpenOffice. LibreOffice is supported by the Document Foundation, which was established after Oracle's acquisition of Sun, the main developer for Open Office. LibreOffice is now the primary open source office software for Linux. Oracle retains control of all the original OpenOffice software and does not cooperate with any LibreOffice development. LibreOffice has replaced OpenOffice as the default Office software for most Linux distributions.

LibreOffice includes word processing, spreadsheet, presentation, and drawing applications (see Table 5-2). Versions of LibreOffice exist for Linux, Windows, and Mac OS. You can obtain information such as online manuals and FAQs as well as current versions from the LibreOffice website at **https://www.libreoffice.org**. The LibreOffice suite of applications is installed as part of the Ubuntu Desktop installation.

Application	Description
Calc (Spreadsheet)	LibreOffice spreadsheet
Draw (Drawing)	LibreOffice drawing application
Writer (Word Processing)	LibreOffice word processor
Math (Formula)	LibreOffice mathematical formula composer
Impress (Presentation)	LibreOffice presentation manager
Base (Database)	Database front end for accessing and managing a variety of different databases.

Table 5-2: LibreOffice Applications

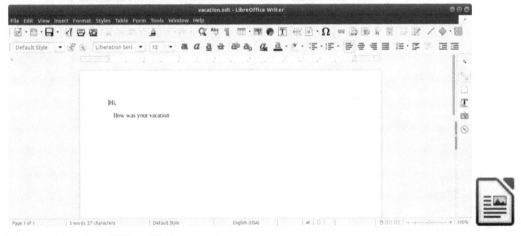

Figure 5-1: LibreOffice Writer word processor

LibreOffice is an integrated suite of applications. You can open the writer, spreadsheet, or presentation application directly. The word processing, spreadsheet, and presentations applications are also accessible from the Dock: Writer, Calc, and Impress. The LibreOffice Writer word processor supports standard word processing features, such as cut and paste, spell-checker, and text formatting, as well as paragraph styles (see Figure 5-1). Context menus let you format text easily. Wizards (Letter, Web page, Fax, and Agenda) let you generate different kinds of documents quickly. You can embed objects within documents, such as using Draw to create figures that you can then drag-and-drop to the Writer document. LibreOffice Writer is compatible with earlier versions of Microsoft Word. It will read and convert Word documents to LibreOffice Writer document, preserving most features including contents, tables, and indexes. Writer documents also can be saved as Word documents.

LibreOffice provides access to many database files. File types supported include ODBC (Open Database Connectivity), JDBC (Java), MySQL, PostgreSQL, and MDB (Microsoft Access) database files. You can also create your own simple databases. Check the LibreOffice Features | Base page (**https://www.libreoffice.org/discover/base/**) for detailed information on drivers and supported databases.

LibreOffice Calc is a professional-level spreadsheet. With LibreOffice Math (LibreOffice Formula), you can create formulas that you can embed in a text document. With the presentation manager (Libre Office Impress), you can create images for presentations, such as circles, rectangles, and connecting elements like arrows, as well as vector-based illustrations. Impress supports advanced features such as morphing objects, grouping objects, and defining gradients. Draw is a sophisticated drawing tool that includes 3-D modeling tools (LibreOffice Drawing). You can create simple or complex images, including animation text aligned on curves. LibreOffice also includes a printer setup tool with which you can select printers, fonts, paper sizes, and page formats.

Scribus is a desktop publishing tool, **https://www.scribus.net** (see Figure 5-2). Scribus is available from the Universe repository.

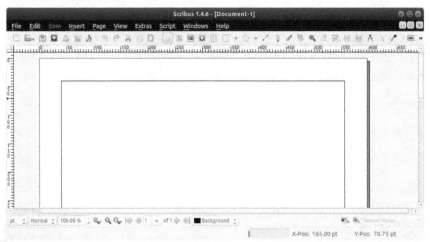

Figure 5-2: Scribus

Calligra

Calligra is an integrated office suite for the K Desktop Environment (KDE) consisting of several office applications, including a word processor, a spreadsheet, and graphics applications. You can download and install it from the Universe repository, using the Synaptic Package Manager (Ubuntu desktop) or the Discover Package Manager (Kubuntu). Calligra allows components from any one application to be used in another, letting you embed a spreadsheet from Calligra Sheets or diagrams from Karbon in a Calligra Words document. It also uses the open document format

(ODF) for its files, providing cross-application standardization. There is also a Windows version available. You can obtain more information about Calligra from **https://www.calligra.org**.

Currently, Calligra includes Calligra Sheets, Calligra Flow, Calligra Words, Karbon, Krita, Plan, Calligra Stage, Braindump, and Kexi (see Table 5-3). The contact application, Kontact, has been spun off as a separate project. Kontact is an integrated contact application including Kmail, Korganizer, Kaddressbook, and Knotes. Calligra Sheets is a spreadsheet, Calligra Stage is a presentation application, Karbon is a vector graphics program, and Calligra Words is a publisher-like word processor. Krita is a paint and image editor. Kexi provides database integration with Calligra applications, currently supporting PostgreSQL and MySQL.

Application	Description
Braindump	Whiteboards for notes, images, and charts
Flow	Flow chart applications
Stage	Presentation application
Words	Word processor (desktop publisher)
Sheets	Spreadsheet
Karbon	Vector graphics program
Kexi	Database integration
Plan	Project management and planning
Krita	Paint and image manipulation program
Kontact (separate project)	Contact application including mail, address book, and organizer

Table 5-3: Calligra Applications

Calligra Sheets is the spreadsheet application, which incorporates the basic operations found in most spreadsheets, with formulas similar to those used in MS Excel. You can also embed charts, pictures, or formulas using Krita and Karbon. With Calligra Stage, you can create presentations consisting of text and graphics modeled using different fonts, orientations, and attributes such as colors. Karbon is a vector-based graphics program, much like Adobe Illustrator and LibreOffice Draw. It supports the standard graphic operations such as rotating, scaling, and aligning objects. Calligra Words can best be described as a desktop publisher, with many of the features found in publishing applications. Although it is a fully functional word processor, Calligra Words sets up text in frames that are placed on the page like objects. Frames, like objects in a drawing program, can be moved, resized, and reoriented. You can organize frames into a frame set, having text flow from one to the other.

GNOME Office Applications

There are several GNOME office applications available including AbiWord, Gnumeric, Evince, and Evolution. GNOME office applications are part of Ubuntu and can be downloaded with Ubuntu Software. A current listing of common GNOME office applications is shown in Table 5-4. All implement the support for embedding components, ensuring drag-and-drop capability throughout the GNOME interface.

AbiWord is an open source word processor that aims to be a complete cross-platform solution, running on Mac, Unix, and Windows, as well as Linux. It is part of a set of desktop productivity applications being developed by the AbiSource project (**https://www.abisource.com**).

Gnumeric is a professional-level GNOME spreadsheet meant to replace commercial spreadsheets. Gnumeric supports standard spreadsheet features, including auto filling and cell formatting, and an extensive number of formats. Gnumeric also supports plug-ins, making it possible to extend and customize its abilities easily.

Dia is a drawing program designed to create diagrams, such as database, circuit object, flow chart, and network diagrams. You can create elements along with lines and arcs, with different types of endpoints such as arrows or diamonds. Data can be saved in XML format, making it transportable to other applications.

GnuCash (**http://www.gnucash.org**) is a personal finance application for managing accounts, stocks, and expenses.

Application	Description
AbiWord	Cross-platform word processor
Gnumeric	Spreadsheet
Evince	Document Viewer
Evolution	Integrated email, calendar, and personal organizer
Dia	Diagram and flow chart editor
GnuCash	Personal finance manager
Glom	Database front end for PostgreSQL database
glabels	Label Designer

Table 5-4: Office Applications for GNOME

Running Microsoft Office on Linux: Wine and CrossOver

One of the concerns for new Linux users is what kind of access they will have to their Microsoft Office files, particularly Word files. The Linux operating system and many applications for it are designed to provide seamless access to Microsoft Office files. The major Linux Office suites, including Calligra, LibreOffice, and Oracle Open Office, all read and manage Microsoft Office files. In addition, these office suites are fast approaching the same level of features and support for office tasks as found in Microsoft Office.

Note: You can, of course, use your browser to run the Microsoft Office Online version, which runs from a remote Microsoft cloud site.

Wine (Windows Compatibility Layer) allows you to run many Windows applications directly, using a supporting virtual windows API. See the Wine website for a list of supported applications, **https://www.winehq.org**, AppDB tab. Well-written applications may run directly from Wine. Sometimes you will have to have a working Windows system from which you can copy system DLLs needed by particular applications. You can also import Windows fonts by directly copying them to the Wine font directory. Each user can install and run their own version of Wine with its own simulated C: partition on which Windows applications are installed. The simulated drive is installed as **drive_c** in your **.wine** directory. The **.wine** directory is a hidden directory. It is not normally displayed with the **ls** command or the GNOME file manager (View | Show Hidden Files). You can also use any of your Linux directories for your Windows application data files instead of your simulated C: drive. These are referenced by Windows applications as the **z:** drive.

In a terminal window, using the **wine** command with an install program will automatically install that Windows application on the simulated C: drive. The following example installs Microsoft Office. Though there may be difficulties with the latest Microsoft Office versions and with the 64-bit versions, Office 2002, 2007, 2010, and 2013 32bit versions should work fine (see **https://www.winehq.org**, AppDB tab, search for Office Suites). Applications are rated platinum, gold, silver, bronze, and garbage. Several of the Microsoft Office suites are gold or platinum.

When you insert the Microsoft Office CD, it will be mounted to the **/media/***username* directory using the disk label as its folder name. Check the **/media** folder under the user's name to see what the actual name is. You then run the **setup.exe** program for Office with wine. Depending on the version of Office you have, there may be further subfolders for the actual Office **setup.exe** program. The following example assumes that the label for Office is OFFICE and that the **setup.exe** program for Office is on the top-level directory of that CD.

```
$ wine /media/richard/OFFICE/setup.exe
```

The install program will start up and you will be prompted to enter your product key. Be sure to use only uppercase as you type. Once installed, choose Applications | Wine | Programs | Microsoft Office, and then choose the application name to start up. The application should start up normally. The application is referenced by Wine on the user's simulated **c:** drive.

The Windows My Documents folder is set up by Wine to be the user's Ubuntu Documents directory. There you will find any files saved to My Documents.

Wine is constantly being updated to accommodate the latest versions of Windows applications. However, for some applications you may need to copy DLL files from a working Windows system to the Wine Windows folder, **.wine/drive_c/windows**, usually to the **system** or **system32** directories. Though effective, Wine support will not be as stable as Crossover.

CrossOver Office is a commercial product that lets you install and run most Microsoft Office applications. CrossOver Office was developed by CodeWeavers, which also supports Windows web browser plug-ins as well as several popular Windows applications like Adobe Photoshop. CrossOver features both standard and professional versions, providing reliable application support. You can find out more about CrossOver Office at **https://www.codeweavers.com**.

CrossOver can be installed either for private multi-user mode or managed multi-user mode. In private multi-user mode, each user installs Windows software, such as full versions of Office. In managed multi-user mode, the Windows software is installed once and all users share it. Once the software is installed, you will see a Windows Applications menu on the main menu, from which you can start your installed Windows software. The applications will run within a Linux window, but they will appear just as if they were running in Windows.

Also, with VMware, you can run Windows under Linux, allowing you to run Windows applications, including Microsoft Office, on your Linux system. For more information, check the VMware website at **http://www.vmware.com**.

Another option, for users with high-powered computers that support virtualization, is to install the Windows OS on a virtual machine using the Virtual Machine Manager. You could then install and run Windows on the virtual machine and install Microsoft Office on it.

GNOME Documents

You can use the GNOME Documents application to access and search for local and cloud-based documents. Documents can be text (word processing), spreadsheets, presentations, or PDF files. Currently, both Google docs and Microsoft SkyDrive documents are supported. You have to enable access from the Online Accounts dialog on GNOME Settings.

GNOME Documents is accessible from the Applications overview. The Documents dialog shows tabs for both Documents and Collections (see Figure 5-3). Documents lists your local and cloud-based documents (see Figure 5-3). The Documents GNOME applications menu lets you view the documents in a grid (icons) or as a list. Collections are categories you can set up to organize your documents. There are buttons at the right of the titlebar for searching, sorting, and editing. Click the Search button to open a search box with a menu that lets you search for source (local or cloud), type, and search target (title or author).

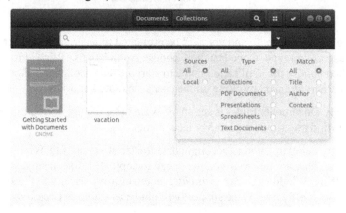

Figure 5-3: GNOME Documents, with search

Click the check mark button at the top right to open a taskbar, which lets you open the document or print it. In the list view, click the check box to the left of the document you want to perform the task on. In the grid view, a check box is displayed at the lower right of each icon. When you click a check box, the taskbar is displayed with buttons to open the document the appropriate application, print the document, and delete it. The properties button displays information about the document. The Collections button lets you place the document in a collection. When finished, click the Done button.

Document Viewers, and DVI)

Though located under Applications overview, PostScript, PDF, DVI, and ebook viewers are more commonly used with Office applications (see Table 5-5). You can install these viewers with Ubuntu Software. Evince (PostScript, PDF and Okular can display both PostScript (**.ps**) and PDF (**.pdf**) files.

Evince is the default document viewer for GNOME. It is started automatically whenever you double-click a PDF file on the GNOME desktop. Okular is the default document viewer for KDE5. Okular, Evince, and Xpdf are PDF viewers. They include many of the standard Adobe reader features such as zoom, two-page display, and full-screen mode.

Viewer	Description
Evince	Document Viewer for PostScript, DVI, and PDF files
Okular	KDE5 tool for displaying PDF, DVI, and postscript files
xpdf	X Window System tool for displaying PDF files only
Acrobat Reader for Linux	Adobe PDF viewer and Ebook reader
Scribus	Desktop publisher for generating PDF documents
Simple Scan	GNOME Scanner interface for scanners

Table 5-5: PostScript, PDF, and DVI viewers

All these viewers have the ability to print documents. To generate PDF documents you can use LibreOffice Writer or the Scribus desktop publisher (**https://www.scribus.net**).

Linux also supports a professional-level typesetting tool, called TeX, commonly used to compose complex mathematical formulas. TeX generates a DVI document that can be displayed by DVI viewers, several of which are available for Linux. DVI files generated by the TeX document application can be viewed by Evince and Okular.

Note: To scan documents directly, you can use Simple Scan which you can save as jpeg, png, or PDF files.

E-book Readers: FBReader and Calibre

To read E-books on Ubuntu, you can use Calibre and FBReader (see Table 5-6). FBReader is an open source reader that can read non-DRM ebooks, including mobipocket, html, chm, EPUB, text, and rtf. The toolbar holds operations that move you through the text and configure your reader, adding books and setting interface preferences (see Figure 5-4). To see your selection of books click the Library Tree icon on the left. You can organize text by author or tag. On the Options window, the Library tab lets you choose where your books are stored. You also can search for public domain books.

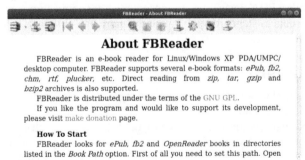

Figure 5-4: FBReader ebook reader

Calibre reads PDF, EPUB, Lit (Microsoft), and Mobipocket ebooks. Calibre functions as a library for accessing and managing your ebooks (see Figure 5-5). Calibre also can convert many document files and ebooks to the EPUB format, the open source standard used by Apple (iPad) and Barnes and Noble (Nook). It can take as conversion input text, HTML, TRF, and ODT (LibreOffice), as well as ebooks.

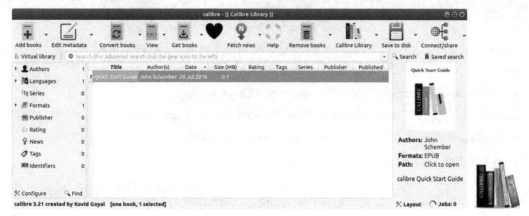

Figure 5-5: Calibre E-book reader, organizer, and converter

Viewer	Description
Calibre	E-book reader and library, also converts various inputs to EPUB ebooks.
E-book reader	FBReader E-book reader

Table 5-6: E-book Readers

PDA Access

For many PDAs, you can use the pilot tools to access your handheld device, transferring information between it and your system. You can use the J-Pilot and Pilot Manager applications to access your PDA from your desktop. J-Pilot provides a desktop interface that lets you perform basic tasks such as synchronizing the address book and writing memos. The **pilot-link** package holds tools you can use to access your PDA. The tool name usually begins with "pilot"; for instance, **pilot-addresses** read addresses from an address book. Other tools whose names begin with "read" allow you to convert PDA device data for access by other applications; **read-expenses**, for instance, outputs expense data as standard text. One of the more useful tools is **pilot-xfer**, used to back up your PDA.

GNOME Notes (bijiben)

The GNOME Notes application lets you create and organize simple notes on your desktop. Install using the **bijiben** package (Synaptic). The Notes window lists your new and recent notes, showing the note title and the first few lines of text (see Figure 5-6). In the header bar, the search button opens a search box that lets you search for notes. The list button lets you switch between icon and list views. The check button lets you delete or organize your notes. A checkbox is displayed at the right lower corner of the note icons. Clicking on that checkbox opens a taskbar at the bottom with buttons to delete the note, add it to a collection (notebooks), or email it. There is also a color button you can use the background color.

Figure 5-6: GNOME Notes

To create a new note, click on the New button on the header bar to open a new text. The first line is the title of your note (see Figure 5-8). Press the ENTER key to move to the next line. A button at the top right opens a dialog that lets you choose the color for a note. The task menu (menu button) provides undo/redo functions, deletion, and email options. You can also add the note to a notebook. You can use notebooks to organize your notes. To delete a note, click on the checkmark button to display a checkbox next to each note. Check the ones you want to delete and click the Done button.

GNOME Clocks and Weather

Two helpful tools are the clocks and weather applications. Clocks has four tabs: World, Alarm, Stopwatch, and Timer. The World tab displays the current time at any city and at your current location (see Figure 5-7). Click the New button to open a dialog where you can add a city. To remove a city, click the check button to display a checkbox in the lower right corner of each time icon. Check the ones you want to delete, and then click the Delete button. The Alarm tab works as an alarm clock. The Stopwatch tab operates a stopwatch, letting you mark laps. The timer counts down in time. You set the start amount.

Figure 5-7: GNOME Clocks: World tab

The GNOME weather tool lets you display the weather in any city. Click the Places button to open a dialog where you can enter the name of a city. A partial entry is matched on, giving you a listing of possible cities. Clicking on a city displays a full image of the weather for that city, with the temperature and forecast for the next several hours, and a sidebar with the forecast for the next five days (see Figure 5-8). The Today and Tomorrow buttons show to the current weather and tomorrow's weather. The current time is displayed in the upper right corner. A reload button on the right side of the header bar lets you refresh the weather display.

The Places dialog shows a list of previous cities you have viewed with the temperature and weather icons (see Figure 5-8). If Automatic location is turned on, the weather at your current location is also listed (first entry).

Figure 5-8: GNOME Weather: city with forecast

GNOME Characters and Fonts

The GNOME Characters utility lets you copy a color character image to use in a document. You can choose from several categories (see Figure 5-9). These characters are open source emojis. You can access GNOME Chartacters form the applications overiview | Utilties as Characters. Click on the character you want to display a dialog promptint you to copy the character to the copy the character to the clipboard. In your text editor, you can then paste it as an inline character. The characters include images, as well as math symbols, punctuation, and currencies.

Figure 5-9: GNOME Characters

Fonts provides a simple listing of your installed fonts, showing the font style (see Figure 5-10)) . You can access Fonts from the applications overview's Utilities sub-folder. Click on a font image to display examples of the font and an info buton at the top right on the title bar, which you can click to display information about the font, including style, type, version, and copyright.

Figure 5-10: Fonts

GNOME Calendar

GNOME Calendar lets you manage a calendar, specifying events (see Figure 5-11) . Events can be imported from Web sources. To add an event, click on a date to open a dialog where you can enter the event name and select a calendar. Click the Edit Details button to display a dialog for setting the time, duration, location and any notes. Personal and Birthday calendars are already set up. Click the calendar button at the right side of the title bar to open a dialog to let you add new calendars.

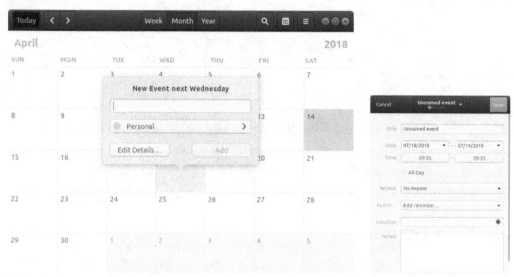

Figure 5-11: GNOME Calendar

Editors

The Ubuntu desktop (GNOME and Kubuntu) supports powerful text editors with full mouse support, scroll bars, and menus. These include basic text editors, such as Gedit and Kate, as well as word processors, such as LibreOffice Word, AbiWord, and Calligra Words. Ubuntu also provides the cursor-based editors Nano, Vim, and Emacs. Nano is a cursor-based editor with an easy-to-use interface supporting menus and mouse selection (if run from a terminal window). Vim is an enhanced version of the Vi text editor used on the Unix system. These editors use simple, cursor-based operations to give you a full-screen format. Table 5-7 lists several desktop editors for Linux. Vi and Emacs have powerful editing features that have been refined over the years. Emacs, in particular, is extensible to a full development environment for programming new applications. Later versions of Emacs and Vim, such as GNU Emacs, XEmacs, and Gvim provide support for mouse, menu, and window operations.

GNOME Text Editor: Gedit

The Gedit editor is a basic text editor for the GNOME desktop. It provides full mouse support, implementing standard desktop operations, such as cut and paste to move text, and click and drag to select and move/copy text. It supports standard text editing operations such as Find and Replace. The editor is accessible from the Applications overview as Text Editor. You can use Gedit to create and modify your text files, including configuration files. Gedit also provides more advanced features such as print preview and configurable levels of undo/redo operations, and it can read data from pipes. It features plug-ins that provide added functionality, including spell checking, document statistics, email, and sorting. Install **gedit-plugins** for more.

Application	Description
Kate	Text and program editor
Calligra Words	Desktop publisher, part of Calligra Suite
Gedit	Text editor
AbiWord	Word processor
OpenWriter	LibreOffice word processor that can edit text files
nano	Easy to use screen-based editor, installed by default
GNU Emacs	Emacs editor with X Window System support
XEmacs	X Window System version of Emacs editor
gvim	Vim version with X Window System support

Table 5-7: Desktop Editors

The nano text editor

The nano editor is a simple screen-based editor that lets you visually edit your file, using arrow and page keys to move around the file. You use control keys to perform actions. **Ctrl-x** will exit and prompt you to save the file, **Ctrl-o** will save it. **Ctrl-k** will cut the current line.

You start nano with the **nano** command entered in a terminal window or on the command line interface. To edit a configuration file, you will need administrative access. Figure 5-12 shows the nano editor being used to edit the GRUB configuration file, **/etc/default/grub**.

```
sudo nano /etc/default/grub
```

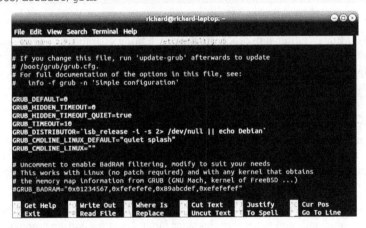

Figure 5-12: Editing with nano

KDE Editor: Kate

The KDE editor Kate provides full mouse support, implementing standard GUI operations, such as cut and paste to move text, and click and drag to select and move/copy text. The editor is accessible from the Applications | Utilities menu on the KDE desktop, and from the Applications overview on the Ubuntu desktop. Kate is an advanced editor, with such features as spell checking, font selection, and highlighting. Most commands can be selected using menus. A toolbar of icons for common operations is displayed across the top of the Kate window. A sidebar displays panels for a file list. Kate also supports multiple views of a document, letting you display segments in their own windows, vertically or horizontally. You can also open several documents at the same time, moving among them with the file list. Kate is designed to be a program editor for editing software programming/development-related source code files. Kate can format the syntax for different programming languages, such as C, Perl, Java, and XML.

The Emacs Editor

Emacs can best be described as a working environment featuring an editor, a mailer, a newsreader, and a Lisp interpreter. The editor is tailored for program development, enabling you to format source code according to the programming language you use. Many versions of Emacs are currently available for use on Unix and Linux systems. The versions usually included with Linux distributions are either GNU Emacs or XEmacs. GNU Emacs is X Window System capable, enabling GUI features such as menus, scroll bars, and mouse-based editing operations. You can find out more information about Emacs at **https://www.gnu.org/software/emacs/**, and for XEmacs at its website, **http://www.xemacs.org**.

The Emacs editor operates much like a standard word processor. The keys on your keyboard represent input characters. Commands are implemented with special keys, such as control (CTRL) keys and alternate (ALT) keys. There is no special input mode, as in Vi. You type in your text, and if you need to execute an editing command, such as moving the cursor or saving text, you use a CTRL key. You invoke the Emacs editor with the command **emacs**. You can enter the name of the file you want to edit, and if the file does not exist, it is created. In the next example, the user prepares to edit the file **mydata** with Emacs:

```
$ emacs mydata
```

The GNU Emacs editor supports basic desktop editing operations such as selection of text with click-and-drag mouse operations, cut/copy/paste, and a scroll bar for moving through text. The Mode line and Echo areas are displayed at the bottom of the window, where you can enter keyboard commands.

The Vi Editor: Vim and Gvim

The Vim editor is an enhanced version of the Vi editor. It includes all the commands and features of the Vi editor. Vi, which stands for *visual,* remains one of the most widely used editors in Linux. On Ubuntu, a basic version of Vi, called **vim-tiny**, is installed as part of the basic installation. For the full version, install the Vim package from Ubuntu Software.

Keyboard-based editors like Vim and Emacs use a keyboard for two different operations: to specify editing commands and to receive character input. Used for editing commands, certain keys perform deletions, some execute changes, and others perform cursor movement. Used for character input, keys represent characters that can be entered into the file being edited. Usually, these two different functions are divided among different keys on the keyboard. Alphabetic keys are reserved for character input, while function keys and control keys specify editing commands, such as deleting text or moving the cursor. Such editors can rely on the existence of an extended keyboard that includes function and control keys.

Editors in Unix were designed originally to assume a minimal keyboard with alphanumeric characters and some control characters, as well as the ESC and ENTER keys. Instead of dividing the command and input functions among different keys, the Vi editor has three separate modes of operation for the keyboard: command and input modes, and a line editing mode. In command mode, all the keys on the keyboard become editing commands; in the input mode, the keys on the keyboard become input characters. Some of the editing commands, such as **a** or **i**, enter the input mode. On typing **i**, you leave the command mode and enter the input mode. Each key now represents a character to be input to the text. Pressing ESC automatically returns you to the command mode, and the keys once again become editor commands. As you edit text, you are constantly moving from the command mode to the input mode and back again. With Vim, you can use the **Ctrl-o** command to jump quickly to the command mode and enter a command, and then automatically return to the input mode. Table 5-8 lists a basic set of Vi commands to get you started.

Although you can create, save, close, and quit files with the Vi editor, the commands for each are not very similar. Saving and quitting a file involves the use of special line editing commands, whereas closing a file is a Vi editing command. Creation of a file is usually specified on the same shell command line that invokes the Vi editor. To edit a file, type **vi** or **vim** and the name of a file on the shell command line. If a file by that name does not exist, the system creates it. In effect, entering the name of a file that does not yet exist instructs the Vi editor to create that file. The following command invokes the Vi editor, working on the file **booklist**. If **booklist** does not yet exist, the Vi editor creates it.

```
$ vim booklist
```

Command	Description
h	Moves the cursor left one character.
l	Moves the cursor right one character.
k	Moves the cursor up one line.
j	Moves the cursor down one line.
CTRL-F	Moves forward by a screen of text; the next screen of text is displayed.
CTRL-B	Moves backward by a screen of text; the previous screen of text is displayed.
Input	*(All input commands place the user in input; the user leaves input with ESC.)*
a	Enters input after the cursor.
i	Enters input before the cursor.
o	Enters input below the line the cursor is on; inserts a new empty line below the one the cursor is currently on.
Text Selection (Vim)	
v	Visual mode; move the cursor to expand selected text by character. Once selected, press key to execute action: **c** change, **d** delete, **y** copy, **:** line-editing command, **J** join lines, **U** uppercase, **u** lowercase.
V	Visual mode; move the cursor to expand selected text by line.

Delete	
x	Deletes the character the cursor is on.
dd	Deletes the line the cursor is on.
Change	*(Except for the replace command, r, all change commands place the user into input after deleting text.)*
cw	Deletes the word the cursor is on and places the user into the input mode.
r	Replaces the character the cursor is on. After pressing **r**, the user enters the replacement character. The change is made without entering input; the user remains in the Vi command mode.
R	First places into input mode, and then overwrites character by character. Appears as an overwrite mode on the screen but actually is in input mode.
Move	Moves text by first deleting it, moving the cursor to the desired place of insertion, and then pressing the **p** command. (When text is deleted, it is automatically held in a special buffer.)
p	Inserts deleted or copied text after the character or line the cursor is on.
P	Inserts deleted or copied text before the character or line the cursor is on.
dw p	Deletes a word, and then moves it to the place you indicate with the cursor (press **p** to insert the word *after* the word the cursor is on).
yy or Y p	Copies the line the cursor is on.
Search	The two search commands open up a line at the bottom of the screen and enable the user to enter a pattern to be searched for; press ENTER after typing in the pattern.
/*pattern*	Searches forward in the text for a pattern.
?*pattern*	Searches backward in the text for a pattern.
n	Repeats the previous search, whether it was forward or backward.
Line Editing Commands	**Effect**
w	Saves file.
q	Quits editor; **q!** quits without saving.

Table 5-8: Vi Editor Commands

After executing the `vim` command, you enter Vi's command mode. Each key becomes a Vi editing command, and the screen becomes a window onto the text file. Text is displayed screen by screen. The first screen of text is displayed, and the cursor is positioned in the upper-left corner. With a newly created file, there is no text to display. When you first enter the Vi editor, you are in the command mode. To add text, you need to enter the input mode. In the command mode, **a** is the editor command for appending text. Pressing this key places you in the input mode. Now the keyboard operates like a typewriter, and you can input text to the file. If you press ENTER, you merely start a new line of text. With Vim, you can use the arrow keys to move from one part of the entered text to another and work on different parts of the text. After entering text, you can leave the input mode and return to the command mode by pressing ESC. Once finished with the editing session, you exit Vi by typing two capital Zs, **zz**. Hold down the SHIFT key and press **z** twice. This sequence first saves the file and then exits the Vi editor, returning you to the Linux shell. To save a file while editing, you use the line editing command **w**, which writes a file to the disk; **w** is equivalent to the Save command found in other word processors. You first type a colon to access the line editing mode, and then type **w** and press ENTER, **:w**.

You can use the **:q** command to quit an editing session. Unlike the **zz** command, the **:q** command does not perform any save operation before it quits. In this respect, it has one major constraint. If any modifications have been made to your file since the last save operation, the **:q** command will fail and you will not leave the editor. You can override this restriction by placing a **!** qualifier after the **:q** command. The command **:q!** will quit the Vi editor without saving any modifications made to the file in that session since the last save (the combination **:wq** is the same as **zz**).

To obtain online help, enter the **:help** command. This is a line editing command. Type a colon, enter the word **help** on the line that opens at the bottom of the screen, and then press ENTER. You can add the name of a specific command after the word **help**. Pressing the **F1** key also brings up online help.

As an alternative to using Vim in a command line interface, you can use gvim, which provides X Window System–based menus for basic file, editing, and window operations. Gvim can be installed from Ubuntu Software. On the Synaptic Package Manager, the package is called the **vim-gui-common** package, which includes several links to Gvim such as **evim**, **gview**, and **gex** (open Ex editor line). To use Gvim, you can enter the **gvim** command at a terminal prompt. The standard Vi interface is shown, but with several menu buttons displayed across the top along with a toolbar with buttons for common commands like search and file saves. All the standard Vi commands work just as described previously. However, you can use your mouse to select items on these menus. You can open and close a file, or open several files using split windows or different windows. The editing menu enables you to cut, copy, and paste text, as well as undo or redo operations. In the editing mode, you can select text with your mouse with a click-and-drag operation, or use the Editing menu to cut or copy and then paste the selected text. Text entry, however, is still performed using the **a**, **i**, or **o** command to enter the input mode. Searches and replacements are supported through a dialog window. There are also buttons on the toolbar for finding next and previous instances. You can also split the view into different windows to display parts of the same file or different files. Use the **:split** command to open a window, and use **:hide** to close the current one. Use **Ctrl-w** with the up and down arrow keys to move between them. On Gvim, you use entries in the Windows menu to manage windows. Configuration preferences can be placed in the user's **.vimrc** file.

Database Management Systems

Several database systems are provided for Ubuntu, including LibreOffice Base, MySQL, SQLite, and PostgreSQL. Ubuntu continues to provide the original MySQL database. In addition, commercial SQL database software is also compatible with Ubuntu. Table 5-9 lists database management systems currently available for Linux. SQLite is a simple and fast database server requiring no configuration and implementing the database on a single disk file. For small embedded databases you can use Berkeley DB (db4). In addition, Ubuntu also supports document-based non-

SQL databases such as MongoDB. MongoDB is a document-based database that can be quickly searched.

SQL Databases (RDBMS)

SQL databases are relational database management systems (RDBMSs) designed for extensive database management tasks. Many of the major SQL databases now have Linux versions, including Oracle and IBM. These are commercial and professional database management systems. Linux has proved itself capable of supporting complex and demanding database management tasks. In addition, many free SQL databases are available for Linux that offer much the same functionality. Most commercial databases also provide free personal versions.

System	Site
LibreOffice	LibreOffice database (Ubuntu repository): **https://www.libreoffice.org/discover/base/**
PostgreSQL	The PostgreSQL database (Ubuntu repository): **https://www.postgresql.org/**
MySQL	MySQL database (Ubuntu repository): **https://www.mysql.com/**
SQLite	Simple SQL database: **www.sqlite.org**
MongoDB	Document-based database: **www.mongodb.org**

Table 5-9: Database Management Systems for Linux

LibreOffice Base

LibreOffice provides a basic database application, LibreOffice Base that can access many database files. You can set up and operate a simple database, as well as access and manage files from other database applications. When you start up LibreOffice Base, you will be prompted either to start a new database or connect to an existing one. File types supported include ODBC (Open Database Connectivity), JDBC (Java), MySQL, PostgreSQL, and MDB (Microsoft Access) database files (install the **unixodbc** and **libmysql-java** packages). You can also create your own simple databases. Check the LibreOffice Base page (**https://www.libreoffice.org/discover/base/**) for detailed information on drivers and supported databases.

PostgreSQL

PostgreSQL is based on the POSTURES database management system, though it uses SQL as its query language. POSTGRESQL is a next-generation research prototype developed at the University of California, Berkeley. Linux versions of PostgreSQL are included in most distributions, including the Red Hat, Fedora, Debian, and Ubuntu. You can find more information on it from the PostgreSQL website at **https://www.postgresql.org**. PostgreSQL is an open source project, developed under the GPL license.

MySQL

MySQL, included with Ubuntu, is a true multi-user, multithreaded SQL database server, supported by MySQL AB. MySQL is an open source product available free under the GPL license.

You can obtain current information on it from its website, **https://www.mysql.com**. The site includes detailed documentation, including manuals and FAQs. Currently, MySQL is owned by Oracle.

E-Mail Clients

You can send and receive email messages in a variety of ways, depending on the type of mail client you use. Although all email utilities perform the same basic tasks of receiving and sending messages, they tend to use different interfaces. Some mail clients are designed to operate on a specific desktop interface such as KDE and GNOME. Several older mail clients use a screen-based interface and can be started only from the command line. For Web-based Internet mail services, such as Gmail and Yahoo, you use a Web browser instead of a mail client to access mail accounts provided by those services. Table 5-10 lists several popular Linux mail clients. Mail is transported to and from destinations using mail transport agents like Sendmail, Exim, and Postfix. To send mail over the Internet, Simple Mail Transport Protocol (SMTP) is used.

Mail Client	Description
Kontact	Includes the K Desktop mail client, KMail; integrated mail, address book, and scheduler (KMail, KAddressbook, KOrganizer)
Evolution	Email client, **https://wiki.gnome.org/Apps/Evolution**
Thunderbird	Mozilla mail client and newsreader
Sylpheed	Gtk mail and news client
Claws-mail	Extended version of sylpheed Email client
GNUEmacs and XEmacs	Emacs mail clients
Mutt	Screen-based mail client
Mail	Original Unix-based command line mail client
Squirrel Mail	Web-based mail client
gnubiff	Email checker and notification tool
Mail Notification	Email checker and notification that works with numerous mail clients, including MH, Sylpheed, Gmail, Evolution, and Mail

Table 5-10: Linux Mail Clients

Thunderbird

Thunderbird is a full-featured stand-alone email client provided by the Mozilla project (**https://www.mozilla.org**). It is installed by default along with LibreOffice. Thunderbird is designed to be easy to use, highly customizable, and heavily secure. It features advanced intelligent spam filtering, as well as security features like encryption, digital signatures, and S/MIME. To protect against viruses, email attachments can be examined without being run. Thunderbird supports both Internet Message Access Protocol (IMAP) and the Post Office Protocol (POP). It also functions as a newsreader and features a built-in RSS reader. Thunderbird also supports the use of the Lightweight Directory Access Protocol (LDAP) for address books. Thunderbird is an extensible application, allowing customized modules to be added to enhance its abilities. You can download extensions such as dictionary search and contact sidebars from the website. GPG encryption can be supported with the enigmail extension (Ubuntu main repository).

Thunderbird is installed by default. You can access it from the dock. It provides better integration with popular online mail services like Gmail, saved searches, and customized tags for selected messages. You can access Thunderbird from the dock and the Applications overview.

The Thunderbird interface uses a standard three-pane format, with a side pane for listing mail accounts and their mailboxes (see Figure 5-13). The top pane is the message list pane and the bottom pane shows a selected message's text. Commands can be run using the toolbar, menus, or keyboard shortcuts. You can even change the appearance using different themes. Thunderbird also supports HTML mail, displaying Web components like URLs in mail messages.

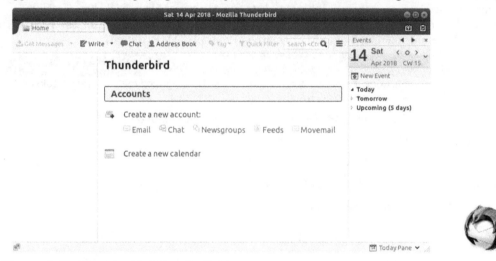

Figure 5-13: Thunderbird Email client

The message list pane shows several fields by which you can sort your messages. Some use just symbols like the Threads, Attachments, and Read icons. Clicking Threads will gather the messages into respective threads with replies grouped together. The last icon in the message list fields is a pop-up menu that lets you choose which fields to display. Thunderbird provides a variety of quick display filters, such as displaying only messages from people included in your address book and display messages with attached files. Search and sorting capabilities also include filters that can match selected patterns in any field, including subject, date, or the message body. To compose a message, click the Write button to open the Write window. The Security button lets you digitally sign and encrypt a message.

When you first start up Thunderbird, The Mail Account Setup dialog opens, which prompts you to create an email account. You can add more email accounts or modify current ones by selecting Account Settings from the Edit menu (Edit | Account Settings). The first page of the Mail Account Setup dialogs prompts you to enter your name, email address, and password. Thunderbird then attempts to detect and configure your email account automatically. Popular email services such as Gmail (Google) and Yahoo will be detected and their incoming and outgoing mail servers configured automatically. If the username entry is wrong you can click the Username Edit button to edit it. For more email configuration options, you can click the Manual Setup button. You can also just choose to abandon the email setup by clicking the Start Over link. If the settings are correct, click the Create Account button to create the account. The account will be accessed. If the account detection fails, you will be prompted to enter the username and password, along with the names of the incoming and outgoing mail servers for that account. For a more detailed configuration, click the Manual Setup button where you can specify the security protocol like SSL/TSL.

To edit an email account, select the Edit | Account Settings menu entry. In the Account Settings window, you will see an entry for your mail account, with tabs for Server Settings, Copies & Folders, Composition & Addressing, Offline & Disk Space, Synchronization & Storage, Return Receipt, and Security. The Server Settings tab has entries for your server name, port, username, and connection and task configurations such as downloading new messages automatically. The Security tab opens the Certificate Manager, where you can select security certificates to use to digitally sign or encrypt messages.

Thunderbird provides an address book where you can enter complete contact information, including email addresses, street addresses, phone numbers, and notes. Select Address Book from the Tools menu to open the Address Book window (Tools | Address Book). There are three panes: one for the address books available; another listing the address entries with field entries like name, email, and organization; and one for displaying address information. You can sort the entries by these fields. Clicking an entry will display the address information, including email address, street addresses, and phone. Only fields with values are displayed. To create a new entry in an address book, click New Contact to open a window with tabs for Contact, Private, Work, Other, and Photo. To create mailing lists from the address book entries, you click the New List button, specify the name of the list, and enter the email addresses.

Once you have set up your address book, you can use its addresses when creating mail messages. On the Write window, when you start to enter an email address in the To text box, the address will auto-complete to the corresponding address in your address book. Alternatively, you can open the address book and drag-and-drop addresses to an address box in the message window.

A user's email messages, addresses, and configuration information are kept in files located in the **.thunderbird** directory within the user's home directory. Backing up this information is as simple as making a copy of that directory. Messages for the different mailboxes are kept in a **Mail** subdirectory. If you are migrating to a new system, you can copy the directory from the older system. To back up the mail for any mail account, just copy the **Mail** subdirectory for that account. Though the default address books, **abook.mab** and **history.mab**, can be interchangeably copied, non-default address books need to be exported to an LDIF format and then imported to the new Thunderbird application. It is advisable to export your address books regularly to LDAP Data Interchange Format (LDIF) files as backups.

Evolution

Evolution is the primary mail client for the GNOME desktop. Though designed for GNOME, it will work equally well on KDE. Evolution is an integrated mail client, calendar, and address book. It supports numerous protocols (SMTP, POP, and IMAP). With Evolution, you can create multiple mail accounts on different servers, including those that use different protocols such as POP or IMAP. You can also decrypt Pretty Good Privacy (PGP) or GNU Privacy Guard (GPG) encrypted messages. Messages are indexed for easy searching. As an added feature, you can display Web calendars within evolution. See the Evolution website for resources and documentation links.

`https://wiki.gnome.org/Apps/Evolution`

The Evolution mailer provides a simple desktop interface, with a toolbar for commonly used commands and a sidebar for shortcuts. A set of buttons on the lower left allows you to access other operations, such as the calendar and contacts. The main screen is divided into two panes, one for listing the mail headers and the other for displaying the currently selected message (see Figure 5-14). You can click any header label to sort your headers by that category. Evolution also supports the use of virtual folders that can be created by the user to hold mail that meets specified criteria. Incoming mail can be automatically distributed to a virtual folder.

With evolution, you can also create search folders to organize access to your messages. A search folder is not an actual folder. It simply collects links to messages based on certain search criteria. Using search folders, you can quickly display messages on a topic, or subject, or from a specific user. In effect, it performs an automatic search on messages as they arrive. To set up a search folder, select Search Folders in the Edit menu (Edit | Search Folders) and click Add to open the Add Rule window. Here you can add criteria for searches and the folders to search. You can also right-click a message header that meets criteria you want searched and select Create Rule from Message, and then select one of the Search Rule entries.

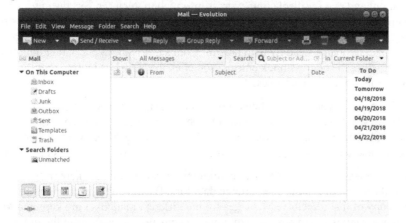

Figure 5-14: Evolution Email client

To configure Evolution, select Preferences from the Edit menu (Edit | Preferences). On the Evolution Preferences window, a sidebar shows icons for mail accounts, contacts, mail preferences, composition preference, calendar and tasks, and certificates. The Mail accounts tab displays a list of current accounts. An Add button lets you add new accounts, and the Edit button allows you to change current accounts. When editing an account, the Account Editor displays tabs for Identity, Receiving email (your incoming mail server), sending email (outgoing mail server), and security (encryption and digital signatures) among others. Mail Preferences lets you configure how Evolution displays and manages messages. The Mail Preferences Automatic Contacts tab is where you can specify whether the addresses of mail you have replied to should be added automatically to the Evolution Contacts list. Composer Preferences lets you set up composition features like signatures, formatting, and spell-checking. Calendar and Tasks lets you configure your calendar, specifying a type zone, work days, display options, and publishing.

Numerous plugins are available to extend Evolution's capabilities. Most are installed and enabled for you automatically, including the SpamAssassin plug-in for handling junk mail. To manage your plug-ins, select the Plugins entry in the Edit menu (Edit | Plugin) to open the Plugin Manager, with plug-ins listed in a left scroll window and configuration tabs located for a selected plug-in on the right side.

Evolution also supports filters. You can use filters to direct some messages automatically to certain folders, instead of having all incoming messages placed in the inbox folder. To create a filter, you can select the Message Filters entry in the Edit menu (Edit | Message Filters) and click Add to open the Add Rule window. You can also right-click the header of a message whose heading meets your criteria, like a subject or sender, and select Create Rule from Message and select a Filter entry for sender, subject, or recipient. On the Add Rule window, you can add other criteria and specify the action to take, like moving the message to a particular folder. You can also add other actions, like assigning a score, changing the color, copying the message, or deleting it.

A user's email messages, addresses, and configuration information are kept in files located in the **.evolution** directory within the user's home directory. Backing up this information is as simple as making a copy of that directory. Messages for the different mailboxes are kept in a **mail** subdirectory. If you are migrating to a new system, you can just copy the directory from the older system. To back up the mail for any given mail account, just copy the **mail** subdirectory for that account. You can also backup the address book, calendar, memos, and tasks subdirectories.

Evolution also supports contact operations like calendars, contact lists, and memos. On the left side pane, the bottom section displays buttons for these different functions: Mail, Contacts, Calendars, Tasks, and Memos. To see and manage your contacts, click the Contacts button on the left sidebar. The Calendar displays a browsable calendar on the left pane to move easily to a specific date (see Figure 5-15). The right pane shows a daily calendar page by the hour with sections for tasks and memos. You can set up several calendars, which you can access at the top of the right pane. A personal calendar is set up for you already. To add a new calendar, select Calendar from the New menu to open a New Calendar dialog where you can choose the type and name.

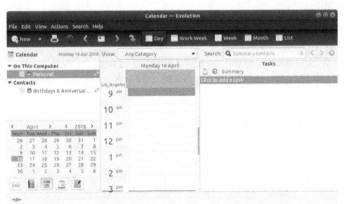

Figure 5-15: Evolution Calendar

Note: Other GNOME mail clients include sylpheed and Claws-mail (both are on the Ubuntu Universe repository). Sylpheed is a mail and news client with an interface similar to Windows mail clients. Claws-mail is an extended version of Sylpheed with many additional features (www.claws-mail.org).

The KDE Mail Client: KMail

The KDE mail client, KMail, provides a full-featured desktop interface for composing, sending, and receiving email messages. KMail is part of the KDE Personal Information Management suite (KDE-PIM) which also includes an address book (KAddressBook), an organizer and scheduler (KOrganizer), and a note writer (KNotes). All these components are also directly integrated on the desktop into Kontact. You can start up KMail directly or as part of the Kontact applications (Mail). KMail is installed as part of the KDE desktop, but you can also install it separately with the Synaptic Package Manager.

The KMail window displays three panes for folders, headers, and messages. The lower-left pane displays your mail folders: an inbox folder for received mail, an outbox folder for mail you have composed but have not sent yet, and a sent-mail folder for messages you have previously sent. You can create your own mail folders and save selected messages in them if you want. You can designate certain folders as favorite folders and have them listed in the Favorite Folders pane (right-click on the Favorite Folders pane and select Add Favorite Folder to choose a folder).

SquirrelMail

You can use the SquirrelMail Webmail tool to access mail from Internet email services using your Web browser. It will display a login screen for mail users. It features an inbox list and message reader, support for editing and sending new messages, and a plug-in structure for adding new features. You can find out more about SquirrelMail at **http://www.squirrelmail.org**. The Apache configuration file is **/etc/httpd/conf.d/squirrelmail.conf**, and SquirrelMail is installed in **/usr/share/squirrelmail**. Be sure that the IMAP mail server is also installed.

To configure SquirrelMail, you use the **config.pl** script in the **/usr/share/squirrelmail/config** directory (run in a terminal window). This displays a simple text-based menu where you can configure settings like the server to use, folder defaults, general options, and organizational preferences.

```
cd /usr/share/squirrelmail/config
./config.pl
```

To access SquirrelMail, use the Web server address with the **/squirrelmail** extension, as in **localhost/squirrelmail** for users on the local system, or **www.mytrek.com/squirrelmail** as an example for remote users.

Command Line Mail Clients

Several mail clients use a simple command line interface. They can be run without any other kind of support, such as the X Window System, desktops, or cursor support. They are simple and easy to use but include an extensive set of features and options. Two of the more widely used mail clients of this type are Mail and Mutt. Mail is the mailx mail client that was developed for UNIX. It is considered a default mail client that can be found on all UNIX and Linux systems. Mutt is a cursor-based client that can be run from the command line.

Mutt

Mutt has an easy-to-use cursor-based interface with an extensive set of features. You can find more information about Mutt from the Mutt website, **http://www.mutt.org**. The Mutt manual is located in the **/usr/doc** directory under Mutt. To use Mutt, enter the **mutt** command in a terminal window or on the command line.

Mail

What is known now as the Mail utility was originally created for BSD Unix and called, simply, mail. Later versions of Unix System V adopted the BSD mail utility and renamed it mailx. Now, it is simply referred to as Mail. Mail functions as a default mail client on most Unix and Linux systems. It is not installed by default on Ubuntu. Install the **bsd-mailx** package with the Synaptic Package Manager.

To send a message with Mail, type **mail** on the command line along with the address of the person to whom you are sending the message. Press ENTER and you are prompted for a subject. Enter the subject of the message and press ENTER again. At this point, you are placed in input mode. Anything you type in is considered the contents of the message. Pressing ENTER adds a new line to the text. When you finish typing your message, press CTRL-D on a line of its own to end the message. You will then be prompted to enter a user to whom to send a carbon copy of the message (Cc). If you do not want to send a carbon copy, just press ENTER. You will then see EOT (end-of-transmission) displayed after you press CTRL-D

You can send a message to several users at the same time by listing those users' addresses as arguments on the command line following the **mail** command. In the next example, the user sends the same message to both **chris** and **aleina**.

```
$ mail chris aleina
```

To receive mail, you first enter the **mail** command and press ENTER. This invokes a Mail shell with its own prompt and mail commands. A list of message headers is displayed. Header information is arranged into fields beginning with the status of the message and the message number. The status of a message is indicated by a single uppercase letter, usually **N** for new or **U** for unread. A message number, used for easy reference to your messages, follows the status field. The next field is the address of the sender, followed by the date and time the message was received, and then the number of lines and characters in the message. The last field contains the subject the sender gave for the message. After the headers, the Mail shell displays its prompt, an ampersand (**&**). At the Mail prompt, you enter commands that operate on the messages. An example of a Mail header and prompt follows:

```
$ mail
Mail version 8.2 01/15/2001. Type ? for help.
"/var/spool/mail/larisa": 3 messages 1 new 2 unread
 1 chris@turtle.mytrek. Thu Jun 7 14:17 22/554 "trip"
>U 2 aleina@turtle.mytrek Thu Jun 7 14:18 22/525 "party"
 U 3 dylan@turtle.mytrek. Thu Jun 7 14:18 22/528 "newsletter"
& q
```

Mail references messages either through a message list or through the current message marker (**>**). The greater-than sign (**>**) is placed before a message considered the current message. The current message is referenced by default when no message number is included with a Mail command. You can also reference messages using a message list consisting of several message numbers.

You use the **R** and **r** commands to reply to a message you have received. The **R** command entered with a message number generates a header for sending a message and then places you into input mode to type the message. The **q** command quits Mail. When you quit, messages you have already read are placed in a file called **mbox** in your home directory. Instead of saving messages in the **mbox** file, you can use the **s** command to save a message explicitly to a file of your choice. Mail has its own initialization file, called **.mailrc**, which is executed each time Mail is invoked, either for sending or receiving messages. Within it, you can define Mail options and create Mail aliases.

Notifications of Received Mail

As your mail messages are received, they are automatically placed in your mailbox file, but you are not automatically notified when you receive a message. You can use a mail client to retrieve any new messages, or you can use a mail monitor tool to tell you when new mail has arrived in your inbox. Several mail notification tools are also available, such as **gnubiff** and Mail Notification. Mail Notification will support Gmail, as well as Evolution (for Evolution, install the separate plug-in package). When you first log in after Mail Notification has been installed, the Mail Notification configuration window is displayed. Here you can add new mail accounts to check, such as Gmail accounts, as well as set other features like summary pop-ups. When you receive mail, a mail icon will appear on your top desktop panel. Move your cursor over it to check for any new mail. Clicking it will display the Mail Notification configuration window, though you can configure this to go directly to your email application. The **gnubiff** tool will notify you of any POP3 or IMAP mail arrivals.

For command line interfaces, you can use the biff utility, which notifies you immediately when a message is received. biff automatically displays the header and beginning lines of messages as they are received. To turn on biff, you enter **biff y** on the command line. To turn it off, you enter **biff n**. To find out if biff is turned on, enter **biff** alone.

Accessing Mail on Remote Mail Servers

Most new mail clients are equipped to access mail accounts on remote servers. Mail clients, such as Evolution, KMail, Sylpheed, and Thunderbird, enable you to set up a mailbox for such an account and access a mail server to check for and download received mail. You must specify what protocol a mail server uses. This is usually either the Post Office Protocol (POP) or the IMAP protocol (IMAP). Using a mail server address, you can access your account with your username and password.

For email clients such as **mail** and **mutt** that do not provide mail server access, you can use Fetchmail to have mail from those accounts sent directly to the inbox maintained by your Linux system for your Linux account. All your mail, whether from other users on your Linux system or from remote mail accounts, will appear in your local inbox. Fetchmail checks for mail on remote mail servers and downloads it to your local inbox, where it appears as newly received mail. Enter **fetchmail** on the command line with the mail server address and any needed options. The mail protocol is indicated with the **-p** option and the mail server type, usually POP3. If your email username is different from your Linux login name, you use the **-u** option and the email name. Once you execute the **fetchmail** command, you are prompted for a password. The syntax for the **fetchmail** command for a POP3 mail server follows:

```
fetchmail -p POP3 -u username mail-server
```

You will see messages telling you if mail is there and, if so, how many messages are being downloaded. You can then use a mail client to read the messages from your inbox. You can run Fetchmail in daemon mode to have it check automatically for mail. You have to include an option specifying the interval in seconds for checking mail.

```
fetchmail -d 1200
```

To have fetchmail run automatically you can set the START DAEMON option to yes in the **/etc/default/fetchmail** file. Edit the file with the **sudo gedit** command.

You can specify options such as the server type, username, and password in a **.fetchmailrc** file in your home directory. You can also include entries for other mail servers and accounts you may have. Once Fetchmail is configured, you can enter **fetchmail** with no arguments; it will read entries from your **.fetchmailrc** file. You can also make entries directly in the **.fetchmailrc** file. An entry in the **.fetchmailrc** file for a particular mail account consists of several fields and their values: poll, protocol, username, and password. The poll field refers to the mail server name. You can also specify your password, instead of having to enter it each time Fetchmail accesses the mail server.

Mailing Lists

Users on mailing lists automatically receive messages and articles sent to the lists. Mailing lists work much like a mail alias, broadcasting messages to all users on the list. Mailing lists were designed to serve specialized groups of people. Numerous mailing lists, as well as other subjects, are available for Linux. By convention, to subscribe to a list, you send a request to the mailing list address with a **-request** term added to its username. For example, to subscribe to **gnome-list@gnome.org**, you send a request to **gnome-list-request@gnome.org**.

You can use the Mailman and Majordomo programs to manage your mailing lists automatically. Mailman is the GNU mailing list manager, included with Ubuntu (**http://www.list.org**).

MIME: /etc/mime.types

MIME (the term stands for Multipurpose Internet Mail Extensions) is used to enable mail clients to send and receive multimedia files and files using different character sets such as those for different languages. Multimedia files can be images, sound clips, or even video. Mail clients that support MIME can send binary files automatically as attachments to messages. MIME-capable mail clients maintain a file called **mailcap** that maps different types of MIME messages to applications on your system that can view or display them. For example, an image file will be mapped to an application that can display images. Your mail clients can then run that program to display the image message. A sound file will be mapped to an application that can play sound files. Most mail clients have MIME capabilities built in and use their own version of the **mailcap** file. Others use a program called metamail that adds MIME support. MIME is used not only in mail clients. Both the KDE and GNOME file managers use MIME to map a file to a particular application so that you can launch the application directly from the file.

Applications are associated with binary files by means of the **mailcap** and **mime.types** files. The **mime.types** file defines different MIME types, associating a MIME type with a certain application. The **mailcap** file then associates each MIME type with a specified application. Your system maintains its own MIME types file, usually **/etc/mime.types**.

Entries in the MIME types file associate a MIME type and possible subtype of an application with a set of possible file extensions used for files that run on a given kind of application. The MIME type is usually further qualified by a subtype, separated from the major type by a slash. For example, a MIME type image can have several subtypes such as jpeg, gif, or tiff. A sample MIME type entry defining a MIME type for JPEG files are shown here. The MIME type is image/jpeg, and the list of possible file extensions is "jpeg jpg jpe":

```
image/jpeg        jpeg jpg jpe
```

The applications specified will depend on those available on your particular system. The application is specified as part of the application type. In many cases, X Window System–based programs are specified. Comments are indicated with a **#**. The following entries associate **odt** files with the LibreOffice writer and **qtl** files with the QuickTime player.

```
application/vnd.oasis.opendocument.text    odt
application/x-quicktimeplayer              qtl
```

Though you can create your own MIME types, a standard set already is in use. The types text, image, audio, video, application, multipart, and message, along with their subtypes, have already been defined for your system. You will find that commonly used file extensions such as **.tif** and **.jpg** for TIFF and JPEG image files are already associated with a MIME type and an application. Though you can easily change the associated application, it is best to keep the MIME types already installed. The current official MIME types are listed at the IANA website (**http://www.iana.org**) under the name Media Types, provided as part of their Assignment Services.

S/MIME and OpenPGP/MIME are authentication protocols for signing and encrypting mail messages. S/MIME was originally developed by the RSA Data Security. OpenPGP is an open standard based on the PGP/MIME protocol developed by the PGP (Pretty Good Privacy) group. Clients like KMail and Evolution can use OpenPGP/MIME to authenticate messages. Check the Internet Mail Consortium for more information, **www.imc.org**.

Usenet News

Usenet is an open mail system on which users post messages that include news, discussions, and opinions. It operates like a mailbox to which any user on your Linux system can read or send messages. Users' messages are incorporated into Usenet files, which are distributed to any system signed up to receive them. Certain Usenet sites perform organizational and distribution operations for Usenet, receiving messages from other sites and organizing them into Usenet files, which are then broadcast to many other sites. Such sites are called backbone sites, and they operate like publishers, receiving articles and organizing them into different groups.

To access Usenet news, you need access to a news server, which receives the daily Usenet newsfeeds and makes them accessible to other systems. Your network may have a system that operates as a news server. There are also many commercial servers you can access for a fee. To read Usenet articles, you use a newsreader, a client program that connects to a news server and accesses the articles. On the Internet and in TCP/IP networks, news servers communicate with newsreaders using the Network News Transfer Protocol (NNTP) and are often referred to as NNTP news servers. You can also create your own news server on your Linux system to run a local Usenet news service or to download and maintain the full set of Usenet articles. News transport agent applications can be set up to create such a server.

Usenet files were originally designed to function like journals. Messages contained in the files are referred to as articles. A user could write an article, post it in Usenet, and have it immediately distributed to other systems. Usenet files themselves were organized as journal publications. Because journals are designed to address specific groups, Usenet files are organized according to groups called newsgroups. When a user posts an article, it is assigned to a specific newsgroup. You can also create articles of your own, which you can then add to a newsgroup for others to read. Linux has newsgroups on various topics. Some are for discussion, and others are sources of information about recent developments. On some, you can ask for help for specific problems. A selection of some of the popular Linux newsgroups is provided here:

Newsgroup	Topic
comp.os.linux.announce	Announcements of Linux developments
comp.os.linux.admin	System administration questions
comp.os.linux.misc	Special questions and issues
comp.os.linux.setup	Installation problems
comp.os.linux.help	Questions and answers for particular problems
linux.help	Obtain help for Linux problems

Newsreaders

You read Usenet articles with a newsreader, such as Pan and tin, which enable you to select a specific newsgroup and then read the articles in it. A newsreader operates like a user interface, letting you browse through and select available articles for reading, saving, or printing. Most newsreaders employ a retrieval feature called threads that pulls together articles on the same discussion or topic. Several popular newsreaders are listed in Table 5-11.

Most newsreaders can read Usenet news provided on remote news servers that use the NNTP protocol. Desktop newsreaders, such as Pan, have you specify the Internet address for the remote news server in their own configuration settings. Shell-based newsreaders such as **tin**, obtain the news server's Internet address from the NNTPSERVER shell variable, configured in the **.profile** file.

```
NNTPSERVER=news.domain.com
export NNTPSERVER
```

Binary Newsreaders and Grabbers

A binary newsreader can convert text messages to binary equivalents, like those found in **alt.binaries** newsgroups. There are some news grabbers, applications designed only to download binaries. The binaries are normally encoded with RAR compression, which have an **.rar** extension. To decode them you first have to install the **unrar-free** package. Binaries normally consist of several rar archive files, some of which may be incomplete. To repair them you can use Par2 recovery program. Install the **par2** package. A binary should have its own set of par2 files also listed on the news server that you can download and use to repair any incomplete **rar** files. The principle works much the same as RAID arrays using parity information to reconstruct damaged data. You can use the PyPar2 application to manually repair rar archive files.

Newsreader	Description
Pan	GNOME Desktop newsreader
Thunderbird	Mail client with newsreader capabilities (X based)
Sylpheed	GNOME Windows-like newsreader
Slrn	Newsreader (cursor based)
Emacs	Emacs editor, mail client, and newsreader (cursor based)
tin	Newsreader (command line interface)
trn4	Newsreader (command line interface)
xpn	Desktop newsreader
nzb	Binary only NZB based news grabber

Table 5-11: Linux Newsreaders

The NZB grabber application works using NZB files to locate and download binaries. You first have to obtain the NZB file to use. But if you can obtain an NZB file, then NZB is by far the easiest to use. Set the server options in Tools | Options (port would be 119). Load the NZB file (File | Open) and then start the download and decode (Action | Start).

slrn

The **slrn** newsreader is cursor-based. Commands are displayed across the top of the screen and can be executed using the listed keys. Different types of screens exist for the newsgroup list, article list, and article content, each with its own set of commands. An initial screen lists your subscribed newsgroups with commands for posting, listing, and subscribing to your newsgroups. When you start slrn for the first time, you may have to create a **.jnewsrc** file in your home directory. Use the following command: **slrn -f .jnewsrc -create**. Also, you will have to set the **NNTPSERVER** variable in your **.profile** file and make sure it is exported.

The slrn newsreader features a utility called **slrnpull** that you can use to download articles in specified newsgroups automatically. This allows you to view your selected newsgroups offline. The slrnpull utility was designed as a simple single-user version of Leafnode; it will access a news server and download its designated newsgroups, making them available through slrn whenever the user chooses to examine them. Newsgroup articles are downloaded to the **SLRNPULL_ROOT** directory. On Ubuntu, this is **/var/spool/slrnpull**. The selected newsgroups to be downloaded are entered in the **slrnpull.conf** configuration file placed in the **SLRNPULL_ROOT** directory. In this file, you can specify how many articles to download for each group and when they should expire. To use **slrn** with **slrnpull**, you will have to configure the **.slrnrc** file to reference the **slrnpull** directories where newsgroup files are kept.

News Transport Agents

Usenet news is provided over the Internet as a daily newsfeed of articles and postings for thousands of newsgroups. This newsfeed is sent to sites that can then provide access to the news for other systems through newsreaders. These sites operate as news servers; the newsreaders used to access them are their clients. The news server software called news transport agents, provide newsreaders with news, enabling you to read newsgroups and post articles. For Linux, several popular news transport agents are INN, Leafnode, Papercut, and sn. Both Papercut and Leafnode are small and simple, and useful for small networks. INN is more powerful and complex, designed with large systems in mind (see **https://www.isc.org/** for more details).

Daily news feeds on Usenet are often large and consume much of a news server's resources in both time and memory. For this reason, you may not want to set up your own Linux system to receive such newsfeeds. If you are operating in a network of Linux systems, you can designate one of them as the news server and install the news transport agent on it to receive and manage the Usenet newsfeeds. Users on other systems on your network can then access that news server with their own newsreaders. If your network already has a news server, you need not install a news transport agent at all. You only have to use your newsreaders to access that server remotely.

You can also use news transport agents to run local versions of news for only the users on your system or your local network. To do this, install INN, Leafnode, or Papercut configure them just to manage local newsgroups. Users on your system could then post articles and read local news.

ubuntu©

6. Graphics and Multimedia

Graphics Applications

Multimedia

Music Applications

Video Applications

Sound Configuration with PulseAudio

Ubuntu includes a wide range of graphics and multimedia applications, including simple image viewers such as the Eye of GNOME, sophisticated image manipulation programs like GIMP, music and CD players like Rhythmbox, and video players like Videos. Several helpful Linux multimedia sites are listed in Table 6-1. There is strong support for graphics and multimedia tasks from image management, video and DVD, to sound and music editing (see Tables 6-1, 6-4 and 6-5). Most are available on Ubuntu's multiverse and universe repositories. In addition, the Ubuntu Studio project has collected popular multimedia development software into several collections for audio, video, and graphics. For information on graphics hardware and drivers, check **https://www.phoronix.com**.

Projects and Sites	Description
Advanced Linux Sound Architecture (ALSA)	The Advanced Linux Sound Architecture (ALSA) project for current sound drivers: **www.alsaproject.org**
Open Sound System	Open Sound System, drives for older devices: **www.opensound.com**
PulseAudio	PulseAudio sound interface, now the default for Ubuntu. **https://www.freedesktop.org/wiki/Software/PulseAudio/**
Phoronix	Site for the latest news and reviews of Linux hardware compatibility, including graphics cards. **https://www.phoronix.com**
Ubuntu Studio	Ubuntu Studio multimedia development applications and desktop, audio, video, and graphics collection installed from ubuntustudio meta packages, Meta Packages (universe) **https://ubuntustudio.org**

Table 6-1: Linux and Ubuntu Multimedia Sites

Support for many popular multimedia operations, specifically MP3, DVD, and DivX, are not included on the Ubuntu Desktop DVD because of licensing and other restrictions. To play MP3, DVD, or DivX files, you will have to download and install support packages manually. For Ubuntu, precompiled packages for many popular media applications and libraries, such as VideoLan and XviD, as well as MP3 and DVD video support, are available on the Ubuntu multiverse and universe repository sections.

Graphics Applications

The GNOME and KDE desktops support an impressive number of graphics applications, including image viewers, window grabbers, image editors, and paint tools. Table 6-2 lists some popular graphics tools for Linux.

Tools	Description
Shotwell	GNOME digital camera application and image and video library manager (**https://wiki.gnome.org/Apps/Shotwell**)
Photos	GNOME photo viewer and organizer
Cheese	GNOME Webcam application for taking pictures and videos
ubuntustudio-graphics	Ubuntu Studio meta package (Meta Packages (universe)), includes a collection of graphics applications. Use Synaptic Package Manager.
Digikam	Digital photo management tool, works with both GNOME and KDE
KDE	
Gwenview	Image browser and viewer (default for KDE)
ShowFoto	Simple image viewer, works with digiKam (**https://www.digikam.org/**)
KSnapshot	Screen grabber
KolourPaint	Paint program
Krita	Image editor (**https://krita.org/en/**)
GNOME	
Eye of Gnome	GNOME Image Viewer (eog package)
GIMP	GNU Image Manipulation Program (**https://www.gimp.org/**)
Inkscape	GNOME Vector graphics application (**https://inkscape.org/en/**)
gpaint	GNOME paint program
Blender	3d modeling, rendering, and animation
LibreOffice Draw	LibreOffice Draw program
X Window System	
Xpaint	Paint program
Xfig	Drawing program
ImageMagick	Image format conversion and editing tool

Table 6-2: Graphics Tools for Linux

Photo Management: Shotwell, Photos, and Cheese

Shotwell provides an easy and powerful way to manage, display, and import, and publish your photos and images (**https://wiki.gnome.org/Apps/Shotwell**). It is the default photo manager for Ubuntu 18.04. See the Shotwell user manual for full details (Help | Contents menu and at **http://yorba.org/shotwell/help/**). Shotwell is accessible as the Shotwell Photo Manager from the Applications overview. Shotwell also supports video files.

You can import folders from cameras or folders (see Figure 6-1). Your Pictures folder is the default library folder, whose photos are imported automatically. Adding an image file to the

Pictures folder also imports it to Shotwell. Photo thumbnails are displayed in the main right pane. The View menu lets you control the thumbnail display, allowing you to sort photos, zoom, show photo filenames (Titles), or select by rating or event. You can adjust the size of the displayed thumbnails using a slider bar in the toolbar located at the bottom right of the Shotwell window. The small figure button to the left of the slider reduces thumbnails to their smallest size, and the large figure button to the right of the slider expands them to the largest size.

Figure 6-1: Shotwell Photo Management

To see a full-screen slide show of the photos, choose the Slideshow entry in the View menu. The slide show starts automatically. During the slideshow, moving your mouse to the center bottom of the screen displays slideshow controls for pausing and stepping through photos. The Settings button opens a dialog where you can set the display time. To end the slide show and return to the desktop, click the full-screen button. The slideshow buttons are shown here.

You can also select photos to work as a desktop slideshow. Select the photos and choose File | Set as Desktop Slideshow (**Ctrl-b**).

Photos are organized automatically by the time they were taken. Dates are listed under the Events entry in the left sidebar, arranged by year, month, and date. To name a photo, right-click on it and choose Edit Title to open a dialog where you can enter the name. You can also tag photos placing them in groups, making them easier to access. To tag a photo, right-click it and choose Add Tags to open a dialog where you can enter a tag name. The tag will show up as a label for the photo. You can access photos by tags using the Tags entries in the left sidebar. For each photo, you can also set a rating indicated by five stars or less. You can also mark a photo as rejected. To rate a photo, right-click it and choose Set Rating which then lists rating options in a submenu. Use the Rating button in the Search toolbar to display photos by rating. You can select several photos at once using click and drag, Ctrl-click, or Shift-click (as you would files in a file manager window), and then right-click to give them the same rating (Set Rating) or same tag (Add Tags).

To search for photos, click the Find button to open a search bar, which displays a text box for entering the search pattern. Buttons to the left let you refine the search by image type, photos or videos, flagged files, and ratings.

When you select a photo or group of photos, the Rotate, Enhance, and Publish buttons in the bottom toolbar become active. The Publish button lets you publish the photo on a Web service: Facebook, Flickr, or Google (use Settings | Online Accounts to set up access). The Rotate button rotates the Photo (from the Photos menu you can also flip the Photo horizontally or vertically). The Enhance button will adjust the photo automatically.

You can perform more complex edits either within the Shotwell window or in full screen. To edit a photo within the Shotwell window, double-click its image to display the edit toolbar, which hold Rotate, Crop, Straighten, Red-eye, Adjust, and Enhance buttons. For full-screen edits, select the photo and then choose View | Fullscreen (F11) to open the photo in the Shotwell photo editor (see Figure 6-2) . Move your mouse to the bottom of the screen to display edit toolbar (Rotate, Crop, Straighten, Red-eye, Adjust, and Enhance buttons). You can also zoom in or out from the photo using the slider bar. The Crop button opens an adjustable border, with a menu for choosing the display proportions you may want such as HD video or postcard. The Adjust button opens a dialog for refined changes such as exposure, saturation, tint, temperature, shadows, and highlights. Edits are stored in a Shotwell database; they are not made to the original photo. To revert to the original photo, right-click and choose "Revert to Original" or choose that entry from the Photos menu.

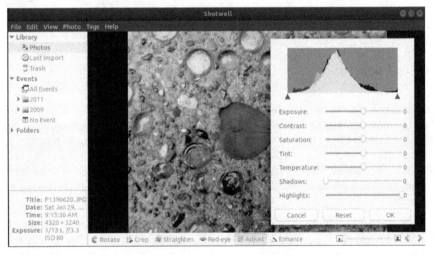

Figure 6-2: Shotwell Photo Editing

The Shotwell Preferences dialog (Edit | Preferences) lets you set the background intensity, choose a photo library folder, and select a photo editor. To open a photo with an external photo editor, right-click the photo thumbnail and select "Open With External Editor." Photos are stored in your Pictures directory under Events subfolders by year and then month. To open a photos folder, right-click and select "Show in File Manager."

Note: You can also set Shotwell display features using the dconf editor's Shotwell keys located at org | yorba | shotwell.

DigiKam (**https://www.digiKam.org**) is a KDE photo manager with many of the same features as Shotwell. DigiKam is accessible from the Applications overview. A side panel allows easy access by album, date, tags, or previous searches (see Figure 6-3). The program also provides image-editing capabilities, with numerous effects. The digiKam configuration (Settings menu) provides extensive options, including image editing, digital camera support, and interface configuration.

Figure 6-3: digiKam Photo Manager

Tip: The Windows version of Photoshop is supported by Wine. You can install Photoshop CS on Ubuntu using Wine. Once started, Photoshop will operate like any Linux desktop application.

Cheese is a Webcam picture-taking and video-recording tool (**https://wiki.gnome.org/Apps/Cheese**). You can snap pictures from your Webcam and apply simple effects. Click the Photo button to manage photos and the Video button to record video (located to the left). Icons of photos and video will appear on the bottom panel, which you can select for effects or removal. The effects tab will show effects that can be turned on or off for the current image. To save a photo, right click on its icon on the lower panel and select Save As from the pop-up menu.

GNOME Photos is a simple image viewer and organizer for the images in your Pictures folder. GNOME Photos has three tabs: Recent, Albums, and Favorites (see Figure 6-4). It opens to the Recent tab. You can also click on the search button at the right side of the menu bar to open a search box at the top of the window to search for photos. A pop-up menu to the right of the search box lets you limit searches by favorites, albums, title, or author.

Click on a photo to open it, and then use arrow buttons to display the next or previous ones (see Figure 6-5). A task menu at the top right lets you open the photo with Shotwell, print it, set it as the background of your desktop, or display it on another device. The Properties dialog displays detailed information about the image and lets you give it a name. Click the back arrow on the menu bar to return to the main dialog. To choose several photos to work on, click on the checkmark button at the top right. Check boxes appear on the lower right corner of each image (see Figure 6-

6). A menu at the top center lets you choose all or deselect all images. If you check a single image, a toolbar appears at the bottom, which lets you print the image, check its properties, add it to an album, delete it, or tag it as a Favorite. If you check several photos, the toolbar only lets you add them to an album, delete them, or mark them as favorites.

Figure 6-4: GNOME Photos

Figure 6-5: GNOME Photos: image display

When you open a photo, you can also tag it as a favorite by clicking on the star button in the lower right corner. Favorite images show a star emblem in the lower right corner of the image. Click on the Favorites tab to show only the favorite images. To remove an image from favorites, click its star to open the photo and then click the Favorites button in the photo's menu bar. Photos can be organized into albums, which are displayed on the Albums tab. When you add a photo to an album, you are prompted to choose an existing album, or create a new one.

Figure 6-6: GNOME Photos selection

GNOME Graphics Applications

GNOME features several powerful and easy-to-use graphics applications. The Eye of GNOME is the GNOME image viewer. It is installed by default.

The image viewer provides basic image display operations such as enlargement, full-screen display, rotation, and slide shows (see Figure 6-7). The Eye of GNOME is accessible as "Image Viewer" on the Applications overview. The image Gallery (icon list of images at the bottom of the screen), the Statusbar (bottom bar with size and position of selected photo), and Side Pane (properties of a selected image) are configured for display from entries in the View menu. Most preferences can be set using the EOG preferences dialog (Edit | Preferences). User interface preferences, such as trash confirmations and the gallery position, can be set using the dconf editor's eog keys at org | gnome | eog | ui.

The gThumb application is an image viewer and browser that lets you browse images using thumbnails, display them, and organize them into catalogs for easy reference.

Figure 6-7: Image Viewer (Eye of Gnome)

Figure 6-8: GIMP

GIMP is the GNU Image Manipulation Program, a sophisticated image application much like Adobe Photoshop (see Figure 6-8). You can use GIMP for such tasks as photo retouching, image composition, and image authoring. It supports features such as layers, channels, blends, and gradients. GIMP makes effective use of the GTK+ widget set. GIMP is accessible as the GIMP Image Editor. You can find out more about GIMP from its website at **https://www.gimp.org**. GIMP is freely distributed under the GNU Public License. You can install GIMP from Ubuntu Software.

Inkscape is a vector graphics application for SVG (Scalable Vector Graphics) images (see Figure 6-9). Inkscape is accessible as Inkscape Image Editor on the Applications overview. It features abilities similar to professional level vector graphics. The SVG format allows easy generation of images for Web use as well as complex art. Though its native format is SVG, it can also export to the Portable Network Graphics (PNG) format. It features layers and easy object creation, including stars and spirals. A color bar lets you quickly change color fills. You can install Inkscape from Ubuntu Software.

Figure 6-9: Inkscape

KDE Graphics Applications

The KDE desktop features the same variety of graphics applications found on the GNOME desktop. Many are available from the Ubuntu main repository. Most do not require a full installation of the KDE desktop. The Spectacle program is a simple screen grabber for KDE. Gwenview is an easy-to-use image browser and viewer supporting slide shows and numerous image formats. It is the default viewer for KDE, but can also be used on GNOME (see Figure 6-10). Gwenview can share photos with social networking sites directly. KolourPaint is a basic paint program with brushes, shapes, and color effects; it supports numerous image formats. Krita is the Calligra professional image paint and editing application, with a wide range of features such as the ability to create web images and modify photographs.

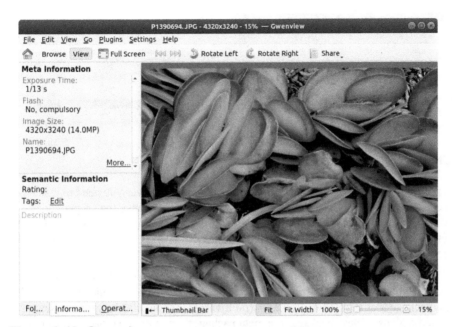

Figure 6-10: Gwenview

X Window System Graphic Programs

X Window System–based applications run directly on the underlying X Window System. These applications tend to be simpler, lacking the desktop functionality found in GNOME or KDE applications. Most are available on the Ubuntu Universe repository. Xpaint is a simple paint program that allows you to load graphics or photographs and then create shapes, add text and colors, and use brush tools with various sizes and colors. Xfig is a drawing program. ImageMagick lets you convert images from one format to another; you can, for instance, to change a TIFF image to a JPEG image.

Multimedia

Many applications are available for both video and sound, including sound editors, MP3 players, and video players (see Tables 6-5 and 6-6). Linux sound applications include mixers, digital audio tools, CD audio writers, MP3 players, and network audio support. To use restricted formats such as commercial DVD video and Blu-Ray see the following site.

`https://help.ubuntu.com/community/RestrictedFormats`

Multimedia support

A listing of popular multimedia codecs available is shown in Table 6-3. Of particular interest may be the liba52, faad2, and lame codecs for sound decoding, as well as the xvidcore, x264, libdvdcss, and libdvbpsi for video decoding.

Figure 6-11: Ubuntu codec wizard selection

Ubuntu provides a codec wizard that automatically detects whenever you need to install a new multimedia codec. If you try to run a media file for which you do not have the proper codec, the codec wizard will appear, listing the codecs you need to download and install. Often there are several choices (see Figure 6-11). The codec wizard will select and install these packages for you, simplifying the process of installing the various multimedia codecs available for Linux.

To install support for most of the commonly used codecs, you can install the Ubuntu restricted packages, **ubuntu-restricted-extras** and **ubuntu-restricted-addons**, which are available from the Synaptic Package Manager (Meta Packages (multiverse) section, ubuntu-restricted-extras and ubuntu-restricted-addons). These packages are meta packages that will download a collection of other packages that provide support for DVD, MP3, MPEG4, DivX, and AC3, as well as Flash (non-free). The **ubuntu-restricted-addons** package will install the GStreamer bad, ugly, and Fluendo packages, as well as Adobe Flash. The **ubuntu-restricted-addons** package will install the Microsoft font collection (**ttf-mscorefonts**), RAR archive extraction (**unrar**), and ffmpeg audio codecs (**libavcodec-extra**). Checking the "Install Third Party codec" option during installation (second screen) only installs the **ubuntu-restricted-addons** package.

```
ubuntu-restricted-addons
ubuntu-restricted-extras
```

For the Kubuntu desktop, you would also install the KDE version (install with the Synaptic Package Manager or the Discover Package Manager).

```
kubuntu-restricted-addons
kubuntu-restricted-extras
```

GStreamer

Many GNOME-based applications make use of GStreamer, a streaming media framework based on graphs and filters (**https://gstreamer.freedesktop.org/**). Using a plug-in structure, GStreamer applications can accommodate a wide variety of media types:

The Videos (Totem) video player uses GStreamer to play DVDs, VCDs, and MPEG media.

Rhythmbox and Banshee provide integrated music management.

Sound Juicer is an audio CD ripper.

A GNOME CD player and sound recorder

Package	Description
`liba52`	HDTV audio (ATSC A/52, AC3)
`faad`	MPEG2/ 4 AAC audio decoding, high quality (faad2)
`faac`	MPEG2/ 4 AAC sound encoding and decoding
`ffmpeg`	Play, record, convert, stream audio and video. Includes digital streaming server, conversion tool, and media player.
`libav extra libraries`	Unrestricted multimedia libraries, includes encoders and additional formats
`gstreamer-ffmpeg`	ffmpeg plug-in for GStreamer
`gstreamer-plugins-bad`	Not fully reliable codecs and tools for GStreamer, some with possible licensing issues
`gstreamer-plugins-ugly`	Reliable video and audio codecs for GStreamer that may have licensing issues
`gstreamer-fluendo-mp3`	Fully licensed MP3 codec from Fluendo for GStreamer
`gstreamer-fluendo-mpegmux`	Fully licensed MPEG2 TS video streams demuxing from Fluendo for GStreamer
`lame`	MP3 playback capability, not an official MP3 decoder
`libdvbpsi`	MPEG TS stream (DVB and PSI) decoding and encoding capability, VideoLAN project
`libdvdcss`	DVD commercial decryption
`libfame`	Fast Assembly MPEG video encoding
`libmad`	MPEG1 audio decoding (Ubuntu main repository)
`libmpeg2`	MPEG video audio decoding (MPEG1/2 audio and video, AC3, IFO, and VOB)
`libquicktime`	QuickTime playback
`mpeg2dec`	MPEG2 and MPEG1 playback
`x264`	H264/AVC encoding (high definition media)
`libxvidcore4`	OpenDivx codec (DivX and Xvid playback)
`libsmpeg`	Smpeg MPEG 1 video and audio decoder
`swfdec-gnome,` `swfdec-mozilla`	Play SWF files (FLASH)
`libxine2-all-plugins`	Added video/ audio playback plugins for Xine

Table 6-3: Multimedia third-party codecs

GStreamer Plug-ins: the Good, the Bad, and the Ugly

Many GNOME multimedia applications like Videos use GStreamer to provide multimedia support. To use such features as DVD-Video and MP3, you have to install GStreamer extra plugins.

You can find more information about GStreamer and its supporting packages at **https://gstreamer.freedesktop.org/**.

GStreamer has four different support packages called the base, the good, the bad, and the ugly. The base package is a set of useful and reliable plug-ins. These are in the Ubuntu main repository. The good package is a set of supported and tested plug-ins that meets all licensing requirements. This is also part of the Ubuntu main repository. The bad package is a set of unsupported plug-ins whose performance is not guaranteed and may crash, but still meet licensing requirements. The ugly package contains plug-ins that work fine, but may not meet licensing requirements, like DVD support.

The base   Reliable commonly used plug-ins

The good   Reliable additional and useful plug-ins

The ugly   Reliable but not fully licensed plug-ins (DVD/MP3 support)

The bad   Possibly unreliable but useful plug-ins (possible crashes)

As an alternative to the ugly package, you can use Fluendo packages for MP3 support, **gstreamer-fluendo-mp3**. Another plug-in for GStreamer that you may want include is **ffmpeg** for Matroska (mkv) and OGG support. The codec wizard will automatically detect the codec you will need to use for your GStreamer application.

GStreamer MP3 Compatibility: iPod

Ubuntu provides support for your iPod and iPod Touch from your desktop directly. For your iPod and other MP3 devices to work with GNOME applications like Banshee, you are prompted to install MP3 support for GStreamer the first time you use them (**gstreamer-fluendo-mp3** (licensed MP3) or **gstreamer-plugins-ugly** packages). MP3 support is not installed initially because of licensing issues.

The **libgpod** library allows player applications like Rhythmbox, Banshee, and Amarok to play songs from your iPod. To synchronize, import, or extract data from your iPod, you can use iPod management software such as **gtkpod** (Universe). For the iPhone, you can use **ifuse**.

Music Applications

Many music applications are currently available for GNOME, including sound editors, MP3 players, and audio players (see Table 6-4). You can use Banshee, Rhythmbox, GNOME Music, and Sound Juicer to play music from different sources, and the GNOME Sound Recorder to record sound sources. Several applications are also available for KDE, including the media players Amarok and Juk, a mixer (KMix), and a CD player (Kscd).

GNOME includes music applications like the Sound Juicer (Audio CD Extractor), GNOME Music, and Rhythmbox. Rhythmbox is the default sound multimedia player, supporting music files, radio streams, video, and podcasts (see Figure 6-12). When you open Rhythmbox, the indicator sound menu on the top panel displays options for Rhythmbox to play or stop playing, and to move to the next or previous audio source, such as a song or radio station.

KDE music applications include Amarok and Juk. Amarok is the primary multimedia player for KDE but will play on the GNOME desktop (see Figure 6-13). It includes access to

Internet sources, local music files, and local devices like Audio CDs. JuK (Music Jukebox) is the KDE music player for managing music collections.

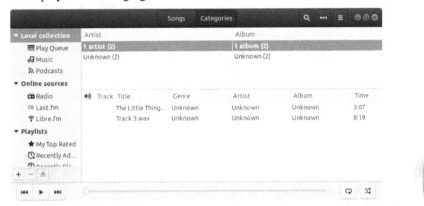

Figure 6-12: Rhythmbox GNOME Multimedia Player

Application	Description
Banshee	Music management (GStreamer)
Rhythmbox	Music management (GStreamer), default Music player with iPod support
Sound Juicer	GNOME CD audio ripper (GStreamer)
Amarok	KDE5 multimedia audio player
GNOME Music	GNOME Music player
Audacious	Multimedia player
Kscd	Music CD player
JuK	KDE5 Music player (jukebox) for managing music collections
GNOME CD Player	CD player
GNOME Sound Recorder	Sound recorder
XMMS2	CD player
ubuntustudio-audio	Ubuntu Studio meta package (Meta Packages (universe)), includes a collection of audio applications. Use Synaptic Package Manager
QMidiRoute	MIDI event router and filter (universe)

Table 6-4: Music players, editors, and rippers

Figure 6-13: Amarok KDE Multimedia Player

GNOME Music is the GNOME Music player with tabs for Albums, Artists, Songs, and Playlists. GNOME Music accesses sound files in your Music folder. On the Songs tab, you can click on a file to play it. A toolbar opens at the bottom with buttons to control the playback. The button to the right opens a menu with shuffle and repeat options. At the top, click on the Search button to search the list of sound files. To add files to the playlist, click on the check button to displays checkbox next to each sound file, which you can check and then click the "Add to Playlist" button.

Figure 6-14: GNOME Music

Due to licensing and patent issues, Ubuntu does not install MP3 support by default. MP3 playback capability has been removed from multimedia players like Banshee and Rhythmbox. The Ubuntu codec wizard will prompt you to install MP3 support when you first try to play an MP3 file, usually the Gstreamer package and the free Fluendo MP3 codec. As an alternative to MP3, you can use Ogg Vorbis compression for music files (**https://xiph.org/vorbis/**).

CD/DVD Burners

Several CD/DVD ripper and writer programs can be used for CD music and MP3 writing (burners and rippers). These include Sound Juicer, Serpentine, Brasero, and K3b (See Table 6-5). GNOME features the CD audio ripper Sound Juicer. You can also use Serpentine to create audio

CDs. For burning DVD/CD music and data discs, you can still use the Brasero CD/DVD burner and for KDE you can use K3b.

Brasero, K3b, and dvdauthor can all be used to create DVD-Video discs. All use mkisofs, cdrecord, and cdda2wav DVD/CD writing programs installed as part of your desktop. OGMrip can rip and encode DVD video. DVD-Video and CD music rippers may require addition codecs installed, for which the codec wizard will prompt you.

Application	Description
Brasero	Full service CD/DVD burner, for music, video, and data discs (no longer supported)
Sound Juicer (Audio CD Extractor)	GNOME music player and CD burner and ripper
ogmrip	DVD ripping and encoding with DivX support
K3b	KDE CD writing interface
dvdauthor	Tools for creating DVDs

Table 6-5: CD/DVD Burners

Video Applications

Several projects provide TV, video, DivX, DVD, and DVB support for Ubuntu (see Table 6-6). Aside from GStreamer applications, there are also several third-party multimedia applications you may want, also available on the Ubuntu repositories, such as MPlayer and vlc.

Video and DVD Players

Most current DVD and media players are provided on the Ubuntu repositories. The default video player is GNOME Videos, whose interface has undergone a major change. The main dialog displays two tabs: Videos and Channels (see Figure 6-15). The Videos tab lists videos on your system and for those at specific sites on the Internet. Click the plus button at the left side of the header bar to display a menu for adding local or Web videos. For a Web video, you enter the video's Web address.

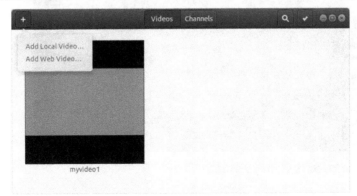

Figure 6-15: GNOME Videos: Videos tab

Projects and Players	Sites
Videos	video and DVD player for GNOME using GStreamer, includes plugins for DVB, YouTube, and MythTV. It is based on the original GNOME Totem video player
Dragon Player	Dragon Player video and DVD player for KDE
VLC Media Player (vlc)	Network multimedia streaming. **www.videolan.org**
MPlayer	MPlayer DVD/multimedia player **www.mplayerhq.hu**
MythTV	Home media center with DVD, DVR, and TV capabilities **https://www.mythtv.org**
tvtime	TV viewer, **http://tvtime.sourceforge.net**
XviD	Open Source DivX, **https://www.xvid.com/**
ubuntustudio-video	Ubuntu Studio meta package (Meta Packages (universe)), includes a collection of video applications. Use Synaptic Package Manager.
Kaffeine	An older KDE media player, including HDTV, DVB, DVD, CD, and network streams (Universe repository, install with Synaptic or Discover)
PiTiVi	Video editor
GNOME Media Player	Basic media player using Gstreamer, vlc, or xine engines

Table 6-6: Video and DVD Projects and Applications

To Play a video, click on it (see Figure 6-16). For full-screen viewing, click the expand icon on the right side of the header bar. Move the mouse toward the bottom of the dialog to display viewing controls, including pause/play, repeat, sound volume, and skipping to the next or previous video. Click the back button (left side of the header bar) to return to the video listing.

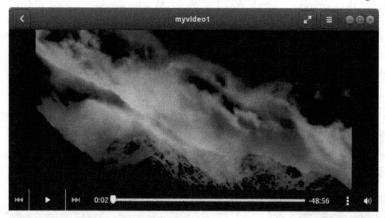

Figure 6-16: GNOME Videos, playing a video

To play several videos in sequence click on the check icon at the right side of the header bar to display checkboxes at the corner of each video icon. Click the checkboxes of the videos you want to see, and then click the Play button on the lower left corner of the dialog. To randomize the sequence, click the Shuffle button instead.

To remove a video, click the check icon at the right side of the header bar to display checkboxes at the corner of each video icon. Click the checkboxes of the videos you want to remove and then click the Delete button on the lower right corner of the dialog.

The Channels tab list streaming services, such as Euronews, Apple Movie Trailers, and media on your system that you want to stream.

Clicking on the search icon opens a text box for searching for videos (see Figure 6-17). The resource searched is shown on the right side of the text box. Clicking on the resource name displays a menu with possible resources you can search, including your file system, YouTube, bookmarks, and supported streaming services.

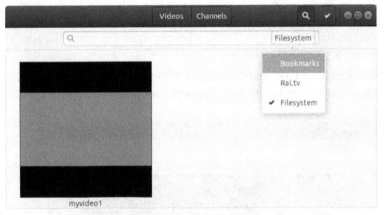

Figure 6-17: GNOME Videos Search

Several popular video players available for Ubuntu are listed here:

Dragon Player is a KDE multimedia player, installed with KDE desktop but will play on the GNOME Ubuntu desktop (see Figure 6-18). (from the Ubuntu desktop, install with the Synaptic Package Manager).

GNOME MPlayer provides a simple interface for playing media files using the xine, vlc, or Gstreamer engines (**gnome-mplayer** package, universe repository).

MPlayer is one of the most popular and capable multimedia/DVD players in use. It is a cross-platform open source alternative to RealPlayer and Windows Media Player (**www.mplayerhq.hu**). MPlayer uses an extensive set of supporting libraries and applications like **lirc, lame, lzo,** and **aalib,** which are also available on the Ubuntu repository. If you have trouble displaying video, be sure to check the preferences for different video devices and select one that works best (**mplayer** package, Multiverse repository).

mpv is a Video player based on Mplayer and supports an extensive selection of codecs and formats.

Videos is the GNOME Video player that uses GStreamer (see Figure 6-15), labeled with the name Videos. To expand Videos capabilities, you need to install added GStreamer plug-ins, as discussed previously. The codec wizard will prompt you to install any needed media codecs and plugins. You can use the dconf editor to modify default settings (org.gnome.Totem) (**totem** package, Ubuntu main repository). Though the name of the application is Videos, the package name is still totem.

The **VideoLAN** project (**http://www.videolan.org**) offers network streaming support for most media formats, including MPEG-4 and MPEG-2 (see Figure 6-19). It includes a multimedia player, VLC, which can work on any kind of system (**vlc** package, Universe repository). VLC supports high-def hardware decoding. Install from Ubuntu Software or the Synaptic Package Manager.

Xine is a multipurpose video engine and for Linux/Unix systems that can play video, DVD, and audio discs. Many applications like Videos and Kaffeine use Xine support to playback DVD Video. See **http://xinehq.de** for more information. (**xine** support packages, universe repository). For the Xine user interface, install the **xine-ui** package with the Synaptic Package Manager.

Kaffeine is an older KDE multimedia player (video and dvb) (**kaffeine** package, Ubuntu Universe repository, install from the Synaptic Package Manager or the Discover Package Manager).

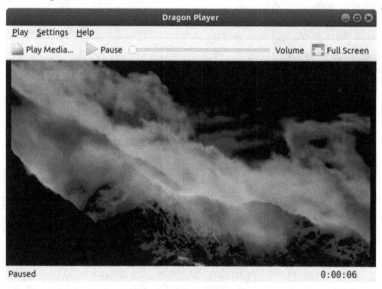

Figure 6-18: KDE Dragon Player

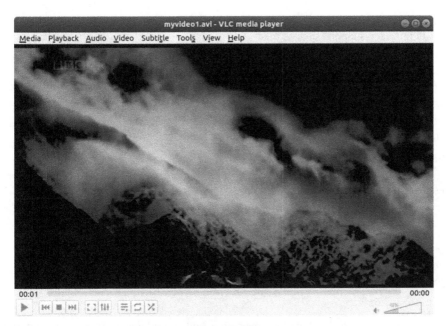

Figure 6-19: VLC Video Player (VideoLAN)

Videos Plugins

The Videos movie player uses plugins to add capabilities like Internet video streaming. Select Preferences from the Videos top bar menu to open the Preferences dialog. On the General tab click on the Plugins button to open the Configure Plugins window (see Figure 6-20). Choose the plugins you want. For added support, install the **totem-plugins-extra** package. This provides the Gromit annotation tool.

Figure 6-20: Videos (Totem) Movie Player plugins

DVD Video support

Unencrypted DVD Video support is provided by three packages available on the Ubuntu repository: **gstreamer-plugins-ugly**, **libdvdnav4**, and **libdvdread4**. These packages are available on the Ubuntu repository and can be installed with Synaptic Package Manager. With the

libdvdnav4 library, these players feature full DVD menu support. The **libdvdread4** library provides basic DVD interface support, such as reading IFO files.

None of the DVD-Video applications will initially play commercial DVD-Video discs. That requires Content Scrambling System (CSS) decryption for commercial DVDs, which is provided by the **libdvdcss** package. This package is not available on the primary Ubuntu repositories. It is only available on the third-party **download.videolan.org** repository. The packages on videolan.org are fully compatible with Ubuntu, but the packages, due to licensing restrictions, are not considered part of the official Ubuntu or Linux software collections.

The **libdvdcss** library works around CSS decryption by treating the DVD as a block device, allowing you to use any of the DVD players to play commercial DVDs. It also provides region-free access. See the following page for complete details.

```
https://help.ubuntu.com/community/RestrictedFormats/PlayingDVDs
```

The easiest way to install the **libdvdcss** package is to use the **libdvd-pkg** package, which is provided on the Ubuntu repository, multiverse. This package will compile the libdvdcss library, prompting you for the automatic upgrades option. You can install it either from the Synaptic Package Manager or from a terminal window with the following command.

```
sudo apt-get install libdvd-pkg
```

Alternatively, you can directly download the source code with your Web browser from the VideoLan site.

```
http://download.videolan.org/pub/libdvdcss/
```

PiTiVi Video editor

The PiTiVi Video editor is an open source application that lets you edit your videos. It is accessible from the Applications overview. Check the PiTiVi website for more details (**http://www.pitivi.org**). You can download a quick-start manual from the Documentation page. Pitivi is a GStreamer application and can work with any video file supported by an installed GStreamer plugin. However, third-party playback plugins designed to be licensed officially such as Fluendo MP3 and MPEG plugins, may not be compatible. These plugins are designed to be playback only and do not provide full codec support. You should use the GStreamer Ugly plugins instead.

The PiTiVi window shows a Clip Library pane on the left, and video playback for a selected video clip on the right (see Figure 6-21). To run a video clip, right click on its icon and select Play Clip. To add a video file to the library, click the Import clips button on the toolbar. You can also drag-and-drop files directly to the Clip Library. The timeline at the bottom of the window displays the video and audio streams for the video clip you are editing, using a rule to shows your position. To edit a video, drag its icon from the Clip Library to the timeline. To trim a video, you pass the mouse over the timeline video and audio streams. Trimming handles will appear that you can use to shorten the video. PiTiVi features ripple editing and rolling editing, splitting, and transitions.

Figure 6-21: Pitivi video editor

TV Players

The following TV players are provided on Ubuntu repositories:

TV player **tvtime** works with many common video capture cards, relying on drivers developed for TV tuner chips on those cards like the Conexant chips. It can only display a TV image. It has no recording or file playback capabilities. Check **http://tvtime.sourceforge.net** for more information.

MythTV is a popular video recording and playback application on Linux systems.

Kaffeine is a popular KDE video recording and playback application on Linux systems. It can also play ATSC over the air digital broadcasts.

Note: To play DivX media on Ubuntu you use the Xvid OpenDivX codec, xvidcore.

DVB and HDTV support

For DVB and HDTV reception, you can use most DVB cards as well as many HDTV cards. The DVB kernel driver is loaded automatically. You can use the **lsmod** command to see if your DVB module is loaded.

Be sure you have installed the restricted add-ons and extras packages (**kubuntu-restricted-extras kubuntu-restricted-addons**, **ubuntu-restricted-extras**, and **ubuntu-restricted-addons**), which provide support for appropriate decoders like mpeg2, FFmpeg, and A52 (ac3) (**liba52**, **libxine1-ffmpeg**, **gstreamer-ffmpeg**, and **libdvbpsi**). You can use the Synaptic Package Manager to install them.

For DVB broadcasts, some DVB-capable players and tools like Kaffeine , as well as vdr, will tune and record DVB broadcasts in t, s, and c formats. Some applications, like Kaffeine, can scan DVB channels directly. Others may require that you first generate a **channels.conf** file. You can do this with the **w_scan** command (**w-scan** package). Then copy the generated **channels.conf** file to the appropriate applications directory. Channel scans can be output in vdr, Kaffeine, and Xine formats for use with those applications as well as others like Mplayer and MythTV. The

w_scan command can also generate **channel.conf** entries for ATSC channels (HDTV), though not all applications can tune ATSC channels (Kaffeine can tune HDTV as well as scan for HDTV channels). You can also use the **dvbscan** tool (**dvb-apps** package) for scanning your channels and the **azap** tool for accessing the signal directly. This tool makes use of channel frequencies kept in the **/usr/share/dvb** directory. There are files for ATSC broadcast as well as cable.

Kaffeine DVB and ATSC tuning

The Kaffeine KDE media player can scan for both DVB and ATSC channels. You will need to have a DVB or ATSC tuner installed on your system. On Kaffeine, from the Television menu choose Configure Television, and on the device tab choose the source such as ATSC. Then from the Television menu, select Channels to open a Channel dialog. Your tuner device is selected on the Search on menu. Click on the Start scan button to begin scanning. Detected channels are listed on the "Scan results" scroll box. Select the ones you want and click Add Selected to place them in the Channels scroll box. Be sure to add the channel you want to watch on the Channel list.

You can use Kaffeine to both tune and record both DVB and ATSC HDTV channels. Kaffeine records an HDTV file as an **m2t** HDV MPEG-2 file, the High Definition Video (HDV) format used for high definition camcorders. The **m2t** files that Kaffeine generates can be played back by most video players, including Videos, Dragon Player, and vlc. To schedule a recording on Kaffeine, click the Television tab or click Digital TV from the Start tab. From the Television menu choose Recording Schedule or click the calendar button in the lower left corner to open the Recording Schedule dialog. Click the New button to open a Schedule Entry dialog where you can name the program, select the channel, set the time and duration, and choose to repeat daily or weekly.

Xvid (DivX) and Matroska (mkv) on Linux

MPEG-4 compressed files provide DVD-quality video with relatively small file sizes. They have become popular for distributing high-quality video files over the Internet. When you first try to play an MPEG-4, the codec wizard will prompt you to install the needed codec packages to play it. Many multimedia applications like VLC already support MPEG-4 files.

MPEG-4 files using the Matroska wrapper, also known by their file extension **mkv**, can be played on most video players including the VideoLan vlc player, Videos, Dragon Player, and Kaffeine. You will need HDTV codecs, like MPEG4 AAC sound codec, installed to play the high definition **mkv** file files. If needed, the codec wizard will prompt you to install them. For the KDE players like Dragon Player, be sure to install the **kubuntu-restricted-extras** and **kubuntu-restricted-addons** packages. To manage and create MKV files you can use the **mkvtoolnix-gui** tools (install with the Synaptic Package Manager).

You use the open source version of DivX known as Xvid to play DivX video (**libxvidcore4** package, Multiverse repository, install with the Synaptic Package Manager). Most DivX files can be run using XviD. XviD is an entirely independent open source project, but it is compatible with DivX files. You can also download the XviD source code from **https://www.xvid.com/**.

Note: Ubuntu provices the Ubuntu Studio flavor for multimedia applications projects.

Ubuntu Studio

Ubuntu Studio features Linux software for multimedia production, including sound, music, video, and graphics applications. You can install Ubuntu Studio as its own installation or as an added desktop on your Ubuntu desktop install.

You can download the Ubuntu Studio install DVD from **https://ubuntustudio.org**. This is a DVD that installs using the text install utility. Use the arrow keys and tabs to move the cursor, the spacebar to choose, and ENTER key to select. The install procedure is the same for the desktop. Use the arrow keys and spacebar to select entries. Select them all for the entire collection.

To add Ubuntu Studio to your current desktop, use the Synaptic Package Manager and find the Meta Package (universe) section. There you will find the **ubuntustudio-desktop** Meta package, which will install the complete Ubuntu Studio desktop. You also install the Ubuntu Studio software collections including **ubuntustudio-audio, ubuntustudio-graphics**, and **ubuntustudio-video**. Ubuntu studio uses its own Ubuntu Studio desktop theme with its own icons, Applications menu categories, and background image.

Sound Settings

Your sound cards are detected automatically for you when you start up your system, by ALSA, which is invoked by udev when your system starts up. Removable devices, like USB sound devices, are also detected. See Table 6-7 for a listing of sound device and interface tools.

Sound tool	Description
KMix	KDE sound connection configuration and volume tool
alsamixer	ALSA sound connection configuration and volume tool
amixer	ALSA command for sound connection configuration
Sound Settings	GNOME Sound Settings, used to select and configure your sound interface
PulseAudio	PulseAudio sound interface, the default sound interface for Ubuntu. **https://www.freedesktop.org/wiki/Software/PulseAudio/**
PulseAudio Volume Control	PulseAudio Volume Control, controls stream input, output, and playback, **pavucontrol** package
PulseAudio Volume Meter	Volume Meter, displays active sound levels
PulseAudio Manager	Manager for information and managing PulseAudio, **pman** package
PulseAudio Preferences	Options for network access and virtual output

Table 6-7: Sound device and interface tools

In addition to hardware drivers, sound systems also use sound interfaces to direct encoded sound streams from an application to the hardware drivers and devices. Ubuntu uses the PulseAudio server for its sound interface. PulseAudio aims to combine and consolidate all sound interfaces into a simple, flexible, and powerful server. The ALSA hardware drivers are still used, but the application interface is handled by PulseAudio. Pulse audio is installed as the default set up for Ubuntu.

Note: Sound devices on Linux are supported by hardware sound drivers. With the Ubuntu kernel, hardware support is implemented by the Advanced Linux Sound Architecture (ALSA) system. ALSA replaces the free version of the Open Sound System used in previous releases, as well as the original built-in sound drivers. You can find more about ALSA at http://alsa-project.org.

PulseAudio is cross-platform sound server, allowing you to modify the sound level for different audio streams separately. See **https://www.freedesktop.org/wiki/Software/PulseAudio/** for documentation and help. PulseAudio offers complete control over all your sound streams, letting you combine sound devices and direct the stream anywhere on your network. PulseAudio is not confined to a single system. It is network capable, letting you direct sound from one PC to another.

As an alternative, you can use the command-line ALSA control tool, **alsamixer**. This will display all connections and allow you to use a keyboard command to select (arrow keys), mute (m key), or set sound levels (Page Up and Down). Press the ESC key to exit. The **amixer** command lets you perform the same tasks for different sound connections from the command line. To actually play and record from the command-line, you can use the **play** and **rec** commands.

Volume Control

Volume control for different applications is displayed on the application's dialog as the speaker icon. You can click it to change your application's output sound volume using a sliding bar. The sliding sound bar on the system status area menu also lets you set the sound volume, as shown here.

To perform volume control for specific devices like a microphone, you use the GNOME Settings Sound dialog.

Sound: PulseAudio

You configure sound devices and set the volume for sound effects, input, output, and applications using the GNOME Settings Sound dialog. The Sound dialog has four tabs: Output, Input, Sound Effects, and Applications (see Figure 6-22). Corresponding sound configuration is available on KDE, which also uses PulseAudio.

Volume Control is integrated into the Sound dialog. A sliding bar at the top of the dialog, above the tabs, lets you set the output volume.

The Sound Effects tab lets you select an alert sound, such as Drip or Sonar. A sliding bar lets you set the volume for your sound alerts, or turn them off by clicking the ON/OFF switch.

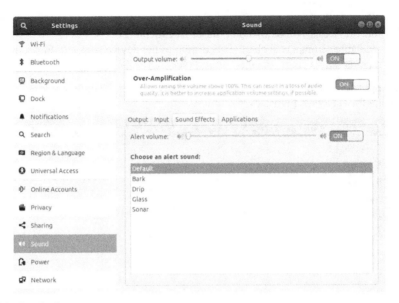

Figure 6-22: Sound

On the Input tab, you set the input volume for an input device such as a microphone. An ON/OFF switch lets you disable it. When speaking or recording, the input level is displayed (see Figure 6-23). If you have more than one input device, they will be listed in the "Choose a device for sound input" section. Choose the one you want to configure.

Figure 6-23: Sound - Input tab

On the Output tab, you can configure balance settings for a selected output device. If you have more than one device, it will be listed in the Profile menu. Choose the one you want to configure. The available settings will change according to the device selected. For a simple Analog Stereo Output, there is only a single balance setting (see Figure 6-24).

The Applications tab will show applications currently using sound devices. You can set the sound volume for each (see Figure 6-25).

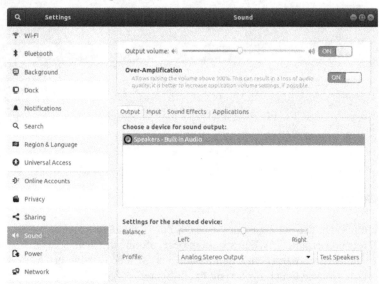

Figure 6-24: Sound - Output tab

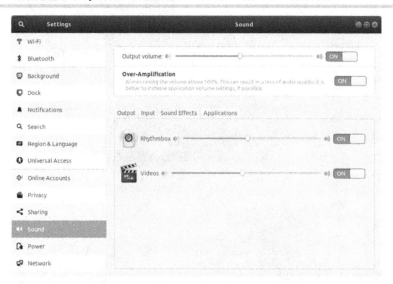

Figure 6-25: Sound - Applications tab

Sound devices that support multiple interfaces like analog surround sound 7.1 and digital SPDIF output, may have an extensive list of interface combinations in the Profile menu. The Input and Output tabs will then display configuration settings for the selected device. With Analog Surround 7.1 Output selected, the Output tab will show settings for Balance, Fade, and Subwoofer. Configuring digital output for SPDIF (digital) connectors is a simple matter of selecting the digital output entry on the Profiles menu.

PulseAudio applications

For additional configuration abilities, you can also install the PulseAudio applications. Most begin with the prefix **pa** in the package name. PulseAudio tools are accessible from the Applications overview. The PulseAudio Manager and PulseAudio Volume Meter menu entries are not listed by default. The PulseAudio tools and their command names are shown in Table 6-8.

PulseAudio Volume Control, **pavucontrol**

PulseAudio Volume Meter, **pavumeter**

PulseAudio Manager, **paman**

PulseAudio Preferences, **paprefs**

You can use the PulseAudio Volume Control tool to set the sound levels for different playback applications and sound devices (choose PulseAudio Volume Control on the Applications overview).

Sound tool	Description
pacat	Play, record, and configure a raw audio stream
pacmd	Generates a shell for entering configuration commands
pactl	Control a PulseAudio server, changing input and output sources and providing information about the server.
padsp	PulseAudio wrapper for OSS sound applications
pamon	Link to pacat
paplay	Playback audio. The -d option specifies the output device, the -s option specifies the server, and the --volume option sets the volume (link to pacat)
parec	Record and audio stream (link to pacat)
parecord	Record and audio stream (link to pacat)
pasuspender	Suspend a PulseAudio server
pax11publish	Access PulseAudio server credentials

Table 6-8: PulseAudio commands (command-line)

The PulseAudio Volume Control applications will show tabs for Playback, Recording, Output Devices, Input Devices, and Configuration. The Playback tab shows all the applications currently using PulseAudio. You can adjust the volume for each application separately. You can use the Output tab panel to set the volume control at the source and select different output devices, such as Headphones. The volume for input and recording devices are set on the Recording and Input Devices tabs. The Configuration tab lets you choose different device profiles, such as selecting Digital output or Surround Sound 5.1.

You can also use the PulseAudio Volume control to direct different applications (streams) to different outputs (devices). For example, you could have two sound sources running—one for video and another for music. The video could be directed through one device to headphones, and the music through another device to speakers, or even to another PC. To redirect an application to a different device, right-click its name in the Playback tab. A pop-up menu will list the available devices and let you select the one you want to use.

The PulseAudio Volume Meter tool will show the actual volume of your devices.

The PulseAudio Manager will show information about your PulseAudio configuration, accessible from the Applications overview. The Devices tab shows the currently active sinks (outputs or directed receivers) and sources. The Clients tab shows all the applications currently using PulseAudio for sound.

Simultaneous output creates a virtual output device to the same hardware device. This lets you channel two sources onto the same output. With PulseAudio Volume Control, you could then channel playback streams to the same output device, but using a virtual device as the output for one. This lets you change the output volume for each stream independently. You could have music and voice directed to the same hardware device, using a virtual device for music and the standard device for voice. You can then reduce the music stream or raise the voice stream.

7. Internet Applications

Web Browsers: Firefox, GNOME Web, Chromium, Lynx

Web-Apps: GNOME

BitTorrent: Transmission

Java for Linux

Network File Transfer: FTP

FTP Clients

Online Accounts

Instant Messenger: Empathy and Pidgin

VoIP: Ekiga and Skype

GNOME Maps

Ubuntu provides powerful Web and FTP clients for accessing the Internet. Some of these applications are installed automatically and are ready to use when you first start up your Ubuntu system. Ubuntu also includes full Java development support, letting you run and construct Java applets. Web and FTP clients connect to sites that run servers, using Web pages and FTP files to provide services to users.

On your Ubuntu system, you can choose from several Web browsers, including Firefox, Epiphany, Chromium, and Lynx. Firefox, Rekonq, Chromium, and Epiphany are desktop browsers that provide full picture, sound, and video display capabilities. The Lynx browser is a line-mode browser that displays only lines of text.

Web browsers and FTP clients are commonly used to conduct secure transactions, such as logging into remote sites, ordering items, or transferring files. Such operations are currently secured by encryption methods provided by the Secure Sockets Layer (SSL). If you use a browser for secure transactions, it should be SSL enabled. Most browsers include SSL support. Ubuntu distributions include SSL (OpenSSL) as part of a standard installation.

URL Addresses

An Internet resource is accessed using a Universal Resource Locator (URL). A URL is composed of three elements: the transfer protocol, the hostname, and the pathname. The transfer protocol and the hostname are separated by a colon and two slashes, **://**. The pathname begins with a single slash:

```
transfer-protocol://host-name/path-name
```

The transfer protocol is usually HTTP (Hypertext Transfer Protocol), indicating a Web page. Other possible values for transfer protocols are **ftp** and **file**. As their names suggest, **ftp** initiates FTP sessions, whereas **file** displays a local file on your own system, such as a text or HTML file. The hostname is the computer on which a particular website is located. You can think of this as the address of the website. By convention, many hostnames begin with **www**, though not necessarily. In the next example, the URL locates a Web page called **guides.html** on the **http://tldp.org** website:

```
http://tldp.org/guides.html
```

If you do not want to access a particular Web page, you can leave the file reference out, and then you access the website's home page automatically. To access a website directly, use its hostname. If no home page is specified for a website, the file **index.html** in the top directory is used as the home page. In the next example, the user brings up the GNOME home page:

```
https://www.gnome.org/
```

The resource file's extension indicates the type of action to be taken on it. A picture has a **.gif** or **.jpeg** extension and is converted for display. A sound file has an **.au** or **.wav** extension and is played. The following URL references a **.gif** file. Instead of displaying a Web page, your browser invokes a graphics viewer to display the picture.

Note: You can install the Adobe version of the Flash plug-in for Linux with the Synaptic Package Manager (adobe-flashplugin). Ubuntu also includes two free and open source versions of Flash: swfdec and gnash. The swfdec version is newer. Be sure the Partners repository is enabled.

Web Browsers

Popular browsers for Ubuntu include Firefox (Mozilla), Chromium (Google), Epiphany, and Lynx (see Table 7-1). Firefox is the default Web browser used on most Linux distributions, including Ubuntu. Rekonq is a KDE Web browser, and Web is the GNOME Web browser (formerly known as Epiphany). Chromium is the open source version of the new Google Web browser. Lynx and ELinks are command line–based browsers with no graphics capabilities, but in every other respect, they are fully functional Web browsers.

Web Site	Description
Firefox	The Mozilla project Firefox Web browser, Ubuntu desktop default browser **https://www.mozilla.org**
Web	GNOME Web browser (formerly called Epiphany) **https://wiki.gnome.org/Apps/Web**
Chromium	Open source version of Google Chrome Web browser **http://www.chromium.org**
Rekonq	KDE desktop Web browser based on Webkit (Universe repository) **https://rekonq.kde.org/**
lynx	Text-based command-line Web browser (Ubuntu supported)
elinks	Text-based command-line Web browser **http://elinks.or.cz**

Table 7-1: Web browsers

The Firefox Web Browser

Ubuntu uses Firefox as its primary browser (see Figure 7-1 The Mozilla project is an open source project based on the original Netscape browser code that provides a development framework for web-based applications, primarily the web browser and e-mail client. The Mozilla project site is https://www.mozilla.org, and the site commonly used for plug-in and extension development is https://www.mozdev.org. You can also sing up for a Firefox account which can then make your bookmarks available to the Firefox browsers on all your devices. Firefox calls this feature the pocket. So you can save a bookmark to your pocket on one of your Firefox browsers, and have it available on the Firefox browsers on all your devices.

Firefox is installed by default with icons on the dock and the Applications overview. When opened, Firefox displays the first tab. Firefox is designed to display tabs, each of which can display a complete Web page, including the Firefox toolbar and sidebar. The tab title is shown at the top, and next to it is a plus button (+) you can click to add a new tab. You can also press Ctrl+t. You can easily switch from one page to another by click its tab. You can re-arrange tabs by clicking and holding on a tab title and moving it to the right or left.

Within a tab, a navigation toolbar is displayed at the top, with an address bar (text box) for entering a URL address and a series of navigation buttons for accessing web pages. On the left side of the toolbar are the Next and Previous buttons for paging through previously accessed web pages, followed by a cancel button for loading a page (X) which becomes a refresh button when the page is fully displayed. Next to it is the Home button to move you to your home page.

Figure 7-1: Firefox Web Browser

When you enter a web page name in the address bar, Firefox performs a dynamic search on previously accessed pages and displays the pages in a drop-down menu, which you can choose from. Within the address bar to the right are buttons for recent history (down arrow), page actions (…), saving to the pocket (down arrow), and marking the page as a bookmark (star). The page actions button displays a menu for tasks such as bookmarking the page, saving to the pocket, and emailing the link.

Firefox provides a search bar (text box) where you can use different search engines for searching the Web, selected sites, or particular items. You have the option to display a search bar either to the right of the address bar or at the bottom of the recent history list. By default, the search bar is only shown at the bottom of the recent history list. It shows a list of icons for the different search services, showing the name of the one your mouse passes over. Upon clicking one, it moves you to that the page for the search service. To the right of the icon list is a gear icon, which you can click to open Firefox Preferences at the entry where you can choose to display the search bar in the toolbar instead. When on the toolbar, the search bar is displayed to the right of the address bar. A pop-up menu lets you select a search engine, showing small icons for the options. Currently included are Google, Bing, Amazon, and eBay.

To the right of the address bar are buttons for history-bookmarks, displaying the sidebar, and the Firefox menu. The history-bookmarks button displays a menu for accessing your bookmarks, history, downloads, and screenshots, as well as Firefox account supported features such as your pocket list and synced tabs.

To add a bookmark for a page, click the bookmark button on the right side of the address bar. This displays an Page Bookmarked dialog with a pop-up menu for folders and tags. The Folder menu is set to the Other Bookmarks folder by default. You can also select the Bookmarks Toolbar or the Bookmarks Menu. Clicking on the down button to the right expands a frame where you can edit your bookmark folders, adding new ones. Selecting Bookmarks on the history/bookmarks menu (accessible form the toolbar) displays the Bookmarks menu, showing a list of your bookmarks from which you can select one to view. Here you can also bookmark a page. The "Show All Bookmarks" entry at the bottom of the list opens the Library dialog where you can edit your bookmarks or delete bookmarks.

To search a current page for certain text, enter Ctrl+f. This opens a search toolbar at the bottom of Firefox from which you can enter a search term. You have search options to highlight found entries or to match character case. The Next and Previous buttons let you move to the next found pattern.

When you download a file using Firefox, the download is managed by the Download Manager. You can download several files at once. Progress is displayed download button on the toolbar, which you can click to see your downloads. You can cancel a download at any time or just pause a download, resuming it later.

Selecting History on the history/bookmarks menu (accessible form the toolbar) displays the History menu, showing a list of your recently accessed Web pages from which you can select one to view. You can also see recently closed tabs and Firefox windows. To clear your recent history, chose the "Clear Recent History" entry. The "Show All History" opens the Library dialog as the history entry, letting you edit, access, bookmark, or remove previous pages.

The Firefox menu lets you perform Web page tasks such as zooming, opening new windows, printing and saving a page, and performing searches on a page. There are also administrative options such as Preference, Add-ons, and the Library. The Library dialog lets you manage all your history and bookmarks. On Preferences you can set your privacy and search options, as well as setting your home page, language, fonts, download location (see Figure 7-2).

Figure 7-2: Firefox Preferences

The Add-ons entry on the menu opens the Add-ons window with tabs for Get Add-ons, Extensions, Themes, and Plugins (see Figure 7-3). Click the one you want to open a brief description and display the Add to Firefox button, which you click to open a download and install dialog. The Extensions tab lists installed Extensions with buttons for Preferences, Disable, and Uninstall for each. On the Plugins tab, you can disable or enable embedded applications, such as DivX, iTunes, QuickTime, and Skype. The Themes tab lets you choose a theme.

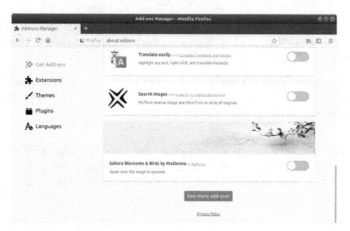

Figure 7-3: Firefox Add-ons Management

Firefox also supports profiles. You can set up different Firefox configurations, each with preferences and bookmarks. This is useful for computers like laptops that connect to different networks or are used for different purposes. You can select and create profiles by starting up the profile manager. Enter the firefox command in a terminal window with the -P option.

```
firefox -P
```

A default profile is already set up. You can create a new profile, which runs the profile wizard to prompt you for the profile name and directory to use. Select a profile to use and click Start Firefox. The last profile you used will be used again the next time you start Firefox. You have the option to prompt for the profile to use at startup, otherwise run the firefox -P command again to change your profile.

Web (Epiphany)

GNOME Web, formerly known as Epiphany, is a GNOME web browser with a simple interface designed to be fast (see Figure 7-4). You can find out more about Epiphany at **https://wiki.gnome.org/Apps/Web**. Web works well as a simple browser with a clean interface. It is also integrated with the desktop, featuring a download applet that will continue after closing Web. Web also supports tabbed panels for multiple web site access. Its applications menu lists options such as New Window, New Incognito Window, the import and export of bookmarks, History, and Preferences. For page-specific operations such as tabs, print, save, zooming, and find, click the menu button at the top right. You can install GNOME Web using Ubuntu Software and searching under "Gnome Web" in Ubuntu Software or **epiphany-browser** in Synaptic. Once installed, you can access it as Web.

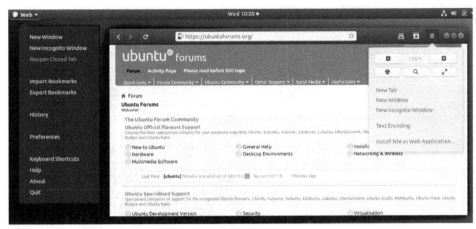

Figure 7-4: Web (Epiphany) Web browser

Chromium

Google's Chromium web browser (**https://www.chromium.org**) provides easy and very secure access to the Web with full Google integration. You can install it using Ubuntu Software, which will enable the Google repository from which it will be downloaded (chromium). You can access Chromium from the Applications overview as Chromium Web Browser. You are first prompted to enter your Google account e-mail and password so that your online preferences and bookmarks can be used, but you can pass.

On Chromium, primacy is afforded to tabs. At the top of the Chromium window are your tabs for open web pages, with a square image button at the end of the tabs for opening a new tab (see Figure 7-3). Chromium features a simple toolbar with navigation buttons and a bookmark button (star icon). To close a tab, click the x button to the right of the tab title.

To the right of the URL box, a menu button displays a drop-down menu for menu items for browser operations such as new tabs, print, zoom, history, bookmarks, and downloads. To configure Chromium, select Settings from this menu to open the Chromium Settings tab. Here you can set your home page, default search service, and themes. Click the Advanced on the sidebar (top left menu icon) to expand the Settings dialog to let you manage passwords, languages, downloads, printing, and accessibility.

When you open a new tab, a thumbnail listing of recently closed and most visited sites is displayed. Clicking a thumbnail moves you to that site. On a new tab, the bookmark toolbar is also displayed, which you can use to access a site.

Figure 7-5: Chromium Web browser (Google Chrome)

The KDE Rekonq Web Browser

Rekonq is a WebKit Web browser for KDE. It is no longer supported directly by Ubuntu, and is now part of the Universe repository (use Synaptic or Discover to install it). Rekonq provides full integration with the KDE Desktop for tasks such as editing and file management. A navigation bar lets you move through accessed pages on a tab, refresh a site, or enter the address of a new site. On the right side of the navigation bar is a menu button that displays Rekonq browser operations, such as open, save, print, panels to display, help, and configuration. Like Chrome, Rekonq is tab-based. Tabs can be reordered with a click-and-drag of their tab thumbnails. To close a tab, click it's x button to the right of its name. You add new tabs by clicking on the new tab button to the right of an open tab.

Lynx and ELinks: Line-Mode Browsers

Linux features two line-mode browsers, Lynx and ELinks, which you can use from a command line interface. You can install them from the Synaptic Package Manager. On these browsers, a Web page is displayed as text only. A text page can contain links to other Internet resources but does not display graphics, video, or sound. Except for the display limitations, Lynx and Elinks are fully functional Web browsers. You can also use them to download files or access local pages. All information on the Web is still accessible to you. Because they do not require as much overhead as desktop-based browsers, they can operate much faster, quickly displaying Web page text. To start the Lynx browser, enter **lynx** on the command line and press ENTER (you can also use a terminal window). ELinks includes features such as frame, form, and table support. It also supports SSL secure encryption. To start ELinks, enter the **elinks** command in a terminal window. You can find out more about elinks at **http://elinks.or.cz**.

Java for Linux

To develop Java applications, use Java tools, and run many Java products, you use the Java 2 Software Development Kit (SDK) and the Java Runtime Environment (JRE). The SDK is a superset of the JRE, adding development tools like compilers and debuggers. Together with other technologies like the Java API, they make up the Java Platform, Standard Edition.

Oracle has open sourced Java as the OpenJDK project and supports and distributes Linux versions. The JRE subset can be installed as OpenJRE. They are directly supported by Ubuntu as packages on the main Ubuntu repository. You can install them with the Synaptic Package Manager. The **openjdk-11-jre** package installs the Java runtime environment, and **openjdk-11-jdk** installs both the JRE and the Java development tools. Java packages and applications are listed in Table 7-2.

Application	Description
Java Development Kit, OpenJDK	An open source Java development environment with a compiler, interpreters, debugger, and more (include the JRE), **http://openjdk.java.net**. Included on the Ubuntu main repository **openjdk-11-jdk**
Java Runtime Environment, OpenJRE	An open source Java runtime environment, including the Java virtual machine, included on the Ubuntu main repository, **openjdk-11-jre**. **http://openjdk.java.net**
Java Platform Standard Edition (JSE)	Complete Java collection, including JRE, JDK, and API, **http://www.oracle.com/technetwork/java/javase/downloads/index.html**
GNU Java Compiler	GNU Public Licensed Java Compiler (GCJ) to compile Java programs, **gcj**

Table 7-2: Java Packages and Java Web Applications

Several compatible GNU packages (Java-like) are also provided that allow you to run Java applets using GNU free Java support. These include GNU Java compiler (**gcj**) and the Eclipse Java compiler (**ecj**).

BitTorrent Clients (transmission)

GNOME and KDE provide very effective BitTorrent clients. With BitTorrent, you can download very large files quickly in a shared distributed download operation where several users participate in downloading different parts of a file, sending their parts of the download to other participants, known as peers. Instead of everyone trying to access a few central servers, all peers participating in the BitTorrent operation become sources for the file being downloaded. Certain peers function as seeders, those who have already downloaded the file, but continue to send parts to those who need them.

Ubuntu installs the GNOME BitTorrent client, Transmission, accessible from the Applications overview. For Kubuntu, you can use the Ktorrent BitTorrent client. To perform a BitTorrent download you need the BitTorrent file for the file you want to download. The BitTorrent file for the Ubuntu Desktop DVD iso image is **ubuntu-18.04-desktop-amd64.iso.torrent**. When you download the file from the **https://www.ubuntu.com/download/alternative-downloads** site. When you doubl-click the file it will open it directly with Transmission.

Figure 7-6: Transmission BitTorrent client

Transmission can handle several torrents at once. On the toolbar are buttons for starting, pausing, and remove a download. The Add button can be used to load a BitTorrent file (**.torrent**), setting up a download. You also can drag-and-drop a torrent file to the Transmission window. When you first open a torrent file, the Torrent Options window opens where you can specify the destination folder and the priority. The option to start the download automatically is selected by default. Figure 7-6 shows Transmission with two BitTorrent operations set up, one of which is active. A progress bar shows how much of the file has been downloaded.

You could set up Transmission to manage several BitTorrent operations, of which only a few may be active, others paused, and still others that have finished but continue to function as seeders. From the first Show menu, you can select All, Active, Downloading, Seeding, Paused, Finished, and Queued torrents. You can also choose those verifying and those that have errors. From the second menu, you can choose Trackers, public or private torrents (Privacy), and select by priority (high, normal, or low).

To remove a torrent, right-click on it and select Remove. Choose Delete Files and Remove to remove what you have downloaded so far.

To see more information about a torrent, select it and then click the Properties button (see Figure 7-7). This opens a Properties window with tabs for Information, Peers, Tracker, Files, and Options. On the Information tab, the Activity section shows statistics like the progress, times, and errors, and the Details section shows the origin, comment, and locations of the download folder. Peers show all the peers participating in the download. Tracker displays the location of the tracker, the server that manages the torrent operation. Files shows the progress of the file download (a torrent could download more than one file). The Options tab lets you set bandwidth and connection parameters, limiting the download or upload, and the number of peers.

Figure 7-7: Transmission BitTorrent client properties

FTP Clients

With File Transfer Protocol (FTP) clients, you can connect to a corresponding FTP site and download files from it. These sites feature anonymous logins that let any user access their files. Basic FTP client capabilities are incorporated into the Dolphin (KDE) and Files (GNOME) file managers. You can use a file manager window to access an FTP site and drag files to local directories to download them. Effective FTP clients are also now incorporated into most Web browsers, making Web browsers the primary downloading tool. Firefox, in particular, has strong FTP download capabilities.

Although file managers and Web browsers provide effective access to public (anonymous login) sites, to access private sites, you may need a stand-alone FTP client like curl, wget, Filezilla, gFTP, lftp, or **ftp**. These clients let you enter usernames and passwords with which you can access a private FTP site. The stand-alone clients are also useful for large downloads from public FTP sites, especially those with little or no Web display support. Popular Linux FTP clients are listed in Table 7-4.

Network File Transfer: FTP

With File Transfer Protocol (FTP) clients, you can transfer extremely large files directly from one site to another (see Table 7-3). FTP can handle both text and binary files. FTP performs a remote login to another account on another system connected to you on a network. Once logged into that other system, you can transfer files to and from it. To log in, you need to know the login name and password for the account on the remote system. Many sites on the Internet allow public access using FTP, however. Such sites serve as depositories for large files anyone can access and download. These sites are often referred to as FTP sites, and in many cases, their Internet addresses begin with the term ftp, such as **ftp.gnome.org**. These public sites allow anonymous FTP login from any user. You can then transfer files from that site to your own system.

FTP Clients	Description
Dolphin	KDE file manager
Files	GNOME file manager (nautilus)
gFTP	GNOME FTP client, **gftp-gtk**
ftp	Command line FTP client
lftp	Command line FTP client capable of multiple connections
curl	Internet transfer client (FTP and HTTP)
Filezilla	Linux version of the open source Filezilla ftp client (Universe repository)

Table 7-3: Linux FTP Clients

Several FTP protocol are available for accessing sites that support them. The original FTP protocol is used for most anonymous sites. FTP transmissions can also be encrypted using SSH2, the SFTP protocol. More secure connections may use FTPS for TLS/SSL encryption. Some sites support a simplified version of FTP called File Service Protocol, FSP. FTP clients may support different protocols like gFTP for FSP and Filezilla for TLS/SSL. Most clients support both FTP and SSH2.

Web Browser–Based FTP

You can access an FTP site and download files from it with any Web browser. Browsers are useful for locating individual files, though not for downloading a large set of files. A Web browser is effective for checking out an FTP site to see what files are listed there. When you access an FTP site with a Web browser, the entire list of files in a directory is listed as a Web page. You can move to a subdirectory by clicking its entry. You can easily browse through an FTP site to download files. To download a file, click the download link. This will start the transfer operation, opening a dialog for selecting your local directory and the name for the file. The default name is the same as on the remote system. On many browsers, you can manage your downloads with a download manager, which will let you cancel a download operation in progress or remove other downloads requested. The manager will show the time remaining, the speed, and the amount transferred for the current download.

GNOME Desktop FTP: Connect to Server

The easiest way to download files from an FTP site is to use the built-in FTP capabilities of the GNOME file manager, GNOME Files. On GNOME, the desktop file manager has a built-in FTP capability much like the KDE file manager. The FTP operation has been seamlessly integrated into standard desktop file operations. Downloading files from an FTP site is as simple as dragging files from one folder window to another, where one of the folders happens to be located on a remote FTP site. Use the GNOME file manager (GNOME Files) to access a remote FTP site, listing files in the remote folder, just as local files are (see Figure 7-8). In a file manager's Location bar (**Ctrl-l**), enter the FTP site's URL using the prefix **ftp://** and press ENTER. A dialog opens prompting you to specify how you want to connect. You can connect anonymously for a public FTP site, or connect as a user supplying your username and password (private site). You can also choose to remember the password.

Folders on the FTP site will be displayed, and you can drag files to a local folder to download them. You can navigate through the folders as you would with any file manager folder, opening folders or returning to the parent folder. To download a file, just drag it from the FTP window to a local folder window. To upload a file, drag it from your local folder to the window for the open FTP folder. Your file will be uploaded to that FTP site (if you have permission to do so). You can also delete files on the site's folders if allowed.

You can also use the Connect to Server bar in the file manager (see Figure 8-9) to connect, which remembers your previous FTP connections. To access the Connect to Server bar, click on the "Other Locations" entry in any file manager sidebar. The Connect to server bar is displayed at the bottom of the file manager window. It shows a text box for the server address, a menu button to display previous addresses, and a Connect button. Enter the server address. The address is remembered and added to the previous servers list. Then click the Connect button. A dialog opens letting you specify an Anonymous login or to enter a username and password. Click the Connect button to access the site.

Figure 7-8: GNOME FTP access with the file manager

Figure 7-9: GNOME FTP access with Connect to Server and the file manager

The top directory of the remote FTP site will be displayed in a file manager window. Use the file manager to progress through the remote FTP site's directory tree until you find the file you want. Then, open another window for the local directory to which you want the remote files copied. In the window showing the FTP files, select those you want to download. Then click and drag those files to the window for the local folder. As files are downloaded, a dialog appears showing the progress.

The file manager window's sidebar will list an entry for the FTP site accessed. An eject button is shown to the right of the FTP site's name. To disconnect from the site, click this button. The FTP entry will disappear along with the FTP sites icons and file listings.

The KDE File Manager: Dolphin

On the KDE Desktop, the desktop file manager Dolphin has built-in FTP capability. The FTP operation has been seamlessly integrated into standard desktop file operations. Downloading files from an FTP site is as simple as copying files by dragging them from one folder window to another, with one of the folders located on a remote FTP site. To download files from an FTP site, you open a window to access that site, entering the URL for the FTP site in the window's location box. Use the **ftp://** protocol for FTP access. Once connected, open the directory you want, and then open another window for the local folder to which you want the remote files copied. In the window showing the FTP files, select the ones you want to download. Then click-and-drag those files to the window for the local directory. A pop-up menu appears with choices for Copy, Link, or Move. Select Copy. The selected files are then downloaded. Another window opens, showing the download progress and displaying the name of each file in turn, along with a bar indicating the percentage downloaded so far.

Filezilla

Filezilla is an open source FTP client originally implemented on Windows systems (**https://filezilla-project.org/**). The Linux version for Ubuntu is available on the Ubuntu Universe repository. Use the Synaptic Package Manager or Ubuntu Software to install. Once installed, you can access it from the Applications overview. The interface displays a left and right pane for local and remote folders. You can navigate through folder trees, with the files of a selected folder displayed below. To download a file, right-click on a file in the Remote site pane (right) and select Download. To upload, right-click on the file in the Local site pane (left) and select Upload. Text boxes at the top let you specify the host, username, password, and port. A Quick connect menu will connect to a preconfigured site.

To configure a remote site connection, use the Site Manager (File | Site Manager). In the Site Manager window, click on the New Site button to create a new site connection. Four configuration tabs become active: General, Advanced, Transfer settings, and Charset. On the General tab, you can specify the host, user, password, and account. The server type menu lets you specify a particular FTP protocol like SFTP for SSH encrypted transmissions or FTPS for TLS/SSL encryption.

gFTP

The gFTP program is an older GNOME FTP client designed to let you make standard FTP file transfers. The package name for gFTP is **gftp-gtk**, and it is located in the Universe repository. You can install it from Ubuntu Software or the Synaptic Package Manager.

The gFTP window consists of several panes. The top-left pane lists files in your local directory, and the top-right pane lists your remote directory. Subdirectories have folder icons preceding their names. The parent directory can be referenced by the double period entry (**..**) with an up arrow at the top of each list. Double-click a directory entry to access it. The pathnames for all directories are displayed in boxes above each pane. A drop down menu to the far right lets you specify the FTP protocol to use such as FTP for a standard transmission, SSH2 for SSH encrypted connections, and FSP for File Service Protocol transmissions. Two buttons between the panes are used for transferring files. The left arrow button, <-, downloads selected files in the remote directory, and the right arrow button, ->, uploads files from the local directory. Menus across the top of the window can be used to manage your transfers. A connection manager enables you to enter login information about a specific site.

wget

The wget tool lets you access Web and FTP sites for particular directories and files. Directories can be recursively downloaded, letting you copy an entire website. The **wget** command takes as its option the URL for the file or directory you want. Helpful options include **-q** for quiet, **-r** for recursive (directories), **-b** to download in the background, and **-c** to continue downloading an interrupted file. One drawback is that your URL reference can be very complex. You have to know the URL already. You cannot interactively locate an item as you would with an FTP client. The following would download the Ubuntu Install DVD in the background.

```
wget -b ftp://releases.ubuntu.com/bionic/ubuntu-18.04-desktop-amd64.iso
```

curl

The **curl** Internet client operates much like **wget**, but with much more flexibility. With curl, you can specify multiple URLs on its command line. You can also use braces to specify multiple matching URLs, like different websites with the same domain name. You can list the different website host names within braces, followed by their domain name (or vice versa). You can also use brackets to specify a range of multiple items. This can be very useful for downloading archived files that have the same root name with varying extensions. **curl** can download using any protocol, and will try to intelligently guess the protocol to use if none is provided. Check the **curl** man page for more information.

ftp

The **ftp** client uses a command line interface, and it has an extensive set of commands and options you can use to manage your FTP transfers. It is the original FTP client used on Unix and Linux systems. See the **ftp** man page for more details. Alternatively, you can use **sftp** for more secure access. The **sftp** client has the same commands as **ftp** but provides SSH (Secure SHell) encryption. Also, if you installed the Kerberos clients (**krb5-clients**), a Kerberized version of ftp is setup, which provides for secure authentication from Kerberos servers. It has the same name as the **ftp** client (an **ftp** link to Kerberos **ftp**) and the same commands.

You start the **ftp** client by entering the command **ftp** at a shell prompt. If you want to connect to a specific site, you can include the name of that site on the command line after the **ftp** keyword. Otherwise, you need to connect to the remote system with the ftp command **open**. You are then prompted for the name of the remote system with the prompt "(to)". When you enter the remote system name, ftp connects you to the system and then prompts you for a login name. After entering the login name, you are prompted for the password. In the next example, the user connects to the remote system **garnet**, and logs in to the **robert** account:

```
$ ftp
ftp> open
(to) garnet
Connected to garnet.berkeley.edu.
220 garnet.berkeley.edu FTP server ready.
Name (garnet.berkeley.edu:root): robert
password required
Password:
user robert logged in
ftp>
```

Once logged in, you can execute Linux commands on either the remote system or your local system. You execute a command on your local system in ftp by preceding the command with an exclamation point. Any Linux commands without an exclamation point are executed on the remote system. One exception exists to this rule. Whereas you can change directories on the remote system with the **cd** command, to change directories on your local system, you need to use a special ftp command called **lcd** (local **cd**). In the next example, the first command lists files in the remote system, while the second command lists files in the local system:

```
ftp> ls
ftp> !ls
```

The ftp program provides a basic set of commands for managing files and directories on your remote site, provided you have the permission to do so. You can use **mkdir** to create a remote directory, and **rmdir** to remove one. Use the **delete** command to erase a remote file. With the **rename** command, you can change the names of files. You close your connection to a system with the **close** command. You can then open another connection if you want. To end the ftp session, use the **quit** or **bye** command.

```
ftp> close
ftp> bye
Good-bye
$
```

To transfer files to and from the remote system, use the **get** and **put** commands. The **get** command receives files from the remote system to your local system, and the **put** command sends files from your local system to the remote system. In a sense, your local system gets files *from* the remote and puts files *to* the remote. In the next example, the file **weather** is sent from the local system to the remote system using the **put** command:

```
ftp> put weather
PORT command successful.
ASCII data connection
ASCII Transfer complete.
ftp>
```

lftp

The **lftp** program is an enhanced FTP client with advanced features such as the abilities to download mirror sites and to run several FTP operations in the background at the same time. You can install it with the Synaptic Package Manager.

It uses a command set similar to that for the ftp client. You use **get** and **mget** commands to download files, with the **-o** option to specify local locations for them. Use **lcd** and **cd** to change local and remote directories.

When you connect to a site, you can queue commands with the **queue** command, setting up a list of FTP operations to perform. With this feature, you could queue several download operations to a site. The queue can be reordered and entries deleted if you wish. You can also connect to several sites and set up a queue for each one. The **mirror** command lets you maintain a local version of a mirror site. You can download an entire site or just update newer files, as well as remove files no longer present on the mirror.

You can tailor lftp with options set in the **.lftprc** file. System-wide settings are placed in the **/etc/lftp.conf** file. Here, you can set features like the prompt to use and your anonymous password. The **.lftp** directory holds support files for command history, logs, bookmarks, and startup commands. The lftp program also supports the **.netrc** file, checking it for login information.

Social Networking

Ubuntu provides integrated social networking support for broadcasting, IM (Instant Messenger), and VoIP (Voice over Internet). User can communicate directly with other users on your network (see Table 7-1). Most of these applications are not supported by Ubuntu and are not installed by default. You can install them from Ubuntu Software.

Instant Messenger

Instant messenger (IM) clients allow users on the same IM service to communicate across the Internet (see Table 7-4). Currently, some of the major IM services are AIM (AOL), Microsoft Network (MSN), Yahoo, ICQ, and Jabber. Some use an XML protocol called XMPP, Extensible Messaging and Presence Protocol. Numerous instant messaging clients are available on Ubuntu Software (Internet | Instant Messaging).

Empathy

Empathy is the GNOME messaging application. Empathy is based on the Telepathy framework, which is designed to provide IM support to any application that wants an IM capability. All major IM services are supported, including Google Talk, AIM, Salut, zephyr, Jabber (XMPP), ICQ, and Yahoo.

Figure 7-10: Empathy IM Client

Clients	Description
Ekiga	VoIP application
Skype	VoIP application (Partner repository)
empathy	GNOME instant messenger
Pidgin	Older instant messenger client used in previous releases and still available.
Jabber	Jabber IM (XMPP)
Finch	Command line cursor-based IM client
Konversation	KDE IRC client

Table 7-4: Instant Messenger, Talk, and VoIP Clients

Empathy is accessible from the Applications overview (see Figure 7-10). Click the Accounts entry in the Empathy menu to open the Online Account dialog, letting you add new accounts for Empathy. Click the plus button to add a new account. Choose the Empathy entry in the drop down menu labeled "Show accounts that integrate with" to show instant messaging services such as AIM, Yahoo, Jabber, and Facebook. A drop down menu on the Contact List window lets you select your status, like Available, Busy, Away, Invisible, or Offline. You can specify a custom message for a particular status.

Pidgin

Pidgin is an older IM client that works with most IM protocols. It is still available on the Universe repository, and can be installed with the Synaptic Package Manager. Pidgin will be accessible from the Applications overview. Pidgin will open a Buddy List window with menus for Buddies, Accounts, Tools, and Help (see Figure 7-11). Use the Buddies menu to send a message or join a chat. The Accounts menu lets you configure and add accounts. The Tools menu provides configuration features, such as preferences, plugin selection, privacy options, and sound.

Figure 7-11: Pidgin Buddy List

The first time you start Pidgin, the Add Account window is displayed with Basic, Advanced, and Proxy tabs for setting up an account. Later you can edit the account by selecting it in the Accounts window (Accounts | Manage) and clicking the Modify button. Pidgin is not supported by Online Accounts.

To create a new account, select Manage Accounts from the Accounts menu (Accounts | Manage). This opens the Accounts dialog, which lists your current accounts. Click the Add button to open the Add Account dialog with a Basic, Advanced, and Proxy tabs. On the Basic panel, you choose the protocol from a pop-up menu that shows items such as AIM, Bonjour, Yahoo!, and IRC, and then enter the appropriate account information. You can also select a buddy icon to use for the account. On the Advanced tab, you specify the server and network connection settings. Many protocols will have a server entered already.

To configure your setup, select Preferences from the Tools menu (Tools | Preferences) to open the Preferences dialog where you can set options for logging, sounds, themes, and the interface display. You can find out more about Pidgin at **http://pidgin.im**. Pidgin is a GNOME front end that used the libpurple library for is actual IM tasks (formerly libgaim). The libpurple library is used by many different IM applications such as Finch.

VoIP Applications

Ubuntu provides two popular VoIP applications: Ekiga, which is open source, and Skype, which is proprietary (available through the Partners repository).

Ekiga

Ekiga is GNOME's VoIP application providing Internet IP Telephone and video conferencing support (see Figure 7-12), **https://www.ekiga.org/**. Ekiga supports both the H.323 and SIP (Session Initiation Protocol) protocols. It is compatible with Microsoft's NetMeeting. H.323 is a comprehensive protocol that includes the digital broadcasting protocols such as digital video broadcast (DVB) and H.261 for video streaming, as well as the supporting protocols like the H.450 series for managing calls. You can access Ekiga from the Applications overview. Ekiga has panel status icons that display circles indicating Online, Away, and Do Not Disturb.

Figure 7-12: Ekiga VoIP

To use Ekiga you will need a SIPaddress. You can obtain a free address from **http://www.ekiga.org**. You will first have to subscribe to the service. When you first start Ekiga, the Ekiga Configuration Assistant prompts you to configure your connection (SIP address, Callout account if you wish, connection type, and audio and video devices). Here you can provide information like contact information, your connection method, sound driver, and video device. Use the address book to connect to another Ekiga user. A white pages directory lets you search for people who are also using Ekiga.

Skype

Skype is part of the Ubuntu Partner repository. Be sure to enable the Canonical Partners repository on the Software & Updates dialog's Other Software tab. You can install Skype using the Ubuntu Software, Synaptic Package Manager, or with the following apt-get command in a terminal window.

```
sudo apt-get install skype
```

Once installed, you can access Skype from the Applications overview. The interface is similar to the Windows version (see Figure 7-13). A Skype panel icon will appear on the panel, once you start Skype. You can use it to access Skype throughout your session. Click to open Skype and right-click to display a menu from which you can change your status and sign out. The panel icon changes according to your status.

Also, the **pidgin-skype** package provides a Skype plugin, which will let you use Ubuntu applications like Pidgin, Finch, and Empathy to operate through Skype connections.

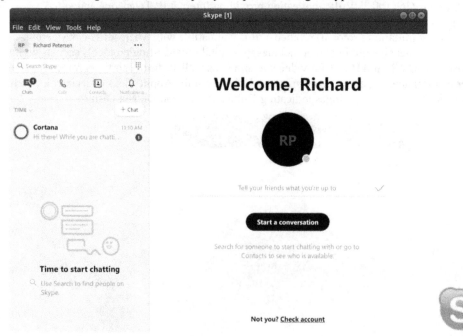

Figure 7-13: Skype VoIP and panel icon

KDE Online Services

On KDE, use the System Settings Online Accounts to set up access to your online services, including Google, AIM, Yahoo Messenger, jabber, ICQ, and KDE talk. On the desktop and panel, you can use the Instant Messaging and Quick Chat widgets. Check the Online Service category in the Widgets dialog. Opening the Instant Messaging settings displays Online Accounts and General tabs. The Online Accounts tab is the same as System Settings Online Accounts, where you can add and configure messaging services. On the General tab, you can set the widget's display options, such as away conditions and the download folder.

For blogging, you can still use the Blogilo blogging client (Universe repository), which features a text editor.

GNOME Maps

GNOME Maps is a GNOME map utility that provides both street and satellite maps. It can also detect your current location or close to it (see Figure 7-14). From the task menu at the left, you can choose a street or satellite view. Use the zoom buttons, also at the left, or mouse scroll button to zoom in and out. To search for a location, enter the name in the search box, and options will be listed. To see your current location, click the Geolocation button to the left. To trace routes click the route planner button to the right to open a dialog where you can enter the source and destination locations.

Figure 7-14: GNOME Map

Part 3: Desktops

Ubuntu Desktop
Kubuntu
Ubuntu MATE
Ubuntu Flavors
The Shell

ubuntu

8. Ubuntu Desktop

Ubuntu GNOME

Favorites

System Status Area

Workspaces

Dash

The GNOME Files File Manager

The Ubuntu desktop is now based on GNOME. Ubuntu GNOME has been deprecated. As discussed in Chapter 3, check the Ubuntu Desktop Guide for a help and documentation. The Ubuntu GNOME desktop uses the GNOME Files file manager, as well as the same GNOME desktop configuration tools (see Chapter 3). The Ubuntu GNOME flavor has been discontinued as it has been incorporated into the official Ubuntu desktop.

GNOME

The GNU Network Object Model Environment, also known as GNOME, is a powerful and easy-to-use environment consisting primarily of a panel, a desktop, and a set of desktop tools with which program interfaces can be constructed. GNOME is designed to provide a flexible platform for the development of powerful applications. Currently, GNOME is supported by several distributions and is the primary interface for Ubuntu Desktop. GNOME is free and released under the GNU Public License. GTK+ is the widget set used for GNOME applications. The GTK+ widget set is entirely free under the Lesser General Public License (LGPL). The LGPL enables developers to use the widget set with proprietary software, as well as free software (the GPL is restricted to free software).

For detailed documentation, check the GNOME documentation site at **https://help.gnome.org**. Documentation is organized by users, administrators, and developers. "GNOME Help" provides a complete tutorial on desktop use. For administrators, the "GNOME Desktop System Administration Guide" details how administrators can manage user desktops. Table 8-1 offers a listing of useful GNOME sites.

Web Site	Description
www.gnome.org	Official GNOME website
https://help.gnome.org	GNOME documentation website for users, administrators, and developers
https://wiki.gnome.org/Personalization	Desktop themes and background art
https://wiki.gnome.org/Apps	GNOME software applications, applets, and tools
https://developer.gnome.org/	GNOME developer's site; see library.gnome.org for developer documentation

Table 8-1: GNOME Resources

GNOME releases new versions on a frequent schedule. The Ubuntu Desktop uses GNOME 3.18, with many features included from GNOME 3.0. Key changes with GNOME 3.28 and GNOME 3.0 are described in detail at the following:

```
https://help.gnome.org/misc/release-notes/3.0/

https://help.gnome.org/misc/release-notes/3.28/
```

The Ubuntu GNOME Desktop

GNOME is based on the gnome-shell, which is a compositing window manager (see Figure 8-1). The key components of the gnome-shell are a top bar, an Activities overview, the

Ubuntu Dock, and a notification/message tray feature. The top bar has a dialog for the date and time, a universal access menu, and a status area menu for sound volume, network connections, power information, and user tasks such as accessing settings and logging out. The Activities overview lets you quickly access favorite applications, locate applications, select windows, and change workspaces. The message tray and notification system notifies you of recent events, such as updates and recently attached USB drives. To the right of the Activities button is the Applications menu, which is a menu for the currently selected open application, such as the Files menu for a file manager window. Most applications have only a Quit entry, while others list key tasks.

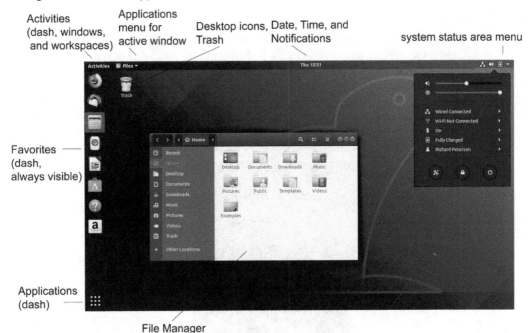

Figure 8-1: GNOME Desktop

You can configure desktop settings and perform most administrative tasks using the GNOME configuration tools (see Table 8-1) listed in the GNOME Settings dialog, accessible from the System Status Area menu (see Figure 8-25). Most use the GNOME 3 configuration and administrative tools such as Background, Lock Screen, Users, and Power.

You can enhance the Ubuntu desktop by adding third-party extensions, as noted in Chapter 4 (see Figures 4-13, 4-14, an 4-15). These extensions are not guaranteed to work, though some are already installed and activated. Open the Ubuntu Software Add-ons category and click the Shell Extensions tab. First, enable the extensions. You will see icons with names and descriptions of different extensions, such as Dash to Dock which places a dash on the desktop instead of the Activities overview. Some extensions work as added items on the top bar, like system monitor. To manage installed extensions, click the Extension Settings button at the top of the Shell Extensions tab to pen a Shell Extension dialog where you can both turn extensions on or off, and configure them if possible.

Top Bar

The screen displays a top bar, through which you access your applications, windows, and such system properties as sound and networking. Clicking the sound and power icons at the right of the top bar displays the system status area menu with options to set the sound level, screen brightness (laptop), wired and wireless connections, Bluetooth, and to shut down or lock the screen (see Figure 8-1). The center of the top bar has a button to display your clock and calendar. To the left is the Activities button, which displays an icon bar for favorite and open applications.

The System Status Area

Once logged in, the System Status Area is displayed on the right side of the top bar (see Figure 8-2) . The area will include status icons for features such as sound and power. Clicking the button showing the sound, power, and down arrow icons displays the System Status Area menu, with items for sound, brightness, wired and wireless connections, the battery, the current user, in addition to buttons at the bottom for opening GNOME Settings, activating the lock screen, and shutting down or rebooting the system. The sound and brightness items feature sliding bars with which you can adjust the volume and brightness. The Wi-Fi, Battery, and current user entries expand to submenus with added entries. The buttons at the bottom open separate dialogs.

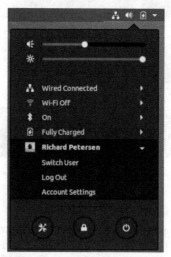

Figure 8-2: System Status Area menu

On systems that are not laptops, there will be no brightness slider or Battery entry on the System Status Area menu. If the system also has no wireless device, the Wi-Fi entry will also be missing. A·system of this kind will only have a sound slider and a user entry.

To log out, you click the current user entry to expand the menu to show Switch User, Log Out, and Account Settings entries. The Log Out returns you to the login screen, where you can log in as another user. To switch to another user, click the Switch User entry to display the login screen. You can then log in as another user. When you log out or choose Switch User, you can then select the original user. When you log back in, your session is restored.

Activities Overview

To access applications and windows, you use the Activities overview mode. Click the Activities button at the left side of the top bar (or move the mouse to the left corner, or press the super (Windows) button). The Activities overview mode consists of a dash listing your favorite and running applications, thumbnails of open windows, and workspace thumbnails (see Figure 8-3). You can use the search box at the top center to locate applications and files. Partially hidden thumbnails of your desktop workspaces are displayed on the right side. Initially, there are two. Moving your mouse to the right side displays the workspace thumbnails.

You can manually leave the Activities overview mode at any time by pressing the ESC key.

Figure 8-3: GNOME Activities Overview

Ubuntu Dock and GNOME Dash

The Ubuntu dock is a bar on the left side of the desktop with icons for your favorite applications (see Figure 8-4). The GNOME Dash is displayed on the Activities overview. The Ubuntu dock is a GNOME extension implemented by Ubuntu and is a modified version of the GNOME Dock to Dash extension, which places a GNOME dash on the desktop. Both the Ubuntu Dock and the GNOME Dash look the same and operate in the same way. Initially, there are icons for the Firefox web browser, Thunderbird mail, Files (the GNOME file manager), Rhythmbox music application, LibreOffice Writer, Ubuntu Software, GNOME help, a link to Amazon, and the Applications overview. To open an application from the dock, click its icon, or right-click and choose New Window from the pop-up menu. You can also click-and-drag the icon to the windows thumbnail area or to a workspace thumbnail on the right side.

Favorites are always displayed on the dock. When you run other applications, they are also placed on the dock during the time they are running. To add a running application to the dock as a favorite, right-click the icon and choose Add to Favorites. You can later remove an application as a favorite by choosing Remove from Favorites. You can also add any application to the dock from the Applications overview, by clicking-and-dragging its icon to the dock, or by right-clicking the icon and choosing Add to Favorites from the menu (see Figure 8-4).

Figure 8-4: Dock/Dash with favorites and running applications

You can configure the Ubuntu dock using the Settings Dock tab (see Figure 8-5). Here you can adjust the size of the icons, the location of the dock on the screen (left, right, bottom), and whether to hide the dock when not in use.

Figure 8-5: Dock Configuration on Settings

Window Thumbnails

You access windows using the window thumbnails on the Activities overview. Thumbnails are displayed of all your open windows (see Figure 8-6). To select a window, move your mouse over the window's thumbnail. The selected window also shows an x (close) button at the top right of the window's thumbnail, which you can use to close the window directly. To access the window, move your mouse over it and click. This displays the window, exiting the overview and returning to the desktop.

Figure 8-6: Window thumbnails

Moving your mouse to the right side of the screen displays the workspace selector showing workspace thumbnails, with the current workspace highlighted (see Figure 8-7). You can switch to another workspace by clicking its thumbnail. You can also move windows or applications directly to a workspace. If your mouse has a scroll wheel, you can press the Ctrl key and use the scroll wheel to move through workspaces, forward or backward.

Figure 8-7: Workspace thumbnails

Applications Overview

Clicking the Applications icon (last icon, grid button) on the dash opens the Applications overview, from which you can locate and open applications. Icons for installed applications are displayed (see Figure 8-8) . The Frequent button at the bottom of the overview lets you see only your most frequently used applications. Click the All button to see them all. A pager consisting of buttons, on the right side, lets you move quickly through the list of applications. You can move anywhere to a page in the list using the buttons. There are two special sub-folders: Utilities and Sundry. Clicking those icons opens another, smaller overview, showing applications in those categories, such as Tweak Tool and Backups in the Utilities overview. You can use the Ubuntu Software Installed tab to create your own sub-folders and place application icons in them (see Chapter 4). Click an application icon to open it and exit the overview. Should you return to the overview mode, you will see its window in the overview. The super key (Windows key) with the **a** key (super+a) will switch automatically from the desktop to the Applications overview. Continuing to press it, switches between the applications overview and the window thumbnails.

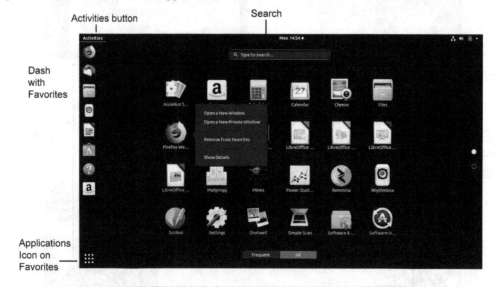

Activities Applications Overview

Figure 8-8: Applications overview

You can also open an application by dragging its icon to a workspace thumbnail on the right side, starting it in that workspace.

Also, as previously noted, to add an application as a favorite on the dash, you can simply drag its icon from the Applications overview to the dash directly.

Activities Search

The Activities search will search applications and files. Should you know the name of the application you want, you can simply start typing, and the matching results are displayed (see Figure 8-9). Your search term is entered in the search box as you type. The results dynamically narrow the more you type. The first application is selected automatically. If this is the one you want, just press ENTER to start it. Results will also show Settings tools and recently accessed files.

The search box for the Activities overview can be configured from the Settings Search tab (see Figure 8-10). Here, you can turn search on or off and specify which applications are to support searches. By default, these include Calendar, Ubuntu Software, the Files file manager, Passwords and Keys, the Firefox Web browser, and terminal.

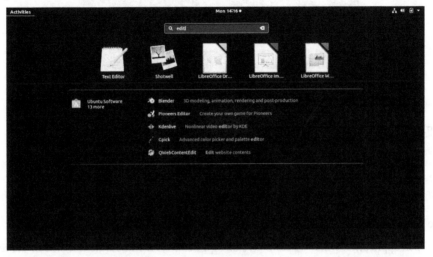

Figure 8-9: Activities - search box

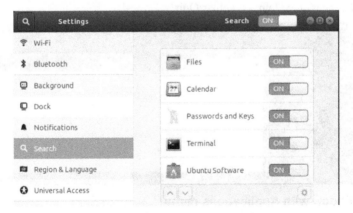

Figure 8-10: Activities - Search configuration

Managing Windows

The title bar and the toolbar for GNOME windows have been combined into a single header bar, as shown in the following for the file manager.

The minimize and maximize buttons have been dropped, and a single close button is always present. You can use Tweak Tool to add the minimize and maximize buttons if you wish. Some applications change the header bar if the function changes, presenting a different set of tools, as shown here for the GNOME Videos application (see Figure 8-11).

Figure 8-11: Windows header bar

Windows no longer have maximize and minimize buttons. These tasks can be carried out by a dragging operation or by double-clicking the header bar. To maximize a window, double-click its header bar or drag the header bar to the top edge of the screen. To minimize, drag the title away from the top edge of the screen. You can also use a window's menu entries to maximize or minimize it. Right-click the header bar or press Alt+spacebar to display the window menu.

Open application windows also have an Applications menu on the left side of the top bar. For many applications, this menu holds only a Quit entry (see Figure 8-12). Others, such as the file manager, list key tasks, such as Bookmarks, Preferences, and Help. The Firefox web browser only lists a Quit button, whereas the GNOME file manager lists items such as New Window, Bookmarks, Preferences, and Help, as well as Quit.

Figure 8-12: Window with Applications menu

To minimize an open window so that it no longer displays on the desktop, right-click the header bar and choose minimize. This will hide the window. You can then maximize the window later, using the window's thumbnails on the activities overview (Activities button).

To close a window, click its close box or choose Close from the Window menu. Many currently selected windows have an Applications menu in the top bar to the left. Should an application not have a close button, you can click the Applications menu button on the top bar and choose the Quit entry (see Figure 8-12).

To tile a window, click-and-drag its header bar to the left or right edge of the screen. When your mouse reaches the edge of the screen, the window is tiled to take up that half of the screen. You can do the same with another window for the other edge, showing two windows side by side.

To resize a window, move the mouse to the edge or corner until it changes to an edge or corner mouse, then click-and-drag.

The scrollbar to the right also features fine scrolling. When scrolling through a large number of items, you can fine scroll to slow the scrolling when you reach a point to search. To activate fine scrolling, click and hold the scrollbar handle, or press the Shift key while scrolling.

You can use the Window Switcher on the desktop to quickly search open windows. Press the Alt+Tab keys to display an icon bar of open windows on the current workspace (see Figure 8-13). While holding down the Alt key, press the Tab key to move through the list of windows. Windows are grouped by application. Instead of the Tab keys, you can use the forward and back arrow keys. For applications with multiple open windows, press the tilde (~) key (above the Tab key) to move through a list of the open windows.

Figure 8-13: Window Switcher (Alt+Tab)

On the GNOME Tweak Tool's Windows tab, you can configure certain windows' actions and components. Attached Modal Dialogs will attach a dialog that an application opens to the application's window (see Figure 8-14). You can use the switch to turn this feature off, allowing you to move a modal dialog away from the application window. Actions on the title bar (Titlebar Actions) are also defined, such as double-click to maximize and secondary-click to display the menu. There are also switches to display the Maximize and Minimize buttons on the title bar.

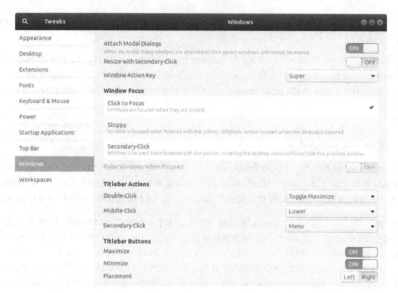

Figure 8-14: GNOME Tweak Tool - Windows (dialogs and title bar)

Workspaces

You can organize your windows into different workspaces. Workspaces are managed using the Workspace selector. In the overview, move your mouse to the right edge of the screen to display the workspace selector, a vertical panel showing thumbnails of your workspaces (see Figure 8-15). Workspaces are generated dynamically. The workspace selector will show an empty workspace as the last workspace (see Figure 8-16). To add a workspace, click-and-drag a window in the overview to the empty workspace on the workspace selector. A new empty workspace appears automatically below the current workspaces.

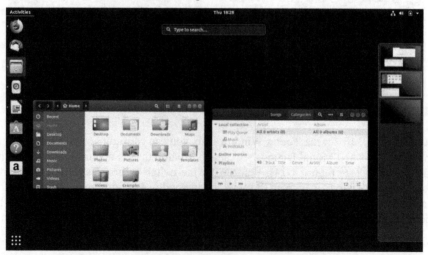

Figure 8-15: Workspace selector

Figure 8-16: Adding workspaces

To remove a workspace, close all its open windows, or move the windows to other workspaces.

To move to another workspace, in the overview mode, move to the right edge to display the workspace selector, then click on the workspace you want. You can also use Ctrl+Alt with the up and down arrow keys to move to the next or previous workspaces.

To move a window to a workspace, on the Windows overview, click-and-drag the window to the workspace selector (right edge) and then to the workspace you want. You can also use the Window menu and choose Move to Workspace Down or Move to Workspace Up. You can also use Ctrl+Alt+Shift and the up or down arrow keys to move the window to the next workspace. Continue pressing the arrow to move it further should you have several workspaces.

You can use the GNOME Tweak Tool's Workspaces tab to change workspace creation from dynamic to static, letting you specify a fixed number of workspaces (see Figure 8-17).

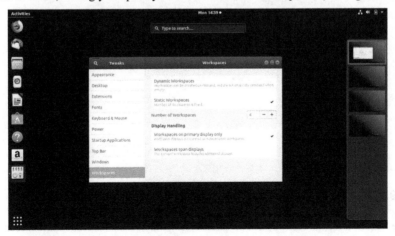

Figure 8-17: GNOME Tweak Tool - Workspaces tab

Notifications and Message dialog

Notifications, such as software updates and removable device activation, are displayed in the message area at the top of the screen (automatically hidden). When you have a notification, a message displaying the number of the message is displayed at the bottom center of the overview. Click on it to open the message tray and display your messages. You can also press the super key with the **m** key to open the message tray.

When you first attach a removable device such as a USB drive or DVD, a notification is displayed asking you what you want to do, such as open it with the file manager (see Figure 8-18).

Figure 8-18: Notifications

GNOME Customization with Tweak Tool: Themes, Icons, Fonts, Startup Applications, and Extensions

You can perform common desktop customizations using the GNOME Tweak Tool. Areas to customize include the desktop icons, fonts, themes, startup applications, workspaces, window behavior, and the time display. You can access Tweak Tool from the Applications overview | Utilities. The GNOME Tweak Tool has tabs for Appearance, Desktop, Extensions, Fonts, Keyboard and Mouse, Power, Startup Applications, Top Bar, Typing, Windows, and Workspaces (see Figure 8-19).

Figure 8-19: GNOME Tweak Tool - Appearance tab (themes)

The Appearance tab lets you set the theme for your windows, icons, and cursor. GNOME 3 uses the Adwaita Theme. This theme has a light and dark variant. The Global Light Theme is the default, but you can use the switch on the Appearance tab to enable the Global Dark Theme. The Global Dark Theme shades the background of windows to a dark gray, while text and button images appear in white.

You may also want to display Home, Trash, and Mounted Volumes like USB drives, on the desktop, as other desktops do. Use the Desktop tab on Tweak Tool to display these icons (see Figure 8-20). Turn on the "Icons on Desktop" switch. Home, Trash, and Mounted Volumes are checked by default. Uncheck an icon in order not to display it. You can also check a Network Servers option to display icons for remotely accessed folders.

Desktop fonts for window titles, interface (application or dialog text), documents, and monospace (terminal windows or code) can be changed in the Fonts tab. You can adjust the size of the font or change the font style. Clicking the font name opens a "Pick a Font" dialog from which you can choose a different font. The quality of text display can be further adjusted with Hinting and Antialiasing options. To simply increase or decrease the size of all fonts on your desktop interface, you can adjust the Scaling Factor.

At times, there may be certain applications that you want started up when you log in, such as the Gedit text editor, the Firefox web browser, or the Videos movie player. On the Startup Applications tab, you can choose the applications to start up. Click the plus (+) button to open an applications dialog from which you can choose an application to start up. Once added, you can later remove the application by clicking its Remove button.

Extensions function much as applets did in GNOME 2. They are third-party programs that enhance or modify the GNOME desktop, such as a window list, workspace indicator, a removable drive menu, and an applications menu. Extensions appear on the top bar or, in the case of the window list, in an added bottom bar. Installed extensions are listed on the Extensions tab of Tweak Tool, where you can turn them on or off.

Figure 8-20: GNOME Tweak Tool - Desktop tab (desktop icons)

GNOME Desktop Help

The GNOME Help browser provides a browser-like interface for displaying the GNOME Desktop Help and various GNOME applications, such as Brasero, Evince, and gedit (Utilities | Help) (see Figure 8-21) . It features a toolbar that enables you to move through the list of previously viewed documents. You can even bookmark specific items. You can search for topics using the search box, with results displayed in the drop-down menu. Initially, the Desktop Help manual is displayed. To see other help pages and manuals, choose All Help from the menu next to the close box (see Figure 8-22).

Figure 8-21: GNOME Help browser

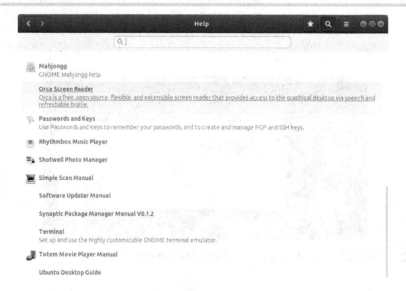

Figure 8-22: GNOME Help - All Documents

The GNOME Files File Manager

The GNOME file manager supports the standard features for copying, removing, and deleting items as well as setting permissions and displaying items. The name used for the file manager is Files, but the actual program name is still nautilus. When you select a file manager window, a Files menu appears as the Applications menu on the top bar to the left (see Figure 8-23). The Files menu has entries for opening a new file manager window, displaying the sidebar, the file manager preferences, displaying the file manager keyboard shorcuts, and help (see Table 8-2).

Figure 8-23: File manager with Files applications menu

Menu Item	Description
New Window	Open a new file manager window
Sidebar	Toggle display of the file manager sidebar
Preferences	Open the file manager Preferences dialog
Keyboard Shortcuts	Display a dialog listing keyboard shortcuts
Help	Open GNOME desktop help
About	Current GNOME release
Quit	Close the file manager

Table 8-2: File Manager GNOME Menu

Home Folder Subfolders

GNOME uses the Common User Directory Structure (xdg-user-dirs at **http://freedesktop.org**) to set up subfolders in the user home directory. Folders include Documents, Music, Pictures, Downloads, and Videos. These localized user folders are used as defaults by many desktop applications. Users can change their folder names or place them within each other using the GNOME file browser. For example, Music can be moved into Videos or Documents into Pictures. Local configuration is held in the **.config/user-dirs.dirs** file. System-wide defaults are set up in the **/etc/xdg/user-dirs.defaults** file. You can edit the local configuration using a text editor and change the directories for the current ones.

File Manager Windows

When you click the Files icon on the dock, a file manager window opens showing your home folder. The file manager window displays several components, including a toolbar and a sidebar (see Figure 8-24). The sidebar displays sections for folder, device, bookmark, and network items showing your file systems and default home folder subfolders. You can choose to display or hide the sidebar toolbar by selecting its entry in the View and Tools menu. The main pane (to the right) displays the icons or lists files and subfolders in the current working folder. When you select a file and folder, a status section at the bottom right of the window displays the number or name of the file or folder selected and the total size.

When you open a new folder, the same window is used to display it, and you can use the forward and back arrows to move through previously opened folders (top left). As you open subfolders, the main toolbar displays buttons for your current folder and its parent folders, as shown here:

You can click a folder button to move to it directly. It also can display a location URL text box instead of buttons, from which you can enter the location of a folder, either on your system or on a remote one. Press Ctrl+l to display the text box. Press the ESC key to revert back to the folder location buttons.

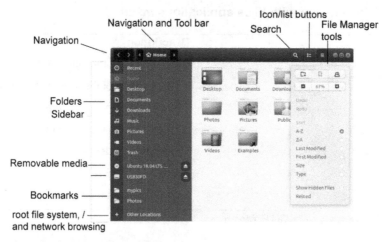

Figure 8-24: File manager with sidebar

You can click anywhere on the empty space on the main pane of a file manager window to display a pop-up menu with entries to create a new folder, open the current folder in a terminal window with a command line prompt, and open the file manager properties dialog (see Table 8-3).

When you create a folder, a New Folder dialog is displayed with a text box where you enter the name of the new folder (see Figure 8-25).

Figure 8-25: File manager New Folder

Menu Item	Description
New Folder	Creates a new subfolder in the current folder
Paste	Pastes files that you have copied or cut, letting you move or copy files between folders, or make duplicates
Select All	Select all files and folders in the current folder
Properties	Opens the Properties dialog for the directory
Open in Terminal	Open a terminal window at the current folder

Table 8-3: File Manager Pop-up Menu

File Manager Sidebar

The file manager sidebar shows file system locations that you would normally access: folders, devices, bookmarks, and network folders (See Figure 8-26) . Selecting the Computer entry places you at the top of the file system, letting you move to any accessible part of it. The Recent folder holds links to your recently used files. Should you bookmark a folder (Tools | Bookmark This Location), the bookmarks will appear on the sidebar. To remove or rename a bookmark, right-click its entry on the sidebar and choose Remove or Rename from the pop-up menu. The bookmark's name changes, but not the original folder name.

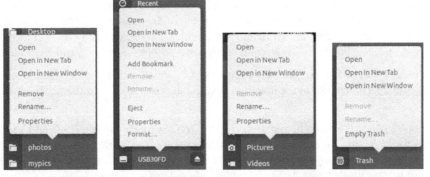

Figure 8-26: File manager sidebar with menus for bookmarks, devices, folders, and trash

Tabs

The GNOME file manager supports tabs with which you can open several folders in the same file manager window. To open a tab, select New Tab from the Tools menu (see Figure 8-24) or press Ctrl+t. You can use the Tabs buttons to move from one tab to another, or to rearrange tabs. You can also use the Ctrl+PageUp and Ctrl+PageDown keys to move from one tab to another. Use the Shift+Ctrl+PageUp and Shift+Ctrl+PageDown keys to rearrange the tabs. To close a tab, click its close (x) button on the right side of the tab (see Figure 8-27), or press Ctrl+w. Tabs are detachable. You can drag a tab out to a separate window.

Figure 8-27: File manager window with tabs

Displaying and Managing Files and Folders

You can view a folder's contents as icons or as a detailed list, which you can choose by clicking the icon/list button between the search and menu buttons on the right side of the toolbar as shown here. This button toggles between icon and list views.

Use the Ctrl key to change views quickly: Ctrl+1 for Icons and Ctrl+2 for list (there is no longer a Compact view). The List view provides the name, permissions, size, date, owner, and group. Buttons are displayed for each field across the top of the main pane. You can use these buttons to sort the list according to that field. For example, to sort the files by date, click the Date button; to sort by size, click Size. Click again to alternate between ascending and descending order.

Certain types of file icons display previews of their contents. For example, the icons for image files display a thumbnail of the image. A text file displays in its icon the first few words of its text.

You can click the menu button at the right of toolbar to display the Tools and View menu with entries for managing and sorting your file manager icons (see Table 8-4). The sort entries allow you to sort your icons by name (A-Z and Z-A), size, type, modification date, and access date. You can also reverse the order by name and modification date (see Figure 8-28).

At the top of the menu is a zoom bar, with zoom in and zoom out buttons, showing the zoom percentage between them. The zoom in button (+ button) enlarges your view of the window, making icons bigger. The zoom out button (- button) reduces your view, making them smaller. You can also use the Ctrl++ and Ctrl+- keys to zoom in and out.

You can also bookmark the folder, create a new folder, create a new tab, and close the file manager window. The top bar of the view menu has buttons to create a new folder, create a bookmark for the current folder, and create a new file manager tab.

Menu Item	Description
New Folder button	Creates a new subfolder in the current folder
Bookmark button	Creates bookmark for current folder
Tab button	Creates a new tab
Zoom In button	Enlarge icon size
Zoom Out button	Reduce icon size
Undo	Undo the previous operation
Redo	Redo an undo operation
A-Z	Sort in alphabetic order
Z-A	Sort in reverse alphabetic order
Last Modified	Sort by last modified date
First Modified	Sort by recent modified date
Size	Sort by file size
Type	Sort by file type
Show Hidden Files	Shows administrative dot files
Reload	Refreshes file and directory list

Table 8-4: File Manager Tools and View Menu

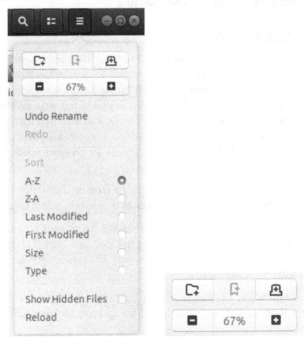

Figure 8-28: File manager View and Tools menu

Menu Item	Description
Open	Opens the file with its associated application. Directories are opened in the file manager. Associated applications are listed.
Open in New Tab	Opens a folder in a new tab in the same window
Open in New Window	Opens a folder in a new file manager window
Open With Other Application	Selects an application with which to open this file. An Open With dialog lists the possible applications
Cut Copy	Cuts or copies the selected file
Copy To	Copies a file to the Home folder, desktop, or to a folder displayed in another pane in the file manager window
Move To	Moves a file to the Home folder, desktop, or to a folder displayed in another pane in the file manager window
Rename (F2)	Renames the file
Move To Trash	Moves a file to the Trash directory, where you can later delete it
Send to	E-mails the file
Compress	Archives the file using File Roller
Properties	Displays the Properties dialog
Open in Terminal	Open a folder in a terminal window

Table 8-5: The File and Folder Pop-up Menu

Navigating in the File Manager

The file manager operates similarly to a web browser, using the same window to display opened folders. It maintains a list of previously viewed folders, and you can move back and forth through that list using the toolbar buttons. The left arrow button moves you to the previously displayed directory, and the right arrow button moves you to the next displayed directory. Use the sidebar to access your storage devices (USB, DVD/CD, and attached hard drives). From the sidebar, you can also access mounted network folders. You can also access your home folders, trash, and recent files. As noted, the Computer entry on the Devices section opens your root (top) system directory.

To open a subfolder, you can double-click its icon or right-click the icon and select Open from the menu (see Table 8-5). To open the folder in a new tab, select Open in New Tab.

You can open any folder or file system listed in the sidebar by clicking it. You can also right-click an entry to display a menu with entries to Open in a New Tab and Open in a New Window (see Table 8-6). The menu for the Trash entry lets you empty the trash. You can also remove and rename the bookmarks.

Entries for removable devices in the sidebar, such as USB drives, also have menu items for Eject and Safely Remove Drive. Internal hard drives have an Unmount option instead.

Menu Item	Description
Open	Opens the file with its associated application. Folders are opened in the file manager. Associated applications are listed.
Open in a New Tab	Opens a folder in a new tab in the same window
Open in a New Window	Opens a folder in a separate window, accessible from the toolbar with a right-click
Remove	Removes the bookmark from the sidebar
Rename	Renames the bookmark

Table 8-6: The File Manager Sidebar Pop-up Menu

Managing Files and Folders

As a GNOME-compliant file manager, Files supports desktop drag-and-drop operations for copying and moving files. To move a file or directory, drag-and-drop from one directory to another. The move operation is the default drag-and-drop operation in GNOME. To copy a file to a new location, press the Ctrl key as you drag-and-drop.

You can also perform remove, rename, and link-creation operations on a file by right-clicking its icon and selecting the action you want from the pop-up menu that appears (see Table 8-5). For example, to remove an item, right-click it and select the Move To Trash entry from the pop-up menu. This places it in the Trash directory, where you can later delete it. To create a link, right-click the file and select Make Link from the pop-up menu. This creates a new link file that begins with the term "Link."

Renaming Files

To rename a file, you can either right-click the file's icon and select the Rename entry from the pop-up menu or click its icon and press the F2 function key. A dialog is displayed with the current name in a small text box (see Figure 8-29). You can overwrite the old one or edit the current name by clicking a position in the name to insert text, as well as by using the Backspace key to delete characters. When renaming a file, be sure to click the Rename button once you have entered the new name. You can also rename a file by entering a new name in its Properties dialog box (Basic tab).

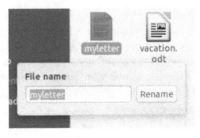

Figure 8-29: File manager Rename dialog

You can also change several filenames at once by selecting the files and then right-clicking and choosing Rename. A dialog opens listing the selected files and a text box for specifying the new names (see Figure 8-30). You can add to the name or choose the "Find and replace" option to change a common part of the names. Clicking the Add button lets you choose from a list of possible automatic number formats to add. The added characters are encased in brackets in the text box, separated by commas, one for each file name. The Original File Name entry add the original file name specifier to the text box, should you remove it.

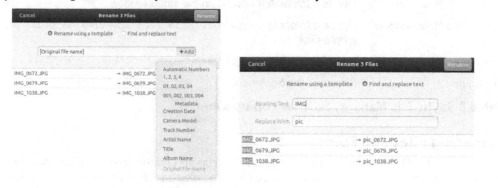

Figure 8-30: File manager - Renaming several files at once

Compress and Archive Files

You can also compress and archive files and folders (see Figure 8-31). Select the files or folders to compress and archive, right-click and choose the Compress option. A Create Archive dialog opens where you can specify the name of the compressed archive and the archive format. Choose the format of the archive from the list below the name (zip, tar, and 7z).

Figure 8-31: File manager - Compress and Archive dialogs

Copying Files

To copy a file to a new location, press the Ctrl key as you drag-and-drop. When copying a large file or many of files, an icon is displayed on the titlebar to the right showing a circle chart and the progress of the copy operation (see Figure 8-32). Clicking on the icon displays a menu showing the progress of the copy operation, with an x to the right you can click to cancel the copy, as shown here. When the copy process for a file is completed, the x becomes a checkmark. When the entire copy process is completed for all files, the icon shows a fully dark circle.

Figure 8-32: File manager - Copying files

Grouping Files

You can select a group of files and folders by clicking the first item and then holding down the Shift key while clicking the last item, or by clicking and dragging the mouse across items you want to select. To select separated items, hold the Ctrl key down as you click the individual icons. If you want to select all the items in the directory, choose the Select All entry from the Tools menu (Tools | Select All), or choose Ctrl+a. You can then copy, move, or delete several files at once. To select items that have a certain pattern in their name, choose Select Items Matching from the Tools menu to open a search box from which you can enter the pattern (Ctrl+s). Use the asterisk (*) character to match partial patterns, as in ***let*** to match on all filenames with the pattern let in them. The pattern **my*** would match filenames beginning with the **my** pattern, and ***.png** would match on all PNG image files (the period indicates a filename extension).

Opening Applications and Files MIME Types

You can start any application in the file manager by double-clicking either the application or a data file used for that application. If you want to open the file with a specific application, you can right-click the file and select one of the Open With entries. One or more Open With entries will be displayed for default and possible application, such as Open With gedit for a text file. If the application you want is not listed, you can select Open With | Other Application to access a list of available applications. Drag-and-drop operations are also supported for applications. You can drag a data file to its associated application icon (say, on the desktop) The application then starts up using that data file.

To change or set the default application to use for a certain type of file, you open a file's Properties dialog and select the Open With tab. Here, you can choose the default application to use for that kind of file. Possible applications will be listed, organized as the default, recommended, related, and other categories. Click the one you want, and click the Set As Default button. Once you choose the default, it will appear in the Open With list for this file.

If you want to add an application to the Open With menu, click the Other Applications entry to list possible applications. Select the one you want, and click the Add button. If there is an application on the Open With tab that you do not want listed in the Open With menu items, right-click it and choose Forget Association.

File and Directory Properties

In a file's Properties dialog, you can view detailed information on a file and set options and permissions (see Figure 8-33) . A file's Properties dialog has three tabs: Basic, Permissions, and Open With. Folders will have an additional Local Network Share tab, instead of an Open With tab. The Basic tab shows detailed information, such as type, size, location, accessed, and date modified. The type is a MIME type, indicating the type of application associated with it. The file's icon is displayed at the top, with a text box showing the file's name. You can edit the filename in the Name text box. If you want to change the icon image used for the file or folder, click the icon image (next to the name) to open a Select Custom Icon dialog and browse for the one you want. The **/usr/share/pixmaps** directory holds the set of current default images, although you can select your own images (click the Computer entry to locate the **pixmaps** folder). In the **pixmaps** folder, click an image file to see its icon displayed in the right pane. Double-click to change the icon image.

The Permissions tab for files shows the read, write, and execute permissions for owner, group, and others, as set for this file. You can change any of the permissions here, provided the file belongs to you. You configure access for the owner, the group, and others, using drop-down menus. You can set owner permissions as Read Only or Read and Write. For group and others, you can also set the None option, denying access. Clicking the group name displays a menu listing different groups, allowing you to select one to change the file's group. If you want to execute this as an application, you check the "Allow executing file as program" entry. This has the effect of setting the execute permission.

The Open With tab for files lists all the applications associated with this kind of file. You can select the one you want to use as the default. This can be particularly useful for media files, for which you may prefer a specific player for a certain file or a particular image viewer for pictures.

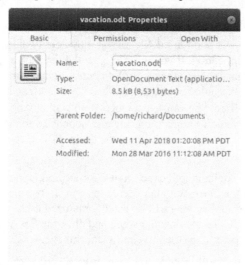

Figure 8-33: File properties

Certain kind of files will have additional tabs, providing information about the file. For example, an audio file will have an Audio tab listing the type of audio file and any other information, such as a song title or the compression method used. An image file will have an Image tab listing the resolution and type of image. A video file will contain an Audio/Video tab showing the type of video file, along with compression and resolution information.

The Permissions tab for folders operates much the same way, with Access menus for Owner, Group, and Others . The Access menu controls access to the folder with options for None, List Files Only, Access Files, and Create and Delete Files. These correspond to the read and execute permissions given to directories. To set the permissions for all the files in the folder accordingly (not just the folder), click the "Change Permissions for Enclosed Files" button to open a dialog where you can specify the owner, group, and others permissions for files and folders in the folder.

File Manager Preferences

You can set preferences for your file manager in the Preferences dialog, accessible by selecting the Preferences item in any file manager window's application menu (Files | Preferences).

The Views tab allows you to select how files are displayed by default, such as a list or icon view. You also can set default zoom levels for icon and list views.

Behavior lets you choose how to select files, manage the trash, and handle scripts.

Display lets you choose what information you want displayed in an icon caption, such as the size or date. You can also choose to have the list view display an expandable tree, showing files and subfolders within and expanded folder.

The List Columns tab lets you choose both the features to display in the detailed list and the order in which to display them. In addition to the already-selected name, size, date, and type, you can add permissions, group, MIME type, location, accessed, and owner.

The Preview tab lets you choose whether you want small thumbnail content displayed in the icons, such as the beginning text for text files.

File Manager Search

Two primary search tools are available for your GNOME desktop: the GNOME dash search and the GNOME file manager search. With GNOME file manager, you enter a pattern to search. You can further refine your search by specifying dates and file types. Click the Search button (looking glass icon) on the toolbar to open a Search box. Enter the pattern to search, then press Enter. The results are displayed (see Figure 8-34). Click the menu button to the right to add file-type (What) and date (When) search parameters, or to search file text or just the file name. Selecting the When entry opens a dialog where you can specify the recency of the document's last use or modification, by day, week, month, or year. A calendar button to the right of the text box for the date opens a calendar to let you choose a specific date. The What entry displays a menu with different file categories such as music, Documents, folders, picture, and PDF.

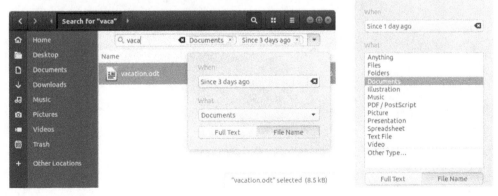

Figure 8-34: GNOME file manager search

kubuntu

9. Kubuntu (KDE Plasma)

The KDE Plasma Desktop

Kickoff Menu and Applications Dashboard

Plasma

Plasmoids (Widgets)

Activities

Desktop Effects

KDE File Manager: Dolphin

Discover Package Manager

KDE System Settings

Plasma is the desktop developed and distributed by KDE (the K Desktop Environment. It is often referred to as simply the KDE desktop. Plasma includes the standard desktop features, such as a window manager and a file manager, as well as an extensive set of applications that cover most Linux tasks. The KDE Plasma version of Ubuntu is called Kubuntu and is available as a separate Desktop DVD, and as the **kubuntu-desktop** meta-package on the Synaptic Package Manager. The KDE Plasma desktop is developed and distributed by the KDE Project. KDE is open source software provided under a GNU Public License and is available free of charge along with its source code. KDE development is managed by the KDE Core Team.

The KDE software development and distribution is organized into three projects: Plasma, Applications, and Frameworks. KDE Applications include numerous applications written specifically for KDE Plasma are accessible from the desktop. These include editors, photo and image applications, sound and video players, and office applications. Some applications have the letter *K* as part of their name, for example, KOrganizer. On a system administration level, KDE provides several tools for managing your system, such as the Discover Software Manager, and the KDE system monitor. KDE applications also feature a built-in Help application. See **https://www.kde.org/applications/** for a list and descriptions of current applications.

KDE Frameworks provides support libraries designed to work with the Qt libraries that KDE Plasma and Applications depend on. Frameworks is designed to be cross-platform, enabling any KDE Application to run on systems that support the Qt libraries. Frameworks can be used as a basis for any custom operating system, such as LXDE. KDE Framework packages have the prefix **kf5**, such as the **kf5-filesystem** that provides support for the KDE filesystem. Development for Plasma, Frameworks, and Applications proceed at different paces. The KDE Frameworks version used in Fedora 28 Plasma Desktop is 5.46.0, whereas the KDE Plasma version is 5.12.5.

Web Site	Description
`https://www.kde.org`	KDE website
`http://www.kubuntu.org`	Kubuntu site
`https://www.kde.org/applications/`	KDE Applications website
`https://www.qt.io/`	Site for the Qt company
`https://store.kde.org`	KDE desktop themes
`https://mail.kde.org/mailman/listinfo/`	KDE mailing lists
`https://www.kde.org/plasma-desktop`	KDE Plasma desktop website
`https://docs.kde.org`	KDE documentation site

Table 9-1: KDE Web Sites

KDE, initiated by Matthias Ettrich in October 1996, is designed to run on any Unix implementation, including Linux, Solaris, HP-UX, and FreeBSD. The official KDE website is **https://www.kde.org**, which provides news updates, download links, and documentation. Detailed documentation for the KDE desktop and its applications is available at **https://docs.kde.org**. Several KDE mailing lists are available for users and developers, including announcements, administration, and other topics. Development support and documentation can be obtained at the KDE Techbase site at **http://techbase.kde.org**. Most applications are available on the Ubuntu repositories and can be installed directly from Discover Software and the Synaptic Package

Manager. Various KDE websites are listed in Table 9-1. KDE uses as its library of GUI tools the Qt library, currently developed and supported by the QT company, owned by Digia (**https://www.qt.io**). It provides the Qt libraries as Open Source software that is freely distributable, though a commercial license is also available.

KDE Plasma 5 and Kubuntu 18.04

The KDE Plasma 5 release is a major reworking of the KDE desktop. KDE Plasma 5.5 is included with the Kubuntu 18.04 distribution. Check the Kubuntu and KDE sites for detailed information on KDE 5.

```
https://www.kde.org/announcements/plasma5.0/
```

For features added with KDE Plasma 5.12, check:

```
https://www.kde.org/announcements/plasma-5.12.0.php
```

KDE development is organized into a plasma, frameworks, and applications releases. The plasma release covers the desktop interface (the Plasma desktop shell), and the applications release covers KDE applications. Plasma has containments and plasmoids (also called widgets). Plasmoids operate similar to applets, small applications running on the desktop or panel. Plasmoids operate within containments. On KDE 5, there are two Plasma containments, the panel and the desktop. In this sense, the desktop and the panel are features of an underlying Plasma operation. They are not separate programs. Each has their own set of plasmoids.

Each containment has a toolbox for configuration. The desktop has a toolbox at the top left corner, and panels will have a toolbox on the right side. The panel toolbox includes configuration tools for sizing and positioning the panel. Kubuntu also supports Activities, multiple plasma desktop containments, each with their own set of active plasmoids (widgets) and open windows.

The Kubuntu edition of Ubuntu installs KDE as the primary desktop from the Kubuntu install disc. Kubuntu 18.04 officially supports and installs KDE Plasma 5.12. The latest features included with Kubuntu 18.04 are discussed at:

```
https://kubuntu.org/news/kubuntu-18-04-has-been-released/
```

Kubuntu 18.04 also uses KDE Applications 5.12, check:

```
https://www.kde.org/announcements/announce-applications-15.12.0.php
```

Installing Kubuntu

You can download the Kubuntu Desktop discs from the Kubuntu site at:

```
http://www.kubuntu.org/
```

You can obtain the ISO image for Kubuntu from:

```
https://kubuntu.org/getkubuntu/
```

You can also add Kubuntu as a desktop to an Ubuntu desktop installation. KDE includes numerous packages. Instead of trying to install each one, you should install KDE using its meta packages on the Synaptic Package Manager, **kubuntu-desktop**.

You will be prompted to keep the GDM display manager for logins, though you can change to SDDM, the Simple Desktop Display Manager. Once installed, KDE will then become an option you can select from the Sessions menu on the Login screen as "Plasma."

If you are installing Kubuntu from the Kubuntu DVD, you will follow the same steps as those used for the Ubuntu Desktop DVD: language, keyboard, partition (Disk Setup), time zone, user and host name (User Info). Installation will begin as soon as you choose the partition configuration. The artwork will be different, but the tasks will be the same. The "Installation type" screen (partitioning) shows lets you choose a default general, LVM, disk encryption, or manual partitioning.

The initial install screen has options for Start Kubuntu, Check disc for defects, Test memory, and boot from first hard disk. Function keys provide options for help, language, keymap, modes, accessibility, and other options. The modes menu allows the use of a driver update disk or an OEM install. The "Other Options" menu displays the boot options, one of which is "Free software only," which installs open source software only. When you start up Kubuntu, you are given the options to try Kubuntu or install it. The Try option starts up the Kubuntu Live DVD/USB.

With an EUFI boot, three options are listed: Start Kubuntu, Install for manufacturers, and Check disk for errors. Once started you are then given the option to try Kubuntu or to install it.

Note: Kubuntu has its own restricted packages, kubuntu-restricted-extras and kubuntu-restricted-addons, for multimedia codecs.

SDDM

KDE Fedora Linux uses the Simple Desktop Display Manager (SDDM) to manage logins. A login greeter is displayed at the center of the screen where you can select a user icon and enter a password (see Figure 9-1). Suspend, Restart, Shutdown, and Different User buttons are displayed below the login button. Use the Different User button to login as a user not displayed in the user list.

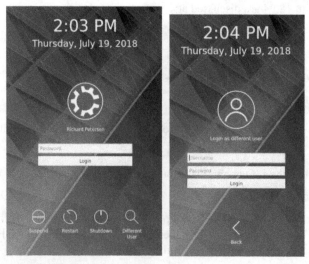

Figure 9-1: SDDM Display Manager, login screen

Upon choosing a user icon and entering the password, press ENTER or clicking the login button at the right end of the password text box. Your KDE session then starts up.

If you have more than one desktop installed on your system, such as Cinnamon, Mate, or Xfce, then a "Plasma" menu item is displayed as one of the alternatives. Use this menu to choose a different desktop to log into. The KDE desktop is called Plasma.

You can change the theme of the login greeter using the Login Screen (SDDM) tab in the Startup and Shutdown dialog (GNOME Settings | Startup and Shutdown in the Workspace section). The theme section lists available theme. Currently, only Breeze is listed. To change the background image, click on a theme to display it in the Customize section to the right. Then click on the Background icon and choose the "Load from file" option from the pop-up menu. On the Advanced tab, you can choose the default user, the desktop for your session, and whether to automatically log in. You can also choose a cursor theme and an alternative desktop (session). You can also manually configure SDDM using the **/etc/sddm.conf** file.

The Plasma Desktop

One of KDE's aims is to provide users with a consistent integrated desktop (see Figure 9-2). Plasma provides its own window manager (KWM), file manager (Dolphin), program manager, and desktop and panel (Plasma). You can run any other X Window System–compliant application, such as Firefox, in Plasma, as well as any GNOME application.

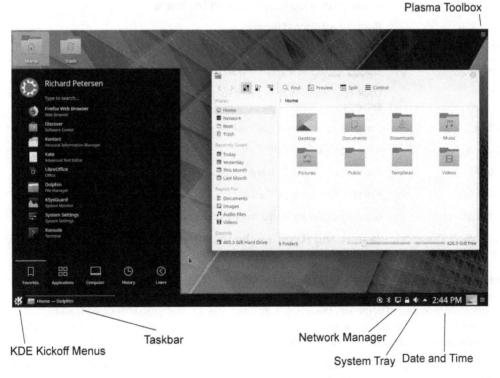

Figure 9-2: The KDE desktop

In turn, you can also run any KDE application, including the Dolphin file manager in GNOME. The Plasma 5 desktop features the Plasma desktop shell with new panel, menu, widgets, and activities. Keyboard shortcuts are provided for many desktop operations, as well as plasmoid (widget) tasks (see Table 9-2).

Keys	Description
Alt-F1	Kickoff menu
Alt-F2	Krunner, command execution, entry can be any search string for a relevant operation, including bookmarks and contacts, not just applications.
up/down arrows	Move among entries in menus, including Kickoff and menus
left/right arrows	Move to submenus menus, including Kickoff and Quick Access submenus menus
ENTER	Select a menu entry, including a Kickoff or QuickAccess
PageUp, PageDown	Scroll up fast
Alt-F4	Close current window
Alt-F3	Window menu for current window
Ctrl-Alt -F6	Command Line Interface
Ctrl-Alt -F8	Return to desktop from command line interface
Ctrl-r	Remove a selected widget
Ctrl-s	Open a selected widget configuration's settings
Ctrl-a	Open the Add Widgets window to add a widget to the desktop
Ctrl-l	Lock your widgets to prevent removal, adding new ones or changing settings
Alt-Tab	Cover Switch or Box Switch for open windows
Ctrl-F8	Desktop Grid
Ctrl-F9	Present Windows Current Desktop
Ctrl-F10	Present Windows All Desktops
Ctrl-F11	Desktop Cube for switching desktops

Table 9-2: Desktop, Plasma, and KWin Keyboard Shortcuts

To configure your desktop, you use the System Settings dialog (Computer| System Settings), which lists icons for dialogs such as Workspace Theme, Font, Icons, Applications Style Desktop Behavior, Search, Application Style, Window Management, Driver Manager, and Bluetooth. Workspace Theme lets you choose desktop, cursor, and splash themes. Desktop Behavior is where you can set desktop effects and virtual desktops. Windows Management controls window display features like window switchers, title bar actions, and screen edge actions.

The desktop supports drag-and-drop and copy-and-paste operations. With the copy-and-paste operation, you can copy text from one application to another. You can even copy and paste from a Konsole terminal window.

The KDE Help Center

The KDE Help Center provides a browser-like interface for accessing and displaying both KDE Help files and Linux Man and info files (see Figure 9-3). It may not be installed by default. Install the **khelpcenter** package. The same documentation is available at **https://docs.kde.org**. You can start the Help Center by searching for "help" in the search box of the Kickoff Applications menu. The Help window displays a sidebar that holds two tabs, one listing contents and one providing a glossary. The main pane displays currently selected document. A help tree on the contents tab in the sidebar lets you choose the kind of Help documents you want to access. Here you can choose KDE manuals, Man pages (UNIX manual pages), or info documents (Browse info Pages), or even application manuals (Application Manuals). Online Help provides links to KDE websites such as the KDE user forum and the KDE tech base sites. Click the "Table of Contents" button to open a listing of all KDE help documents, which you can browse through and click on to open.

A navigation toolbar enables you to move through previously viewed documents. KDE Help documents contain links you can click to access other documents. The Back and Forward buttons move you through the list of previously viewed documents. The KDE Help system provides an effective search tool for searching for patterns in Help documents, including Man and info pages. Click the Find button on the toolbar or choose the Find entry from the Edit menu, to open a search box at the bottom of the Help window where you can enter a pattern to search on the current open help document. The Options menu lets you refine your search with regular expressions, case sensitive queries, and whole words-only matches.

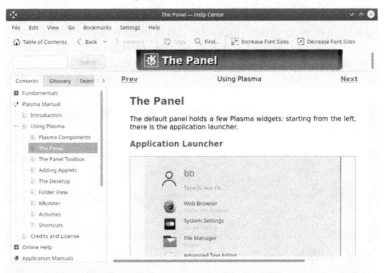

Figure 9-3: KDE Help Center

Desktop Backgrounds (Wallpaper)

The background (wallpaper) is set from the desktop menu directly. Right-click on the desktop to display the desktop menu and then select Configure Desktop to open the Desktop Settings dialog (see Figure 9-4).

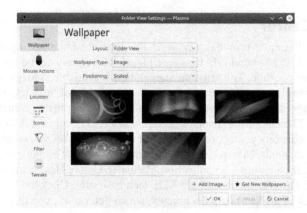

Figure 9-4: Default Desktop Settings, wallpaper

You can also select Desktop Settings from the activities menu in the upper left corner of the desktop. The background is called wallpaper in KDE and can be changed in the Wallpaper tab. You can select other wallpapers from the wallpaper icons listed or select your own image by clicking the Open button.

You can add more wallpaper by clicking the "Get New Wallpaper" button to open a "Get Hot New Stuff" dialog, which lists and downloads wallpaper posted on the **https://store.kde.org** site (see Figure 9-5). Each wallpaper entry shows an image, description, and rating. Buttons at the upper right of the dialog let you view the entries in details (list) or icon mode. You can refine the wallpaper listing by size (category), newest, rating, and popularity (most downloads). Click the Install button to download the wallpaper and add it to your Desktop Setting's Wallpaper tab. The wallpaper is downloaded and the Install button changes to Uninstall. To remove a wallpaper, you can select installed wallpapers to find the entry quickly. You can also search by pattern for a wallpaper.

Figure 9-5: Default Desktop Settings, Get New Wallpapers

Themes

For your desktop, you can also select a variety of different themes, icons, and window decorations. A theme changes the entire look and feel of your desktop, affecting the appearance of desktop elements, such as scrollbars, buttons, and icons. Themes and window decorations are provided for workspaces. Access the System Settings dialog from the KDE Kickoff Computer menu or the Applications | Settings menu. On the System Settings dialog, click the Workspace Theme icon in the "Appearance" section. The Workspace Theme dialog lets you choose overall look and feel, cursor themes, desktop themes, and a splash screen (startup) themes. The Desktop Themes tab lists installed themes, letting you choose the one you want. Click the Get New Themes button to open a Get Hot New Stuff dialog, listing desktop themes from **https://store.kde.org** (see Figure 9-6). Click a theme's Install button to download and install the theme.

For window decorations, you use the Application Style dialog, Window Decorations tab, where you can select window decoration themes. Click the Get New Decorations button to download new decorations. Icons styles are chosen using the Icons dialog, Icons tab, where you can choose the icon set to use, and even download new sets (Get New Themes).

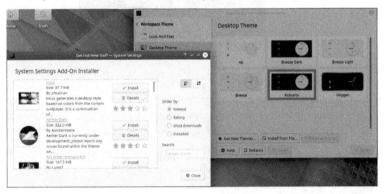

Figure 9-6: System Settings | Workspace Theme | Desktop Theme, Get New Themes

Leave KDE

To leave KDE, click the Leave tab on the KDE Kickoff menu (see Figure 9-7). Here you will find options to log out, lock, switch user, suspend, shutdown, and restart. There are Session and System sections. The Session section has entries for Logout, Lock, and Switch User. The System section lists the system-wide operations: Shut Down, Reboot, Hibernate, and Suspend. When you select a leave entry, a dialog for that action appears on the desktop, which you then click. The Shut Down entry will display the Shutdown and Logout dialog with the Shutdown button selected (see Figure 9-8). The Logout option displays the same dialog with the Logout button selected. The Switch User option displays a dialog with the currently logged in users to choose from, along with a plus button for a new login.

Figure 9-7: The Kickoff Menu Leave

The Lock, and Switch User display manager (SSDM) screens display both a button for the current user and a plus button for starting a new session (Switch User shows the icon for the user you selected). The new session button displays the login screen with its list of users to log in as.

If you logout and more than one user is logged in from a previous Switch User operation, then the Log Out display manager screen will show a logged in user button and a plus button. Use the plus button to display the main login screen.

Figure 9-8: Shutdown and Logout dialog

If you have installed the Application Dashboard widget, you can click the logout, shutdown, and restart button on the lower left. For a complete selection choose the Power/Session category on the right (see Figure 9-9).

Figure 9-9: The Application Dashboard Menu Power/Session

You can also right-click anywhere on the desktop and select the Leave entry from the pop-up menu, to open a leave dialog with the Logout button selected, as shown here. Buttons to the left let you choose between the suspend, reboot, and shutdown operations.

If you just want to lock your desktop, you can select the Lock Screen entry (Lock on the Kickoff and Application Dashboard menus), and your screen saver will appear. To access a locked desktop, click on the screen and a box appears prompting you for your login password. When you enter the password, your desktop re-appears.

KDE Kickoff menus

The Kickoff application Dock (see Figure 9-10) organizes menu entries into tabs that are accessed by icons at the bottom of the Kickoff menu. There are tabs for Favorites, Applications, Computer, History, and Leave. You can add an application to the Favorites tab by right-clicking on the application's Kickoff entry and selecting Add to Favorites. To remove an application from the Favorites menu, right-click on it and select Remove from Favorites. The Applications tab shows application categories. Click the Computer tab to list all your fixed and removable storage. The History tab shows previously accessed documents and applications. Kickoff also provides a Search box where you can search for a particular application instead of paging through menus. As you move through sub-tabs, they are listed at the top of the Kickoff menu, below the search box, allowing you to move back to a previous tab quickly. Click on a tab name to move directly to that tab.

Figure 9-10: The Kickoff Menu Favorites

The Computer menu has Applications, Places, and Removable Storage sections (see Figure 9-11). The Applications section has an entry for System Settings and Run Command (Krunner). The Places section is similar to the Places menu in GNOME, with entries for your home folder, root folder, network, and the trash. The root folder is the same as the system folder on GNOME, the top level directory in the Linux file system. The Removable Storage section shows removable devices like USB drives and DVD/CD discs.

Figure 9-11: The Kickoff Menu Computer

The Applications menu has most of the same entries as those found on GNOME (see Figure 9-12). You can find entries for categories such as Internet, Graphics, and Office. These menus list both GNOME and KDE applications you can use. However, some of the KDE menus contain entries for alternate KDE applications, like KMail on the Internet menu. Other entries will invoke the KDE version of a tool, like the Terminal entry in the System menu, which will invoke the KDE terminal window, Konsole. There is no Preferences menu.

Figure 9-12: The Kickoff Menu Applications

KDE Application Dashboard menus

You can install the Application Dashboard as a desktop or panel widget. The Applications Dashboard menu launcher displays menu entries on a full-screen dashboard, showing sections for applications, favorites, logout/shutdown options, and categories (see Figure 9-13). Press the Esc key to leave the dashboard without making a selection. You can add an application to the Favorites section by right-clicking on the application's icon and selecting Add to Favorites. To remove an application from the Favorites section, right-click on it and select Remove from Favorites. The Applications section shows categories to the right. and the icons for a selected category to the left. There are also categories for recent applications and documents. The Power/Section category lists the complete set of leave options, including lock, suspend, and new session. The All Applications category lists all your applications under alphabetic headings (see Figure 9-14).

Figure 9-13: The Application Dashboard Menu - Office

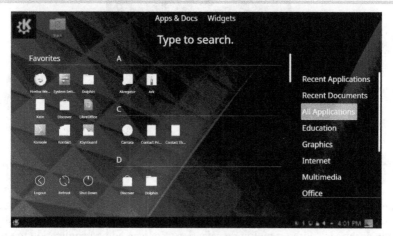

Figure 9-14: Application Dashboard Menu - All Applications

Krunner

For fast access to applications, bookmarks, contacts, and other desktop items, you can use Krunner. The Krunner widget operates as a search tool for applications and other items such as bookmarks. To find an application, enter a search pattern and a listing of matching applications is displayed. Click on an application entry to start the application. You can also place an icon (application launcher) for an entry on the desktop by simply clicking and dragging its entry for the list to the desktop. For applications where you know the name, part of the name, or just its basic topic, Krunner is a very fast way to access the application. To start Krunner, press Alt-F2, Alt-space, or right-click on the desktop to display the desktop menu and select "Run Command." Enter the pattern for the application you want to search for and press enter. The pattern "software" or "package" would display an entry for Discover Software. Entering the pattern "office" displays entries for all the LibreOffice applications, as well as additional office applications you can install (see Figure 9-15).

Clicking the settings button at the left opens the Configure Search dialog, which lists plugins for searching applications, widgets, and bookmarks, as well as providing capabilities such a running shell commands, opening files, and spell checking. The Clear History button deletes earlier search results. You can also configure Krunner search using the Plasma Search tab on System Settings Search (Workspace section).

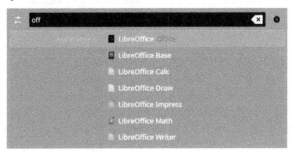

Figure 9-15: Krunner application search

Removable Devices: Device Notifier

Installed on the system tray to the right is the Device Notifier. When you insert a removable device like a CD/DVD disc or a USB drive, the New Device Notifier briefly displays a dialog showing all your removable devices, including the new one. The Device Notifier icon is displayed on the system tray. You can click on the New Device Notifier any time to display this dialog. Figure 9-16 shows the New Device Notifier displayed on the panel and its panel icon. The New Device Notifier is displayed only if at least one removable device is attached.

Removable devices are not displayed as icons on your desktop. Instead, to open the devices, you use the New Device Notifier. Click on the Device Notifier icon in the panel to open its dialog. The device is unmounted initially with an unmount button displayed. Click on this button to mount the device. An eject button is then displayed which you can later use to unmount and eject the device. Opening the device with an application from its menu will mount the device automatically. Clicking on the eject button for a DVD/CD disc will physically eject it. For a USB drive, the drive will be unmounted and prepared for removal. You can then safely remove the USB drive.

To open a device, click on its entry in the Device Notifier, like one for your DVD/CD disc or your USB drive (see Figure 9-16).

Removable media are also displayed on the File manager window's side pane. You can choose to eject removable media from the file manager instead of from the Device Notifier by right-clicking on the removable media entry, and select "Safely remove" from the popup menu.

Figure 9-16: Device Notifier and its panel widget icon

KDE Network Connections: Network Manager

On KDE, the Network Manager plasma widget provides panel access for Network Manager. This is the same Network Manager application but adapted to the KDE interface. The widget icon image changes for wireless only and wired connections. Clicking on the widget icon in the panel opens a dialog listing your current available wireless and wired connections. When you pass the mouse over an active connection, a Disconnect buttons appear (see Figure 9-17). For entries not connected, Connect buttons are displayed. To rescan your available connections, click the rescan button (circle) located to the right of the "Available connections" heading. Clicking on a connected entry opens tabs for Speed and Details (see Figure 9-18).

Figure 9-17: Network Manager connections and panel icons:

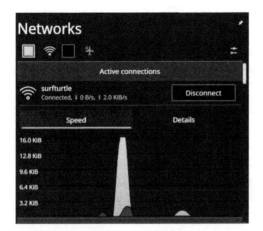

Figure 9-18: KDE Network Manager connection information - speed and details:

The toolbar at the top of the network plasma widget has buttons for wireless and airplane mode connections (shown below). Checkboxes next to each connection icon show if it is enabled. Clicking on the checkbox for a connection will enable or disable the connection. Disabled connections have an empty checkbox and a red icon.

You can use the "Connection editor" to configure your established connections. Either click the settings button on the right side of the toolbar at the top of the network dialog or right-click on the network dialog to display a menu where you can choose "Configure Network Connections." The Connection editor then opens, which lists your connections (see Figure 9-19). Select a connection and then click the Edit button on the toolbar to open the Network Manager editor for KDE, with the same General, Wired, Security, and IPv tabs for a wired or wireless connections as described in Chapter 15 (see Figure 9-17). To add a new connection manually, click the Add button on the Connection editor to display a menu for different connection types.

Figure 9-19: KDE connection editor and KDE Network Manager

Desktop Plasmoids (Widgets)

The KDE desktop features the Plasma desktop that supports plasmoids. Plasmoids are integrated into the desktop on the same level as windows and icons. Just as a desktop can display windows, it can also display plasmoids. Plasmoids can take on desktop operations, running essential operations, even replacing, to a limited extent, the need for file manager windows. The name for plasmoids used on the desktop is widgets. The tools and commands on the desktop that manage plasmoids, refer to them as widgets. For that reason, they will be referred to as widgets.

Managing desktop widgets

When you long click (click and hold for several seconds) your mouse on a widget, its sidebar is displayed with buttons for resizing, rotating, settings, and removing the widget (see Figure 9-18). Click and drag the resize button to change the widget size. Clicking the settings button opens that widget's settings dialog (see Figure 9-20).

To move a widget, long click on it to display its sidebar and while holding the click, drag the icon to the position you want.

Figure 9-20: Clock Widget with task sidebar and configuration dialog

To add a widget (plasmoid) to the desktop, right-click anywhere on the desktop and select Add Widgets from the pop-up menu. This opens the Widgets dialog at the left side of the desktop that lists widgets you can add (see Figure 9-21). Clicking on the Categories button opens a pop-up menu with different widget categories like Date and Time, Online Services, and Graphics. Double-click or drag a widget to the desktop to add it to the desktop. You can enter a pattern to search for a widget using the search box located at the top of the dialog.

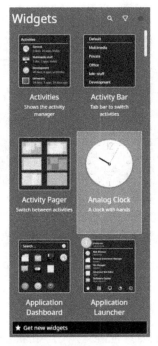

Figure 9-21: Adding a widget - Widgets dialog

To remove a widget, long click on the widget to display its toolbar, and then click on the red Remove button at the bottom of the toolbar. When you remove a widget, a notification message is displayed with an Undo button, as shown here. Clicking on the Undo button will restore the widget.

Figure 9-22 shows the folder, digital clock, notes, calculator, and cpu monitor widgets. The desktop folder widget is just a folder widget set initially to the desktop folder.

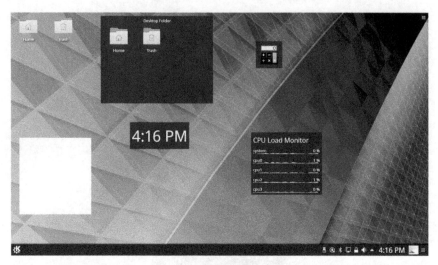

Figure 9-22: Folder, Calculator, Digital clock, CPU Load monitor, and Notes widgets:

Folder and Icon Widgets

You can place access to any folders on the desktop by simply dragging their icons from a file manager window to the desktop (see Figure 9-23). A small menu will appear that includes options for the Icon and Folder widgets. The Folder option sets up a Folder widget for the folder showing icons for subfolders and files. The Icon entry creates an Icon widget, as shown here.

 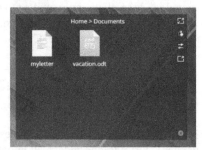

Figure 9-23: Folder and Icon widgets:

For any Folder widget, you can use that widget's settings dialog to change the folder it references. A Folder widget has options for showing the desktop folder, a folder on your Places list, or a specific folder. You can also specify a title. You can easily create a Folder widget for your home folder.

Activities

KDE is designed to support multiple activities. Activities are different plasma containments, each with its set of widgets. An activity is not the same as virtual desktop. Virtual desktops affect space, displaying additional desktops. An activity has its own set of widgets (widgets) and windows, displaying a different set of widgets and windows for each activity. In effect, each activity has a different desktop and set of virtual desktops. Technically, each activity is a Plasma containment that has its own collection of widgets and windows. You can switch to a different activity (containment) and display a different collection of widgets and windows on your desktop.

An activity if often tailored for a certain task. You could have one activity for office work, another for news, and yet another for media. Each activity could have its own set of appropriate widgets, like clock, calculator, notes, and folder widgets for an office activity. A media activity might have a Media Player widget and media applications open.

Multiple activities are managed using the Activities Manager, which is accessed through the Activities entry on the desktop toolbox menu, the desktop menu, or the Activities widget, which you can install on the panel or desktop. The toolbox menu and Activities widget are shown here.

Files and folders can be attached to an activity, displaying them only on that activity. Right-click on the folder or file icon in the File Manager, and choose the Activities submenu to choose an activity. Windows are set by default to display on the activity they are opened on. The window switcher is configured to work only on the current activity. The setting is configured in the Window Management dialog (Workspace section of the System settings dialog). On the Task Switcher tab, the 'Filter windows by" section has Activities checked and Current activity selected.

To add an activity, click the "Activities" entry in the toolbox or desktop menus. If you have added and Activities widget to the panel, you can click the Activities button. The Activities Manager is displayed listing your activities on the left side of the screen (see Figure 9-24). A default activity icon for your desktop will already be displayed. Click the Create Activity button (plus button) to add a new activity. A "Create a new activity" window opens with entries for the name and description (see Figure 9-25). Click on the Icon image to open a dialog where you can choose an icon for your activity. On the Other tab, you can choose not track usage and to set up a keyboard shortcut for the activity. Click the Create button to add the new activity. An activity entry then appears on the Activity Manager. To switch to another activity, click its icon.

Note: If you cannot add activities, install the kactivitymanagerd package.

Figure 9-24: Activity toolbar and icons

Moving the mouse over an activity icon displays Configure and Stop buttons. The Configure button opens the "Activity settings" dialog for that activity, which is the same as the create dialog, with Name, description, and icon settings. The Stop button deactivates the activity and places it at the bottom of the Activity Manager under the "Stopped activities" heading. To start a stopped activity, simply click its icon in the "Stopped activities" list.

To remove an activity, first stop it, then move your mouse over the activity icon in the Stopped activities section (see Figure 9-26). A remove button appears to the right of the activity entry. Click it to remove the activity. You are prompted to confirm the deletion.

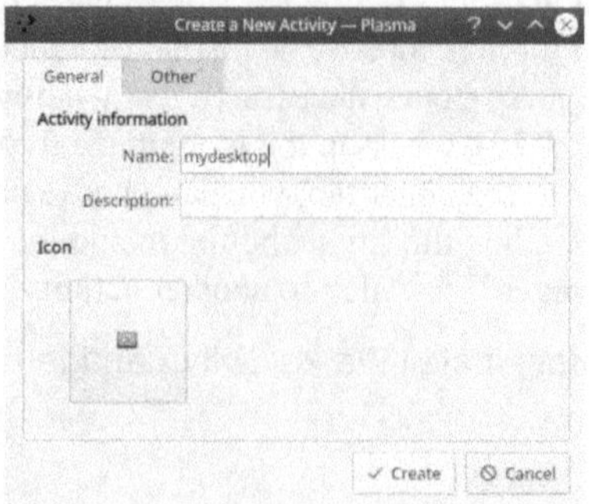

Figure 9-25: Create an activity

To add widgets to an activity, first, click the activity to make it the current activity, and then click the Add Widgets button to display the Widgets dialog. Widgets you add are placed in the current activity.

To switch from one activity to another, first, display the Activities Manager by choosing Activities from the desktop toolbox menu (right-click on desktop) or the Activates button on the panel (if installed). Then click on the activity icon you want. The new Activity becomes your desktop (see Figure 9-27). To change to another activity, open the Activities Manager again, and click the activity icon you want. Your original desktop is the first icon (Default).

Figure 9-26: stop Activity icons

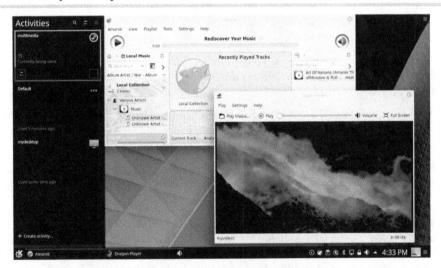

Figure 9-27: Activity Manager and screen of selected activity

To move easily between activities, you can add the Activity bar widget, either to the panel or to the desktop. On the panel, the Activity bar displays buttons for each activity. Click to move to a different activity. On the desktop, the Activity bar displays a dialog with an arrow button for moving from one activity to another.

KDE Windows

A KDE window has the same functionality you find in other window managers and desktops. You can re-size the window by clicking and dragging any of its corners or sides. A click-and-drag operation on a side extends the window in that dimension, whereas a corner extends both height and width at the same time. The top of the window has a title bar showing the name of the window, the program name in the case of applications, and the current directory name for the file manager windows. The active window has the title bar highlighted. To move the window, click the title bar and drag it where you want. Right-clicking the window title bar displays a pop-up menu with entries for window operations, such as minimize, maximize, and moving the window to a different desktop or activity. The More Actions submenu includes closing or resizing the window, the shade option to roll up the window to the title bar, and full screen. Within the window, menus, icons, and toolbars for the particular application are displayed.

You can configure the appearance and operation of a window by selecting the Window Manager Settings from the More Actions submenu in the Window menu (right-click the title bar). Here you can set appearance (Window Decoration), button and key operations (Actions), the focus policy, such as a mouse-click on the window or just passing the mouse over it (Focus), and how the window is displayed when moving it (Moving). All these features can be configured also using the System Setting's Window Behavior tool in the Workspace section.

Opened windows are shown as buttons on the KDE taskbar located on the panel. The taskbar shows buttons for the different programs you are running or windows you have open. This is essentially a docking mechanism that lets you change to a window or application by clicking its button. When you minimize a window, it is reduced to its taskbar button. You can then restore the window by clicking its taskbar button. A live thumbnail of a window on the taskbar is displayed as your mouse passes over its taskbar button, showing its name, desktop, and image.

Taskbar buttons also function as progress bars, showing the progress of copy and download operations. Music and video players also show basic multimedia controls, such as pause, start, next, and previous.

To the right of the title bar are three small buttons for minimizing, maximizing, or closing the window (down, up, and x symbols). You can switch to a window at any time by clicking its taskbar button. You can also maximize a window by dragging it to the top edge of the screen.

From the keyboard, you can use the ALT-TAB key combination to display a list of current open windows. Holding down the ALT key and sequentially pressing TAB moves you through the list.

A window can be displayed as a tile on one-half of the screen. Another tile can be set up for a different window on the other side of the screen, allowing you to display two windows side by side on the full screen (see Figure 9-28). You can tile a window by dragging it to the side of the screen (over the side edge to the middle of the window). A tile outline will appear. Add a second tile by moving a window to the other side edge. You can add more windows to a tile by moving them to that edge. Clicking on a window's taskbar button will display it on its tile.

The same process works for corners. You can tile a window to a corner by moving it to that corner. You can then have four tiled windows open at each corner. You could even have server windows open on the same corner, displaying the one you want by clicking its taskbar icon.

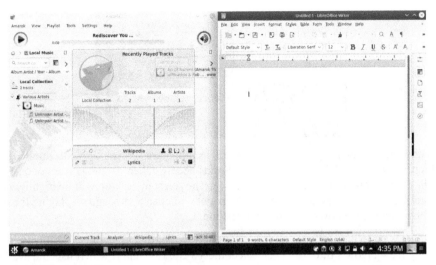

Figure 9-28: Window tiles

Applications

You can start an application in KDE in several ways. If an entry for it is in the Kickoff Applications menu or Application dashboard, you can select that entry to start the application. You can right-click on any application entry in the Applications menu to display a pop-up menu with "Add to Panel" and "Add to Desktop" entries. Select either to add a shortcut icon for the application to the desktop or the panel. You can then start an application by single-clicking its desktop or panel icon.

An application icon on the desktop is implemented as a desktop widget. Performing a long click on the application icon on the desktop displays a sidebar with the icon for the widget settings. This opens a Settings window that allows you to specify a keyboard shortcut.

You can also run an application by right-clicking on the desktop and selecting the Run Command (or press Alt-F2 or Alt-space) which will display the Krunner tool consisting of a box to enter a single command. Previous commands can be accessed from a pop-up menu. You need only enter a pattern to search for the application. Results will be displayed in the Krunner window. Choose the one you want.

Virtual Desktops: Pager

KDE supports virtual desktops, extending the desktop area on which you can work. You could have a Web browser running on one desktop and be using a text editor in another. KDE can support up to 16 virtual desktops. To use virtual desktops, add the Pager widget to your panel or desktop. On the panel, you can use the panel editor (toolbox, right side) to move it to the location you want on the panel. The panel and desktop pagers are shown here.

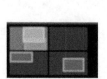

The Pager represents your virtual desktops as miniature screens showing small squares for each desktop. It works much like the GNOME Workspace Switcher. To move from one desktop to another, click the square for the destination desktop. The selected desktop will be highlighted. Just passing your mouse over a desktop image on the panel will open a message displaying the desktop number along with the windows open on that desktop.

If you want to move a window to a different desktop, first open the window's menu by right-clicking the window's title bar. Then select the To Desktop entry, which lists the available desktops. Choose the one you want.

You can also configure KDE so that if you move the mouse over the edge of a desktop screen, it automatically moves to the adjoining desktop. You need to imagine the desktops arranged next to each. You enable this feature by enabling the "Switch desktop on edge" feature in the System Settings | Desktop Behavior | Screen Edges tab. This feature will also allow you to move windows over the edge to an adjoining desktop.

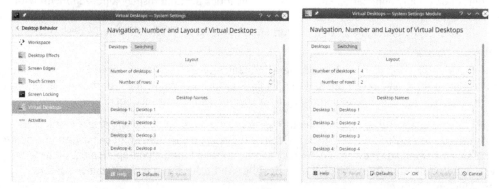

Figure 9-29: Virtual desktop configuration (Desktop Behavior) and Pager widget icon:

To change the number of virtual desktops, right-click on the Desktop Pager widget, select Add Virtual Desktop. To configure the amount displayed select the Configure Desktops entry in the pop-up menu to open the Virtual Desktops dialog, and choose the Desktops tab, which displays entries for your active desktops. You can also access the Virtual Desktops dialog from System Settings | Desktop Behavior in the Workspace section (see Figure 9-29). The text box labeled "Number of Desktops" controls the number of active desktops. Use the arrows or enter a number to change the number of active desktops. You can change any of the desktop names by clicking an active name and entering a new one.

To change how the pager displays desktops on the pager, right-click on the pager and choose Pager Settings to open the Pager Settings dialog (see Figure 9-30). Here you can configure the pager to display numbers or names for desktops, or show icons of open windows.

Figure 9-30: Pager Settings:

Tip: Use CTRL key in combination with a function key to switch to a specific desktop: for example, CTRL-F1 switches to the first desktop and CTRL-F3 to the third desktop.

KDE Panel

The KDE panel, located at the bottom of the screen, provides access to most KDE functions (see Figure 9-31). The panel is a specially configured Plasma containment, just like the desktop. The panel can include icons for menus, folder windows, specific programs, and virtual desktops. These are widgets that are configured for use on the panel. At the left end of the panel is a button for the Kickoff menu, a KDE *K* icon.

To add an application to the panel, right-click on its entry in the Kickoff menu to open a pop-up menu and select Add to Panel.

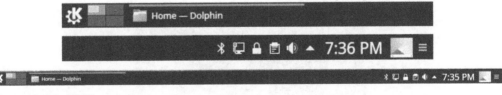

Figure 9-31: KDE panel

To add a widget to the panel, right-click on any panel widget on the panel to open a pop-up menu, and select Panel Options submenu from which you can select the Add Widgets entry. This opens the Add Widgets dialog that lists widgets you can add to the panel (see Figure 9-32). A drop-down menu at the top of the window lets you see different widget categories like Date and Time, Online Services, and Graphics. Another way to open the Add Widgets dialog is to click on the panel toolbox at the right side of the panel and click the Add widgets button

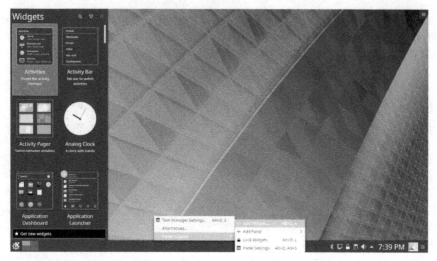

Figure 9-32: KDE Add Widgets for panel

The Plasma panel supports several kinds of Windows and Tasks widgets, including the taskbar (Task Manager) and system tray. To the right of the system tray is the digital clock. The system tray holds widgets for desktop operations like update notifier, the clipboard, Bluetooth, device notifier, sound settings (kmix), media player (if a multimedia player is active), and network manager, as shown here.

The pop-up menu (arrow icon) on the right side of the system tray display widgets that are not in use, or not often used (see Figure 9-33). The Battery and Brightness entry displays a dialog to see battery charges and set screen brightness.

Figure 9-33: System Tray

To configure the system tray, right-click on the system tray menu (arrow icon) and choose System Tray Settings to open the system tray configuration dialog at the General tab, where you can decide what items to display or entries to make visible or remove (see Figure 9-34). In the "Extra Items" list you can check items that you also want displayed on the system tray, such as Printers and Instant Messaging. When you click the Apply button the items are displayed. Items not in use are in the menu. The Entries tab shows how selected items are to be displayed (auto, shown, or hidden).

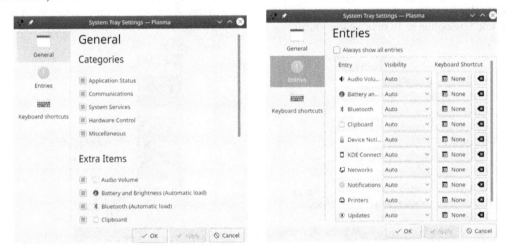

Figure 9-34: KDE panel system tray settings

KDE Panel Configuration

To configure a panel, changing its position, size, and display features, you use the panel's toolbox, located at the right side of the panel. Click on it to open an additional configuration panel with buttons for adding widgets, moving the panel, changing its size, and a More Settings menu for setting visibility and alignment features. Figure 9-35 shows the configuration panel as it will appear on your desktop. Figure 9-36 provides a more detailed description, including the More Settings menu entries.

Figure 9-35: KDE Panel Configuration

With the configuration panel activated, you can also move widgets around the panel. Clicking on a widget will overlay a movement icon, letting you then move the widget icon to a different location on the panel.

As you move your mouse over a widget in the panel, a pop-up dialog opens showing the widget's name, a settings button, and a delete button (see Figure 9-35). To remove the widget from the panel, click its delete button.

The lower part of the configuration panel is used for panel position settings. On the left side is a slider for positioning the panel on the edge of the screen. On the right side are two sliders for the minimum (bottom) and maximum (top) size of the panel.

The top part of the panel has buttons for changing the location and the size of the panel. The Screen Edge button lets you move the panel to another side of the screen (left, right, top, bottom). Just click and drag. The height button lets you change the panel size, larger or smaller. The Add Widgets button will open the Add Widgets dialog, letting you add new widgets to the panel. The Add Spacer button adds a spacer to separate widgets. Right-click on the spacer to set the flexible size option or to remove the spacer.

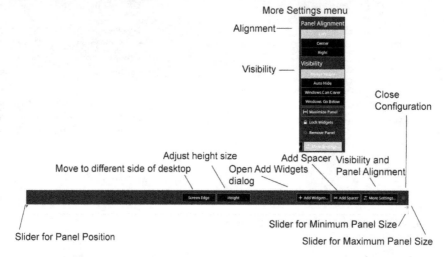

Figure 9-36: KDE Panel Configuration details and display features

The More Setting menu lets you set Visibility and Alignment features. You can choose an AutoHide setting that will hide the panel until you move the mouse to its location. The "Windows can cover" option lets a window overlap the panel. For smaller panels, you can align to the right, left, or center of the screen edge. The More Settings menu also has an entry to remove the panel. Use this entry to delete a panel you no longer want.

When you are finished with the configuration, click the red x icon the upper right side.

Desktop Effects

Desktop effects can be enabled on the System Settings Desktop Effects tab in the Desktop Behavior dialog in the Workspace section (System Settings | Desktop Behavior). For virtual desktop switching you can choose Slide, Fade Desktop, and Desktop Cube Animation (see Figure 9-37). The more dramatic effects are found in the Windows Management section. Desktop Effects requires the support of a capable graphics chip (GPU). You may have to install the proprietary graphics driver (System Settings | Driver Manager).

Figure 9-37: Desktop Effects selection

KEY	Operation
ALT-TAB	Cover Switch, Thumbnail, or Breeze for open windows
CTRL-F8	Desktop Grid (use mouse to select a desktop)
CTRL-F9	Present Windows Current Desktop
CTRL-F10	Present Windows All Desktops
CTRL-F11	Desktop Cube (use mouse or arrow keys to move, ESC to exit)

Table 9-3: KWin desktop effects keyboard shortcuts

Several Windows effects are selected by default, depending on whether your graphics card can support them. A check box is filled next to active effects. If there is a dialog icon to the right of the effects entry, it means the effect can be configured. Click on the icon to open its configuration dialog. Figure 9-38 shows the configuration dialog for the Desktop Grid effect. For several effects, you use certain keys to start them. The more commonly used effects are Cover Switch, Desktop Grid, Present Windows, and Desktop Cube. The keys for these effects are listed in Table 9-3.

Figure 9-38: Desktop Effects configuration

Figure 9-39: Thumbnail and Breeze Switch - Alt-Tab

Window switching using Alt-Tab is controlled on the Windows Management dialog's Task Switcher tab, not from Desktop Behavior's Desktop Effects tab. In the Visualization section, you can choose the window switching effect you want to use from the drop-down menu. These include Breeze, Thumbnails, Grid, Cover Switch, and Flip Switch, as well as smaller listings such as informative, compact, text icons, and small icons. The Alt-Tab keys implement the effect you have chosen. Continually pressing the Tab key while holding down the Alt key moves you through the windows. Thumbnails displays windows in a boxed dialog (see Figure 9-39), whereas Cover Switch arranges windows stacked to the sides, and Flip Switch arranges the windows to one side (see Figure 9-40). The default is Breeze, which arranges the window images to the left side of the screen (see Figure 9-39).

The Present Windows effect displays images of the open windows on your screen with the selected one highlighted (see Figure 9-41). You can use your mouse to select another. This provides an easy way to browse your open windows. You can also use Ctrl-F9 to display windows on your current virtual desktop statically and use the arrow key to move between them. Use Ctrl-F10 to display all your open windows across all your desktops. Press the ESC key to return to the desktop.

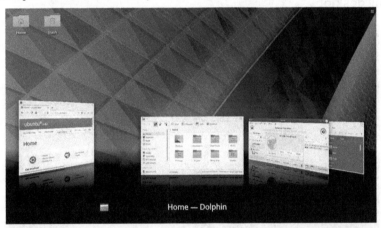

Figure 9-40: Cover Switch - Alt-Tab

Desktop Grid will show a grid of all your virtual desktops (Ctrl-F8), letting you see all your virtual desktops on the screen at once (see Figure 9-42). You can then move windows and open applications between desktops. Clicking on a desktop makes it the current one. The plus and minus keys allow you to add or remove virtual desktops.

Figure 9-41: Present Windows (Windows effects) Ctrl-F9 for current desktop and Ctrl-f10 for all desktops

Figure 9-42: Desktop Grid - Ctrl-F8

Desktop Cube will show a cube of all your virtual desktops, letting you move to different desktops around a cube (see Figure 9-43). Stop at the side you want to select. Press Ctrl-F11 to start the Desktop Cube. You can then move around the cube with the arrow keys or by clicking and dragging your mouse. Alternatively, if you have a touchpad, you can use a two-finger drag to start and move through the Desktop Cube. When you are finished, press the ESC key to return you the desktop. Desktop Cube Animation will use cube animation whenever you switch to a different desktop using the Desktop Pager.

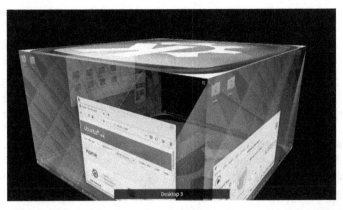

Figure 9-43: Desktop Cube - Ctrl-F11, drag-mouse or right/left arrow keys (or two-finger drag on touchpad)

KDE File Manager: Dolphin

Dolphin is KDE's dedicated file manager (see Figure 9-44). A navigation bar shows the current directory either in a browser or edit mode. In the browse mode it shows icons for the path of your current directory, and in the edit mode, it shows the path name in a text-editable box. You can use either to move to different folders and their subfolders. Use the **Ctrl-l** key or click to the right of the folder buttons to use the edit mode. You can also choose Control | Location Bar | Editable Location. Clicking on the checkmark at the end of the editable text box returns you to the browser mode.

Figure 9-44: The KDE file manager (Dolphin)

The Dolphin menubar has been hidden by default. The menus are displayed when clicking the Control button on the right end of the toolbar (see Figure 9-45). You can redisplay the menubar by choosing "Show Menubar" from the Control (or View) menu (**Ctrl-m**). You can hide the menubar again by choosing Show Menubar from the Settings menu (or pressing **Ctrl-m**).

You can open a file either by clicking it or by right-clicking it, and choosing the "Open With" submenu to list applications to open it with. If you want to just select the file or folder, you need to hold down the CTRL key while you click it. A single-click will open the file. If the file is a program, that program starts up. If it is a data file, such as a text file, the associated application is run using that data file. Clicking a text file displays it with the Kate editor while clicking an image file displays it with the Gwenview image viewer. If Dolphin cannot determine the application to use, it opens a dialog box prompting you to enter the application name. You can click the Browse button on this box to use a directory tree to locate the application program you want.

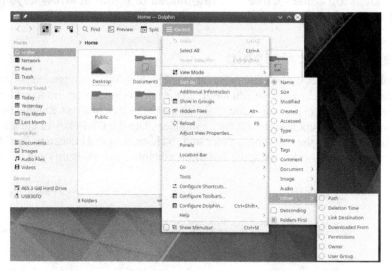

Figure 9-45: The KDE file manager menus

Dolphin can display panels to either side (Dolphin refers to these as panels, though they operate more like stand-alone tabs). The Places panel will show icons for often-used folders like Home, Network, and Trash, as well as removable devices. To add a folder to the Places panel, just drag it there. The files listed in a folder can be viewed in several different ways, such as icons, detailed listing (Details), and columns (Control | View Mode menu). See Table 9-4 for keyboard shortcuts.

The Additional information submenu in the Control menu (or View menu) lets you display additional information about files such as the size, date, type, and comments. Type specific information can also be displayed such as album, track, and duration for audio files, and word and line counts for documents. You can also display the full path, permissions, and group information (Other submenu).

Keys	Description
ALT-LEFT ARROW, ALT-RIGHT ARROW	Backward and Forward in History
ALT-UP ARROW	One directory up
ENTER	Open a file/directory
LEFT/RIGHT/UP/DOWN ARROWS	Move among the icons
PAGE UP, PAGE DOWN	Scroll fast
CTRL-C	Copy selected file to clipboard
CTRL-V	Paste files from clipboard to current directory
CTRL-S	Select files by pattern
CTRL-L	URI text box location bar
CTRL-F	Find files
CTRL-Q	Close window

Table 9-4: KDE File Manager Keyboard Shortcuts

You can display additional panels by selecting them from the Control | Panels submenu. The Information panel displays detailed information about a selected file or folder, and the Folders panel displays a directory tree for the file system. The panels are detachable from the file manager window (see Figure 9-46). Be sure to choose "Unlock Panels" the panels in the Panels menu to make them detachable.

Figure 9-46: The KDE file manager with panels

The Places panel makes use of file metadata to provide easy access to files by category and date. The Places panel has four sections: Places, Recently Saved, Search For, and Devices. As in previous versions, the Places section holds your folders, including root, trash, and network, and the Devices section holds your attached devices, including removable devices. The Recently Saved section lets you display files you access fairly recently: today, yesterday, this month, and last month (see Figure 9-47). The Search For section lets you displays files of specified types: documents, images, audio files, and videos.

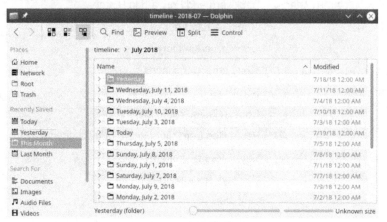

Figure 9-47: The KDE file manager panel Recently Saved

Dolphin supports split views, where you can open two different folders in the same window. Click the Split button in the toolbar. You can then drag folder and files from one folder to the other (see Figure 9-48).

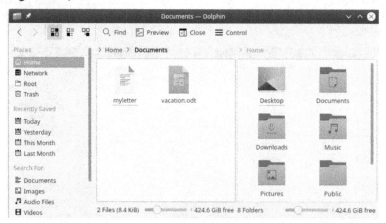

Figure 9-48: The KDE file manager with split views

Dolphin also supports file sharing with Samba. To share a folder, right-click on the folder icon and choose Properties to open the Properties dialog. Then on the Share tab, you can choose to share the folder with Samba (Microsoft Windows). You can also set permissions for users: Read Only, Full Control, and Deny (See Figure 9-49). For the Everyone entry, you would usually set the permission to Read Only.

Figure 9-49: The KDE file manager share dialog for folders

To configure Dolphin, click Configure Dolphin from the Control menu to open the Dolphin Preferences dialog with tabs for Startup, View Modes, Navigation, Services, Trash, and General (see Figure 9-50).

Figure 9-50: Dolphin file manager configuration

On the Startup tab, you can specify features like the split view and the default folder to start up with. On the View Modes tab, you can set display features for the different display modes (Icons, Details, and Column), like the icon size, font type, and arrangement. The Navigation tab sets features like opening archives as folders. The Services tab is where you specify actions supported for different kinds of files, like play a DVD with Dragon Player, install a true type font file or display Tiff image files. The Trash tab lets you configure trash settings like deleting items in the trash after a specified time and setting the maximum size of the trash. The General tab has sub-tabs for Behavior, Previews, Confirmations, and Status Bar. The Behavior tab is where you can enable tool tips and show selection markers. Preview lets you choose which type of files to preview. The image, jpeg, and directories types are already selected. On Confirmations, you can require confirmation prompts for file deletion, moving files to the trash, or closing multiple tabs. On the Status tab, you can choose to show the zoom slider and the amount of free storage.

Navigating Directories

Within a file manager window, a single-click on a folder icon moves to that folder and displays its file and sub-folder icons. To move back up to the parent folder, you click the back arrow button located on the left end of the navigation toolbar. A single-click on a folder icon moves you down the folder tree, one folder at a time. By clicking the back arrow button, you move up the tree. The Navigation bar can display either the folder path for the current folder or an editable location box where you can enter in a pathname. For the folder path, you can click on any displayed folder name to move you quickly to an upper-level folder. To use the location box, click to the right of the folder path. The Location box is displayed. You can also select Show Full Location in the View | Location Bar | Editable Location menu item (or press Ctrl-L or F6). The navigation bar changes to an editable textbox where you can type a path name. To change back to the folder path, click the check mark to the right of the text box.

Like a Web browser, the file manager remembers the previous folder it has displayed. You can use the back and forward arrow buttons to move through this list of prior folders. You can also use several keyboard shortcuts to perform such operations, like Alt-back-arrow to move up a folder, and the arrow keys to move to different icons.

Copy, Move, Delete, Rename, and Link Operations

To perform an operation on a file or folder, you first have to select it by clicking the file's icon or listing. To select more than one file, hold down the CTRL key down while you click the files you want. You can also use the keyboard arrow keys to move from one file icon to another.

To copy and move files, you can use the standard drag-and-drop method with your mouse. To copy a file, you locate it by using the file manager. Open another file manager window to the folder to which you want the file copied. Then drag-and-drop the file icon to that window. A pop-up menu appears with selections for Move Here, Copy Here, or Link Here. Choose Copy Here. To move a file to another directory, follow the same procedure, but select Move Here from the pop-up menu. To copy or move a folder, use the same procedure as for files. All the folder's files and subfolders are also copied or moved. Instead of having to select from a pop-up menu, you can use the corresponding keys: **Ctrl** for copy, **Shift** for move, and **Ctrl-Shift** for link, same as for GNOME.

To rename a file, Ctrl-click its icon and press F2, or right-click the icon and select Rename from the pop-up menu. A dialog opens where you can enter the new name for the file or folder.

You can delete a file either by selecting it and deleting it, or placing it in the Trash folder to delete later. To delete a file, select it and then choose the Delete entry in the File menu, File | Delete (also SHIFT-DEL key). To place a file in the Trash folder, drag-and-drop it to the Trash icon on the Places panel, or right-click the file and choose "Move To Trash" from the pop-up menu. You can later open the Trash folder and delete the files. To delete all the files in the Trash folder, right-click the Trash icon in Dolphin file manager Places panel, and select Empty Trash from the pop-up menu. To restore files in the Trash bin, open the Trash window and right click on the file to restore and select Restore.

Each file or directory has properties associated with it that include permissions, the filename, and its directory. To display the Properties dialog for a given file, right-click the file's icon and select the Properties entry. On the General tab, you see the name of the file displayed. To change the filename, replace the name there with a new one. Permissions are set on the Permissions tab. Here, you can set read, write, and execute permissions for user, group, or other access to the file. The Group entry enables you to change the group for a file.

Search Bar and Filter Bar

The Dolphin search tool provides a simplified search bar for files and folders. KDE also supports a filter bar to search files and folders in the current folder. You can also use the Filter Panel to refine searches by metadata such as type, date, ratings, and tags. For quick access to basic categories and recent use you can use the Places panel's Recently Accessed and Search For entries, as noted previously.

Search Bar

To search for files, click the Find button on the icon bar to open the search bar, which displays a search text box. You can also choose Find from the Edit menu or press Ctrl-f. The search bar displays a search text box where you enter the pattern of the file or folder you are searching for. Click the red x button to the left to close the find bar, and use the black x button in the text box to clear the search pattern.

Buttons below the search box provide options to qualify the search. The Filename button (the default) searches on the filename. The Content button will search the contents of text files for the pattern. The "From Here" button searches the user's home folders, and the Everywhere button (the default) searches the entire file system (see Figure 9-51).

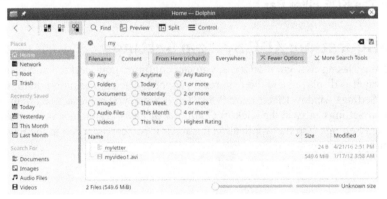

Figure 9-51: The KDE Search Bar

The search results are displayed in the main pane. You can click a file to have it open with its appropriate application. Text files are displayed by the Kate text editor, images by Gwenview, and applications are run. When you are finished searching, click the Close button.

When you pass your mouse over an icon listed in the Query Results, information about it is displayed on the information panel to the right (if the information panel is displayed). Links are shown for adding tags and comments. Right-clicking on this panel lets you open a configure dialog where you can specify what information to display.

The search operation makes use of the KDE implementation of Baloo desktop search. To configure desktop search, choose System Settings | Workspace | Search, File Search tab. On the File Search tab, you can enable or disable file searching, and choose folders not to search.

Filter Bar

For a quick search of the current folder, you can activate the Filter bar (Control | Tools | Show Filter Bar or **Ctrl-i**), which opens a Filter search box at the bottom of the window. Enter a pattern, and only those file and directory names containing that pattern are displayed. Click the x button at the right of the Filter box to clear it (see Figure 9-52).

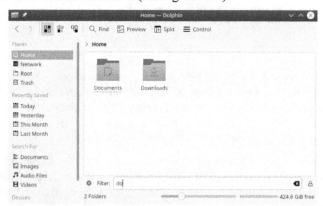

Figure 9-52: The KDE Filter Bar

KDE Configuration: KDE System Settings

With the Plasma configuration tools, you can configure your desktop and system, changing the way it is displayed and the features it supports. The configuration dialogs are accessed on the System Settings window (See Figure 9-53). On Plasma, you can access System Settings from the System Settings entry in the Kickoff Computer or Favorites menus, or from Applications | Settings | System Settings. On the Application dashboard, you can access it in the Favorites section and in the Settings category.

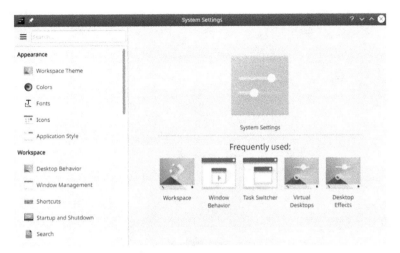

Figure 9-53: Plasma System Settings - Sidebar view

The System Settings window can be displayed three ways: tree view, icon view, and sidebar view. Use the Configure dialog | General tab to choose the view you want. You can access the Configure dialog from the menu on the sidebar view (upper left corner) or the Configure button on the icon view (top toolbar). The sidebar view is the current default (see Figure 9-53). The icon view was the default in previous releases (see Figure 9-54). With the sidebar view, System Settings shows an icon list of setting categories arranged in several sections: Appearance, Workspace, Personalization, Network, Hardware, and System Administration (see Figure 9-55). Click an entry to display a new icon list in the sidebar with configuration entries for that category. Selecting an entry shows the configuration settings on the right pane (see Figure 9-56).

The Appearance section lets you set the desktop theme, manage fonts, choose icon sets, and select application and window styles. The Workspace section lets you set desktop effects, virtual desktops, window actions, startup applications, desktop search. The Network section holds icons for configuring networking preferences, Bluetooth connections, and sharing. Personalization lets you set the settings for user management, the date and time, notifications, online accounts, and file/application associations. Hardware lets you set the printer configuration, power management, multimedia devices (sound), your display resolution, and to manage drivers.

Alternatively, you can display the System Settings window using the classic tree format. Click the System Settings Configure entry from the menu to open the configuration dialog, and select Classic tree on the General tab. Setting sections are displayed as expandable trees on the left pane, with dialogs for a selected section displayed to the right.

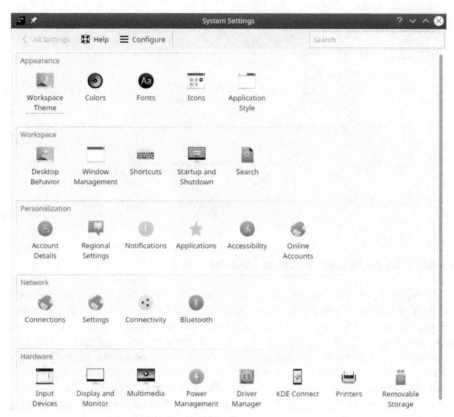

Figure 9-54: Plasma System Settings - Icon view

Figure 9-55: Plasma System Settings - Sidebar icon list

Figure 9-56: KDE System Settings | Application Style, Widget Style

KDE has administration tools comparable to the Mate desktop. For example, User management is provided by Kuser, accessible from System Settings | Account Details (Personalization section), User Manager tab. It works much the same way as User Accounts on the Mate desktop (see Chapter 14) (see Figure 9-57).

Figure 9-57: KDE System Settings | User Manager

Plasma Software Management: Discover

Discover is Plasma's corresponding application to Ubuntu Software. It uses a simple interface to let you quickly locate and install software). Applications can be easily removed with a click. With Discover, you can also install Plasma (KDE) desktop add-ons, including widgets for desktop and panel. Discover shows a sidebar on the left and a list of applications to the right (see Figure 9-58). You use the Discover sidebar to locate software packages. The Applications entry expands to software categories on the sidebar, which, when selected, will display a list of available and installed packages in the right pane. Clicking on a package entry expands it to a software description with an Install button (installed packages have a Remove button) (see Figure 9-59).

On the Installed entry lists all your installed packages with Remove button for easy deletion. You can also use the Search box at the top of the sidebar to locate a package. The Settings enter lists your repositories, which you can enable or disable.

The Plasma addons entry on the sidebar provides an extensive set of addons to different parts of the Plasma desktop. There are categories for fonts, themes, icons, window effects, window switching, and wallpapers, among others. You use the Plasma Widgets entry to manage your desktop and panel widgets.

The Application Addons entry lists addons for particular applications, such as calendar events for Korganizer.

Figure 9-58: Discover Software Manager

Figure 9-59: Discover Software Manager - Application Description

10. Ubuntu MATE

MATE Desktop

Windows

Workspaces

Main Menu

MATE Menu

MATE Panel

Applets

The Caja File Manager

Preferences (desktop configuration)

The MATE desktop is a simplified and easy to use version of the GNOME 2.4 desktop. MATE's official file manager is Caja. Those familiar with GNOME 2 will find most of the same features, with a few changes. The Ubuntu MATE desktop use the MATE desktop with Ubuntu software repositories. Ubuntu MATE is an official Ubuntu Flavour, supported by Ubuntu. The Ubuntu MATE website is:

```
https://ubuntu-mate.org
```

The Ubuntu MATE Guide provides detailed documentation on using MATE (see Figure 10-1). It is accessible from the Accessories menu, Ubuntu Mate Guide entry. The "All Help" option on the menu displays a lists of documentation for applications.

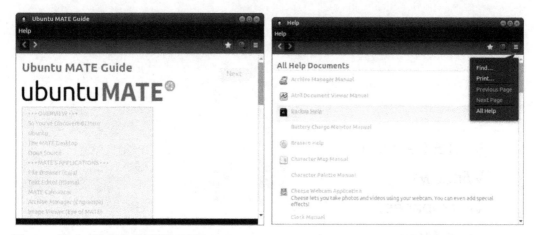

Figure 10-1: Ubuntu MATE Guide

The first time you access Ubuntu MATE, the Welcome dialog is displayed (see Figure 10-2), with links for information and online sites about Ubuntu MATE (you are initially asked whether to send system information to Ubuntu MATE or not). Be sure to check the Getting Started link, which covers key post-install topics such as updates, drivers, firewalls, backups, and user configuration, as well as customization links to background settings (wallpaper), the control center, and the desktop configuration dialog (MATE Tweak). You can redisplay the Welcome dialog anytime from Welcome entry in the System menu.

Figure 10-2: Ubuntu MATE Welcome dialog

Ubuntu MATE also provides a software manager called Software Boutique, which provides the MATE applications available on the Ubuntu repositories (see Figure 10-3). Use the icon bar at the top to move to different categories, such as Graphics, Office, Sound & Video, and Servers. Software Boutique only provides a small subset of applications available from Ubuntu, though these are the ones most compatible with MATE. Click the install button to install a package. Use the Filter menu to reduce the selection by subcategory.

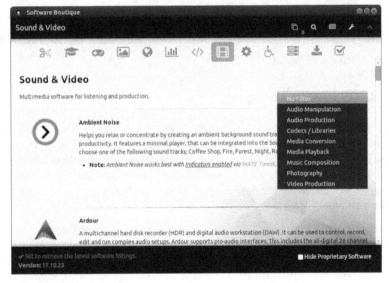

Figure 10-3: Software Boutique

The applications listed are known to work best with the MATE desktop. You can install most other software, such as those used on the Ubuntu Desktop, or the Kubuntu desktop, as well as network servers. To do so, access the More Software category, where you can install the Synaptic Package Manager.

The MATE Desktop

The MATE desktop is designed to be very simple, with a single panel and desktop icons (see Figure 10-4). The panel appears as a long bar across the bottom of the screen. It holds menus, program launchers, and applet icons. You can display the panel horizontally or vertically, and have it automatically hide to show you a full screen.

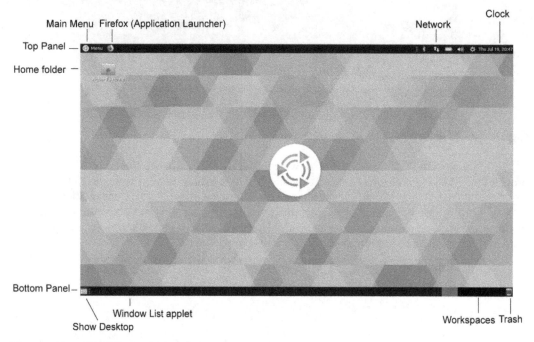

Figure 10-4: MATE desktop and panel

On the left side of the top panel is the button for the main menu. On the right side of the panel are system tools such as icons for the Network Manager, Update Manager, Power, sound volume, and the clock. With this menu, you can access places and applications. On the bottom panel to the left is the Show Desktop button, which hides your open windows, followed by the Window List applet, which shows buttons for open windows. On the right side is the workspace switcher and the trash.

The remainder of the screen is the desktop, where you can place folders, files, and application launchers. You can use a click-and-drag operation to move a file from one window to another or to the desktop. A drag-and-drop with the CTRL key held down will copy a file. A drag-and-drop operation with both the CTRL and SHIFT keys held down (Ctrl-Shift) creates a link on the desktop to that folder or file. Your home directory is accessed from the Home Folder icon on the desktop. Double clicking it opens a file manager window for your home directory. A right-click anywhere on the desktop displays a desktop menu with which you can align your desktop icons, change the background, and create new folders.

To quit the desktop, you click the Power button at the bottom of the menu (the Familiar menu). This opens a menu with options to Suspend, Restart, and Shut Down.

MATE Components

From a user's point of view, the desktop interface has four components: the desktop, the panels, the main menu, and the file manager (see Figure 10-5). You have two panels displayed, used for menus, application icons, and managing your windows. When you open a window, a corresponding button for it will be displayed in the lower panel, which you can use to minimize and restore the window.

To start a program, you can select its entry from the Main menu. You can also click its application icon in the panel (if one is present) or drag-and-drop data files to its icon. To add an icon for an application to the desktop, right-click on its entry in the Main menu and select "Pin to desktop".

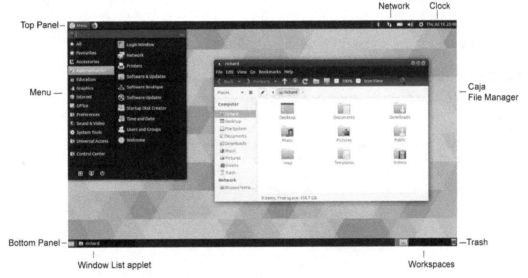

Figure 10-5: MATE with Main Menu and Caja file manager

Drag-and-Drop Files to the Desktop

Any icon for an item that you drag-and-drop from a file manager window to the desktop also appears on the desktop. However, the default drag-and-drop operation is a move operation. If you select a file in your file manager window and drag it to the desktop, you are actually moving the file from its current directory to the desktop folder, which is located in your home folder and holds all items on the desktop. The desktop folder is **Desktop**. In the case of dragging folders to the desktop, the entire folder and its subfolders will be moved to the desktop folder.

To remove an icon from the desktop, you right-click and choose "Move to Trash." If you choose to display the trash icon on the desktop, you can simply drag-and-drop it in the trash.

You can copy a file to your desktop by pressing the CTRL key and then clicking and dragging it from a file manager window to your desktop. You will see the mouse icon change to hand with a small + symbol, indicating that you are creating a copy, instead of moving the original.

You can also create a link on the desktop to any file. This is useful if you want to keep a single version in a folder and just be able to access it from the desktop. You could also use links for customized programs that you may not want to appear on the menu or panel. There are two ways to create a link. While holding down the Ctrl and Shift keys, CTRL-SHIFT, drag the file to where you want the link created. A copy of the icon then appears with a small arrow in the right corner indicating it is a link. You can click this link to start the program, open the file, or open the folder, depending on the type of file to which you linked. Alternatively, first click and drag the file out of the window, and after moving the file but before releasing the mouse button, press the ALT key. This will display a pop-up menu with selections for Move Here, Copy Here, and Link Here. Select the Link Here option to create a link.

The drag-and-drop file operation works on virtual desktops provided by the Workspace Switcher. The Workspace Switcher creates icons for each virtual desktop in the panel, along with task buttons for any applications open on them. The Workspace Switcher is not added by default. You will have to add it to the panel.

MATE Tweak

You can configure desktop and window display settings using the MATE Tweak dialog, which you can access from the Preferences menu, or from the Control Center (see Figure 10-6). The MATE Tweak dialog has three tabs: Desktop, Panel, and Windows. The Desktop tab lets you choose which system icons to display on the desktop. The Computer and Home folder icons are initially selected, along with Mounted volumes for external file systems such as USB drives and DVDs that you insert. You can also choose to display the Computer, Network, and Trash icons. The first option lets disable this feature, hiding all the desktop icons.

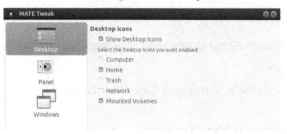

Figure 10-6: MATE Tweak

The Panel tab lets you

configure your panel, choosing from a panel layout style, possible features for the panel chosen (Panel Menu Features), and added panel features such as using a dock, displaying a keyboard LED, and choosing the size of icons in the panel.

On Windows tab, you can turn off compositing (change the window manager) and change the location of the minimize, maximize, and close buttons from the right side of the title bar to the left side. You can also enable or disable window features such as window snapping and animations.

Applications on the Desktop

In some cases, you will want to create another way on the desktop to access a file without moving it from its original folder. You can do this either by using an application launcher icon or by creating a link to the original program. Application launcher icons are the components used in menus and panels to display and access applications. To place an application icon on your desktop for an entry in the menus, you can simply drag-and-drop the application entry from the menu to the desktop, or right-click and select "Pin to desktop."

For applications that are not on a menu, you can either create an application launcher button or create a direct link for it. To create an application launcher, right-click the desktop background to display the desktop menu, and then select the "Create Launcher" entry. To create a simple link, click-and-drag a program's icon while holding the Ctrl-Shift keys down to the desktop.

The Desktop Menu

You can right-click anywhere on the empty desktop to display the GNOME desktop menu that includes entries for common tasks, such as creating an application launcher, creating a new folder, or organizing the icon display. Keep in mind that the New Folder entry creates a new folder on your desktop, specifically in your GNOME desktop folder (**Desktop**), not your home folder. The entries for this menu are listed in Table 10-1.

Menu Item	Description
Create Folder	Creates a new directory on your desktop, within your DESKTOP directory.
Create Launcher	Creates a new desktop icon for an application.
Create Document	Creates files using installed templates or a simple text file
Organize Desktop by Name	Arranges your desktop icons.
Keep Aligned	Aligns your desktop icons.
Cut, Copy, Paste	Cuts, copies, or pastes files, letting you move or copy files between folders.
Change Desktop Background	Opens a Background Preferences dialog to let you select a new background for your desktop.
Restore Missing Files	Restore files from backup
Open in Terminal	Open Desktop folder in a terminal window

Table 10-1: The GNOME Desktop Menu

Windows

You can resize a window by clicking any of its sides or corners and dragging. You can move the window with a click-and-drag operation on its title bar. You can also ALT-click and drag anywhere on the window. The upper-right corner of a window shows the Minimize, Maximize, and Close buttons (minus, square, and x buttons) (see Figure 10-4). Clicking the Minimize button no longer displays the window on the desktop. A button for it remains on the bottom panel (the Window list applet) that you can click to restore it. The panel button for a window works like a display toggle. If the window is displayed when you click the panel button, it will no longer be shown. If not displayed, it will then be shown. On the left side of the title bar is a drop-down menu that displays a window menu with entries for window operations (you can also right-click anywhere on the title bar to display the menu) (see Figure 10-7). The options include workspace entries to move the window to another workspace (virtual desktop) or make visible on all workspaces, which displays the window no matter to what workspace you move.

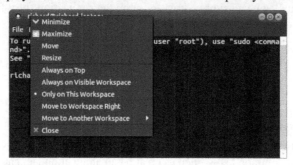

Figure 10-7: MATE window

You can quickly move between windows by pressing the Alt-Tab keys. A window switcher bar opens displaying thumbnails of open windows (see Figure 10-8). Continue pressing the Alt-Tab keys to move through them. To enable thumbnails, be sure that the Compositing Manager on the Windows Preferences dialog's General tab is enabled (Preferences | Windows). You also have the option to disable thumbnails for the switcher, displaying only small icons for the open windows.

Figure 10-8: Switching Windows with thumbnails

You can configure window behavior using the Window Preferences dialog's Behavior tab accessible from the Preference menu and the Control Center. You choose features such as to select windows by moving the mouse over them and use the Super key instead of the Alt key to move a window. From a menu, you can choose the action to perform when the title bar is double-clicked. The default is maximize, but other options include to roll up the window and minimize it.

On the Placement tab, you can choose to center new windows and to enable window snapping (side by side tiling).

Window List

The Window List applet on the left side of the bottom panel shows currently opened windows (see Figure 10-9). The Window List arranges opened windows in a series of buttons, one for each window. A window can include applications such as a Web browser or a file manager window displaying a folder. You can move from one displayed window to another by clicking its button. When you minimize a window, you can later restore it by clicking its entry in the Window List.

Right clicking a window's Window List button opens a menu that lets you Minimize or Unminimize, Move, Resize, Maximize, or Close the window, and move the window to another workspace. The Minimize operation will reduce the window to its Window List entry. Right clicking the entry will display the menu with an Unminimize option instead of a Minimize one, which you can then use to redisplay the window. The Close entry will close the window, ending its application. There are also entries for moving the window to another workspace.

Figure 10-9: Window List applet

The Window List applet is represented by a small area at the beginning of the window list applet (see Figure 10-9). To configure the Window List applet, right-click on this area and select the Preferences entry to open the Window List Preferences dialog (see Figure 10-10). Here, you can set features such as whether to group windows on the panel, whether to show all open windows or those from just the current workspace, and which workspace to restore windows to.

Figure 10-10: Window List Preferences

If you choose to group windows, then common windows are grouped under a button that will expand like a menu, listing each window in that group. For example, all open terminal windows would be grouped under a single button, which when clicked would pop up a list of their buttons. The button shows the number of open windows. You can also choose to group only if there is not enough space on the Window List applet to display a separate button for each window.

Workspace Switcher

The Workspace Switcher applet, located on the right side of the bottom panel, lets you switch to different virtual desktops (see Figure 10-11). You can add the Workspace Switcher to any panel by selecting it from that panel's Add To dialog. The Workspace Switcher shows your entire virtual desktop as separate rectangles listed next to each other. Open windows show up as small rectangles in these squares. You can move any window from one virtual desktop to another by clicking and dragging its image in the Workspace Switcher from one workspace to another.

Figure 10-11: Workspace switcher, one row and two rows

In addition to the Workspace Switcher, you can use the scroll button on your mouse, or the Ctrl-Alt-*arrow* keys to move from one workspace to another . When you use the Ctrl-Alt-arrow keys, the right and left arrows move you through a row, and the up and down keys move you from one row to another. A small workspace bar appears at the center of the screen, highlighting the current workspace and displaying its name (see Figure 10-12).

Figure 10-12: Switching workspaces, Ctrl-Alt-*arrow*

To configure the Workspace Switcher, right-click on the applet to display a menu, and then select Preferences to display the Workspace Switcher Preferences dialog box (see Figure 10-13). Here, you can select the number of workspaces and name them. The default is four. You can also choose the number of rows for the workspace and whether to show their names.

Figure 10-13: Workspace Switcher Preferences

MATE Panel Menus

Ubuntu Mate provides a variety of panel layouts to choose from. You can choose the panel layout using the Panel tab on the MATE Tweak dialog (Preferences menu) (see Figure 10-14). Available layouts include Familiar (the default), Contemporary, Cupertino, Mutiny, Netbook, Pantheon, Redmond, and Traditional. The Traditional layout is the one used in previous releases of Ubuntu Mate. You can activate certain features for a panel, as well as add applets to the panel, and then save it as your own, using the "Save as" button.

Figure 10-14: MATE Tweaks, Panel tab

Several different types of menus are available for Ubuntu Mate. These are incorporated into the different panel layouts. The menus include Main menu (Familiar, Contemporary, Netbook, and Pantheon), Mate Menu (Redmond), Menu Bar (Traditional), and Brisk menu with dash layout

(Mutiny and Cupertino). You can add any of these menus to a panel by using the Add to Panel dialog. The Cupertino and Pantheon layouts will also include the Mate Dock, which operates much like the dock on Apple systems.

You can edit any of the menus using the Main Menu editor, with which you can add and remove applications from the menus, create new menus, and add or remove submenus (see Figure 10-15). You can open the editor by right-clicking on the Main Menu menubar and choosing "Edit Menus" from the pop-up menu. Menus are listed to left and items shown in a selected menu are check marked on the right. Click a checkmark to no longer display an entry.

Figure 10-15: Main Menu Editor

Main Menu (traditional Brisk)

Ubuntu MATE uses the Main menu on the top panel for the Familiar, Contemporary, Netbook and Pantheon panel layouts. The Main Menu is a traditional Brisk menu. The Familiar panel layout is the default. Application categories are lists to the left and applications in a selected category are shown on the right (see Figure 10-16). The All category lists all the applications. The Favorites category lists only those application you have selected as your favorites. You can also access the Control Center and Universal Access dialog directly. Buttons at the bottom of the menu let you logout, lock, or shut down (power button) our system. At the top of the menu is a search box where you can search directly for an application. The search is dynamic, reducing the selection of found applications as you add more characters to the search pattern. If you right-click on an application, a menu is displayed with "Pint to favorites menu" and Pin to desktop" options.

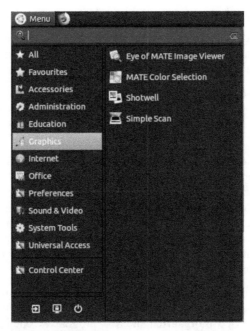

Figure 10-16: Main Menu: Applications

Menu Bar menu

Ubuntu MATE uses the Menu Bar menu on the top panel for the Traditional panel layouts. It was the default panel layout used in previous release of Ubuntu Mate. The Menu Bar is a menubar that has three menus: Applications, Places, and System (See Figure 10-17). From the Applications menu, you can access your installed software applications. They are arranged by category with submenus for Internet, Graphics, Office, Sound & Video, and Accessories. The Places menu lets you access locations such as your home folder and removable devices. On the System menu you can access Administration tools from the Administration submenu, and Preferences dialogs from the Preferences submenu.

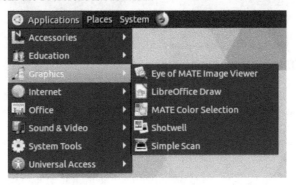

Figure 10-17: Menu Bar

MATE Menu (advanced)

You can install the Mate (advanced) menu as an applet on any panel. It is also the default panel for Redmond panel layout (MATE Tweak dialog's Panel tab). The menu is located on the left side of the panel, as the Menu button.

The MATE menu has three sections: Places, System, and Favorites/Applications (see Figure 10-18). The Places section displays buttons for accessing commonly used locations: the computer window for your devices and mounted folder, your home folder, the network window for shared devices and folders, your trash folder, and the Desktop folder.

The System section has buttons for software management, the Control Center, a terminal window, and for lock, logout, and shut down (Quit) operations. Package Manager opens the Ubuntu MATE Software Boutique Software Manager, letting you install software for MATE from Ubuntu repositories. The Control Center button opens the GNOME Control Center, which shows icons for system and desktop configuration and administration. Many of the administrative tools are the same as those used for the Ubuntu Desktop. The Lock Screen button locks your system, displaying the lock screen. The Logout button logs you out to the login screen. The Quit button opens the shutdown dialog with options to suspend, restart, and shut down.

The Applications/Favorites section is a toggle showing either your favorite applications or all installed applications. You can toggle between the two using the button in the upper right side of the menu. The Applications view is organized into two scroll boxes, one for software categories and the other for applications in those categories. You can use the scroll wheel on your mouse to scroll through the larger listings.

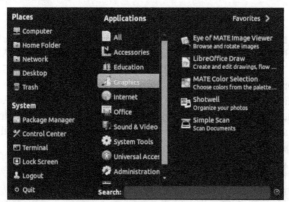

Figure 10-18: MATE Menu (advanced menu)

The MATE menu supports a search operation, using the Search text box in the bottom right corner. When you click on the Search text box, the All category is selected. As you type, matching applications are displayed in the Applications section of the menu. If there are no matches, then entries are listed to search Google, Wikipedia, your dictionary, and your computer for that term.

Several actions can be performed on a menu application item using its pop-up menu. Right-click on the item to display the menu (see Figure 10-19). You can add an application launcher to the panel or the desktop by dragging its icon from the menu to the desktop or panel. You can also right-click on the application icon and choose "Add to Desktop" or "Add to Panel".

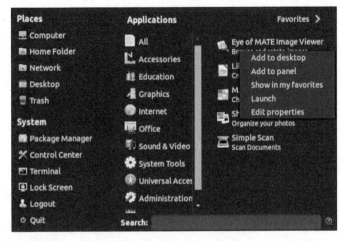

Figure 10-19: MATE Menu Applications pop-up menu

The Favorites section lists default favorites you may want. Click on the Favorites button in the top right corner to display your favorites. You can add any application to the favorites list by right-clicking on its entry and choosing "Show in my favorites" (see Figure 10-20). You can reorder favorites on the menu by simply clicking and dragging them to new locations. To remove a favorite, right-click and choose "Remove from favorites."

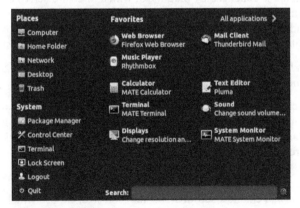

Figure 10-20: MATE Menu Favorites

You can configure the MATE menu using the Menu preferences dialog, which you can access by right-clicking on the Menu button on the panel and choosing "Preferences" from the pop-up menu. Menu Preferences has seven tabs: Main button, Plugins, Theme, Applications, Favorites, Places, and System (see Figure 10-21). On the "Main button" tab you can specify the advanced menu applet's name (text) and whether to show an icon. You can choose a different icon, and specify the keyboard command to use to display the menu (meta-l is the default).

Figure 10-21: MATE Menu Preferences dialog

The MATE menu is enhanced by plugins, of which three are active by default. You can specify the plugins to use on the Plugins tab. The "Show Recent Documents" entry lets you activate an added pane in the advanced menu for recent documents. The "Always start with favorites pane" will display the Favorites pane instead of the Applications pane, when you first display the menu.

The Theme tab lets you choose custom colors for headings, borders, and background. You can also choose a theme.

On the Applications tab, you can configure the Applications pane, choosing to display category icons, show application comments in pop-up notes, and to let mouse hovering select an entry. You can also configure the search function to search for uninstalled packages, and to remember the last search.

For Favorites, you can configure the number of columns and the icons size.

For Places, you can enable a scrollbar, set the icon size, choose which default items to display, and whether to display your bookmarks. You can also add custom places (folders) for the menu. Click the New button to open a dialog where you can enter the place's name and the path name of the folder.

On the System tab, you can choose to allow a scrollbar, set the icon size, and choose the default items to display.

Brisk Menu with dash layout

Both the Mutiny and Cupertino panel layouts use the Brisk Menu with a dash layout. Like GNOME, it displays an overview of icons for applications in different categories. Categories are listed at the top, along with a search box for locating applications. Click the menu button on the top panel to display the menu. The Cupertino panel layout is shown in Figure 10-22.

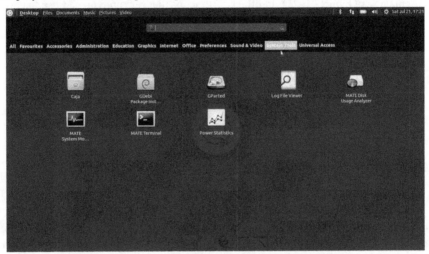

Figure 10-22: Brisk Menu with dash layout, Cupertino panel layout

The Mutiny layout style uses the same dash layout, but adds an application launcher, much like the GNOME Dock extension (see Figure 10-23). Click the Ubuntu icon above the launcher to display the menu.

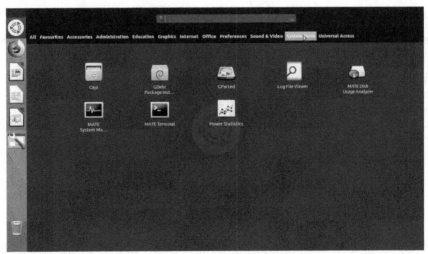

Figure 10-23: Brisk Menu with dash layout and launcher, Mutiny panel layout

Mate Dock

The Mate Dock applet sets up a dock on the panel for applications. As you open applications, icons for them appear on the panel (see Figure 10-24). In this way, the dock operates like the window list. If you minimize an application, you can maximize it again by clicking its dock icon. When the application closes, the icon disappears. You can right-click on an icon to have the application remain (see Figure 10-25). In effect, with icons that remain, you can use the dock more as a launcher for favorite applications.

Figure 10-24: Mate Dock applet

Figure 10-25: Mate Dock on panel layout with applications

In the Cupertino and Pantheon panel layout, a dock is set up at the bottom of the screen that operates more like docks in other operating systems. A set of favorite applications is already displayed.

MATE Panel

The panel is the main component of the MATE interface. Through it, you can start your applications, run applets, and access desktop areas. You can think of the MATE panel as a type of tool you can use on your desktop. You can have several MATE panels displayed on your desktop, each with applets and menus you have placed in them. In this respect, MATE is flexible, enabling you to configure your panels any way you want. The MATE panel work the same as the GNOME 2 panel. You can easily add applets to the panel, along with application launchers.

Ubuntu MATE uses the traditional GNOME 2 top and bottom panels by default, though you can add more. The top panel applets for the Main Menu (MATE Main menubar), a launcher for the Firefox Web browser, and several system applets (see Figure 10-26). The system applets display buttons for the Bluetooth, Network Manager, volume control, the power manager, the clock, and shutdown. If you are using the MATE menu (advanced menu) a Menu button is shown.

Figure 10-26: MATE Top Panel

The bottom panel has applets for the menu, Show Desktop and the window list on the left, and the workspace switcher and the Trash on the right (see Figure 10-27).

Figure 10-27: MATE Panel

Panel configuration tasks such as adding applications, selecting applets, setting up menus, and creating new panels are handled from the Panel pop-up menu (see Figure 10-28). Just right-click anywhere on the empty space your panel to display a menu with entries for Properties, New Panel, Add To Panel, and Delete This Panel, along with Help and About entries. New Panel lets you create other panels; Add To Panel lets you add items to the panel such as application launchers, applets for simple tasks like the Workspace Switcher, and menus like the MATE menu. The Properties entry will display a dialog for configuring the features for that panel, like the position of the panel and its hiding capabilities.

To add a new panel, select the New Panel entry in the Panel pop-up menu (see Figure 10-28). A new expanded panel is automatically created and displayed at the top of your screen. You can then use the panel's properties box to set different display and background features, as described in the following sections.

Figure 10-28: MATE Panel pop-up menu

Panel Properties

To configure individual panels, you use the Panel Properties dialog box (see Figure 10-29). To display this dialog box, you right-click a particular panel and select the Properties entry in the pop-up menu. For individual panels, you can set general configuration features and the background. The Panel Properties dialog box displays two tabs, General and Background.

Displaying Panels

On the General tab of a panel's properties box, you determine how you want the panel displayed. Here you have options for orientation, size, and whether to expand, auto-hide, or display hide buttons. The Orientation entry lets you select which side of the screen you want the panel placed on. You can then choose whether you want a panel expanded or not. An expanded panel will fill the edges of the screen, whereas a non-expanded panel is sized to the number of items in the panel and shows handles at each end. Expanded panels will remain fixed to the edge of the screen, whereas unexpanded panels can be moved.

Figure 10-29: MATE Panel Properties

Moving and Hiding Expanded Panels

Expanded panels can be positioned at any edge of your screen. You can move expanded panels from one edge of a screen to another by selecting an edge from the Orientation menu on the Panel Properties General tab. If a panel is already there, the new one will stack on top of the current one. You cannot move unexpanded panels in this way. You can hide expanded panels either automatically or manually. These are features specified in the panel properties General box as the Autohide and "Show hide buttons" option. To automatically hide panels, select the Autohide feature. The panel will be hidden. To display the panel, move your mouse to the edge where the panel is located.

If you want to hide a panel manually, select the "Show hide buttons" option. Two hide buttons showing arrows will be displayed at either end of the panel. You can further choose whether to have these buttons display arrows or not (displaying arrows is the default). You can then hide the panel at any time by clicking either of the hide buttons located on each end of the panel. The arrows show the direction in which the panel will hide.

Unexpanded Panels: Movable and Fixed

Whereas an expanded panel is always located at the edge of the screen, an unexpanded panel is movable. It can be located at the edge of a screen, working like a shrunken version of an expanded panel, or you can move it to any place on your desktop, just as you would an icon.

An unexpanded panel will shrink to the number of its components, showing handles at either end (on the default Ambient-MATE theme for Ubuntu MATE, the handles show up as simply blank areas). You can then move the panel by dragging its handles. To access the panel menu with its properties entry, right-click either of its handles.

To fix an unexpanded panel at its current position, select the "Show hide buttons" option on its properties box. This will replace the handles with hide buttons and make the panel fixed.

Clicking a Hide button will hide the panel to the edge of the screen, just as with expanded panels. If another expanded panel is already located on that edge, the button for a hidden unexpanded panel will be on top of it. The Autohide feature will also work for unexpanded panels placed at the edge of a screen.

If you want to fix an unexpanded panel to the edge of a screen, make sure it is placed at the edge you want, and then set its "Show hide buttons" option.

Panel Background

With a panel's Background pane on its properties box, you can change the panel's background color or image. For a color background, click the "Solid color" option, and then click the Color button to display a color selection window where you can choose a color from a color wheel or a list of color boxes, or you can enter its number. Once your color is selected, you can use the Style slide bar to make it more transparent or opaque. To use an image instead of a color, select the "Background image" option and use the browse button to locate the image file you want. For an image, you can also drag and drop an image file from the file manager to the panel; that image then becomes the background image for the panel.

Panel Objects

A panel can contain several different types of objects. These include menus, launchers, applets, drawers, and special objects.

Menus   A panel menu has launchers that are buttons used to start an application or execute a command.

Launchers   You can select any application entry in the Applications menu and create a launcher for it on the panel.

Applets   An applet is a small application designed to run within the panel. The Workspace Switcher showing the different desktops is an example of a GNOME applet.

Drawers   A drawer is an extension of the panel that can be open or closed. You can think of a drawer as a shrinkable part of the panel. You can add anything to it that you can to a regular panel, including applets, menus, and even other drawers.

Special objects   These are used for special tasks not supported by other panel objects. For example, the Logout and Lock buttons are special objects.

Moving, Removing, and Locking Objects

To move any object within the panel, right-click it and choose the Move entry. You can move it either to a different place on the same panel or to a different panel. For launchers, you can just drag the object directly where you want it to be. To remove an object from the panel, right-click it to display a pop-up menu for it, and then choose the "Remove From Panel" entry. To prevent an object from being moved or removed, you set its lock feature. Right-click the object and select the "Lock To Panel" entry. For a locked object, a checkmark appears before the "Lock to Panel" entry. To later allow it to be moved, you first have to unlock the object, Right-click it and select "Lock to Panel" to remove the checkmark and making the Move entry active.

Adding Objects

To add an object to a panel, select the object from the panel's "Add to Panel" dialog (see Figure 10-30). To display the Add To Panel dialog, right-click on the panel and select the "Add to Panel" entry. The "Add to Panel" dialog displays a lengthy list of common objects, such as the MATE Menu (advanced menu), Log Out, and Clock. For Application applets, you can click on the Applications Launcher entry and click the Forward button to list all your installed applications. Launchers can also be added to a panel by just dragging them directly. Launchers include applications, windows, and files. The Custom Application Launcher lets you create a custom launcher, choosing an application or script you generated.

Application Launchers

To add an application that already has an application launcher to a panel is easy. You just have to drag the application launcher to the panel. This will automatically create a copy of the launcher for use on that panel. Launchers can be menu items or desktop icons. All the entries in the Main or MATE menus are application launchers. To add an application from the menu, just select it and drag it to the panel. You can also drag any desktop application icon to a panel to add a copy of it to that panel.

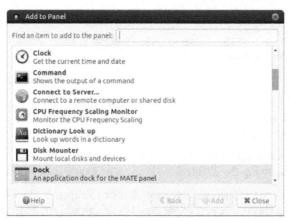

Figure 10-30: MATE Panel "Add to Panel" dialog for panel applets

For any menu item, you can also go to its entry and right-click it, and then select the "Add to panel" entry. An application launcher for that application is then automatically added to the panel. Suppose you use the Pluma text editor frequently and want to add its icon to the panel, instead of having to go through the Application menu all the time. Right-click the Text Editor menu entry in the Accessories menu, and select the "Add this launcher to panel" entry. The Pluma text editor icon now appears in your panel.

Also, as previously noted, you can open the "Add to Panel" dialog, and then choose the Application Launcher entry and click the Forward button. This will display a dialog with a listing of all the Application menu entries along with Preferences and Administration menus, expandable to their items. Just find the application you want added, select it, and click the Add button.

Adding Drawers

You can also group applications under a Drawer icon. Clicking the Drawer icon displays a list of the different application icons you can then select. To add a drawer to your panel, right-click the panel and select the "Add to panel" entry to display the "Add to Panel" dialog. From that list select the Drawer entry. This will create a drawer on your panel. You can then drag any items from desktop, menus, or windows (folders or launchers) to the drawer icon on the panel to have them listed in the drawer.

You can also add applets and applications to a drawer using the "Add to Drawer" dialog. Right-click on the drawer and choose the "Add to Drawer" entry to open the dialog. Then click the applet you want added to the drawer. To add applications, select the Applications Launcher entry and click for Forward to list your application menu categories, which are expandable to list applications. You can add an entire menu to the drawer by choosing the application category and clicking the Add button.

Adding Menus

A menu differs from a drawer in that a drawer holds application icons instead of menu entries. You can add application menus to your panel, much as you add drawers. To add an application menu to your panel, open the "Add to Panel" dialog and select the Application Launcher entry, clicking Forward to open the list of Application categories. Select the category you want, and click the Add button. That menu category with all its application items is added to your panel as a menu.

Adding Folders and Files

You can also add files and folders to a panel. For folders, click and drag the folder icon from the file manager window to your panel. Whenever you click this folder button, a file manager window opens, displaying that directory. You can also add folders to any drawer on your panel. To add a file, also drag it directly to the panel. To add a file (except for images), click and drag the file to the panel or drawer. When you click on the file icon, the file opens with its application.

Adding Applets

Applets are small programs that perform tasks within the panel. To add an applet, right-click the panel and select "Add to Panel" from the pop-up menu. This displays the "Add To Panel" dialog listing common applets along with other types of objects, such as launchers. Select the one you want. For example, to add the clock to your panel, select Clock. Once added, the applet will show up in the panel. If you want to remove an applet, right-click it and select the "Remove From Panel" entry. To configure an applet, right-click on the applet and select the Preferences entry.

MATE features a number of helpful applets. Some applets monitor your system, such as the Battery Charge Monitor, which checks the battery in laptops, and System Monitor, which shows a graph indicating your current CPU and memory use.

Caja File Manager

The Caja file manager supports the standard features for copying, removing, and deleting items as well as setting permissions and displaying items. The program name for the file manager is **caja**. You can enhance Caja using extensions such as "Open terminal" to open the current folder in a new terminal window, and Engrampa that allows you to create (compress) and extract archives. Several extensions already installed are enabled by default, and will display entries in appropriate menus. Extensions are enabled on the Extension tab of the File Management Preferences dialog (Edit | Preferences). To add more extension, use the Software Manager to install the caja extension packages. Extension packages have the prefix **caja-**, such as **caja-share**, **caja-dropbox**, and **caja-wallpaper**. A helpful extension that you may want to add is the Caja Share extension to integrate folder sharing from the Caja file manager (install the Caja Share package, Software Boutique | Servers). The **deja-dup-caja** package (installed by default), integrates backup restore operations into the file manager as the "Revert to Previous Version" entry in the Caja Edit menu and the "Restore Missing Files" in the File menu.

Home Folder Sub-folders and Bookmarks

Like Ubuntu, MATE uses the Common User Directory Structure (xdg-user-dirs at **http://freedesktop.org**) to set up sub-folders in the user home directory. Folders will include **Documents**, **Music**, **Pictures**, **Downloads**, and **Videos**. These localized user folders are used as defaults by many desktop applications. Users can change their folder names or place them within each other. For example, Music can be moved into **Documents**, **Documents/Music**. Local configuration is held in the **.config/user-dirs.dirs** file. System-wide defaults are set up in the **/etc/xdg/user-dirs.defaults** file. The icons for these folders are displayed in Figure 10-31.

Figure 10-31: Caja file manager home folders

The folders are also default bookmarks. You can access a bookmarked folder directly from the Caja window sidebar. You can also add your own bookmarks for folders by opening the folder and choosing "Add Bookmark" from the Bookmarks menu. Your folder will appear in the Bookmarks section of the Caja side pane Places menu and on the Bookmarks menu. Use the Edit Bookmarks dialog to remove bookmarks. Here you can remove a bookmark or change its name and location.

You use Desktop Settings to display basic folders such as the home, network, and trash folders on the desktop area.

File Manager Windows

When you click Home folder icon on the desktop or the Home folder entry on the MATE menu Places section, a file manager window opens showing your home folder. The file manager window displays several components, including a menubar, a main toolbar, and a side pane (see Figure 10-32). The side pane works like the sidebar in the Nemo and Nautilus (Files) file managers, but with a menu, like the file manager in GNOME 2. The file manager window's main pane (to the right) displays the icons or listing of files and sub-folders in the current working folder. When you select a file and folder, the status bar at the bottom of the window displays the name of the file or folder selected and for files the size, and for folders the number of items contained. The status bar also displays the remaining free space on the current file system.

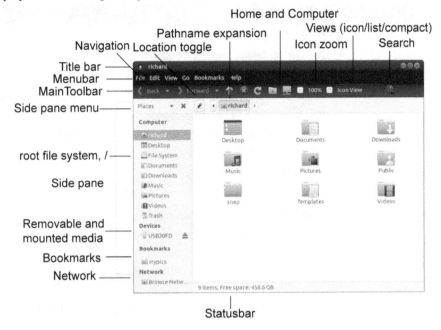

Figure 10-32: Caja file manager with sidebar

Note: Caja works as an operational FTP browser. You can use the Connect to Server entry on the Caja Files menu to open a "Connect to Server" dialog, where you can enter the URL for the FTP site.

When you open a new folder, the same window is used to display it, and you can use the Forward and Back buttons to move through previously opened folders (top left on the main toolbar) (see Figure 10-33). A down triangle to the right of the Forward button displays a menu of previously accessed folders, which you can use to access a previous folder directly. There is also an up arrow to move to the parent directory, and a Home folder button to move directly to your home folder. The Computer button displays the computer window showing your file systems and attached devices. You can also access these operations from the file manager's Go menu (see Table 10-2). Stop and Refresh buttons let you cancel and update display operations. The Go menu will also display a list of folders you have previously opened and searches you have performed. Use the "Clear History" option to reset this list.

Figure 10-33: Caja navigation buttons: back, forward, parent, home, computer

As you open sub-folders, the main toolbar displays buttons for your current folder and its parent folders (see Figure 10-30). You can click on a folder button to move to it directly. Initially, the button shows a path of subdirectories from your home folder. Clicking on the small triangle arrow to the left expands the path to the top level, from the root directory (the hard disk icon).

Menu Item	Description
Open Parent	Move to the parent folder
Back	Move to the previous folder viewed in the file manager window
Forward	Move to the next folder viewed in the file manager window
Paste	Paste files that you have copied or cut, letting you move or copy files between folders, or make duplicates.
Same Location as Other Pane	If you have two panes open on the window, you can make both panes view the same folder
Home Folder	Move to the Home folder
Computer	Move to the Computer folder, showing icons for your devices
Templates	Move to the Templates folder
Trash	Open the trash folder to see deleted files and folders, which can be restored.
Network	Move to the network folder showing connected systems on your network and open remote folders.
Location	Open the location navigation box for entering the path name of a file or folder
Search for Files	Search for files and folders using the file manager window
Clear History	Clear list of previous searches, folders visited, and shared folders

Table 10-2: File Manager Go Menu

You can also display a location URL text box instead of buttons, where you can enter the location of a folder, either on your system or on a remote system. To display the location text box, press **Ctrl-l**, or from the Go menu select Location or click the Location toggle (pencil icon) at the beginning of the location path on the main toolbar (see Figure 10-34). These access methods operate as toggles that move you a back and forth from the location text box to the button path.

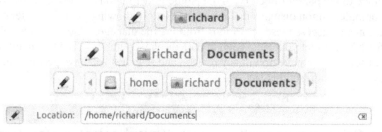

Figure 10-34: Caja locations: unexpanded, expanded, and location path

The File menu has entries for opening a new tab (Ctrl-t), opening a new file manager window (Ctrl-n), creating a new folder (Shift-Ctrl-n), connecting to a remote FTP server, and displaying the properties of the current folder (Alt-ENTER). Most have corresponding keys (see Table 10-3).

Menu Item	Description
New Tab	Creates a new tab.
New Window	Open a new file manager window
Create Folder	Creates a new subdirectory in the directory.
Create Document	Creates a text document.
Open	When a folder is selected the Open item is displayed showing also the "Open in New Tab" and "Open in New Window" items, along with the Open With submenu.
Open With	When a file is selected the Open With item is displayed showing possible applications to open the file with
Connect to server	Connect to an FTP server using the file manager
Properties	Properties for the currently open folder
Empty Trash	Empty the trash folder
Restore Missing Files	Restore files from backup
Open as Administrator	Open a folder or file with administrative access (useful for system folders)
Open in Terminal	Open the current folder in a new terminal window (Open Terminal extension)
Close All Windows	Close all file manage windows
Close	Close the file manager window.

Table 10-3: File Manager File Menu

File Manager Side Pane

The file manager side pane has a menu from which you can choose to display places (Places), the tree view of the file system (Tree), information on the current or selected folder or file (Information), the history of previously opened folders for that login session (History), notes (Notes), and emblems you can place on a file or folder (Emblems).

The default for the side pane is the Places view, which displays sections for Computer, Devices, Bookmarks, and Network items showing your file systems and default home folder sub-folders (see Figure 10-35). You can choose to display or hide the side pane by selecting the "Side Pane" entry in the View menu, or by clicking the close button on the right side of the side pane menu. You can also use F9 to toggle the side pane on and off.

Figure 10-35: File manager side pane menu and views (Caja)

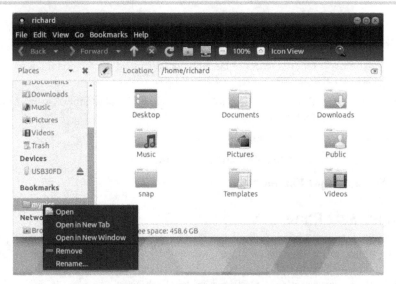

Figure 10-36: File manager side pane with bookmarks menu (Caja)

Selecting the File System entry in the side pane places you at the top of the file system, letting you move to any accessible part of it. In the Computer section, you can search your default folders, such as Documents and Pictures. Should you bookmark a folder (Bookmarks menu, "Add Bookmark" entry (Ctrl-d)), a Bookmark section appears on the side pane with the bookmark. To remove or rename a bookmark, right-click on its entry on the side pane and choose Remove or Rename from the pop-up menu (see Figure 10-36). The bookmark name changes, but not the original folder name. You can also remove a bookmark using the Edit Bookmarks dialog (Go menu, Edit Bookmarks).

Tabs

The Caja file manager supports tabs with which you can open up several folders in the same file manager window. To open a tab, select New Tab from the File menu or press **Ctrl-t**. A tab bar appears with tab buttons for each tab, displaying the name of the folder open, and an x close button (see Figure 10-37). You can re-arrange tabs by clicking and dragging their tab buttons to the right or left. You can also use the Ctrl-PageUp and Ctrl-PageDown keys to move from one tab to another. Use the Shift-Ctrl-PageUp and Shift-Ctrl-PageDown keys to rearrange the tabs. To close a tab, click its close **x** button on the right side of the tab button.

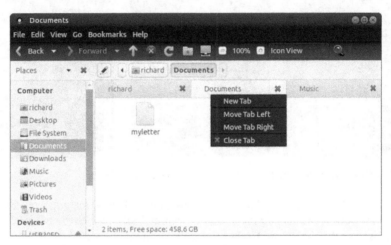

Figure 10-37: File manager window with tabs (Caja)

Displaying Files and Folders

You can view a folder's contents as icons, a compact list, or as a detailed list, which you can choose from the view menu on the right side of the main toolbar: icon, list, and compact views, as shown here.

Use the control keys to change views quickly: **Ctrl-1** for Icons, **Ctrl-2** for list, and **Ctrl-3** for compact view. The List view provides the name, size, type, and date. Buttons are displayed for each field across the top of the main pane. You can use these buttons to sort the list according to that field. For example, to sort the files by date, click the Date Modified button; to sort by size, click Size button. Click again to alternate between ascending and descending order.

Certain types of file icons will display previews of their contents. For example, the icons for image files will display a thumbnail of the image. A text file will display in its icon the first few words of its text.

The View menu has entries for managing and arranging your file manager icons (see Table 10-4) (see Figure 10-38). You can choose Icons, List, and Compact views. In the Icon view, the "Arrange items" submenu appears, which provides entries for sorting icons by name, size, type, emblem, and modification date. You can also simply reverse the order, or position icons manually.

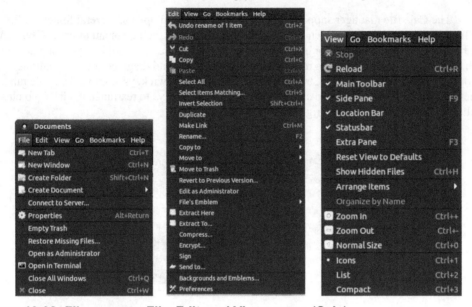

Figure 10-38: File manager File, Edit, and View menus (Caja)

The View | Zoom In entry enlarges your view of the window, making icons bigger, and Zoom Out reduces your view, making them smaller. Normal Size restores them to the standard size. You can also use the **Ctrl-+** and **Ctrl--** keys, and the zoom buttons on the main toolbar (to the left of the view menu) to zoom in and out.

File manager tools and menus

From the Edit menu, you can paste files you have cut or copied to move or copy them between folders, or make duplicates (see Table 10-5 and see Figure 10-28). The selection menu items let you select all files and folders, those matching a simple regular expression, and to invert a selection, choosing all those not selected.

In the icon view, you can click anywhere on the empty space on the main pane of a file manager window to display a pop-up menu with entries to create a new folder, arrange icons, zoom icons, and open the folder properties dialog (see Table 10-4).

Navigating in the file manager

The file manager operates similarly to a Web browser, using the same window to display opened folders. It maintains a list of previously viewed folders, and you can move back and forth through that list using the toolbar navigation buttons (left side). The left arrow button moves you to the previously displayed directory, the right arrow button moves you to the next displayed directory, and the up arrow moves to the parent directory. The home icon opens your home directory, and the computer icon (monitor) opens the Computer window, which lists icons for your file system and removable devices.

Menu Item	Description
Stop	Stop current task
Reload	Refresh file and directory list
Main Toolbar	Displays main toolbar
Side Pane	Displays side pane
Location Bar	Displays location bar
Statusbar	Displays status bar at bottom of folder window
Extra Pane	Display dual panes for file manager window, with separate folders open in each
Reset View to Defaults	Displays files and folders in default view
Show Hidden Files	Show administrative dot files.
Arrange Items: By Name, Size, Type, Modification Date, and Emblems	Arrange files and directory by specified criteria
Organize by Name	Sort icons in Icon view by name
Zoom In	Provides a close-up view of icons, making them appear larger.
Zoom Out	Provides a distant view of icons, making them appear smaller.
Normal Size	Restores view of icons to standard size.
Icons	Displays icons
List	Displays file list with name, size, type, and date. Folders are expandable.
Compact	Displays compact file list using only the name and small icons

Table 10-4: File Manager View Menu (Caja)

Use the side pane's Places view to access your bookmarked folders, storage devices (USB, CD/DVD disc, and attached hard drives), and mounted network folders. On the Computer section of the side pane, you can access your home folders, trash, the file system (root directory). On the Bookmarks section, you can access any additional bookmarks you created.

To open a subdirectory, you can double-click its icon or right-click the icon and select Open from the menu. You can also open the folder in a new tab or a new window. You can also click on the folder to select it, and then choose Open from the File menu (File | Open). The tab, new window, and open with items are also listed when a folder is selected. Figure 10-39 shows the File menu with the different Open items and Open With submenu for a folder and a file. Table 10-3 lists the File menu options.

Menu Item	Description
Cut, Copy	Move or copy a file or directory
Paste	Paste files that you have copied or cut, letting you move or copy files between folders, or make duplicates.
Undo, Redo	Undo or Redo a paste operation
Select All	Select all files and folders in this folder
Select Items Matching	Quick search for files using basic pattern matching.
Invert Selection	Select all other files and folders not selected, deselecting the current selection.
Duplicate	Make a copy of a selected file
Make Link	Make a link to a file or folder
Rename	Rename a selected file or folder
Copy to	Copy a file or folder to one of the default bookmarks
Move to	Move a file or folder to one of the default bookmarks
Move To Trash	Move a file for folder to the trash folder for later deletion
Revert to Previous Version	Restore to a previous backed up version
Edit as Administrator	Edit a file with administrative privileges (useful for system files)
Files's Emblem	Choose a status emblem for a file such as important, favorite, finished, or new.
Open as Administrator	Open a folder with administrative privileges (useful for sytem folders)
Folder's Color	Color of a folder icon
Extract Here Extract To	When an archive is selected, these entries appear
Compress	Compress selected files and folders to a compressed archive file such as a tar, cpio, or zip file (Engrampa extension).
Encrypt	Encrypt a file using encryption keys set up with "Passwords and Keys"
Sign	Sign a file using encryption keys set up with "Passwords and Keys"
Open in terminal	Open a terminal window at the folder
Send To	Send as an email, or copy to a removable disk
Backgrounds and Emblems	Choose a background for the file manager windows. Add emblems to any folder or file in the file manager window.
Preferences	The Caja File Manager preferences for your account.

Table 10-5: File Manager Edit Menu (Caja)

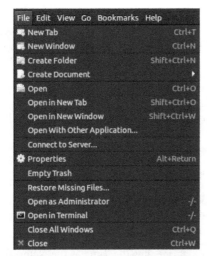

Figure 10-39: File manager File | Open with submenu for folders and files

Menu Item	Description
Create Folder	Creates a new subdirectory in the directory.
Create Document	Creates a text document.
Restore Missing Files	Restore files from a previous backup
Open as Administrator	Open a folder with administrative access (useful for system folders)
Open in Terminal	Open a terminal window at that folder (Open terminal extension)
Arrange Items: By Name, Size, Type, Modification Date, and Emblems	Arrange files and directory by specified criteria
Organize by Name	Sort icons in Icon view by name
Zoom In	Provides a close-up view of icons, making them appear larger.
Zoom Out	Provides a distant view of icons, making them appear smaller.
Normal Size	Restores view of icons to standard size.
Properties	Opens the Properties dialog for the directory

Table 10-6: File Manager Pop-up Menu (Caja)

You can open any folder or file system listed in the side pane Places view by clicking on its folder or bookmark. You can also right-click on a bookmark or folder to display a menu with entries to Open, "Open in a New Tab", and "Open in a New Window" (see Table 10-7). The "Open in a New Window" item is an easy way to access devices from the file manager. The menu for the Trash entry lets you empty the trash. For any bookmark, you can also remove and rename the entry. Entries for removable devices in the sidebar such as USB drives also have menu items for Eject and Safely Remove Drive. Internal hard drives have an Unmount entry instead.

Menu Item	Description
Open	Opens the file with its associated application. Directories are opened in the file manager. Associated applications are listed.
Open In A New Tab	Opens a directory in a new tab in the same window.
Open In A New Window	Opens a directory in a separate window, accessible from the toolbar, right-click.
Remove	Remove bookmark from the sidebar.
Rename	Rename a bookmark.

Table 10-7: The File Manager Side Pane Pop-Up Menu (Caja)

Caja File Manager Search

The Caja file manager provides a search tool that operates the same as the Nemo file manager search. From a file manager window, click the Search button on the toolbar (Looking glass at right), or select Go | Search for Files, to open a Search box below the toolbar. Enter the pattern to search and press ENTER or click the looking glass button on the right side of the text box. The results are displayed.

Drop-down menus for location and file type will appear in the folder window, with + and - buttons for adding or removing location and file type search parameters. Click the plus + button to add more location and file type search parameters. The search begins from the folder opened, but you can specify another folder to search (a Location menu). To search multiple folders at once, click the + button to add a Location menu for each folder, and specify that folder. You can do the same for multiple file types, specifying only files with certain types.

Managing Files and Folders

As a GNOME-compliant file manager, Caja supports desktop drag-and-drop operations for copying and moving files. To move a file or directory, drag-and-drop from one directory to another as you would on Windows or Mac interfaces. The move operation is the default drag-and-drop operation in GNOME. To copy a file to a new location, press the Ctrl key as you drag.

Using a file's pop-up menu

You can also perform remove, rename, and link creation operations on a file by right-clicking its icon and selecting the action you want from the pop-up menu that appears (see Table 10-8). For example, to remove an item, right-click it and select the Move To Trash entry from the pop-up menu. This places it in the Trash directory, where you can later delete it. To create a link, right-click the file and select Make Link from the pop-up menu. This creates a new link file that begins with the term "Link." If you select an archive file, the pop-up menu also displays entries to "Extract Here" and "Extract to".

Renaming Files

To rename a file, you can either right-click the file's icon and select the Rename entry from the pop-up menu, or click its icon and press the F2 function key. The name of the icon will be bordered, encased in a small text box. You can overwrite the old one, or edit the current name by clicking a position in the name to insert text, as well as use the backspace key to delete characters. You can also rename a file by entering a new name in its Properties dialog box (Basic tab).

Menu Item	Description
Open	Opens the file with its associated application. Directories are opened in the file manager. Associated applications are listed.
Open In A New Tab	Opens a folder in a new tab in the same window.
Open In A New Window	Opens a folder in a new window
Open With Other Application	Selects an application with which to open the file, or a file manager to use to open a folder.
Cut Copy	Entries to cut and copy the selected file.
Paste into Folder	Paste the selected folder
Make Link	Creates a link to that file in the same directory.
Rename (F2)	Renames the file.
Copy To	Copy a file to the Home Folder, Desktop, or to a folder displayed in another pane in the file manager window.
Move To	Move a file to the Home Folder, Desktop, or to a folder displayed in another pane in the file manager window.
Move To Trash	Moves a file to the Trash directory, where you can later delete it.
Revert to Previous Version	Restore to a previous backed up version
Edit as Administrator	Edit a file with administrative privileges (useful for system files)
Open as Administrator	Open a folder with administrative privileges
Folder's Color	Color of a folder icon
Files's Emblem	Choose a status emblem for a file
Extract Here Extract To	When an archive is selected, these entries appear
Compress	Archives files
Encrypt	Encrypt a file using encryption keys set up with "Passwords and Keys"
Sign	Sign a file using encryption keys set up with "Passwords and Keys"
Open in terminal	Open a terminal window at the folder (useful for performing command line tasks such as running shell commands)
Send To	Send as an email, or copy to a removable disk
Properties	Displays the Properties dialog.

Table 10-8: The File and Directory Pop-Up Menu

Grouping Files

You can select a group of files and folders by clicking the first item and then hold down the SHIFT key while clicking the last item, or by clicking and dragging the mouse across items you want to select. To select separated items, hold the CTRL key down as you click the individual icons. If you want to select all the items in the folder, choose the Select All entry in the Edit menu (Edit | Select All) (**Ctrl-a**). You can then copy, move, or even delete several files at once. To select items that have a certain pattern in their name, choose Select Items Matching from the Edit menu to open a search box where you can enter the pattern (**Ctrl-s**). Use the * character to match partial patterns, as in *let* to match on all filenames with the pattern "let" in them. The pattern **my*** would match on filenames beginning with the "my" pattern, and *.png would match on all PNG image files (the period indicates a filename extension).

Opening Applications and Files MIME Types

You can start any application in the file manager by double-clicking either the application itself or a data file used for that application. If you want to open the file with a specific application, you can right-click the file and select one of the Open With entries. One or more Open with entries will be displayed for default and possible application, like "Open with Text Editor" for a text file. If the application you want is not listed, you can select Open with | Other Application to open a dialog listing available applications. Drag-and-drop operations are also supported for applications. You can drag a data file to its associated application icon (say, on the desktop); the application then starts up using that data file.

To change or set the default application to use for a certain type of file, you open a file's Properties dialog (File menu, Properties) and select the Open With tab. Here you can choose the default application to use for that kind of file. Possible applications will be listed with a radio button next to each entry. The default has its radio button turned on. Click the radio button of the one you want to change to the default. Once you choose the default, it will appear in the Open With item for this type of file. If there is an application on the Open With tab you do not want listed in the Open With menu, select it and click the Remove button.

If you want to add an application to the Open With menu, click the "Add" button to open the Add Application dialog, which lists possible applications. Select the one you want and click the Add button. You can use the "Use a custom command" text box to enter a command. The Browse button lets you locate a command.

File and Directory Properties

In a file's Properties dialog, you can view detailed information on a file and set options and permissions (see Figure 10-40). A file's Properties dialog has eight tabs: Basic, Emblems, Permissions, Open With, Notes, Access Control List, Extended user attributes, and Digests. Folders do not have an Open With tab. The Basic tab shows detailed information such as type, size, location, and date modified. The type is a MIME type, indicating the type of application associated with it. The file's icon is displayed at the top with a text box showing the file's name. You can edit the filename in the Name text box, changing that name.

Figure 10-40: File properties on Caja

If you want to change the icon image used for the file or folder, click the icon image (next to the name) to open a Select Custom Icon dialog to browse for the one you want. The **/usr/share/pixmaps** directory holds the set of current default images, though you can select your own images (click **pixmaps** entry in the Places side pane). Click an image file to see its icon displayed in the right pane. Double-click to change the icon image.

The Permissions tab for files shows the read, write, and execute permissions for owner, group, and others, as set for this file. You can change any of the permissions here, provided the file belongs to you. You configure access for the owner, the group, and others, using drop-down menus. You can set owner permissions as Read Only or Read And Write. For group and others, you can also set the None option, denying access. Clicking on the group name displays a menu listing different groups, allowing you to select one to change the file's group. If you want to execute this as an application, you check the "Allow executing file as program" entry. This has the effect of setting the execute permission.

The Open With tab for files lists all the applications associated with this kind of file. You can select the one you want to use as the default. This can be particularly useful for media files, where you may prefer a specific player for a certain file or a particular image viewer for pictures.

Certain kinds of files will have additional tabs, providing information about the file. For example, an audio file will have an Audio tab listing the type of audio file and any other information like a song title or compression method used. An image file will have an Image tab listing the resolution and type of image.

The Access Control List (ACL) tab allows you to designate what user or group can have access to your file, as well as specify what permissions they will have. The "Extended user attributes" tab lets you add your own attributes to a file. The Digests tab lets you validate checksums and message digests.

The Permissions tab for folders operates much the same way, but it includes two access entries: Folder Access and File Access. The Folder Access entry controls access to the folder with options for None, List Files Only, Access Files, and Create And Delete Files. These correspond to read, read and execute permissions given to directories. The File Access entry lets you set permissions for all those files in the folder. They are the same as for files: for the owner, Read or Read and Write; for the group and others, the entry adds a None option to deny access. To set the permissions for all the files in the folder accordingly (not just the folder), you click the "Apply Permissions To Enclosed Files" button.

The Share tab for folders allows you to share folders as network shares (requires that the **caja-share** extension is installed, Software Boutique | Servers). If you have Samba or NFS, these will allow your folders and files to be shared with users on other systems. You have the option to specify whether the shared folder or file will be read-only or allow write access. To allow write access check the "Allow other to create and delete files in this folder" entry. To open access to all users, check the Guest access entry.

Caja Preferences

You can set preferences for your Caja file manager in the Preferences dialog, accessible by selecting the Preferences item in any Caja file manager window's Edit menu (Edit | Preferences).

The Views tab allows you to select how files are displayed by default, such as the list, icon, or compact view. You can set default zoom levels for icon, compact, and list views.

Behavior lets you choose how to select files, manage the trash, and handle scripts.

Display lets you choose what added information you want displayed in an icon caption, like the size or date.

The List Columns tab lets you choose both the features to display in the list view and the order in which to display them. In addition to the already-selected Name, Size, Date, and Type, you can add features such as permissions, group, MIME type, and owner.

The Preview tab lets you choose whether you want small preview content displayed in the icons, like beginning text for text files.

The Media tab lets you choose what applications to run for certain media, such as run the VLC media player for DVD videos, or Rhythmbox for audio files.

Extensions lists extensions installed for Caja.

Control Center

Both Preference and Administration tools can be accessed either from the MATE or Main menus or from the Control Center (see Figure 10-41). You can access the Control Center from the System section on the MATE menu, and from the Main Menu's System menu. The Control Center opens a window listing the different applications by section: Personal, Hardware, Administration, Look and Feel, and Internet and Network. Icons for the tools are displayed. Single-click on an icon to open it. The Control Center also has a dynamic search capability. A side pane holds a filter search box and links for the groups. As you enter a pattern in the Filter search box, matching applications appear at the right. Commonly used applications can be listed under Common Tasks. If you want an application to be started when your system starts, you can right-click on its icon and choose "Add to Startup Programs" to add it directly to the Startup Applications dialog. Several of the tools are administration applications such as Software Boutique, Backups, Users and Groups, and Printers. Others are GNOME preferences used for MATE, such as Appearance, About Me, Screensaver, and Keyboard. Others are the same as Ubuntu tools, such as Software & Updates and Software Updater.

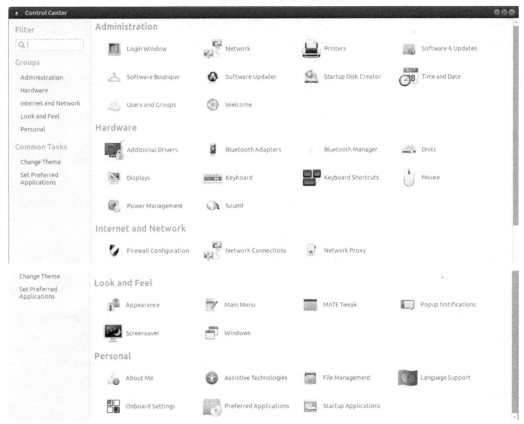

Figure 10-41: GNOME Control Center

MATE Preferences

You can configure different parts of your MATE interface using tools listed in the Preferences menu on the MATE and Main menus, and from the Control Center. Ubuntu MATE provides several tools for configuring your MATE desktop. The MATE preferences are listed in Table 10-9. On some preferences tools, a Help button displays detailed descriptions and examples. Some of the more important tools are discussed here. For administration tasks check the Administration menu (see Table 10-10).

Preferences	Description
About Me	Personal information like image, addresses, and password.
Assistive Technologies	Enables features like accessible login and keyboard screen.
Appearance	Desktop Appearance configuration: Themes, Fonts, Backgrounds, and Visual Effects.
Bluetooth Adapters	Manage visibility of Bluetooth adapters
Bluetooth Manager	Configure Bluetooth devices
Disks	Opens the GNOME Disks utility.
Displays	Change your screen resolution, refresh rate, and screen orientation.
File Management	File Manager options including media handling applications, icon captions, and the default view.
Firewall Configuration	Gufw firewall configuration (see Chapter 15)
Keyboard	Configure your keyboard
Keyboard Shortcuts	Configure keys for special tasks, like multimedia operations.
Language Support	Specify a language
Main Menu	Add or remove categories and menu items for the Applications, Preferences, and System menus.
Mate Tweak	Basic settings
Mouse	Mouse and touchpad configuration: select hand orientation, speed, and accessibility.
Network Connection	Network Manager Connection editor
Network Proxy	Specify proxy configuration if needed: manual or automatic
Popup Notifications	Placement and display theme for notifications.
Power Management	The GNOME power manager for configuring display, suspend, and shutdown options.
Preferred Applications	Set default Web browser, mail application, music player, and terminal window.
Screensaver	Select and manage your screen saver, including the activation time.
Sound	Configure sound
Startup Applications	Manage your session with startup programs and save options.
Windows	Enable window abilities like roll up on the titlebar, movement key, window selection.

Table 10-9: MATE Preferences menu

The keyboard shortcuts configuration (Keyboard Shortcuts) lets you map keys to certain tasks, like mapping multimedia keys on a keyboard to media tasks like play and pause. Just select the task and then press the key. There are tasks for the desktop, multimedia, and window management. In the window management section, you can also map keys to perform workspace switching. Keys that are already assigned will be shown.

The Windows configuration (Windows, in Look and Feel) is where you can enable features like window roll-up (Titlebar Action), window movement key, and mouse window selection.

Administration	Description
Login Window	Configure login window
Network	Network Settings: configure host name, DNS servers, Search domains, and hosts.
Printers	Configure printers with system-config-printer
Software & Updates	Configure repositories, updates, and additional drivers
Software Boutique	Ubuntu MATE software manager
Software Update	Update software
Startup Disk Creator	Create USB live Linux system
Time and Date	Set the time, date, and time zone.
Welcome	Displays the Ubuntu MATE welcome dialog with links to the user guide, tutorial, and software manager.

Table 10-10: MATE Administration menu

Mouse and Keyboard Preferences

The Mouse and Keyboard preferences are the primary tools for configuring your mouse and keyboard. Mouse preferences lets you choose its speed, hand orientation, and double-click times. Accessibility features include simulated secondary clicks and movement-based clicks (dwell clicks). For laptops, you can configure your touchpad, enabling touchpad clicks and edge scrolling (left side). Keyboard preferences shows several tabs for selecting your keyboard model (Layouts), configuring keys (Layouts tab, Options button), repeat delay (General tab), and enforcing breaks from power typing as a health precaution (Typing Break) (see Figure 10-42).

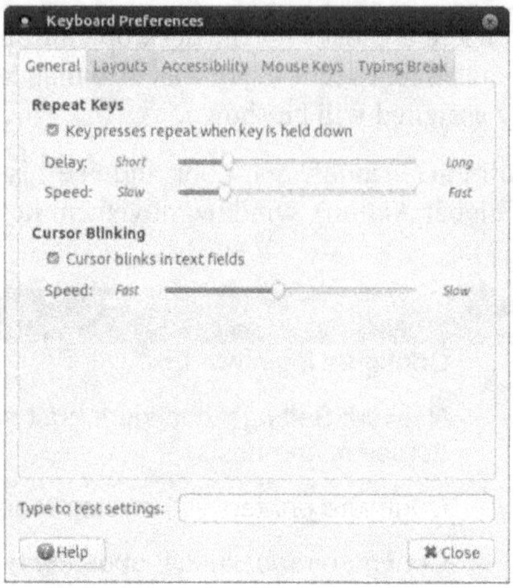

Figure 10-42: Keyboard Preferences

To configure your sound devices, you use the Sound Preferences dialog (Sound, PulseAudio), see Chapter 6. MATE uses sound themes to specify an entire set of sounds for different effects and alerts.

Configuring your personal information

To set up personal information, including the icon to be used for your graphical login, you use the About Me preferences dialog. You can access it from the MATE and Main menu's Preferences menu (Preferences | About Me). The About Me preferences dialog lets you change your password (see Figure 10-43) and the icon or image used to represent the user. Should you want to change your password, you can click on the Change Password button to open a change password dialog.

Clicking on the image icon in the top left corner opens a browser window where you can select a personal image. The **faces** directory is selected by default, which displays several images. The selected image displays at the right on the browser window. For a personal photograph, you can select the Picture folder. This is the Pictures folder on your home directory. Should you place a photograph or image there, you could then select if for your personal image. The image will be used in the login screen when showing your user entry.

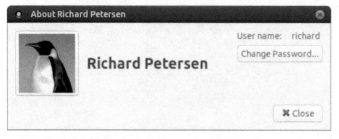

Figure 10-43: About Me information: Preferences | About Me

Appearance

Several appearance-related configuration tasks are combined into the Appearance tool. These include Themes, Background, and Fonts. To change your theme or background image, or configure your fonts, use the Appearance dialog (Preferences | Appearance, or Appearance icon on the Control Center's Personal section). The Appearance window shows four tabs: Theme, Background, Fonts, and Interface (see Figure 10-11). The Interface tab controls the display of icon images and names on the buttons and entries on application menus and toolbars. By default both the name and icons are shown (Text beside items) on a toolbar. You could just display the icon or just the name. For menus, you can choose to also display icons with to the entries.

Desktop Themes

You use the Themes tab on the Appearance Preferences tool to select or customize a theme. Themes control your desktop appearance. The Themes tab will list icons for currently installed themes (see Figure 10-44). The icons show key aspects or each theme such as window, folder, and button images, in effect previewing the theme for you. The default theme for Ubuntu MATE is Ambiance-MATE, which is based on the Ubuntu Desktop's Ambiance theme. You can move through the icons to select a different theme if you wish. If you have downloaded additional themes from **https:/www.gnome-look.org**, you can click the install button to locate and install them. Once installed, the additional themes will also be displayed in the Theme tab. If you download and install a theme or icon set from the Ubuntu repositories, it will be automatically installed for you.

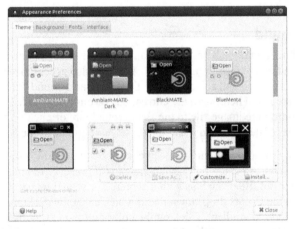

Figure 10-44: Appearance - Selecting GNOME themes

The true power of Themes is shown its ability to let users customize any given theme. Themes are organized into five components: controls, colors, window border, icons, and pointer. Controls covers the appearance of window and dialog controls like buttons and slider bars. Window border lets you choose title bars, borders, window buttons sets. Icons lets you choose different icon sets. Pointers provides different pointer sets to use. Colors lets you choose the background and text color for windows, input boxes, selections, and tool tips. You can even download and install separate components like specific icon sets, which you can then use in a customized theme.

Clicking the Customize button opens a Customize Theme window with tabs for different theme components. The components used for the current theme are selected by default. A color tab lets you set the background and text colors for windows, input boxes, and selected items. In the Controls, Window Border, and Icon tabs you will see listings of the different themes. You can then mix and match different components from those themes, creating your own customized theme, using window borders from one theme and icons from another. Upon selecting a component, your desktop changes automatically showing you how it looks. If you have added a component, like a new icon set, it also is shown.

Once you have created a new customized theme, a Custom theme icon appears in the list on the Theme tab. To save the customized theme, click the Save As button. This opens a dialog where you can enter the theme name, any notes, and specify whether you also want to keep the theme background.

Customized themes and themes installed directly by a user are placed in the **.themes** directory in the user's home directory. Should you want these themes made available for all users, you can move them from the **.themes** directory to the **/usr/share/themes** directory. In a terminal window run a **cp** command as shown here for the **mytheme** theme. The operation requires administrative access (**sudo**).

```
sudo cp -r .themes/mytheme  /usr/share/themes
```

You can do the same for icon sets you have downloaded. Such sets will be installed in the user's **.icons** directory. You can then copy them to the **/usr/share/icons** directory to make them available to all users.

Desktop Background

You use the Background tab on the Appearance Preferences tool to select or customize your desktop background image (see Figure 10-45). You can also access the Background tab by clicking the desktop background and select Change Desktop Background from the desktop menu. Installed backgrounds are listed here, with the current background selected. To add your own image, either drag-and-drop the image file to the Background tab, or click on the Add button to locate and select the image file. To remove an image, select it and click the Remove button.

From the Style drop-down menu, you can choose display options such as Zoom, Center, Scale, Tile, Stretch, or Span. A centered or scaled image will preserve the image proportions. Span may distort it. Any space not filled, such as with a centered or scaled images, will be filled in with the desktop color. From the Colors drop-down menu, you can set the desktop color to a solid color, horizontal gradient, or vertical gradient. Click on the color button next to the Colors drop-down menu to open a "Pick a Color" dialog where you can select a color from a color wheel. For gradients, two color buttons are displayed for selecting a color at each end of the gradient.

Initially, the Ubuntu MATE and MATE backgrounds are listed. Install the **gnome-background** package to add a collection of GNOME backgrounds. To download more backgrounds, click the "Get more backgrounds online" link. Click a Go button to display the background image, then right-click on the image and choose "Set as Desktop Background."

Figure 10-45: Choosing a desktop background, Preferences | Appearance

Fonts

On the Font tab, you can change font sizes, select fonts, and configure rendering options (see Figure 10-46). Fonts are listed for Applications, Documents, Desktop, Window title, and Fixed width. The default font is Ubuntu. Click on a font button to open a "Pick a Font" dialog where you can select a font, choose its style (regular, italic, or bold), and change its size. You can further refine your font display by clicking the Details button to open a window where you can set features like the dots-per-inch, hinting, smoothing, and subpixel order.

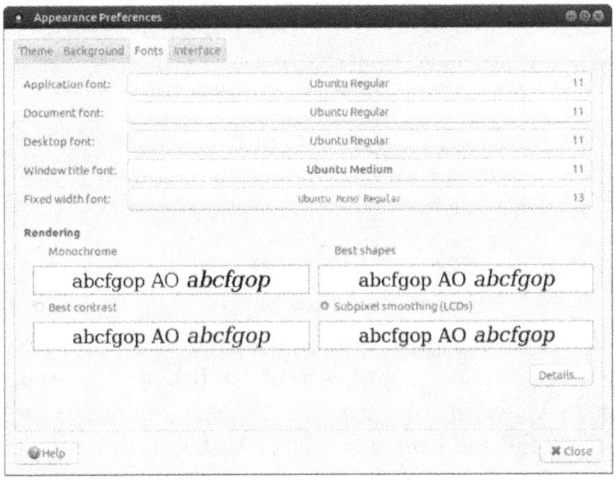

Figure 10-46: Fonts

Numerous font packages are available on the Linux repositories. When you install the font packages, the fonts are installed automatically on your system and ready for use. True type font packages begin with **ttf-** prefix. Microsoft true type fonts are available from the **ttf-mscorefonts-installer** package. Fonts are installed in the **/usr/share/fonts** directory. This directory will have subdirectories for different font collections like true type and X11. You can install fonts manually yourself by copying fonts to the **/user/share/fonts** directory (use the **sudo** command).

MATE Power Manager

For power management, MATE uses the MATE Power Manager, **mate-power-manager**, which makes use of Advanced Configuration and Power Interface (ACPI) support provided by a computer to manage power use (see Figure 10-47). The GNOME Power Manager can display an icon on the panel showing the current power source, a battery (laptop) or lightning (desktop). Clicking on the battery icon displays a menu showing the power charge of your wireless devices, both your laptop and any other wireless devices like a wireless mouse.

The GNOME Power manager is configured with Power Management Preferences, accessible from Preferences | Hardware | Power Management, and by right clicking on the GNOME Power Management panel icon and selecting Preferences from the pop-up menu (also on the GNOME Control Center | Hardware section). Power Manager preferences can be used to configure both a desktop and a laptop. Should you make any changes, and you want to retain your settings, click the Make Default button.

For a desktop, two tabs appear on the Power Management Preferences window, On AC Power and General. The AC Power tab offers two sleep options, one for the computer and one for the display screen. You can put each to sleep after a specified interval of inactivity. On the General tab, you set desktop features like actions to take when you press the power button or whether to display the power icon.

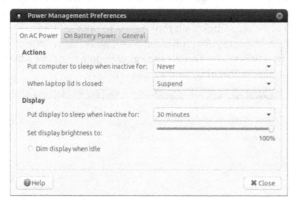

Figure 10-47: MATE Power Manager

Display of the Power Management icon on the panel is configured on the General tab. In the Notification Area section, you can set options to never display, always display the icon, displaying the icon when the battery is low, or when it is charging or discharging, or only if there is a battery. The default is to display the icon only when a battery is present.

A laptop will also have an On Battery Power tab where you can set additional options for the battery and display, such as shutting down if the battery is too low, or dimming the display when the system is idle (see Figure10-43). The laptop On AC Power tab will also have an Actions option for actions to take when the laptop lid is closed, like suspend, blank screen, and shutdown.

To see how your laptop or desktop is performing with power, you can use Power statistics, accessible from the Applications | System Tool menu. The Power Statistics window will display a sidebar listing your different power devices. A right pane will show tabs with power use information for a selected device. The Laptop battery device will display three tabs: Details,

History, and Statistics. The History tab will show your recent use, with graph options for Time to empty (time left), Time to full (recharging), Charge, and Rate. The Statistics tab can show charge and discharge graphs.

Preferred Applications

Certain types of files will have default applications already associated with them. For example, double-clicking a Web page file will open the file in the Firefox Web browser. If you prefer to set a different default application, you can use the Preferred Applications tool (see Figure 10-44). This tool will let you set default applications for Web pages, mail readers, accessibility tools, multimedia, office applications, and the system tools. Available applications are listed in popup menus. In Figure 10-48 the default mail reader is Thunderbird. You access the Preferred Applications tool from the Preferences menu (Preferences | Personal | Preferred Applications). The Preferred applications tool has tabs for Internet, Multimedia, System, Office, and Accessibility. On the Multimedia tab, you can select default multimedia applications to run, such as VLC as the default video player. On the Office tab, you can specify the default word processor, document viewer, and spreadsheet application. On the System tab, you can choose a default text editor, file manager, and terminal. The Accessibility tab lets you select a magnifier.

Figure 10-48: Preferred Applications tool

Default Applications for Media

Caja directly handles preferences for media operations. You set the preferences using the File Management Preferences dialog. It is accessible from either the Edit | Preferences menu item on any Caja file manager window, from the Main and MATE menus Preferences menu as File Management, or from the Control Center as File Management (under the Personal section) .

The Media tab of the File Management Preferences dialog lists entries for CD Audio, DVD Video, Music Player, Photos, and Software. Pop-up menus let you select the application to use for the different media (see Figure 10-49). You also have options for Ask what to do, Do

Nothing, and Open folder. The Open Folder options will just open a window displaying the files on the disc. A segment labeled "Other media" lets you set up an association for less used media like Blu-Ray discs. Initially, the "Ask what to do" option will be set for all entries. Possible options are listed for each menu, like the Rhythmbox Music Player for Cd Audio discs and VLC media player for DVD Video. Photos can be opened with the Shotwell Photo-manager. Once you select an option, when you insert removable media, like a CD Audio discs, its associated application is automatically started.

Figure 10-49: File Management Preferences for Media

If you just want to turn off the startup for a particular kind of media, you can select the Do Nothing entry from its application pop-up menu. If you want to be prompted for options, then set the "Ask what to do" entry in the Media tab's pop-up menu. When you insert a disc, a dialog with a pop-up menu for possible actions is displayed. The default application is already selected. You can select another application or select the Do Nothing or Open Folder options.

You can turn the automatic startup off for all media by checking the box for "Never prompt or start programs on media insertion" at the bottom of the Media tab. You can also enable the option "browse media when inserted" to just open a folder showing its files.

Screen Saver and Lock

With the Screensaver Preferences, you can control when the computer is considered idle and what screen saver to use if any (see Figure 10-50). You can access the Screensaver Preferences dialog from the Main and MATE menus Preferences menu as Screensaver, or from the Control Center in the "Look and Feel" section. You can choose from various screen savers, using the scroll box to the left, with a preview displayed at the right. You can also control whether to lock the screen or not, when idle. You can turn off the Screensaver by unchecking the "Activate screensaver when computer is idle" box.

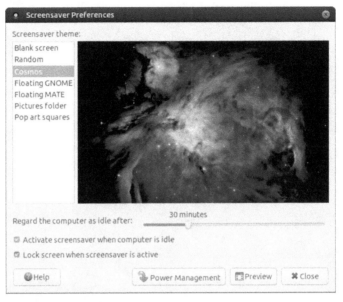

Figure 10-50: Screensaver Preferences

Assistive Technologies

On MATE, the Assistive Technologies dialog is a simple set of buttons for accessing accessibility tabs for other tools (see Figure 10-51). In the Assistive Technologies section, use the "Enable assistive technologies" checkbox to turn assistive technologies on and off. The Preferred Applications button opens the Accessibility tab on the Preferred Applications dialog.

In the Preferences section, there are buttons to open the accessibility tabs for the keyboard, and Mouse dialogs. On the keyboard accessibility tab, you can configure features such as sticky, slow, and bounce keys. The mouse button simply opens the mouse preferences dialog.

Figure 10-51: Assistive Technologies Preferences

ubuntu

11. Ubuntu Flavors

Xubuntu (Xfce)

Lubuntu (LXDE)

Ubuntu Studio

Ubuntu Budgie

Ubuntu Flavors are based on the Ubuntu Linux distribution, but use different desktops and initial software collections. These are common desktops that are used for other Linux distribution, but have been adapted for Ubuntu and the Ubuntu software repositories. These include Kubuntu based on the KDE Plasma desktop (see Chapter 9), Ubuntu MATE which uses the Mate desktop (see Chapter 10), Xubuntu which uses the Xfce desktop, Lubuntu adapts the LXDE desktop, Ubuntu Budgie uses the Budgie desktop, which is based on the Ubuntu GNOME desktop. Ubuntu Studio is a customized collection of multimedia production software from the Ubuntu repository and uses the Xubuntu desktop. Ubuntu Kylin is designed specifically for Chinese users.

The Ubuntu Flavors are available at:

```
https://www.ubuntu.com/download/flavours
```

They are also available at:

```
http://releases.ubuntu.com
```

Xubuntu (Xfce)

Xubuntu uses the Xfce desktop, with the Ubuntu repositories. The Xfce desktop is a lightweight desktop designed to run fast without the kind of overhead required for full featured desktops like KDE and GNOME. You can think of it as a window manager with desktop functionality. It includes its own file manager and panel, but the emphasis is on modularity and simplicity. Like GNOME, Xfce is based on GTK+ GUI tools. The desktop consists of a collection of modules like the thunar file manager, xfce4-panel panel, and the xfwm4 window manager. Keeping with its focus on simplicity, Xfce features only a few common applets on its panel. It small scale makes it appropriate for laptops or dedicated systems, that have no need for complex overhead found in other desktops. Xfce is useful for desktops designed for just a few tasks, like multimedia desktops.

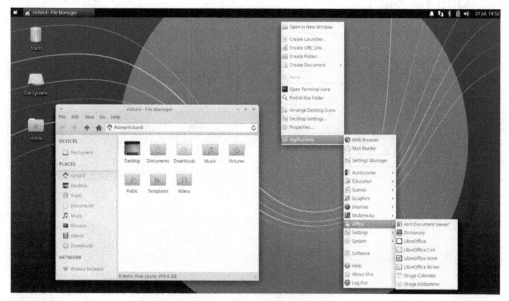

Figure 11-1: Xubuntu (Xfce) Desktop

You can find out more about Xubuntu and download it from:

`https://www.xubuntu.org`

You can find out more about Xfce from:

`https://xfce.org/`

To install Xubuntu as an alternative desktop on a system, select the **xubuntu-desktop** package in the Synaptic Package Manager.

The desktop displays icons for your Home directory, file system, and trash (see Figure 11-1). The top panel holds a menu button on the left side. From the menu, you can access any applications along with administration tools. Next to the menu button are the window list buttons for open windows. The right side of the panel has buttons for the time and date (calendar), volume control, network connections, and power status. You can add more items by clicking on the panel and selecting Add new items. This opens a window with several applets like the clock and workspace switcher, as well as Applications menu and Indicator plugins applet. The Indicator plugins applet displays the Ubuntu Network Manager, sound volume, and messaging indicators. To move an applet, right-click on it and choose Move from the pop-up menu, and then move the mouse to the new insertion location and click.

Clicking the power button on the main menu or the Log Out entry in the desktop Applications menu, opens a dialog with buttons for logout, shut down, suspend, hibernate, and restart. You can also choose to save your current session, restoring your open windows when you log back in.

Figure 11-2: Xubuntu (Xfce) Applications Menu

You can access applications from the Applications menu (left side of the top panel). Categories are shown to the right, and the items in the category are listed to the left (see Figure 11-2). You can use a search box at the top to find an application. The name of the current user is listed at the bottom of the menu. At the lower right are the Settings, Lock Screen, and Log Out buttons.

Clicking the Log Out button displays a menu of log out and shut down buttons. You can also access applications by right-clicking on the desktop background to display the desktop menu.

Xfce file manager is called Thunar. The file manager will open a side pane in the shortcuts view that lists entries for not just for the home directory, but also your file system, desktop, and trash contents (see Figure 11-1). The File menu lets you perform folder operations like creating new directories. From the Edit menu, you can perform tasks on a selected file like renaming the file or creating a link for it. You can change the side pane view to a tree view of your file system by selecting from the menubar View | Side Pane | Tree, (Ctrl-e). The Shortcuts entry changes the view back (Ctrl-b).

To configure the Xubuntu desktop, you use the Settings Manager, accessible from the Applications menu by clicking the Settings button at the bottom right. This opens the Settings window, which shows icons for your desktop, display, panel, user interface, among others (see Figure 11-3). Use the Appearance tool to select themes, icons, and toolbar styles. The Panel tool lets you add new panels and control features like fixed for freely movable and horizontally or vertically positioned. You can also access the Settings tools from the Applications menu's Settings menu.

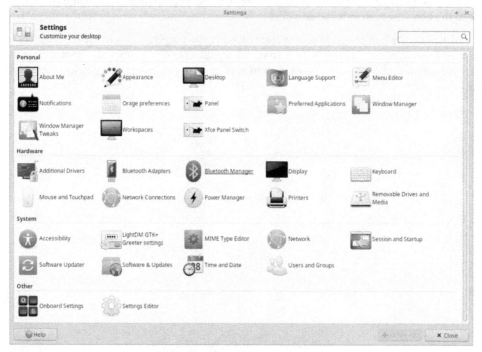

Figure 11-3: Xubuntu (Xfce) Settings Manager

To configure the desktop, select the Desktop icon on the Settings window or right-click on the desktop and select Desktop Settings from the pop-up menu (you can also select Settings | Desktop). This opens the Desktop window where you can select the background image, control menu behavior, and set icon sizes (see Figure 11-4).

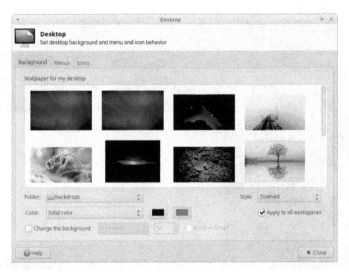

Figure 11-4: Xubuntu (Xfce) Desktop Configuration

Lubuntu (LXDE)

Lubuntu uses the LXDE desktop. The LXDE desktop provides another small desktop designed for use on minimal or low power systems like laptops, netbooks, or older computers.

You can find out more about Lubuntu and download it from:

https://lubuntu.me/

You can find out more about LXDE at:

https://lxde.org/

To install Lubuntu as an alternative desktop on a system, select the **lubuntu-desktop** package on the Synaptic Package Manager.

The desktop displays a single panel at the bottom with application applets to the left, followed by the windows taskbar, and system applets to the right (see Figure 11-5). From the panel applications menu, you can access any applications.

Note: Lubuntu will be using LXQt instead of LXDE for their next release (18.10), **https://lxqt.org/**.

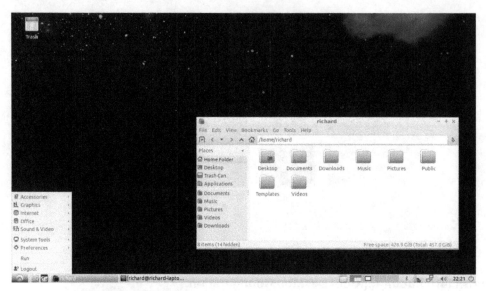

Figure 11-5: Lubuntu (LXDE) desktop

The bottom panel shows applets for the applications menu, the PC-Man file manager, Web browser, minimize windows, workspace manager, and window list. On the right side of the panel are applets for volume control, Network Manager, power, the clock, and the logout button (see Figure 11-6).

Figure 11-6: Lubuntu (LXDE) panel

The logout entry on the applications menu, and the logout button on the right side of the panel opens a dialog with buttons for logout, shutdown, suspend, hibernate, and reboot.

Lubuntu uses the PC-Man file manager as shown in Figure 11-5. The button bar performs browser tasks like moving backward and forward to previously viewed folders. The Home button moves you to your home folder. The side pane has a location (Places) and directory tree view. You can switch between the two using the button at the top of the pane.

To configure your panel your panel, right-click on the panel and select Panel Settings. This open the Panel Preferences window with tabs for General, Appearance, Panel Applets, and Advanced (see Figure 11-7). The Geometry tab lets you set the position and size of the panel. The Appearance tab lets you set the background, theme, and font for the panel. The Panel Applets tab is where you can add applets to the panel. The applets are referred to as plugins. Currently, loaded applets are listed, along with format features like spacers. Some applets have the option to stretch to take up any available space on the panel. By default, only the Task Bar (Window List) is configured to do this. To remove an applet or feature, select it and click the Remove button. To configure an applet, click the Preferences button to open the applet's configuration dialog. This will vary among applets. To set the time display format, select the clock and click Preferences to open the Digital Clock settings dialog. Applets settings can also be configured directly from the panel.

Right-click on the applet and choose the Settings entry, like "Digital Clock Settings" for the digital clock applet.

To add a new applet to the panel, click the Add button to open the "Add plugin to panel" window, which will list all available applets and panel features like spaces and separators. Select the one you want and click the Add button (see Figure 11-7).

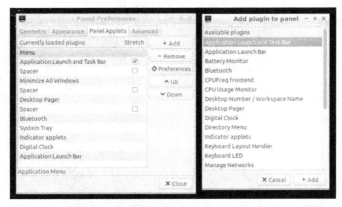

Figure 11-7: Lubuntu (LXDE) Panel Preferences and Plugins

To configure the desktop, right-click anywhere on the desktop and choose Desktop Settings from the pop-up menu. This opens the Desktop Preferences window with tabs for Appearance, Desktop Icons, and Advanced (see Figure 11-8). The Appearance tab lets you set the background. The Desktop Icons tab lets you choose what icons to display on the desktop (trash, Documents folder, and attached devices). On the Advanced tab, you choose whether to display any of these icons.

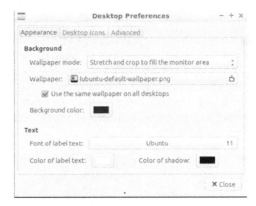

Figure 11-8: Lubuntu (LXDE) Desktop Preferences

Ubuntu Studio

Ubuntu Studio provides a collection of Linux-based multimedia software for graphic design, audio production, and video production (see Figure 11-9). Applications include Blender 3d modeling, Inkscape vector graphics, Audacity sound editor, and Openshot video editor. Ubuntu Studio is based on the Xubuntu release.

You can download Ubuntu Studio from:

```
https://ubuntustudio.org/
```

The site also has documentation and support links for applications.

Figure 11-9: Ubuntu Studio

Ubuntu Budgie

Ubuntu Budgie uses the Budgie desktop, developed for the Solus Linux distribution (see Figure 11-10) . It installs the full set of applications, though some of the default applications are different. The Web Browser is Chromium instead of Firefox, the media player is MPV instead of Videos, and the email application is Geary instead of Thunderbird. Ubuntu Budgie uses Ubuntu Software for managing software, and GNOME Settings (Budgie Desktop Settings) to configure your system. Ubuntu Budgie features immediate updates, as they become available. This ensures a more secure system.

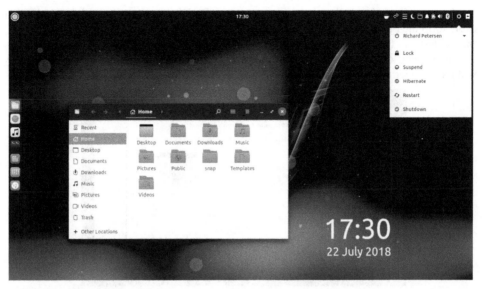

Figure 11-10: Ubuntu Budgie

You can download Ubuntu Budgie from:

```
https://ubuntubudgie.org/downloads
```

The Plank dock to the left has favorite applications. The top panel has applets on the right and the time and date in the center. When you open an application, an icon for it appears on the dock. You can right-click on it to have it shown permanently.

The Welcome dialog's Getting Started button has links for common tasks such as updates, drivers, and customization (see Figure 11-11).

Figure 11-11: Ubuntu Budgie Welcome

For Budgie applets and themes you can use the Budgie Themes and Budgie Applet dialog accessible form the menu (see Figure 11-12). Budgie applets include Show Time to display the time on the desktop, Hot Corners that set up corners to activate features when you move your mouse to one, and Clockworks which provides a world clock display, Places for moving directly to a bookmarked folder or device, and Window Shuffler for moving and arranging windows.

Figure 11-12: Ubuntu Budgie Applets and Themes

ubuntu

12. Shells

The Command Line

History

Filename Expansion: *, ?, [ ]

Standard Input/Output and Redirection

Linux Files

The File Structure

Listing, Displaying, and Printing Files

Managing Directories: mkdir, rmdir, ls, cd, pwd

File and Directory Operations: find, cp, mv, rm, ln

The shell is a command interpreter that provides a line-oriented interactive and non-interactive interface between the user and the operating system. You enter commands on a command line; they are interpreted by the shell and then sent as instructions to the operating system (the command line interface is accessible from Gnome and KDE through a Terminal windows – Applications/Accessories menu). You can also place commands in a script file to be consecutively executed, much like a program. This interpretive capability of the shell provides for many sophisticated features. For example, the shell has a set of file expansion characters that can generate filenames. The shell can redirect input and output, as well as run operations in the background, freeing you to perform other tasks.

Shell	Web Site
`www.gnu.org/software/bash`	BASH website with online manual, FAQ, and current releases
`www.gnu.org/software/bash/manual/bash.html`	BASH online manual
`www.zsh.org`	Z shell website with referrals to FAQs and current downloads.
`www.kornshell.com`	Korn shell site with manual, FAQ, and references

Table 12-1: Linux Shells

Several different types of shells have been developed for Linux: the Bourne Again shell (BASH), the Korn shell, the TCSH shell, and the Z shell. All shells are available for your use, although the BASH shell is the default. You only need one type of shell to do your work. Ubuntu Linux includes all the major shells, although it installs and uses the BASH shell as the default. If you use the command line shell, you will be using the BASH shell unless you specify another. This chapter discusses the BASH shell, which shares many of the same features as other shells.

You can find out more about shells at their respective websites as listed in Table 12-1. In addition, a detailed online manual is available for each installed shell. Use the **man** command and the shell's keyword to access them, **bash** for the BASH shell, **ksh** for the Korn shell, **zsh** for the Z shell, and **tsch** for the TSCH shell. For example, the command **man bash** will access the BASH shell online manual.

Note: You can find out more about the BASH shell at www.gnu.org/software/bash. A detailed online manual is available on your Linux system using the `man` command with the `bash` keyword.

The Command Line

The Linux command line interface consists of a single line into which you enter commands with any of their options and arguments. From GNOME or KDE, you can access the command line interface by opening a terminal window (Applications | Accessories | Terminal). Should you start Linux with the command line interface, you will be presented with a BASH shell command line when you log in.

By default, the BASH shell has a dollar sign (**$**) prompt, but Linux has several other types of shells, each with its own prompt (like **%** for the C shell). The root user will have a different prompt, the #. A shell *prompt,* such as the one shown here, marks the beginning of the command line:

```
$
```

You can enter a command along with options and arguments at the prompt. For example, with an **-l** option, the **ls** command will display a line of information about each file, listing such data as its size and the date and time it was last modified. In the next example, the user enters the **ls** command followed by a **-l** option. The dash before the **-l** option is required. Linux uses it to distinguish an option from an argument.

```
$ ls -l
```

If you wanted only the information displayed for a particular file, you could add that file's name as the argument, following the **-l** option:

```
$ ls -l mydata
-rw-r--r-- 1 chris weather 207 Feb 20 11:55 mydata
```

Tip: Some commands can be complex and take some time to execute. When you mistakenly execute the wrong command, you can interrupt and stop such commands with the interrupt key—CTRL-C.

You can enter a command on several lines by typing a backslash just before you press ENTER. The backslash "escapes" the ENTER key, effectively continuing the same command line to the next line. In the next example, the **cp** command is entered on three lines. The first two lines end in a backslash, effectively making all three lines one command line.

```
$ cp -i \
mydata \
/home/george/myproject/newdata
```

You can also enter several commands on the same line by separating them with a semicolon (;). In effect, the semicolon operates as an execute operation. Commands will be executed in the sequence in which they are entered. The following command executes an **ls** command followed by a **date** command.

```
$ ls ; date
```

You can also conditionally run several commands on the same line with the **&&** operator. A command is executed only if the previous command is true. This feature is useful for running several dependent scripts on the same line. In the next example, the **ls** command is run only if the **date** command is successfully executed.

```
$ date && ls
```

TIP: Command can also be run as arguments on a command line, using their results for other commands. To run a command within a command line, you encase the command in back quotes.

Command Line Editing

The BASH shell, which is your default shell, has special command line editing capabilities that you may find helpful as you learn Linux (see Table 12-2). You can easily modify commands you have entered before executing them, moving anywhere on the command line and inserting or deleting characters. This is particularly helpful for complex commands.

Movement Commands	Operation
CTRL-F, RIGHT-ARROW	Move forward a character
CTRL-B, LEFT-ARROW	Move backward a character
CTRL-A or HOME	Move to beginning of line
CTRL-E or END	Move to end of line
ALT-F	Move forward a word
ALT-B	Move backward a word
CTRL-L	Clear screen and place line at top
Editing Commands	**Operation**
CTRL-D or DEL	Delete character cursor is on
CTRL-H or BACKSPACE	Delete character before the cursor
CTRL-K	Cut remainder of line from cursor position
CTRL-U	Cut from cursor position to beginning of line
CTRL-W	Cut the previous word
CTRL-C	Cut entire line
ALT-D	Cut the remainder of a word
ALT-DEL	Cut from the cursor to the beginning of a word
CTRL-Y	Paste previous cut text
ALT-Y	Paste from set of previously cut text
CTRL-Y	Paste previous cut text
CTRL-V	Insert quoted text, used for inserting control or meta (Alt) keys as text, such as CTRL-B for backspace or CTRL-T for tabs
ALT-T	Transpose current and previous word
ALT-L	Lowercase current word
ALT-U	Uppercase current word
ALT-C	Capitalize current word
CTRL-SHIFT-_	Undo previous change

Table 12-2: Command Line Editing Operations

You can press CTRL-F or the RIGHT ARROW key to move forward a character, or the CTRL-B or LEFT ARROW key to move back a character. CTRL-D or DEL deletes the character the cursor is on, and CTRL-H or BACKSPACE deletes the character preceding the cursor. To add text, you use the arrow keys to move the cursor to where you want to insert text and type the new characters.

You can even cut words with the CTRL-W or ALT-D key, and then press the CTRL-Y key to paste them back in at a different position, effectively moving the words. As a rule, the CTRL version of the command operates on characters, and the ALT version works on words, such as CTRL-T to transpose characters and ALT-T to transpose words. At any time, you can press ENTER to execute the command. For example, if you make a spelling mistake when entering a command, rather than re-entering the entire command, you can use the editing operations to correct the mistake. The actual associations of keys and their tasks, along with global settings, are specified in the **/etc/inputrc** file.

The editing capabilities of the BASH shell command line are provided by Readline. Readline supports numerous editing operations. You can even bind a key to a selected editing operation. Readline uses the **/etc/inputrc** file to configure key bindings. This file is read automatically by your **/etc/profile** shell configuration file when you log in. Users can customize their editing commands by creating an **.inputrc** file in their home directory (this is a dot file). It may be best to first copy the **/etc/inputrc** file as your **.inputrc** file and then edit it. **/etc/profile** will first check for a local **.inputrc** file before accessing the **/etc/inputrc** file. You can find out more about Readline in the BASH shell reference manual at **www.gnu.org/bash/manual**.

Command and Filename Completion

The BASH command line has a built-in feature that performs command line and filename completion. Automatic completions can be displayed by pressing the TAB key. If you enter an incomplete pattern as a command or filename argument, you can press the TAB key to activate the command and filename completion feature, which completes the pattern. A directory will have a forward slash (/) attached to its name. If more than one command or file has the same prefix, the shell simply beeps and waits for you to press the TAB key again. It then displays a list of possible command completions and waits for you to add enough characters to select a unique command or filename. For situations where you know multiple possibilities are likely, you can just press the ESC key instead of two TABs. In the next example, the user issues a **cat** command with an incomplete filename. When the user presses the TAB key, the system searches for a match and, when it finds one, fills in the filename. The user can then press ENTER to execute the command.

```
$ cat pre <tab>
$ cat preface
```

The automatic completions also work with the names of variables, users, and hosts. In this case, the partial text needs to be preceded by a special character, indicating the type of name. A listing of possible automatic completions follows:

Filenames begin with any text or /.

Shell variable text begins with a $ sign.

Username text begins with a ~ sign.

Host name text begins with a @.

Commands, aliases, and text in files begin with normal text.

Variables begin with a **$** sign, so any text beginning with a dollar sign is treated as a variable to be completed. Variables are selected from previously defined variables, like system shell variables. Usernames begin with a tilde (~). Host names begin with a @ sign, with possible names taken from the **/etc/hosts** file. For example, to complete the variable HOME given just $HOM, simply press a tab key.

```
$ echo $HOM <tab>
$ echo $HOME
```

If you entered just an **H**, then you could press TAB twice to see all possible variables beginning with H. The command line is redisplayed, letting you complete the name.

```
$ echo $H <tab> <tab>
$HISTCMD $HISTFILE $HOME $HOSTTYPE HISTFILE $HISTSIZE $HISTNAME
$ echo $H
```

You can also specifically select the kind of text to complete, using corresponding command keys. In this case, it does not matter what kind of sign a name begins with.

Command (CTRL-R for listing possible completions)	Description
TAB	Automatic completion
TAB TAB or ESC	List possible completions
ALT-/, CTRL-R-/	Filename completion, normal text for automatic
ALT-$, CTRL-R-$	Shell variable completion, $ for automatic
ALT-~, CTRL-R-~	Username completion, ~ for automatic
ALT-@, CTRL-R-@	Host name completion, @ for automatic
ALT-!, CTRL-R-!	Command name completion, normal text for automatic

Table 12-3: Command Line Text Completion Commands

For example, the pressing ALT-~ will treat the current text as a username. Pressing ALT-@ will treat it as a hostname, and ALT-$, as a variable. Pressing ALT-! will treat it as a command. To display a list of possible completions, press the CTRL-X key with the appropriate completion key, as in CTRL-X-$ to list possible variable completions. See Table 12-3 for a complete listing.

History

The BASH shell keeps a *history list,* of your previously entered commands. You can display each command, in turn, on your command line by pressing the UP ARROW key. Press the DOWN ARROW key to move down the list. You can modify and execute any of these previous commands when you display them on the command line.

Tip: The ability to redisplay a command is helpful when you have already executed a command you had entered incorrectly. In this case, you would be presented with an error message and a new, empty command line. By pressing the UP ARROW key, you can redisplay the previous command, make corrections to it, and then execute it again. This way, you would not have to enter the whole command again.

History Events

In the BASH shell, the *history utility* keeps a record of the most recent commands you have executed. The commands are numbered starting at 1, and a limit exists to the number of commands remembered—the default is 500. The history utility is a kind of short-term memory, keeping track of the most recent commands you have executed. To see the set of your most recent commands, type **history** on the command line and press ENTER. A list of your most recent commands is then displayed, preceded by a number.

```
$ history
1 cp mydata today
2 vi mydata
3 mv mydata reports
4 cd reports
5 ls
```

History Commands	Description
CTRL-N or DOWN ARROW	Moves down to the next event in the history list
CTRL-P or UP ARROW	Moves up to the previous event in the history list
ALT-<	Moves to the beginning of the history event list
ALT->	Moves to the end of the history event list
ALT-N	Forward Search, next matching item
ALT-P	Backward Search, previous matching item
CTRL-S	Forward Search History, forward incremental search
CTRL-R	Reverse Search History, reverse incremental search
fc *event-reference*	Edits an event with the standard editor and then executes it **Options** -l List recent history events; same as **history** command -e *editor event-reference* Invokes a specified editor to edit a specific event
History Event References	
! *event num*	References an event with an event number
! !	References the previous command
! *characters*	References an event with beginning characters
!? *pattern***?**	References an event with a pattern in the event
! *-event num*	References an event with an offset from the first event
! *num-num*	References a range of events

Table 12-4: History Commands and History Event References

Each of these commands is technically referred to as an event. An *event* describes an action that has been taken—a command that has been executed. The events are numbered according to their sequence of execution. The most recent event has the highest number. Each of these events can be identified by its number or beginning characters in the command.

The history utility lets you reference a former event, placing it on your command line so you can execute it. The easiest way to do this is to use the UP ARROW and DOWN ARROW keys to place history events on the command line, one at a time. You need not display the list first with **history**. Pressing the UP ARROW key once places the last history event on the command line. Pressing it again places the next history event on the command line. Pressing the DOWN ARROW key places the previous event on the command line.

You can use certain control and meta keys to perform other history operations like searching the history list. A meta key is the ALT key, and the ESC key on keyboards that have no ALT key. The ALT key is used here. Pressing ALT-< will move you to the beginning of the history list; ALT-N will search it. CTRL-S and CTRL-R will perform incremental searches, display matching commands as you type in a search string. Table 12-4 lists the different commands for referencing the history list.

Tip: If more than one history event matches what you have entered, you will hear a beep, and you can then enter more characters to help uniquely identify the event.

You can also reference and execute history events using the **!** history command. The **!** is followed by a reference that identifies the command. The reference can be either the number of the event or a beginning set of characters in the event. In the next example, the third command in the history list is referenced first by number and then by the beginning characters:

```
$ !3
mv mydata reports
$ !mv my
mv mydata reports
```

You can also reference an event using an offset from the end of the list. A negative number will offset from the end of the list to that event, thereby referencing it. In the next example, the fourth command, **cd mydata**, is referenced using a negative offset, and then executed. Remember that you are offsetting from the end of the list—in this case, event 5—up toward the beginning of the list, event 1. An offset of 4 beginning from event 5 places you at event 2.

```
$ !-4
vi mydata
```

To reference the last event, you use a following !, as in **!!**. In the next example, the command **!!** executes the last command the user executed—in this case, **ls**:

```
$ !!
ls
mydata today reports
```

Filename Expansion: *, ?, [ ]

Filenames are the most common arguments used in a command. Often you will know only part of the filename, or you will want to reference several filenames that have the same extension or begin with the same characters. The shell provides a set of special characters that search out, match, and generate a list of filenames. These are the asterisk, the question mark, and brackets (*, ?, []). Given a partial filename, the shell uses these matching operators to search for files and expand to a list of filenames found. The shell replaces the partial filename argument with the expanded list of matched filenames. This list of filenames can then become the arguments for commands such as ls, which can operate on many files. Table 12-5 lists the shell's file expansion characters.

Common Shell Symbols	Execution
ENTER	Execute a command line.
;	Separate commands on the same command line.
`command`	Execute a command.
$ (command)	Execute a command.
[]	Match on a class of possible characters in filenames.
\	Quote the following character. Used to quote special characters.
|	Pipe the standard output of one command as input for another command.
&	Execute a command in the background.
!	Reference history command.
File Expansion Symbols	**Execution**
*	Match on any set of characters in filenames.
?	Match on any single character in filenames.
[]	Match on a class of characters in filenames.
Redirection Symbols	**Execution**
>	Redirect the standard output to a file or device, creating the file if it does not exist and overwriting the file if it does exist.
>!	The exclamation point forces the overwriting of a file if it already exists.
<	Redirect the standard input from a file or device to a program.
>>	Redirect the standard output to a file or device, appending the output to the end of the file.
Standard Error Redirection Symbols	**Execution**
2>	Redirect the standard error to a file or device.
2>>	Redirect and append the standard error to a file or device.
2>&1	Redirect the standard error to the standard output.

Table 12-5: Shell Symbols

Matching Multiple Characters

The asterisk (*) references files beginning or ending with a specific set of characters. You place the asterisk before or after a set of characters that form a pattern to be searched for in filenames.

If the asterisk is placed before the pattern, filenames that end in that pattern are searched for. If the asterisk is placed after the pattern, filenames that begin with that pattern are searched for. Any matching filename is copied into a list of filenames generated by this operation.

In the next example, all filenames beginning with the pattern "doc" are searched for and a list generated. Then all filenames ending with the pattern "day" are searched for and a list is generated. The last example shows how the * can be used in any combination of characters.

```
$ ls
doc1 doc2 document docs mydoc monday tuesday
$ ls doc*
doc1 doc2 document docs
$ ls *day
monday tuesday
$ ls m*d*
monday
$
```

Filenames often include an extension specified with a period and followed by a string denoting the file type, such as **.c** for C files, **.cpp** for C++ files, or even **.jpg** for JPEG image files. The extension has no special status, and is only part of the characters making up the filename. Using the asterisk makes it easy to select files with a given extension. In the next example, the asterisk is used to list only those files with a **.c** extension. The asterisk placed before the **.c** constitutes the argument for **ls**.

```
$ ls *.c
calc.c main.c
```

You can use * with the **rm** command to erase several files at once. The asterisk first selects a list of files with a given extension, or beginning or ending with a given set of characters, and then it presents this list of files to the **rm** command to be erased. In the next example, the **rm** command erases all files beginning with the pattern "doc":

```
$ rm doc*
```

Caution: Use the * file expansion character carefully and sparingly with the rm command. The combination can be dangerous. A misplaced * in an rm command without the -i option could easily erase all the files in your current directory. The -i option will first prompt you to confirm whether the file should be deleted.

Matching Single Characters

The question mark (?) matches only a single incomplete character in filenames. Suppose you want to match the files **doc1** and **docA**, but not the file **document**. Whereas the asterisk will match filenames of any length, the question mark limits the match to one extra character. The next example matches files that begin with the word "doc" followed by a single differing letter:

```
$ ls
doc1 docA document
$ ls doc?
doc1 docA
```

Matching a Range of Characters

Whereas the * and ? file expansion characters specify incomplete portions of a filename, the brackets ([]) enable you to specify a set of valid characters to search for. Any character placed within the brackets will be matched in the filename. Suppose you want to list files beginning with "doc", but only ending in *1* or *A*. You are not interested in filenames ending in *2* or *B,* or any other character. Here is how it is done:

```
$ ls
doc1 doc2 doc3 docA docB docD document
$ ls doc[1A]
doc1 docA
```

You can also specify a set of characters as a range, rather than listing them one by one. A dash placed between the upper and lower bounds of a range of characters selects all characters within that range. The range is usually determined by the character set in use. In an ASCII character set, the range "a-g" will select all lowercase alphabetic characters from *a* through *g,* inclusive. In the next example, files beginning with the pattern "doc" and ending in characters *1* through *3* are selected. Then, those ending in characters *B* through *E* are matched.

```
$ ls doc[1-3]
doc1 doc2 doc3
$ ls doc[B-E]
docB docD
```

You can combine the brackets with other file expansion characters to form flexible matching operators. Suppose you want to list only filenames ending in either a **.c** or **.o** extension, but no other extension. You can use a combination of the asterisk and brackets: * [co]. The asterisk matches all filenames, and the brackets match only filenames with extension **.c** or **.o**.

```
$ ls *.[co]
main.c  main.o  calc.c
```

Matching Shell Symbols

At times, a file expansion character is actually part of a filename. In these cases, you need to quote the character by preceding it with a backslash (\) to reference the file. In the next example, the user needs to reference a file that ends with the ? character, called **answers?**. The **?** is, however, a file expansion character and would match any filename beginning with "answers" that has one or more characters. In this case, the user quotes the **?** with a preceding backslash to reference the filename.

```
$ ls answers\?
answers?
```

Placing the filename in double quotes will also quote the character.

```
$ ls "answers?"
answers?
```

This is also true for filenames or directories that have white space characters like the space character. In this case, you could either use the backslash to quote the space character in the file or directory name, or place the entire name in double quotes.

```
$ ls My\ Documents
My Documents
$ ls "My Documents"
My Documents
```

Generating Patterns

Though not a file expansion operation, { } is often useful for generating names that you can use to create or modify files and directories. The braces operation only generates a list of names. It does not match on existing filenames. Patterns are placed within the braces and separated with commas. Any pattern placed within the braces will be used to generate a version of the pattern, using either the preceding or following pattern, or both. Suppose you want to generate a list of names beginning with "doc", but ending only in the patterns "ument", "final", and "draft". Here is how it is done:

```
$ echo doc{ument,final,draft}
document docfinal docdraft
```

Since the names generated do not have to exist, you could use the { } operation in a command to create directories, as shown here:

```
$ mkdir {fall,winter,spring}report
$ ls
fallreport springreport winterreport
```

Standard Input/Output and Redirection

The data in input and output operations is organized like a file. Data input at the keyboard is placed in a data stream arranged as a continuous set of bytes. Data output from a command or program is also placed in a data stream and arranged as a continuous set of bytes. This input data stream is referred to in Linux as the standard input, while the output data stream is called the standard output. A separate output data stream reserved solely for error messages is called the standard error.

Because the standard input and standard output have the same organization as that of a file, they can easily interact with files. Linux has a redirection capability that lets you easily move data in and out of files. You can redirect the standard output so that, instead of displaying the output on a screen, you can save it in a file. You can also redirect the standard input away from the keyboard to a file, so that input is read from a file instead of from your keyboard.

When a Linux command is executed that produces output, this output is placed in the standard output data stream. The default destination for the standard output data stream is a device—in this case, the screen. *Devices,* such as the keyboard and screen, are treated as files. They receive and send out streams of bytes with the same organization as that of a byte-stream file. The screen is a device that displays a continuous stream of bytes. By default, the standard output will send its data to the screen device, which will then display the data.

For example, the **ls** command generates a list of all filenames and outputs this list to the standard output. Next, this stream of bytes in the standard output is directed to the screen device. The list of filenames is then printed on the screen. The **cat** command also sends output to the standard output. The contents of a file are copied to the standard output, whose default destination is the screen. The contents of the file are then displayed on the screen.

Command	Execution
ENTER	Execute a command line.
;	Separate commands on the same command line.
command *opts args*	Enter backslash before carriage return to continue entering a command on the next line.
`` `command` ``	Execute a command.
Special Characters for Filename Expansion	**Execution**
*	Match on any set of characters.
?	Match on any single characters.
[]	Match on a class of possible characters.
\	Quote the following character. Used to quote special characters.
Redirection	**Execution**
command > filename	Redirect the standard output to a file or device, creating the file if it does not exist and overwriting the file if it does exist.
command < filename	Redirect the standard input from a file or device to a program.
command >> filename	Redirect the standard output to a file or device, appending the output to the end of the file.
command 2> filename	Redirect the standard error to a file or device
command 2>> filename	Redirect and append the standard error to a file or device
command 2>&1	Redirect the standard error to the standard output in the Bourne shell.
command >& filename	Redirect the standard error to a file or device in the C shell.
Pipes	**Execution**
*command	command*	Pipe the standard output of one command as input for another command.

Table 12-6: The Shell Operations

Redirecting the Standard Output: > and >>

Suppose that instead of displaying a list of files on the screen, you would like to save this list in a file. In other words, you would like to direct the standard output to a file rather than the screen. To do this, you place the output redirection operator, the greater-than sign (>), followed by the name of a file on the command line after the Linux command. Table 12-6 lists the different ways you can use the redirection operators. In the next example, the output of the `ls` command is redirected from the screen device to a file:

```
$ ls -l *.c > programlist
```

The redirection operation creates the new destination file. If the file already exists, it will be overwritten with the data in the standard output. You can set the `noclobber` feature to prevent overwriting an existing file with the redirection operation. In this case, the redirection operation on an existing file will fail. You can overcome the `noclobber` feature by placing an exclamation point after the redirection operator. You can place the `noclobber` command in a shell configuration file to make it an automatic default operation. The next example sets the `noclobber` feature for the BASH shell and then forces the overwriting of the **oldarticle** file if it already exists:

```
$ set -o noclobber
$ cat myarticle >! oldarticle
```

Although the redirection operator and the filename are placed after the command, the redirection operation is not executed after the command. In fact, it is executed before the command. The redirection operation creates the file and sets up the redirection before it receives any data from the standard output. If the file already exists, it will be destroyed and replaced by a file of the same name. In effect, the command generating the output is executed only after the redirected file has been created.

In the next example, the output of the `ls` command is redirected from the screen device to a file. First, the `ls` command lists files, and in the next command, `ls` redirects its file list to the **listf** file. Then the `cat` command displays the list of files saved in **listf**. Notice the list of files in **listf** includes the **listf** filename. The list of filenames generated by the `ls` command includes the name of the file created by the redirection operation—in this case, **listf**. The **listf** file is first created by the redirection operation, and then the `ls` command lists it along with other files. This file list output by `ls` is then redirected to the **listf** file, instead of being printed on the screen.

```
$ ls
mydata intro preface
$ ls > listf
$ cat listf
mydata intro listf preface
```

Tip: Errors occur when you try to use the same filename for both an input file for the command and the redirected destination file. In this case, because the redirection operation is executed first, the input file, because it exists, is destroyed and replaced by a file of the same name. When the command is executed, it finds an input file that is empty.

You can also append the standard output to an existing file using the **>>** redirection operator. Instead of overwriting the file, the data in the standard output is added at the end of the file. In the next example, the **myarticle** and **oldarticle** files are appended to the **allarticles** file. The **allarticles** file will then contain the contents of both **myarticle** and **oldarticle**.

```
$ cat myarticle >> allarticles
$ cat oldarticle >> allarticles
```

The Standard Input

Many Linux commands can receive data from the standard input. The standard input itself receives data from a device or a file. The default device for the standard input is the keyboard. Characters typed on the keyboard are placed in the standard input, which is then directed to the Linux command. Just as with the standard output, you can also redirect the standard input, receiving input from a file rather than the keyboard. The operator for redirecting the standard input is the less-than sign (**<**). In the next example, the standard input is redirected to receive input from the **myarticle** file, rather than the keyboard device (use CTRL-D to end the typed input). The contents of **myarticle** are read into the standard input by the redirection operation. Then the **cat** command reads the standard input and displays the contents of **myarticle**.

```
$ cat < myarticle
hello Christopher
How are you today
$
```

You can combine the redirection operations for both standard input and standard output. In the next example, the **cat** command has no filename arguments. Without filename arguments, the **cat** command receives input from the standard input and sends output to the standard output. However, the standard input has been redirected to receive its data from a file, while the standard output has been redirected to place its data in a file.

```
$ cat < myarticle > newarticle
```

Redirecting the Standard Error: >&, 2>, |&

When you execute commands, it is possible for an error to occur. You may give the wrong number of arguments or some kind of system error could take place. When an error occurs, the system will issue an error message. Usually, such error messages are displayed on the screen along with the standard output. Error messages are placed in another standard byte stream called the standard error. In the next example, the cat command is given as its argument the name of a file that does not exist, **myintro**. In this case, the **cat** command will simply issue an error. Redirection operators are listed in Table 12-6.

```
$ cat myintro
cat : myintro not found
```

Because error messages are in a separate data stream from the standard output, this means that if you have redirected the standard output to a file, error messages will still appear on the screen for you to see. Though the standard output may be redirected to a file, the standard error is still directed to the screen. In the next example, the standard output of the **cat** command is redirected to the file **mydata**. The standard error, containing the error messages, is still directed toward the screen

```
$ cat myintro > mydata
cat : myintro not found
```

Like the standard output, you can also redirect the standard error. This means that you can save your error messages in a file for future reference. This is helpful if you need to save a record of the error messages. Like the standard output, the standard error's default destination is the display. Using special redirection operators, you can redirect the standard error to any file or device that you choose. If you redirect the standard error, the error messages will not be displayed on the screen. You can examine them later by viewing the contents of the file in which you saved them.

All the standard byte streams can be referenced in redirection operations with numbers. The numbers 0, 1, and 2 reference the standard input, standard output, and standard error respectively. By default an output redirection, >, operates on the standard output, 1. You can modify the output redirection to operate on the standard error by preceding the output redirection operator with the number 2, **2>**. In the next example, the **cat** command again will generate an error. The error message is redirected to the standard byte stream represented by number 2, the standard error.

```
$ cat nodata 2> myerrors
$ cat myerrors
cat : nodata not found
```

You can also append the standard error to a file by using the number 2 and the redirection append operator, **>>**. In the next example, the user appends the standard error to the **myerrors** file, which then functions as a log of errors.

```
$ cat nodata 2>> myerrors
$ cat compls 2>> myerrors
$ cat myerrors
cat : nodata not found
cat : compls not found
$
```

To redirect both the standard output as well as the standard error, you would need a separate redirection operation and file for each. In the next example, the standard output is redirected to the file **mydata**, and the standard error is redirected to **myerrors**. If nodata were to exist, then **mydata** would hold a copy of its contents.

```
$ cat nodata 1> mydata 2> myerrors
cat myerrors
cat : nodata not found
```

If, however, you want to save a record of your errors in the same file as that used for the redirected standard output, you need to redirect the standard error into the standard output. You can reference a standard byte stream by preceding its number with an ampersand. **&1** references the standard output. You can use such a reference in a redirection operation to make a standard byte stream a destination file. The redirection operation **2>&1** redirects the standard error into the standard output. In effect, the standard output becomes the destination file for the standard error. Conversely, the redirection operation **1>&2** would redirect the standard input into the standard error.

Pipes: |

You may encounter situations in which you need to send data from one command to another. In other words, you may want to send the standard output of a command to another command, rather than to a destination file. Suppose you want to send a list of your filenames to the printer to be printed. You need two commands to do this: the **ls** command to generate a list of filenames and the **lpr** command to send the list to the printer. In effect, you need to take the output of the **ls** command and use it as input for the **lpr** command. You can think of the data as flowing from one command to another. To form such a connection in Linux, you use what is called a pipe. The pipe operator (|, the vertical bar character) placed between two commands forms a connection between them. The standard output of one command becomes the standard input for the other. The pipe operation receives output from the command placed before the pipe and sends this data as input to the command placed after the pipe. As shown in the next example, you can connect the `ls` command and the `lpr` command with a pipe. The list of filenames output by the `ls` command is piped into the `lpr` command.

```
$ ls | lpr
```

You can combine the **pipe** operation with other shell features, such as file expansion characters, to perform specialized operations. The next example prints only files with a **.c** extension. The `ls` command is used with the asterisk and ".c" to generate a list of filenames with the **.c** extension. Then this list is piped to the `lpr` command.

```
$ ls *.c | lpr
```

In the preceding example, a list of filenames was used as input. What is important to note is that pipes operate on the standard output of a command, whatever that might be. The contents of whole files, or even several files, can be piped from one command to another. In the next example, the **cat** command reads and outputs the contents of the **mydata** file, which are then piped to the **lpr** command:

```
$ cat mydata | lpr
```

Linux has many commands that generate modified output. For example, the **sort** command takes the contents of a file and generates a version with each line sorted in alphabetic order. The **sort** command works best with files that are lists of items. Commands such as **sort** that output a modified version of its input are referred to as filters. Filters are often used with pipes. In the next example, a sorted version of **mylist** is generated and piped into the **more** command for display on the screen. The original file, **mylist**, has not been changed and is not sorted. Only the output of **sort** in the standard output is sorted.

```
$ sort mylist | more
```

The standard input piped into a command can be more carefully controlled with the standard input argument (-). When you use the dash as an argument for a command, it represents the standard input.

Linux Files

You can name a file using any letters, underscores, and numbers. You can also include periods and commas. Except in certain special cases, you should never begin a filename with a period. Other characters, such as slashes, question marks, or asterisks, are reserved for use as special characters by the system and should not be part of a filename. Filenames can be as long as 256 characters. Filenames can also include spaces, though to reference such filenames from the command line, be sure to encase them in quotes. On a desktop like GNOME or KDE, you do not need to use quotes.

You can include an extension as part of a filename. A period is used to distinguish the filename proper from the extension. Extensions can be useful for categorizing your files. You are probably familiar with certain standard extensions that have been adopted by convention. For example, C source code files always have a **.c** extension. Files that contain compiled object code have an **.o** extension. You can make up your own file extensions. The following examples are all valid Linux filenames. Keep in mind that to reference the name with spaces on the command line, you would have to encase it in quotes as "New book review":

```
preface
chapter2
9700info
New_Revisions
calc.c
intro.bk1
New book review
```

Special initialization files are also used to hold shell configuration commands. These are the hidden, or dot, files, which begin with a period. Dot files used by commands and applications have predetermined names, such as the **.mozilla** directory used to hold your Mozilla data and configuration files. Recall that when you use **ls** to display your filenames, the dot files will not be displayed. To include the dot files, you need to use **ls** with the **-a** option.

The **ls -l** command displays detailed information about a file. First, the permissions are displayed, followed by the number of links, the owner of the file, the name of the group to which the user belongs, the file size in bytes, the date and time the file was last modified, and the name of the file. Permissions indicate who can access the file: the user, members of a group, or all other users. The group name indicates the group permitted to access the file object. The file type for **mydata** is that of an ordinary file. Only one link exists, indicating the file has no other names and no other links. The owner's name is **chris**, the same as the login name, and the group name is **weather**. Other users probably also belong to the **weather** group. The size of the file is 207 bytes, and it was last modified on February 20 at 11:55 A.M. The name of the file is **mydata**.

If you want to display this detailed information for all the files in a directory, simply use the **ls -l** command without an argument.

```
$ ls -l
-rw-r--r-- 1 chris weather 207 Feb 20 11:55 mydata
-rw-rw-r-- 1 chris weather 568 Feb 14 10:30 today
-rw-rw-r-- 1 chris weather 308 Feb 17 12:40 monday
```

All files in Linux have one physical format, a byte stream, which is simply a sequence of bytes. This allows Linux to apply the file concept to every data component in the system. Directories are classified as files, as are devices. Treating everything as a file allows Linux to organize and exchange data more easily. The data in a file can be sent directly to a device such as a screen because a device interfaces with the system using the same byte-stream file format used by regular files.

This same file format is used to implement other operating system components. The interface to a device, such as the screen or keyboard, is designated as a file. Other components, such as directories, are themselves byte-stream files, but they have a special internal organization. A directory file contains information about a directory, organized in a special directory format. Because these different components are treated as files, they can be said to constitute different *file types*. A character device is one file type. A directory is another file type. The number of these file types may vary according to your specific implementation of Linux. Five common types of files exist, however: ordinary files, directory files, first-in first-out (FIFO) pipes, character device files, and block device files. Although you may rarely reference a file's type, it can be useful when searching for directories or devices.

Although all ordinary files have a byte-stream format, they may be used in different ways. The most significant difference is between binary and text files. Compiled programs are examples of binary files. However, even text files can be classified according to their different uses. You can have files that contain C programming source code or shell commands, or even a file that is empty. The file could be an executable program or a directory file. The Linux **file** command helps you determine what a file is used for. It examines the first few lines of a file and tries to determine a classification for it. The **file** command looks for special keywords or special numbers in those first few lines, but it is not always accurate. In the next example, the **file** command examines the contents of two files and determines a classification for them:

```
$ file monday reports
monday: text
reports: directory
```

If you need to examine the entire file byte by byte, you can do so with the **od** (octal dump) command, which performs a dump of a file. By default, it prints every byte in its octal representation. However, you can also specify a character, decimal, or hexadecimal representation. The **od** command is helpful when you need to detect any special character in your file or if you want to display a binary file.

The File Structure

Linux organizes files into a hierarchically connected set of directories. Each directory may contain either files or other directories. In this respect, directories perform two important functions. A *directory* holds files, much like files held in a file drawer, and a directory connects to other directories, much as a branch in a tree is connected to other branches. Because of the similarities to a tree, such a structure is often referred to as a *tree structure*.

The Linux file structure branches into several directories beginning with a root directory, /. Within the root directory, several system directories contain files and programs that are features of the Linux system. The root directory also contains a directory called **home** that contains the home directories of all the users in the system. Each user's home directory, in turn, contains the directories the user has made for their own use. Each of these can also contain directories. Such nested directories branch out from the user's home directory.

Note: The user's home directory can be any directory, though it is usually the directory that bears the user's login name. This directory is located in the directory named /home on your Linux system. For example, a user named dylan will have a home directory called dylan located in the system's /home directory. The user's home directory is a subdirectory of the directory called /home on your system.

Home Directories

When you log in to the system, you are placed within your home directory. The name given to this directory by the system is the same as your login name. Any files you create when you first log in are organized within your home directory. Within your home directory, you can create more directories. You can then change to these directories and store files in them. The same is true for other users on the system. Each user has a home directory, identified by the appropriate login name. Users, in turn, can create their own directories.

You can access a directory either through its name or by making it your working directory. Each directory is given a name when it is created. You can use this name in file operations to access files in that directory. You can also make the directory your working directory. If you do not use any directory names in a file operation, the working directory will be accessed. The working directory is the one from which you are currently working. When you log in, the working directory is your home directory, which usually has the same name as your login name. You can change the working directory by using the **cd** command to move to another directory.

Directory	Function
/	Begins the file system structure, called the *root*.
/home	Contains users' home directories.
/bin	Holds all the standard commands and utility programs.
/usr	Holds those files and commands used by the system; this directory breaks down into several subdirectories.
/usr/bin	Holds user-oriented commands and utility programs.
/usr/sbin	Holds system administration commands.
/usr/lib	Holds libraries for programming languages.
/usr/share/doc	Holds Linux documentation.
/usr/share/man	Holds the online Man files.
/var/spool	Holds spooled files, such as those generated for printing jobs and network transfers.
/sbin	Holds system administration commands for booting the system.
/var	Holds files that vary, such as mailbox files.
/dev	Holds file interfaces for devices such as the terminals and printers (dynamically generated by udev, do not edit).
/etc	Holds system configuration files and any other system files.

Table 12-7: Standard System Directories in Linux

Pathnames

The name you give to a directory or file when you create it is not its full name. The full name of a directory is its *pathname*. The hierarchically nested relationship among directories forms paths, and these paths can be used to identify and reference any directory or file uniquely or absolutely. Each directory in the file structure can be said to have its own unique path. The actual name by which the system identifies a directory always begins with the root directory and consists of all directories nested below that directory.

In Linux, you write a pathname by listing each directory in the path separated from the last by a forward slash. A slash preceding the first directory in the path represents the root. The pathname for the **chris** directory is **/home/chris**. If the **chris** directory has a subdirectory called

reports, then the full the pathname for the **reports** directory would be **/home/chris/reports**. Pathnames also apply to files. When you create a file within a directory, you give the file a name. The actual name by which the system identifies the file, however, is the filename combined with the path of directories from the root to the file's directory. As an example, the pathname for **monday** is **/home/chris/reports/monday** (the root directory is represented by the first slash). The path for the **monday** file consists of the root, **home**, **chris**, and **reports** directories and the filename **monday**.

Pathnames may be absolute or relative. An *absolute pathname* is the complete pathname of a file or directory beginning with the root directory. A *relative pathname* begins from your working directory; it is the path of a file relative to your working directory. The working directory is the one you are currently operating in. Using the previous example, if **chris** is your working directory, the relative pathname for the file **monday** is **reports/monday**. The absolute pathname for **monday** is **/home/chris/reports/monday**.

The absolute pathname from the root to your home directory can be especially complex and, at times, even subject to change by the system administrator. To make it easier to reference, you can use the tilde (**~**) character, which represents the absolute pathname of your home directory. You must specify the rest of the path from your home directory. In the next example, the user references the **monday** file in the **reports** directory. The tilde represents the path to the user's home directory, **/home/chris**, and then the rest of the path to the **monday** file is specified.

```
$ cat ~/reports/monday
```

System Directories

The root directory that begins the Linux file structure contains several system directories that contain files and programs used to run and maintain the system. Many also contain other subdirectories with programs for executing specific features of Linux. For example, the directory **/usr/bin** contains the various Linux commands that users execute, such as **lpr**. The directory **/bin** holds system level commands. Table 12-7 lists the basic system directories.

Listing, Displaying, and Printing Files: ls, cat, more, less, and lpr

One of the primary functions of an operating system is the management of files. You may need to perform certain basic output operations on your files, such as displaying them on your screen or printing them. The Linux system provides a set of commands that perform basic file-management operations, such as listing, displaying, and printing files, as well as copying, renaming, and erasing files. These commands are usually made up of abbreviated versions of words. For example, the **ls** command is a shortened form of "list" and lists the files in your directory. The **lpr** command is an abbreviated form of "line print" and will print a file. The **cat**, **less**, and **more** commands display the contents of a file on the screen. Table 12-8 lists these commands with their different options. When you log in to your Linux system, you may want a list of the files in your home directory. The **ls** command, which outputs a list of your file and directory names, is useful for this. The **ls** command has many possible options for displaying filenames according to specific features.

Displaying Files: cat, less, and more

You may also need to look at the contents of a file. The `cat` and `more` commands display the contents of a file on the screen. The name `cat` stands for *concatenate*.

```
$ cat mydata
computers
```

The `cat` command outputs the entire text of a file to the screen at once. This presents a problem when the file is large because its text quickly speeds past on the screen. The `more` and `less` commands are designed to overcome this limitation by displaying one screen of text at a time. You can then move forward or backward in the text at your leisure. You invoke the `more` or `less` command by entering the command name followed by the name of the file you want to view (`less` is a more powerful and configurable display utility).

```
$ less mydata
```

When `more` or `less` invoke a file, the first screen of text is displayed. To continue to the next screen, you press the F key or the SPACEBAR. To move back in the text, you press the B key. You can quit at any time by pressing the Q key.

Command or Option	Execution
`ls`	This command lists file and directory names.
`cat` *filenames*	This filter can be used to display a file. It can take filenames for its arguments. It outputs the contents of those files directly to the standard output, which, by default, is directed to the screen.
`more` *filenames*	This utility displays a file screen by screen. Press the SPACEBAR to continue to the next screen and **q** to quit.
`less` *filenames*	This utility also displays a file screen by screen. Press the SPACEBAR to continue to the next screen and **q** to quit.
`lpr` *filenames*	Sends a file to the line printer to be printed; a list of files may be used as arguments. Use the **-P** option to specify a printer.
`lpq`	Lists the print queue for printing jobs.
`lprm`	Removes a printing job from the print queue.

Table 12-8: Listing, Displaying, and Printing Files

Printing Files: lpr, lpq, and lprm

With the printer commands such as `lpr` and `lprm`, you can perform printing operations such as printing files or canceling print jobs (see Table 12-8). When you need to print files, use the `lpr` command to send files to the printer connected to your system. In the next example, the user prints the **mydata** file:

```
$ lpr mydata
```

If you want to print several files at once, you can specify more than one file on the command line after the `lpr` command. In the next example, the user prints out both the **mydata** and **preface** files:

```
$ lpr mydata preface
```

Printing jobs are placed in a queue and printed one at a time in the background. You can continue with other work as your files print. You can see the position of a particular printing job at any given time with the **lpq** command, which gives the owner of the printing job (the login name of the user who sent the job), the print job ID, the size in bytes, and the temporary file in which it is currently held.

If you need to cancel an unwanted printing job, you can do so with the **lprm** command, which takes as its argument either the ID number of the printing job or the owner's name. It then removes the print job from the print queue. For this task, **lpq** is helpful, for it provides you with the ID number and owner of the printing job you need to use with **lprm**.

Managing Directories: mkdir, rmdir, ls, cd, pwd

You can create and remove your own directories, as well as change your working directory, with the **mkdir**, **rmdir**, and **cd** commands. Each of these commands can take as its argument the pathname for a directory. The **pwd** command displays the absolute pathname of your working directory. In addition to these commands, the special characters represented by a single dot, a double dot, and a tilde can be used to reference the working directory, the parent of the working directory, and the home directory, respectively. Taken together, these commands enable you to manage your directories. You can create nested directories, move from one directory to another, and use pathnames to reference any of your directories. Those commands commonly used to manage directories are listed in Table 12-9.

Creating and Deleting Directories

You create and remove directories with the **mkdir** and **rmdir** commands. In either case, you can also use pathnames for the directories. In the next example, the user creates the directory **reports**. Then the user creates the directory **articles** using a pathname:

```
$ mkdir reports
$ mkdir /home/chris/articles
```

You can remove a directory with the **rmdir** command followed by the directory name. In the next example, the user removes the directory **reports** with the **rmdir** command:

```
$ rmdir reports
```

To remove a directory and all its subdirectories, you use the **rm** command with the **-r** option. This is a very powerful command and could be used to erase all your files. You will be prompted for each file. To remove all files and subdirectories without prompts, add the **-f** option. The following example deletes the **reports** directory and all its subdirectories:

```
rm -rf reports
```

Displaying Directory Contents

You have seen how to use the **ls** command to list the files and directories within your working directory. To distinguish between file and directory names, however, you need to use the **ls** command with the **-F** option. A slash is then placed after each directory name in the list.

```
$ ls
weather reports articles
$ ls -F
weather reports/ articles/
```

The **ls** command also takes as an argument any directory name or directory pathname. This enables you to list the files in any directory without first having to change to that directory. In the next example, the **ls** command takes as its argument the name of a directory, **reports**. Then the **ls** command is executed again, only this time the absolute pathname of **reports** is used.

```
$ ls reports
monday tuesday
$ ls /home/chris/reports
monday tuesday
$
```

Command	Execution
mkdir *directory*	Creates a directory.
rmdir *directory*	Erases a directory.
ls -F	Lists directory name with a preceding slash.
ls -R	Lists working directory as well as all subdirectories.
cd *directory name*	Changes to the specified directory, making it the working directory. **cd** without a directory name changes back to the home directory: **$ cd reports**
pwd	Displays the pathname of the working directory.
directory name/*filename*	A slash is used in pathnames to separate each directory name. In the case of pathnames for files, a slash separates the preceding directory names from the filename.
..	References the parent directory. You can use it as an argument or as part of a pathname: **$ cd ..** **$ mv ../larisa oldarticles**
.	References the working directory. You can use it as an argument or as part of a pathname: **$ ls .**
~/*pathname*	The tilde is a special character that represents the pathname for the home directory. It is useful when you need to use an absolute pathname for a file or directory: **$ cp monday ~/today**

Table 12-9: Directory Commands

Moving Through Directories

The **cd** command takes as its argument the name of the directory to which you want to move. The name of the directory can be the name of a subdirectory in your working directory or the full pathname of any directory on the system. If you want to change back to your home directory, you need to enter only the **cd** command by itself, without a filename argument.

```
$ cd reports
$ pwd
/home/chris/reports
```

Referencing the Parent Directory

A directory always has a parent (except, of course, for the root). For example, in the preceding listing, the parent for **reports** is the **chris** directory. When a directory is created, two entries are made: one represented with a dot (.), and the other with double dots (..). The dot represents the pathnames of the directory, and the double dots represent the pathname of its parent directory. Double dots, used as an argument in a command, reference a parent directory. The single dot references the directory itself.

You can use the single dot to reference your working directory, instead of using its pathname. For example, to copy a file to the working directory retaining the same name, the dot can be used in place of the working directory's pathname. In this sense, the dot is another name for the working directory. In the next example, the user copies the **weather** file from the **chris** directory to the **reports** directory. The **reports** directory is the working directory and can be represented with the single dot.

```
$ cd reports
$ cp /home/chris/weather .
```

The .. symbol is often used to reference files in the parent directory. In the next example, the **cat** command displays the **weather** file in the parent directory. The pathname for the file is the .. symbol (for the parent directory) followed by a slash and the filename.

```
$ cat ../weather
raining and warm
```

Tip: You can use the cd command with the .. symbol to step back through successive parent directories of the directory tree from a lower directory.

File and Directory Operations: find, cp, mv, rm, ln

As you create more and more files, you may want to back them up, change their names, erase some of them, or even give them added names. Linux provides several file commands that you can use to search for files, copy files, rename files, or remove files (see Table 12-5). If you have a large number of files, you can also search them to locate a specific one. The commands are shortened forms of full words, consisting of only two characters. The **cp** command stands for "copy" and copies a file, **mv** stands for "move" and renames or moves a file, **rm** stands for "remove" and erases a file, and **ln** stands for "link" and adds another name for a file, often used as a shortcut to the original. One exception to the two-character rule is the **find** command, which performs searches of your filenames to find a file. All these operations can be handled by the GUI desktops, like GNOME and KDE.

Searching Directories: find

Once a large number of files have been stored in many different directories, you may need to search them to locate a specific file, or files, of a certain type. The **find** command enables you to perform such a search from the command line. The **find** command takes as its arguments directory names followed by several possible options that specify the type of search and the criteria for the search; it then searches within the directories listed and their subdirectories for files that meet these criteria. The **find** command can search for a file by name, type, owner, and even the time of the last update.

```
$ find directory-list -option criteria
```

The **-name** option has as its criteria a pattern and instructs **find** to search for the filename that matches that pattern. To search for a file by name, you use the **find** command with the directory name followed by the **-name** option and the name of the file.

```
$ find directory-list -name filename
```

Command or Option	Execution
find	Searches directories for files according to search criteria. This command has several options that specify the type of criteria and actions to be taken.
-name *pattern*	Searches for files with the *pattern* in the name.
-lname *pattern*	Searches for symbolic link files.
-group *name*	Searches for files belonging to the group *name*.
-gid *name*	Searches for files belonging to a group according to group ID.
-user *name*	Searches for files belonging to a user.
-uid *name*	Searches for files belonging to a user according to user ID.
-mtime *num*	Searches for files last modified *num* days ago.
-context *scontext*	Searches for files according to security context (SE Linux).
-print	Outputs the result of the search to the standard output. The result is usually a list of filenames, including their full pathnames.
-type *filetype*	Searches for files with the specified file type. File type can be **b** for block device, **c** for character device, **d** for directory, **f** for file, or **l** for symbolic link.
-perm *permission*	Searches for files with certain permissions set. Use octal or symbolic format for permissions.
-ls	Provides a detailed listing of each file, with owner, permission, size, and date information.
-exec *command*	Executes command when files found.

Table 12-10: The find Command

The **find** command also has options that merely perform actions, such as outputting the results of a search. If you want **find** to display the filenames it has located, you simply include the

-print option on the command line along with any other options. The **-print** option is an action that instructs **find** to write to the standard output the names of all the files it locates (you can also use the **-ls** option instead to list files in the long format). In the next example, the user searches for all the files in the **reports** directory with the name **monday**. Once located, the file, with its relative pathname, is printed.

```
$ find reports -name monday -print
reports/monday
```

The **find** command prints out the filenames using the directory name specified in the directory list. If you specify an absolute pathname, the absolute path of the found directories will be output. If you specify a relative pathname, only the relative pathname is output. In the preceding example, the user specified a relative pathname, **reports**, in the directory list. Located filenames were output beginning with this relative pathname. In the next example, the user specifies an absolute pathname in the directory list. Located filenames are then output using this absolute pathname.

```
$ find /home/chris -name monday -print
/home/chris/reports/monday
```

Tip: Should you need to find the location of a specific program or configuration file, you could use `find` to search for the file from the root directory. Log in as the root user and use / as the directory. This command searched for the location of the `more` command and files on the entire file system: `find / -name more -print`.

Searching the Working Directory

If you want to search your working directory, you can use the dot in the directory pathname to represent your working directory. The double dots would represent the parent directory. The next example searches all files and subdirectories in the working directory, using the dot to represent the working directory. If your working directory is your home directory, this is a convenient way to search through all your own directories. Notice that the located filenames that are output begin with a dot.

```
$ find . -name weather -print
./weather
```

You can use shell wildcard characters as part of the pattern criteria for searching files. The special character must be quoted, however, to avoid evaluation by the shell. In the next example, all files (indicated by the asterisk, *) with the **.c** extension in the **programs** directory are searched for and then displayed in the long format using the **-ls** action:

```
$ find programs -name '*.c' -ls
```

Locating Directories

You can also use the **find** command to locate other directories. In Linux, a directory is officially classified as a special type of file. Although all files have a byte-stream format, some files, such as directories, are used in special ways. In this sense, a file can be said to have a file type. The **find** command has an option called **-type** that searches for a file of a given type. The **-type** option takes a one-character modifier that represents the file type. The modifier that represents a directory is a **d**. In the next example, both the directory name and the directory file type are used to search for the directory called **travel**:

```
$ find /home/chris -name travel -type d -print
/home/chris/articles/travel
```

File types are not so much different types of files, as they are the file format applied to other components of the operating system, such as devices. In this sense, a device is treated as a type of file, and you can use **find** to search for devices and directories, as well as ordinary files. Table 12-10 lists the different types available for the **find** command's **-type** option.

You can also use the find operation to search for files by ownership or security criteria, like those belonging to a specific user or those with a certain security context. The **-user** option lets to locate all files belonging to a certain user. The following example lists all files that the user **chris** has created or owns on the entire system. To list those just in the users' home directories, you would use **/home** for the starting search directory. This would find all those in a user's home directory as well as any owned by that user in other user directories.

```
$ find / -user chris -print
```

Copying Files

To make a copy of a file, you simply give **cp** two filenames as its arguments (see Table 12-11). The first filename is the name of the file to be copied—the one that already exists. This is often referred to as the *source file.* The second filename is the name you want for the copy. This will be a new file containing a copy of all the data in the source file. This second argument is often referred to as the *destination file.* The syntax for the **cp** command follows:

```
$ cp source-file destination-file
```

Command	Execution
cp *filename filename*	Copies a file. **cp** takes two arguments: the original file and the name of the new copy. You can use pathnames for the files to copy across directories:
cp -r *dirname dirname*	Copies a subdirectory from one directory to another. The copied directory includes all its own subdirectories:
mv *filename filename*	Moves (renames) a file. The **mv** command takes two arguments: the first is the file to be moved. The second argument can be the new filename or the pathname of a directory. If it is the name of a directory, then the file is moved to that directory, changing the file's pathname:
mv *dirname dirname*	Moves directories. In this case, the first and last arguments are directories:
ln *filename filename*	Creates added names for files referred to as links. A link can be created in one directory that references a file in another directory:
rm *filenames*	Removes (erases) a file. Can take any number of filenames as its arguments. Literally removes links to a file.

Table 12-11: File Operations

In the next example, the user copies a file called **proposal** to a new file called **oldprop**:

```
$ cp proposal oldprop
```

You could unintentionally destroy another file with the **cp** command. The **cp** command generates a copy by first creating a file and then copying data into it. If another file has the same name as the destination file, that file is destroyed and a new file with that name is created. By default, Ubuntu configures your system to check for an existing copy by the same name (**cp** is aliased with the **-i** option). To copy a file from your working directory to another directory, you need to use that directory name as the second argument in the **cp** command. In the next example, the **proposal** file is overwritten by the **newprop** file. The **proposal** file already exists.

```
$ cp newprop proposal
```

You can use any of the wildcard characters to generate a list of filenames to use with **cp** or **mv**. For example, suppose you need to copy all your C source code files to a given directory. Instead of listing each one individually on the command line, you could use an * character with the **.c** extension to match on and generate a list of C source code files (all files with a **.c** extension). In the next example, the user copies all source code files in the current directory to the **sourcebks** directory:

```
$ cp *.c sourcebks
```

If you want to copy all the files in a given directory to another directory, you could use * to match on and generate a list of all those files in a **cp** command. In the next example, the user copies all the files in the **props** directory to the **oldprop** directory. Notice the use of a **props** pathname preceding the * special characters. In this context, **props** is a pathname that will be appended before each file in the list that * generates.

```
$ cp props/* oldprop
```

You can, of course, use any of the other special characters, such as **.**, **?**, or **[]**. In the next example, the user copies both source code and object code files (**.c** and **.o**) to the **projbk** directory:

```
$ cp *.[oc] projbk
```

When you copy a file, you can give the copy a name that is different from the original. To do so, place the new filename after the directory name, separated by a slash.

```
$ cp filename directory-name/new-filename
```

Moving Files

You can use the **mv** command to either rename a file or to move a file from one directory to another. When using **mv** to rename a file, you simply use the new filename as the second argument. The first argument is the current name of the file you are renaming. If you want to rename a file when you move it, you can specify the new name of the file after the directory name. In the next example, the **proposal** file is renamed with the name **version1**:

```
$ mv proposal version1
```

As with **cp**, it is easy for **mv** to erase a file accidentally. When renaming a file, you might accidentally choose a filename already used by another file. In this case, that other file will be erased. The **mv** command also has an **-i** option that checks first to see if a file by that name already exists.

You can also use any of the special characters to generate a list of filenames to use with **mv**. In the next example, the user moves all source code files in the current directory to the **newproj** directory:

```
$ mv *.c newproj
```

If you want to move all the files in a given directory to another directory, you can use * to match on and generate a list of all those files. In the next example, the user moves all the files in the **reports** directory to the **repbks** directory:

```
$ mv reports/* repbks
```

Note: The easiest way to copy files to a CD-R/RW or DVD-R/RW disc is to use the built-in GNOME Files burning capability. Just insert a blank disk, open it as a folder, and drag-and-drop files on to it. You will be prompted automatically to burn the files.

Copying and Moving Directories

You can also copy or move whole directories at once. Both **cp** and **mv** can take as their first argument a directory name, enabling you to copy or move subdirectories from one directory into another (see Table 12-11). The first argument is the name of the directory to be moved or copied, and the second argument is the name of the directory within which it is to be placed. The same pathname structure used for files applies to moving or copying directories.

You can just as easily copy subdirectories from one directory to another. To copy a directory, the **cp** command requires you to use the **-r** option, which stands for "recursive." It directs the **cp** command to copy a directory, as well as any subdirectories it may contain. In other words, the entire directory subtree, from that directory on, will be copied. In the next example, the **travel** directory is copied to the **oldarticles** directory. Now two **travel** subdirectories exist, one in **articles** and one in **oldarticles**.

```
$ cp -r articles/travel oldarticles
$ ls -F articles
/travel
$ ls -F oldarticles
/travel
```

Erasing Files and Directories: the rm Command

As you use Linux, you will find the number of files you use increases rapidly. Generating files in Linux is easy. Applications such as editors, and commands such as **cp**, can easily be used to create files. Eventually, many of these files may become outdated and useless. You can then remove them with the **rm** command. The **rm** command can take any number of arguments, enabling you to list several filenames and erase them all at the same time. In the next example, the file **oldprop** is erased:

```
$ rm oldprop
```

Be careful when using the **rm** command, because it is irrevocable. Once a file is removed, it cannot be restored (there is no undo). With the **-i** option, you are prompted separately for each file and asked whether you really want to remove it. If you enter **y**, the file will be removed. If you enter anything else, the file is not removed. In the next example, the **rm** command is instructed to erase the files **proposal** and **oldprop**. The **rm** command then asks for confirmation for each file. The user decides to remove **oldprop**, but not **proposal**.

```
$ rm -i proposal oldprop
Remove proposal? n
Remove oldprop? y
$
```

Links: the ln Command

You can give a file more than one name using the **ln** command. You might do this because you want to reference a file using different filenames to access it from different directories. The added names are often referred to as *links*. Linux supports two different types of links, hard and symbolic. Hard links are literally another name for the same file, whereas symbolic links function like shortcuts referencing another file. Symbolic links are much more flexible and can work over many different file systems, while hard links are limited to your local file system. Furthermore, hard links introduce security concerns, as they allow direct access from a link that may have public access to an original file that you may want protected. Links are usually implemented as symbolic links.

Symbolic Links

To set up a symbolic link, you use the **ln** command with the **-s** option and two arguments: the name of the original file and the new, added filename. The **ls** operation lists both filenames, but only one physical file will exist.

```
$ ln -s original-file-name added-file-name
```

In the next example, the **today** file is given the additional name **weather**. It is just another name for the **today** file.

```
$ ls
today
$ ln -s today weather
$ ls
today weather
```

You can give the same file several names by using the **ln** command on the same file many times. In the next example, the file **today** is assigned the names **weather** and **weekend**:

```
$ ln -s today weather
$ ln -s today weekend
$ ls
today weather weekend
```

If you list the full information about a symbolic link and its file, you will find the information displayed is different. In the next example, the user lists the full information for both **lunch** and **/home/george/veglist** using the **ls** command with the **-l** option. The first character in the line specifies the file type. Symbolic links have their own file type, represented by an **l**. The file type for **lunch** is **l**, indicating it is a symbolic link, not an ordinary file. The number after the term "group" is the size of the file. Notice the sizes differ. The size of the **lunch** file is only 4 bytes. This is because **lunch** is only a symbolic link—a file that holds the pathname of another file—and a pathname takes up only a few bytes. It is not a direct hard link to the **veglist** file.

```
$ ls -l lunch /home/george/veglist
lrw-rw-r-- 1 chris group 4 Feb 14 10:30 lunch
-rw-rw-r-- 1 george group 793 Feb 14 10:30 veglist
```

To erase a file, you need to remove only its original name (and any hard links to it). If any symbolic links are left over, they will be unable to access the file. In this case, a symbolic link would hold the pathname of a file that no longer exists.

Hard Links

You can give the same file several names by using the **ln** command on the same file many times. To set up a hard link, you use the **ln** command with no **-s** option and two arguments: the name of the original file and the new, added filename. The **ls** operation lists both filenames, but only one physical file will exist.

```
$ ln original-file-name added-file-name
```

In the next example, the **monday** file is given the additional name **storm**. It is just another name for the **monday** file.

```
$ ls
today
$ ln monday storm
$ ls
monday storm
```

To erase a file that has hard links, you need to remove all its hard links. The name of a file is actually considered a link to that file—hence the command **rm** that removes the link to the file. If you have several links to the file and remove only one of them, the others stay in place and you can reference the file through them. The same is true even if you remove the original link—the original name of the file.

Part 4: Administration

System Tools
System Administration
Network Connections

ubuntu

13. System Tools

GNOME System Monitor

Scheduling Tasks

System Log

Disk Usage Analyzer

Virus Protection

Hardware Sensors

Disk Utility

Plymouth

Logical Volume Management

OpenZFS

Useful system tools, as well as user specific configuration tools, can be found in the Applications overview and its| Utilities sub-view (see Table 13-1). Mouse and keyboard configurations are handled by GNOME or KDE directly (System Settings). The Utilities sub-view lists specialized tools like the ClamTK Virus Scanner (Virus Scanner) and the Disk Usage Analyzer.

Ubuntu System Tools	Name	Description
gnome-system-monitor	System Monitor	GNOME System Monitor
gnome-logs	Logs	GNOME Logs
gnome-terminal	Terminal	GNOME Terminal Window
baobab	Disk Usage Analyzer	Disk usage analyzer with graphic representation
gnome-nettool	Network Tools	Network analysis
KDE task scheduler	Task Scheduler	KDE schedule manager (KDE desktop only)
ClamTK	Virus Scanner	Clam Virus scanner
Disk Utility	Disk Utility	Udisks utility for managing hard disks and removable drives

Table 13-1: Ubuntu System Tools

GNOME System Monitor

Ubuntu provides the GNOME System Monitor for displaying system information and monitoring system processes, accessible from the Applications overview. There are three tabs: Processes, Resources, and File Systems (see Figure 13-1). The Resources tab displays graphs for CPU History, Memory and Swap History, and Network History. If your system has a multi-core CPU, the CPU History graph shows the usage for each CPU. The Memory and Swap Memory graph shows the amount of memory in use. The Network History graph displays both the amount of sent and received data, along with totals for the current session. The File Systems tab lists your file systems, where they are mounted, and their type, as well as the amount of disk space used and how much is free. Double clicking on a file system entry will open that file system in a file manager window.

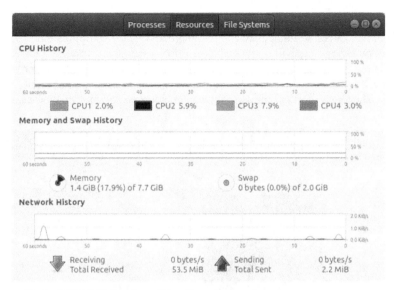

Figure 13-1: GNOME System Monitor: Resources

The Processes tab lists your processes, letting you sort and search processes. You can use field buttons to sort by name (Process Name), process ID (ID), percentage of use (%CPU), and memory used (Memory), among others. The menu (right side of the menu bar) lets you select all processes, just your own (My Processes), or active processes. You can stop any process by selecting it and then clicking the End Process button (lower-right corner) or by right-clicking on it and choosing End. You can right-click a process entry to display a menu with actions you can take on the selected process, such as stopping (Stop), ending (End), killing (Kill), and continuing a process (Continue), as well as changing the priority of the process (Change Priority). The Open Files entry opens a dialog listing all the files, sockets, and pipes the process is using. The Properties entry displays a dialog showing all the details for a process, such as the name, user, status, memory use, CPU use, and priority. Memory Maps display, selected from the Memory Maps entry, shows information on virtual memory, inodes, and flags for a selected process.

Display features such as the colors used for CPU graphs can be set using the dconf editor's gnome-system-monitor keys at org | gnome | gnome-system-monitor.

Managing Processes

Should you have to force a process or application to quit, you can use the Gnome System Monitor Processes tab to find, select, and stop the process. You should be sure of the process you want to stop. Ending a critical process could cripple your system. Application processes will bear the name of the application, and you can use those to force an application to quit. Ending processes manually is usually performed for open-ended operations that you are unable to stop normally. In Figure 13-2, the Firefox application has been selected. Clicking the End Process button on the lower left will then force the Firefox Web browser to end.

The pop-up menu for a process (right-click) provides several other options for managing a selected process: stop, continue, end, kill, and change priority. There are corresponding keyboard keys for most options. The stop and continue operations work together. You can stop (Stop) a process, and then later start it again with the Continue option. The End option stops a process safely, whereas a Kill option forces an immediate end to the process. The End option is preferred, but if it does not work, you can use the Kill option. Change Priority can give a process a lower or higher priority, letting it run faster or slower. The Properties option opens a dialog listing process details such as the name, user, status, different types of memory used, CPU usage, start time, process id, and priority. The Open Files option lists all the files, sockets, and pipes the process is using.

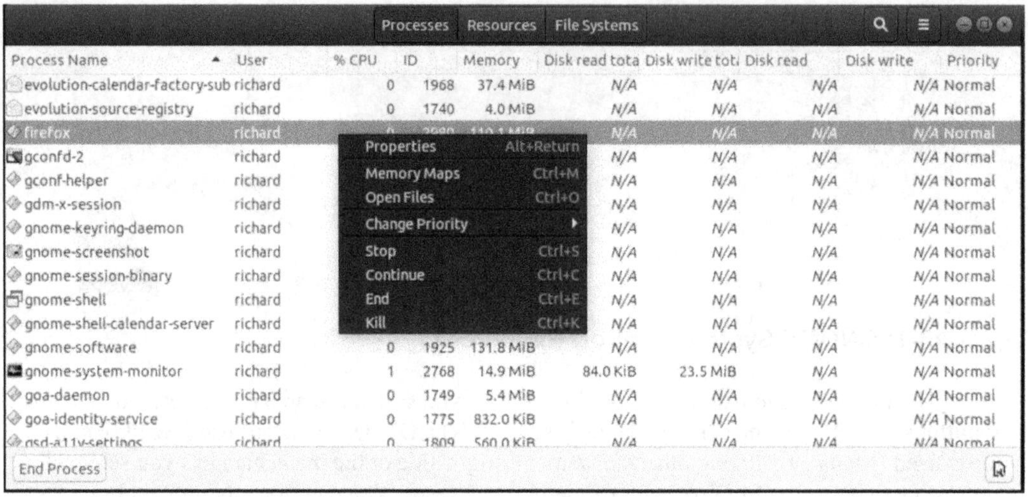

Figure 13-2: GNOME System Monitor: Processes

You can also use the **pkill** command with a process name or a process ID to end a process. To use a process name, enter the process name with the **-n** option for the most recent process for that name.

```
pkill -n firefox
```

You can also use the **kill** command in a terminal window to end a process. The **kill** command takes as its argument a process number. Be sure you obtain the correct one. Use the **ps** command to display a process id. Entering in the incorrect process number could cripple your system. The **ps** command with the **-C** option searches for a particular application name. The **-o** **pid=** option will display only the process id, instead of the process id, time, application name, and tty. Once you have the process id, you can use the **kill** command with the process id as its argument to end the process.

```
$ ps -C firefox -o pid=
5555
$ kill 5555
```

One way to ensure the correct number is to use the **ps** command to return the process number directly as an argument to a **kill** command. In the following example, an open-ended process was started with the **mycmd** command. An open-ended process is one that will continue until you stop it manually.

```
mycmd > my.ts
```

The process is then ended by first executing the **ps** command to obtain the process id for the **mycmd** process (back quotes), and then using that process id in the **kill** command to end the process. The **-o pid=** option displays only the process id.

```
kill `ps -C mycmd -o pid=`
```

Glances

Glances is a comprehensive system monitoring tool run from the command line in a terminal window with the **glances** command. Install with the Synaptic Package Manager (**glances** and **glances-doc** packages). Glances shows detailed resource use for the system, network, disk, file system, sensors, and processes. (see Figure 13-3). It also warns you of any critical alerts. The system section covers detailed memory, CPU, swap and load usage. The network section shows the activity on each network device. The Disk I/O section lists your storage devices and their read/write usage. The File Sys section shows al your partitions and how much memory is used. The Sensors section shows the temperature detected by your sensors such as those for CPU, GPU, and the ambient temperature. The Tasks section lists your active processes by CPU usage, showing memory used, pid, user and the command. Press **q** to end your glances session.

Glances is organized into modules which you can disable to show only a limited set of reports. For example, if you are not interested in the disk I/O reports, you can disable the diskio module with the **--disable-diskio** option. See the **glances** man page for a complete list of module options you can use.

```
glances -- disable-diskio.
```

There are also several runtime commands you can use to show and hide modules, such as **f** to toggle the file system reports on an off, **d** to toggle disk I/O, **n** for network stats, **s** for showing sensors, and **p** to sort processes by name.

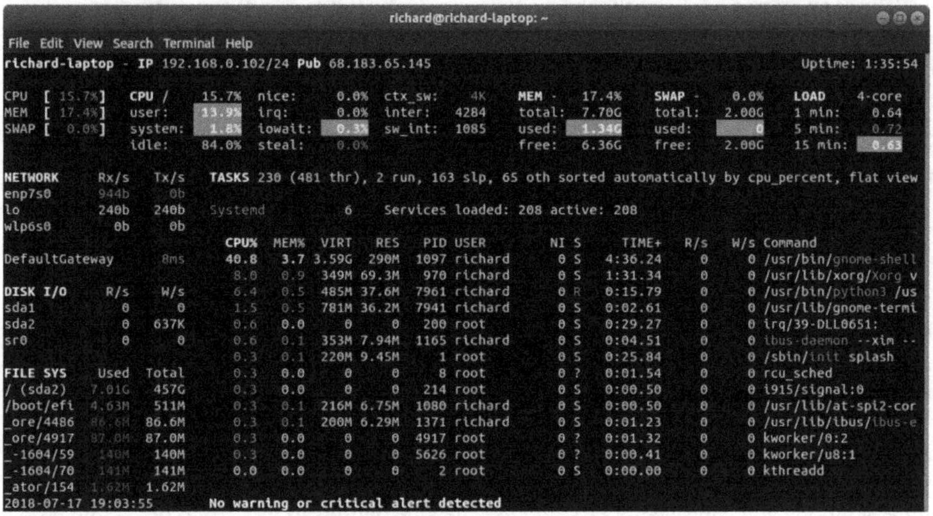

Figure 13-3: Glances System Monitor

Scheduling Tasks

Scheduling regular maintenance tasks, such as backups, can be managed either by using the systemd timers or by the cron service. The systemd timers are systemd files that run service files. Check the man page for **systemd.timers** for a detailed description of timers. They have the extension **.timer**. A timer file will automatically run a corresponding service file that has the same name. For example, the **dnf-automatic.timer** will run the **dnf-automatic.service** file. The timer file only contains scheduling information. Its filename determines which service file to run. It is possible to designate a different service file with the Unit directive in the timer file. If you want to run a command line operation for which there is no service file, you can create your own with an ExecStart entry for that command.

The timer files have a timer section in which you define when the service file is run. There are options that are relative to certain starting points like when system booted up, and the **OnCalendar** option that that reference calendar dates. The **OnCalendar** option uses calendar event expressions as defined on the **systemd.time** man page. A calendar even expression consists of a weekday, year, month, and time. The time is specified in hour, minute, and second, separated by colons. A range of weekdays is separated by two periods, and specific weekdays by commas. Leaving out the year or month selects any year or month. The following references weekdays in May at 2 pm.

```
OnCalendar=Mon..Fri 05 14:00
```

You can create timer files and place them in the **/etc/systemd/system** directory. If you also have to set up a service file for it, you can place it in the same directory. To activate a timer be sure to enable it with **systemctl**. If you created a service file, be sure to enable that also.

You can still use the older cron service to schedule tasks. The cron service is implemented by the cron daemon that constantly checks for certain actions to take. These tasks are listed in the **crontab** file. The **cron** daemon constantly checks the user's **crontab** file to see if it is time to take these actions. Any user can set up a **crontab** file. The root user can set up a **crontab** file to take system administrative actions, such as backing up files at a certain time each week or month.

Creating cron entries can be a complicated task, using the **crontab** command to make changes to crontab files in the **/etc/crontab** directory. Instead, you can use desktop cron scheduler tools to set up cron actions.

KDE Task Scheduler

On KDE you can use the KDE Task Scheduler to set up user and system-level scheduled tasks (install the **kde-config-cron** package). You access the Task Scheduler on the KDE System Settings window in the System Administration section as Task Scheduler. The Task Scheduler window will list your scheduled tasks. Task can be either personal or system-wide. Click the New Task button to open a New Task window where you can enter the command to run, add comments, and then specify the time in months, days, hours, and minutes from simple arranged buttons. On the Task Scheduler window, you can select a task and use the side buttons to modify it, delete the task, run it now, or print a copy of it. For tasks using the same complex commands or arguments, you can create a variable, and then use that variable in a command. Variables are listed in the Environment Variables section. To use a variable in a scheduled task, precede its name with the **$**

character when you enter the command. Entering just the **$** symbol in the Command text box will display a drop-down list of pre-defined system variables you can use like **$PATH** and **$USER**.

Logs

Various system logs for tasks performed on your system are stored in the **/var/log** directory. Here you can find logs for mail, news, and all other system operations, such as Web server logs (see Figure 8-4). This usually includes startup tasks, such as loading drivers and mounting file systems. If a driver for a device failed to load at startup, you will find an error message for it here. Logins are also recorded in this file, showing you who attempted to log into what account. The **/var/log/mail.log** file logs mail message transmissions and news transfers.

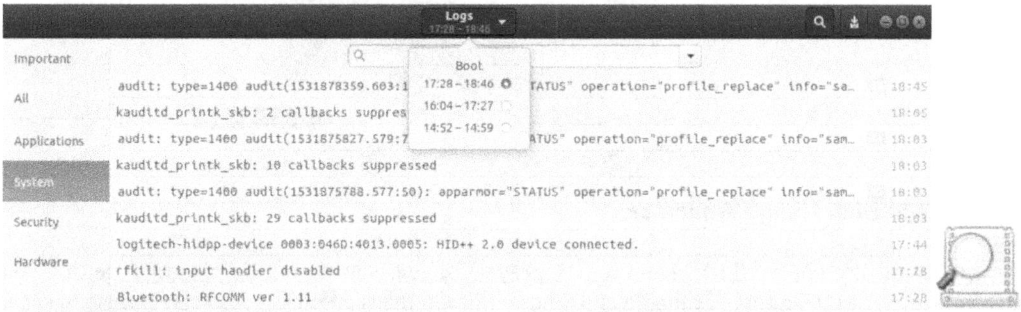

Figure 13-4: System Log

To view logs, you can use Gnome Logs accessible as Logs on the Applications overview. A side panel lists different log categories. Selecting one displays the log messages to the right. Critical messages are listed under the Important category. The "Logs" label on the title bar is a button you can click to display a list of recent boot sessions. You can select one to refine the messages displayed. By default, the most recent one is chosen. A search button on the top right opens a search box where you can search for messages in the selected log. Search has options (menu to the right) for refining the search by fields and by time. A tools button on the top right lets you perform tasks such as zooming, copying, selection, and filters.

Disk Usage Analyzer

The disk usage analyzer lets you see how much disk space is used and available on all your mounted hard disk partitions (see Figure 13-5). You can access it from the Applications | Utilities overview.

Figure 13-5: Disk Usage Analyzer

It will also check all LVM and RAID arrays. Usage is shown in a simple graph, letting you see how much overall space is available and where it is. On the scan dialog, you can choose to scan your home directory (Home Folder, your entire file system (disk drive icon), an attached device like a floppy or USB drive, or a specific or remote folder (see Figure 13-6). To scan a folder click the gear button (top right) to open a menu with the option "Scan Folder." When you scan a directory or the file system, disk usage for your directory is analyzed and displayed. Each file system is shown with a graph for its usage, as well as its size and the number of top-level directories and files. Then the directories are shown, along with their size and contents (files and directories).

A representational graph for disk usage on is displayed on the right pane. The graph can be either a Ring Chart or a Treemap. The Ring Chart is the default. Choose the one you want from the buttons on the lower right. For the Ring Chart, directories are shown, starting with the top level directories at the center and moving out to the subdirectories. Passing your mouse over a section in the graph displays its directory name and disk usage, as well as all its subdirectories. The Treemap chart shows a box representation, with greater disk usage in larger boxes, and subdirectories encased within directory boxes.

Figure 13-6: Disk Usage Analyzer: Scan dialog

Virus Protection

For virus protection, you can use the Linux version of ClamAV, which uses a GNOME front-end called ClamTk, **https://www.clamav.net**. This Virus scanner is included on the Ubuntu main repository. You can install ClamTk from Ubuntu Software. The supporting ClamAV packages (System category) will also be selected and installed for you (clamav-base and clamav-freshclam). You can also install ClamAV using the Synaptic Package Manager, choose the clamav, clamav-base, clamav-freshclam (online virus definitions), and ClamTK packages (Klamav for KDE); selecting just ClamTk will automatically select the other clamav packages for installation. The **clamav-freshclam** package retrieves current virus definitions from the ClamAV servers. For ClamAV to check your mail messages automatically, you need to install the ClamAV scanner daemon (**clamav-daemon** package).

Figure 13-7: The ClamTK tool for ClamAV virus protection

You can access ClamTk from the Applications overview as ClamTk. With ClamTk, you can scan specific files and directories, as well as your home directory (see Figure 13-7). Searches can be recursive, including subdirectories (Settings). You have the option to check configuration files (scan files with a dot). You can also perform quick or recursive scans of your home directory. Infected files are quarantined.

Your virus definitions will be updated automatically. If you want to check manually for virus definitions, you need to click Update Assistant and choose to update the signatures yourself. Then click Updates and click the OK button next to "Check for updates."

Hardware Sensors

A concern for many users is the temperatures and usage of computer components. You can install different software packages to enable certain sensors (see Table 13-2) .

Sensor application	Description
lm-sensors	Detects and accesses computer (motherboard) sensors like CPU and fan speed. Run **sensors-detect** once to configure.
hddtemp	Detects hard drive temperatures (also detected by Disk Utility)
Disk Utility	Disk Utility provides SMART information for hard disks showing current hard disk temperatures as well as detailed disk health information and checks.
Psensor	Application to detect and display system and hard drive temperatures.
Xsensors	Application to detect and display system temperatures and fans.
indicator-cpufreq	CPU Frequency Scaling Indicator for monitoring and changing CPU frequency.

Table 13-2: Sensor packages and applications

You can install the shell extensions CPU Freq, CPU Fequency, CPU Power Manager, or cpufreq (Add ons category in Ubuntu Software) to monitor and control the frequency. Most current CPUs support frequency scaling, which will lower the CPU frequency when it has few tasks to perform.

For CPU, system, fan speeds, and any other motherboard supported sensors, you can use Psensor, Xsensors, or the **lm-sensors** tools. Psensors installs the hddtemp hard drive temperature server and displays your CPU, graphics card, and hard drive temperatures. You can set temperature thresholds for alerts. Xsensors displays your CPU temperature.

If not already installed, install the **lm-sensors** package. Then you have to configure your sensor detection. In a terminal window enter following and press ENTER to answer yes to the prompts:

```
sudo sensors-detect
```

Disk Utility lets you know your hard disk temperature. Disk Utility uses Udisks to access SMART information about the disk drive, including the temperature and overall health. Open Disk Utility, select the hard disk to check, and then, on the right pane, click on the "SMART Data" link located middle right. A hard disk dialog opens showing the disk temperature along with other details.

Disk Utility and Udisks

Disk Utility is a Udisks supported user configuration interface for your storage media, such as hard disks, USB drives, and DVD/CD drives (**gnome-disk-utility** package, installed by default). Tasks supported include disk labeling, mounting disks, disk checks, and encryption. You can also perform more advanced tasks, like managing RAID and LVM storage devices, as well as partitions. Disk Utility is accessible on GNOME from the Applications | Utility overview. Users can use Disk Utility to format removable media like USB drives. Disk Utility is also integrated into GNOME Files, letting you format removable media directly.

The Disk Utility window shows a sidebar with entries for your storage media (see Figure 13-8). Clicking on an entry displays information for the media on the right pane. Removable devices such as USB drives display power and eject buttons, along with a task menu with an entry to format the disk. If you are formatting a partition, like that on removable media, you can specify the file system type to use.

Figure 13-8: Disk Utility

Warning: Disk Utility will list your fixed hard drives and their partitions, including the partitions on which your Ubuntu Linux system is installed. Be careful not to delete or erase these partitions.

If you select a hard disk device, information about the hard disk is displayed on the right pane at the top, such as the model name, serial number, size, partition table type, and SMART status (Assessment) (see Figure 13-9). Click the menu button to display a menu on the upper right with tasks you can perform on the hard drive: Format, Benchmark, and SMART Data.

Figure 13-9: Disk Utility, hard drive

The Volumes section on the hard disk pane shows the partitions set up on the hard drive (see Figure 13-10). Partitions are displayed in a graphical icon bar, which displays each partition's size and location on the drive. Clicking on a partition entry on the graphical icon bar displays information about that partition such as the file system type, device name, partition label, and partition size. The "Contents" entry tells if a partition is mounted. If in use, it displays a "Mounted at:" entry with a link consisting of the path name where the file system is mounted. You can click on this path name to open a folder with which you can access the file system. The button bar below the Volumes images provides additional task you can perform, such as unmounting a file system (square button) and deleting a partition (minus button). From the more tasks menu, you can choose entries to change the partition label, type, and mount options. Certain partitions, like extended and swap partitions, display limited information and have few allowable tasks.

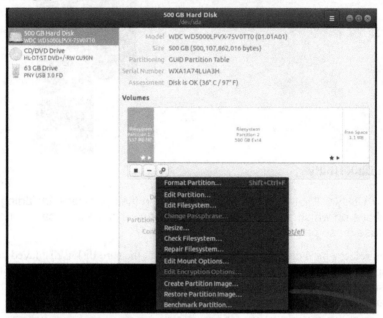

Figure 13-10: Disk Utility, Volumes

For more detailed hardware information about a hard drive, you can click on the "SMART Data and Tests" entry from the task menu in the upper right. This opens a SMART data dialog with hardware information about the hard disk (see Figure 13-11) including temperature, power cycles, bad sectors, and the overall health of the disk. The Attributes section lists SMART details such as the Read Error Rate, Spinup time, temperature, and write error rate. Click the switch on to enable the tests, and off to disable testing. Click the "Refresh" button to manually run the tests. Click the "Start Self-test" button to open a menu with options for short, extended, and conveyance tests.

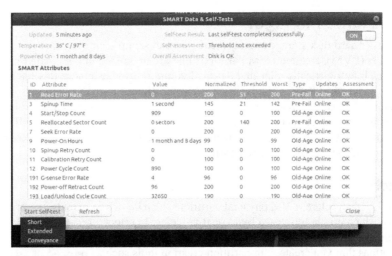

Figure 13-11: Disk Utility: Hard Disk hardware SMART data

Plymouth

Plymouth provides a streamlined, efficient, and faster graphical boot that does not require X server support. It relies on the kernel's Kernel Modesettings (KMS) feature that provides direct support for basic graphics. With the Direct Rendering Manager driver, Plymouth can make use of different graphical plugins. KMS support is currently provided for AMD, Nvidia, and Intel graphics cards.

The Plymouth Ubuntu logo theme is installed by default. You can install others like solar, glow, or kubuntu-logo. The theme packages begin with the prefix **plymouth-theme**. You can search for them on the Synaptic Package Manager. You can also install them from Ubuntu Software (search on Plymouth).

Choosing to use a Plymouth theme involves using the Debian alternatives system, which is designed to designate an application to use when there are several alternative versions to select. A link is set up for the application to use in the **/etc/alternatives** directory. For Plymouth, this link is named **default.plymouth**. You can choose a Plymouth theme by entering the **update-alternatives** command with the **--config** option, the **default.plymouth** link, and the **sudo** command in a terminal window as shown here.

```
sudo update-alternatives --config default.plymouth
```

This displays a numbered menu listing your installed themes. An asterisk indicates the current theme. Enter the number of the theme you want to use. The **default.plymouth** link is then set to the theme you choose. When your system starts up again, it will use that Plymouth theme.

Some of the non-Ubuntu themes may hang on start up. In that case, you can edit the boot kernel line to remove the **splash** option and then boot to your system (see Chapter 3). Then use **update-alternatives** to change your Plymouth theme.

Logical Volume Manager

For easier hard disk storage management, you can set up your system to use the Logical Volume Manager (LVM), creating LVM partitions that are organized into logical volumes, to which free space is automatically allocated. Logical volumes provide a more flexible and powerful way of dealing with disk storage, organizing physical partitions into logical volumes in which you can easily manage disk space. Disk storage for a logical volume is treated as one pool of memory, though the volume may, in fact, contain several hard disk partitions spread across different hard disks. Adding a new LVM partition merely increases the pool of storage accessible to the entire system. Check the LVM HOWTO at **www.tldp.org** for detailed examples.

LVM Structure

In an LVM structure, LVM physical partitions, also known as extents, are organized into logical groups, which are, in turn, used by logical volumes. In effect, you are dealing with three different levels of organization. At the lowest level, you have physical volumes. These are physical hard disk partitions that you create with partition creation tools such as `parted` or `fdisk`. The partition type will be a Linux LVM partition, **fdisk** code **8e**. These physical volumes are organized into logical groups, known as volume groups that operate much like logical hard disks. You assign collections of physical volumes to different logical groups.

Once you have your logical groups, you can then create logical volumes. Logical volumes function much like hard disk partitions on a standard setup. For example, on the **turtle** group volume, you could create a **/var** logical volume, and on the **rabbit** logical group, you could create **/home** and **/projects** logical volumes. You can have several logical volumes on one logical group, just as you can have several partitions on one hard disk.

You treat the logical volumes as you would any ordinary hard disk partition. Create a file system on it with the `mkfs` command, and then you can mount the file system to use it with the `mount` command. For Ubuntu, the file system type would be **ext4**.

Storage on logical volumes is managed using what are known as extents. A logical group defines a standard size for an extent, say 4MB, and then divides each physical volume in its group into extents of that size. Logical volumes are, in turn, divided into extents of the same size, which are then mapped to those on the physical volumes.

Logical volumes can be linear, striped, or mirrored. The mirror option will create a mirror copy of a logical volume, providing a restore capability. The striped option lets you automatically distribute your Logical volume across several partitions, as you would a RAID device. This adds better efficiency for very large files but is complicated to implement. Like a RAID device, stripe sizes have to be consistent across partitions. As LVM partitions can be of any size, the stripes sizes have to be carefully calculated. The simplest approach is just to use a linear implementation, much like a RAID 0 device, just treating the storage as one large ordinary drive, with storage accessed sequentially.

There is one restriction and recommendation for logical volumes. The boot partition cannot be part of a logical volume. You still have to create a separate hard disk partition as your boot partition with the **/boot** mountpoint in which your kernel and all needed boot files are installed. In addition, it is recommended that you not place your root partition on a logical volume. Doing so can complicate any needed data recovery. This is why a default partition configuration set up during Ubuntu installation for LVM will include a separate /**boot** partition of type **ext4**, whereas the root and swap partitions will be installed on Logical volumes. There will be two partitions, one for the logical group (LVM physical volume, **pv**) holding both swap and root volumes, and another for the boot partition (**ext4**). The logical volumes will in turn both be **ext4** file systems.

LVM Tools: using the LVM commands

Instead of using system-config-lvm, you could use a collection of LVM tools to manage your LVM volumes, adding new LVM physical partitions and removing current ones. The system-config-lvm system tool is actually a GUI interface for the LVM tools. For the LVM tools, you can either use LVM tools directly or use the `lvm` command to generate an interactive shell from which you can run LVM commands. There are Man pages for all the LVM commands. LVM maintains configuration information in the /**etc/lvm/lvm.conf** file, where you can configure LVM options such as the log file, the configuration backup directory, or the directory for LVM devices (see the **lvm.conf** Man page for more details).

Note: For desktop LVM administration, you can try using the system-config-lvm application, but it is an older application that may not work.

Displaying LVM Information

You can use the `pvdisplay`, `vgdisplay`, and `lvdisplay` commands to show detailed information about a physical partition, volume groups, and logical volumes. The `pvscan`, `vgscan`, and `lvscan` commands list your physical, group, and logical volumes.

Managing LVM Physical Volumes with the LVM commands

A physical volume can be any hard disk partition or RAID device. A RAID device is seen as a single physical volume. You can create physical volumes either from a single hard disk or from partitions on a hard disk. On very large systems with many hard disks, you would more likely use an entire hard disk for each physical volume.

You would first use a partition utility like **fdisk**, **parted**, or **gparted** to create a partition of the LVM partition type (**8e**). Then, you can initialize the partition as a physical volume using the **pvcreate** command.

To initialize a physical volume on an entire hard disk, you use the hard disk device name, as shown here:

```
pvcreate /dev/sdc
```

This will initialize one physical partition, **pv**, called **sdc1** on the **sdc** hard drive (the third Serial ATA drive, c).

If you are using a particular partition on a drive, you create a new physical volume using the partition's device name, as shown here:

```
pvcreate /dev/sda3
```

To initialize several drives, just list them. The following create two physical partitions, sdc1 and sdd1.

```
pvcreate /dev/sdc /dev/sdd
```

You could also use several partitions on different hard drives. This is a situation in which your hard drives each hold several partitions. This condition occurs often when you are using some partitions on your hard drive for different purposes like different operating systems, or if you want to distribute your Logical group across several hard drives. To initialize these partitions at once, you simply list them.

```
pvcreate /dev/sda3 /dev/sdb1 /dev/sdb2
```

Once you have initialized your partitions, you have to create LVM groups on them.

Managing LVM Groups

Physical LVM partitions are used to make up a volume group. You can manually create a volume group using the **vgcreate** command and the name of the group along with a list of physical partitions you want in the group.

If you are then creating a new volume group to place these in, you can include them in the group when you create the volume group with the **vgcreate** command. The volume group can use one or more physical partitions. The configuration described in the following example used only one physical partition for the **VolGroup00**. In the following example, a volume group called **mymedia** that is made up two physical volumes, **sdc** and **sdd**.

```
vgcreate mymedia  /dev/sdc /dev/sdd
```

The previous example sets up a logical group on two serial ATA hard drives, each with its own single partition. Alternatively, you can set up a volume group to span partitions on several hard drives. If you are using partitions for different functions, this approach gives you the flexibility for using all the space available across multiple hard drives. The following example creates a group called **mygroup** consisting of three physical partitions, **/dev/sda3**, **/dev/sdb4**, and **/dev/sdb4**:

```
vgcreate mygroup  /dev/sda3 /dev/sdb2 /dev/sdb4
```

If you later want to add a physical volume to a volume group you would use the **vgextend** command. The **vgextend** command adds a new partition to a logical group. In the following example, the partition **/dev/sda4** is added to the volume group **mygroup**. In effect, you are extending the size of the logical group by adding a new physical partition.

```
vgextend mygroup  /dev/sda4
```

To add an entire new drive to a volume group, you would follow a similar procedure. The following example adds a fifth serial ATA hard drive, **sde**, first creating a physical volume on it and then adding that volume, sde, to the **mymedia** volume group.

```
pvcreate /dev/sde
vgextend mymedia /dev/sde
```

To remove a physical partition, first, remove it from its logical group. You may have to use the **pmove** command to move any data off the physical partition. Then use the **vgreduce** command to remove it from its logical group.

You can remove an entire volume group by first deactivating it with **vgchange -a n** and then using the **vgremove** command.

Activating Volume Groups

Whereas in a standard file system structure you mount and unmount hard disk partitions, with an LVM structure, you activate and deactivate entire volume groups. The group volumes are accessible until you activate them with the **vgchange** command with the **-a** option. To activate a group, first, reboot your system, and then enter the **vgchange** command with the **-a** option and the **y** argument to activate the logical group (an **n** argument will deactivate the group).

```
vgchange -a  y  mygroup
```

Managing LVM Logical Volumes

To create logical volumes, you use the **lvcreate** command and then format your logical volume using the standard formatting command like **mkfs.ext4**. Keep in mind that all these actions can be performed at once by system-config-lvm.

With the **-n** option you specify the volume's name, which functions like a hard disk partition's label. You use the **-L** or **--size** options to specify the size of the volume. Use a size suffix for the measure, **G** for Gigabyte, **M** for megabyte, and **K** for kilobytes. There are other options for implementing features like whether to implement a linear, striped, or mirrored volume, or to specify the size of the extents to use. Usually, the defaults work well. The following example creates a logical volume named **projects** on the **mygroup** logical group with a size of 20GB.

```
lvcreate -n projects  -L 20GB mygroup
```

The following example sets up a logical volume on the **mymedia** volume group that is 540GB in size. The mymedia volume group is made up of two physical volumes, each on 320GB hard drives. In effect, the two hard drives are logically seen as one.

```
lvcreate -n myvideos  -L 540GB mymedia
```

Once you have created your logical volume, you then need to create a file system to use on it. The following creates an ext4 file system on the myvideos logical volume.

```
mkfs.ext4 myvideos
```

You could also use:

```
mkfs -t ext4 myvideos
```

With **lvextend**, you can increase the size of the logical volume if there is unallocated space available in the volume group.

Should you want to reduce the size of a logical volume, you use the **lvreduce** command, indicating the new size. Be sure to reduce the size of any file systems (**ext4**) on the logical volume, using the **resize2fs** command.

To rename a logical volume use the **lvrename** command. If you want to completely remove a logical volume, you can use the **lvremove** command.

Steps to create a new LVM group and volume

Physical Partition   First create a physical partition on your hard drive. You can use GParted, QTparted, or fdisk with the disk device name to create the partition. For example, to use fdisk to create a new partition on a new hard drive, whose device name is **/etc/sde**, you would enter:

```
fdisk /etc/sde
```

Then, in the fdisk shell, use the fdisk **n** command to create a new partition, set it as a primary partition (**p**), and make it the first partition. If you plan to use the entire hard drive for your LVM, you would need only one partition that would cover the entire drive.

Then use the **t** command to set the partition type to 8E. The 8E type is the LVM partition type. To make your changes, enter **w** to write changes to the disk.

Physical Volume   Next create a physical volume (pv) on the new and empty LVM partition, using the **pvcreate** command and the device name.

```
pvcreate /dev/sde
```

Volume Group   Then, create your volume group with **vgcreate** command, with the volume group name and the hard disk device name.

```
vgcreate mynewgroup  /dev/sde
```

Be sure the volume group is activated. Use the **vgs** command to list it. If not listed, use the following command to activate it.

```
vgchange -a  y  mynewgroup
```

Logical Volume   Then, create a logical volume, or volumes, for the volume group, using the **lvcreate** command. The **--size** or **-L** options determines the size and the **--name** option specifies the name. To find out the available free space, use the **vgs** command. You can have more than one logical volume in a volume group, or just one if you prefer. A logical volume is conceptually similar to logical volumes in an extended partition on Windows systems.

```
lvcreate --size --name mynewvol1
```

Format the Logical volume. You then use the **mkfs** command with the **-t** option to format the logical volume. The logical volume will be listed in a directory for the LVM group, within the /dev directory, **/dev/mynewgroup/mynewvol1**.

```
mkfs -t ext4 /dev/mynewgroup/mynewgroup-mynewvol1
```

Steps to add a new drive to an LVM group and volume

Physical Partition   First create a physical partition on your hard drive. You can use GParted, QTparted, or fdisk with the disk device name to create the partition. For the type specify LVM (**8E**).

Physical Volume   Next, create a physical volume (pv) on the new and empty LVM partition, using the pvcreate command and the device name.

```
pvcreate /dev/sdf
```

Add to Logical Group   Use the **vgextend** command to add the new physical volume to your existing logical group (LG).

```
vgextend mynewgroup  /dev/sdf
```

Add to Logical Volume Then, you can create new logical volumes in the new space, or expand the size of a current logical volume. To expand the size of a logical volume to the new space, first, unmount the logical volume. Then use the **lvextend** command to expand to the space on the new hard drive that is now part the same logical group. With no size specified, the entire space on the new hard drive will be added.

```
umount /dev/mynewgroup/mynewvol1
lvextend /dev/mynewgroup/mynewvol  /dev/sdf
```

Use the **-L** option to specify a particular size, **-L +250G** . Be sure to add the + sign to have the size added to the current logical volume size. To find out the available free space, use the **vgs** command.

Add to file system Use the **resize2fs** command to extend the linux file system (ext4) on to logical volume to include the new space, formatting it. Unless you specify a size (second parameter), all the available unformatted space is used.

```
resize2fs /dev/mynewgroup/mynewvol1
```

LVM Device Names: /dev/mapper

The **device-mapper** driver is used by LVM to set up tables for mapping logical devices to hard disk. The device name for a logical volume is kept in the **/dev/mapper** directory and has the format *logical group –logical volume*. The default LVM setup for Ubuntu has the names **ubuntu-root** and **ubuntu-swap_1**. The **mypics** logical volume in the **mymedia** logical group in the following example has the device name, **/dev/mapper/mymedia-mypics**. In addition, there will be a corresponding device folder for the logical group, which will contain logical volume names. For the **ubuntu** logical group, there is a device folder called **/dev/ubuntu**.

Note: You can backup volume group metadata (configuration) using the vgcfgbackup command. This does not backup your logical volumes (no content). Metadata backups are stored in /etc/lvm/backup, and can be restored using vgcfgrestore.

Using LVM to replace drives

LVM can be very useful when you need to replace an older hard drive with a new one. Hard drives are expected to last about six years on the average. You could want to replace the older drive with a larger one (hard drive storage sizes double every year or so). Replacing additional hard drives is easy. To replace a boot drive is much more complicated.

To replace the drive, simply incorporate the new drive to your logical volume (see Steps to add a new drive to an LVM group and volume). The size of your logical volume will increase accordingly. You can use the **pmove** command to move data from the old drive to the new one. Then, issue commands to remove the old drive (**vgreduce**) from the volume group. From the user and system point of view, no changes are made. Files from your old drive will still be stored in the same directories, though the actual storage will be implemented on the new drive.

Replacement with LVM become more complicated if you want to replace your boot drive, the hard drive from which your system starts up and which holds your linux kernel. The boot drive contains a special boot partition and the master boot record. The boot partition cannot be part of any LVM volume. You would first have to create a boot partition on the new drive using a partition tool such as Parted or fdisk, labeling it as boot (the boot drive is usually very small, about 200 MB).

Then mount the partition on your system, and copy the contents of your **/boot** directory to it. Then add the remainder of the disk to your logical volume and logically remove the old disk, copying the contents of the old disk to the new one. You would still have to boot with linux rescue DVD (or install DVD in rescue mode), and issue the **grub-install** command to install the master boot record on your new drive. You can then boot from the new drive.

LVM Snapshots

A snapshot records and defines the state of the logical volume at a designated time. It does not create a full copy of data on the volume, but only just changes since the last snapshot. A snapshot defines the state of the data at a given time. This allows you to back up the data in a consistent way. Should you need to restore a file to its previous version, you can use the snapshot of it. Snapshots are treated as a logical volume and can be mounted, copied, or deleted.

To create a snapshot, use the lvcreate command with the -s option. In this example, the snapshot is given the name mypics-snap1 (**-n** option). You need to specify the full device name for the logical group you want to create the snapshot for. Be sure there is enough free space available in the logical group for the snapshot. In this example, the snapshot logical volume is created in the **/dev/mymedia** logical group. It could just as easily be created in any other logical group. Though a snapshot normally uses very little space, you have to guard against overflows. If the snapshot is allocated the same size as the original, it will never overflow For systems where little of the original data changes, the snapshot can be very small. The following example allocates one-third the size of the original (60GB).

```
sudo lvcreate -s -n mypics-snap1 -l 20GB /dev/mymedia
```

You can then mount the snapshot as you would any other file system.

```
sudo mount /dev/mymedia/mypic-snap1 /mysnaps
```

To delete a snapshot you use the lvremove command, removing it like you would any logical volume.

```
sudo lvremove -f /dev/mymedia/mypics-nap1
```

Snapshots are very useful for making backups while a system is still active. You can use tar or dump to backup the mounted snapshot to a disk or tape. All the data from the original logical volume will be included, along with the changes noted by the snapshot.

Snapshots also allow you to perform effective undo operations. You can create a snapshot of a logical volume, then unmount the original and mount the snapshot in its place. Any changes you make will be performed on the snapshot, not the original. Should problems occur, unmount the snapshot and then mount the original. This restores the original state of your data. You could also do this using several snapshots, restoring to a previous snapshot. With this procedure, you could test new software on a snapshot, without endangering your original data. The software would be operating on the snapshot, not the original logical volume.

You can also use them as alternative versions of a logical volume. You can read and write to a snapshot. A write will change only the snapshot volume, not the original, creating, in effect, an alternate version.

OpenZFS

The ZFS file system incorporates the features of a logical volume manager (LVM), RAID systems, and file systems. ZFS abstracts a file system, much like LVM, setting up a pool of storage from which a file system can be generated. Checksums for data blocks are saved outside the data blocks and are checked for any corruption within the blocks. This makes ZFS very effective in protecting against silent data corruption from problems such as write interrupts, driver bugs, and access failures. If an RAID-Z support has been set up, corrupted blocks can be recovered. RAID-Z implements a data-oriented RAID-like support with automatic mirroring of your data within the file system. In addition, the LVM-like abstraction of ZFS allows for very large files. Writes are performed with a copy-on-write transaction method, where data is not overwritten directly, but added.

ZFS was developed by SUN, which is now controlled by Oracle. Since 2010, OpenZFS provides an open source version of ZFS for Linux systems. Ubuntu now supports the ZFS file system, using the OpenZFS kernel module. Tools to manage ZFS file systems can be installed with the **zfsutils-linux** package (Universe repository, Synaptic Package Manager). See the following for more information:

```
https://wiki.ubuntu.com/Kernel/Reference/ZFS
```

Much like an LVM system, you have the physical devices (called virtual devices, VDEVs) that are combined and striped into a data pool (**zpool** command), which can then be used to create the ZFS file system. At the pool level, you can implement RAIDZ options. With the **zfs** command, you can then create file systems in your pool. With the **zfs** command, you can also create snapshots (read-only copy) of a ZFS file system, or a clone (writeable copy). To perform an integrity check of the pool, use the **zpool** command's **scrub** option.

14. System Administration

Most administrative configurations tasks are performed for you automatically. Devices like printers, hard drive partitions, and graphics cards are detected and set up for you. There are cases where you may need to perform tasks, manually like adding new users and installing software. Such administrative operations can be performed with user-friendly system tools. Most administration tools are listed on the Applications overview and its Utilities sub-view.

Ubuntu Administration Tools	Description
Ubuntu Software	Software management using online repositories (GNOME Software)
Software Updater	Update tool using Ubuntu repositories
Synaptic Package Manager	Software management using online repositories (no longer supported by Ubuntu, available on the Universe repository)
Network Manager	Detects, connects, and configures your network interfaces
clock	GNOME Time & Date tool (see Chapter 3)
User Accounts	GNOME 3 User configuration tool
users-admin	Older User and Group configuration tool, install gnome-system-tools.
system-config-printer	Printer configuration tool
system-config-samba	Configures your Samba server. User level authentication support.
gnome-language-selector	Selects a language to use
Gufw	Configures your network firewall
Deja-dup	Backup tool using rsync

Table 14-1: Ubuntu Administration Tools

Ubuntu Administrative Tools

On Ubuntu, administration is handled by a set of specialized administrative tools, such as those for user management and printer configuration (see Table 14-1). To access the desktop-based administrative tools, you need to log in as a user who has administrative access. You created this user when you first installed Ubuntu. On the Ubuntu desktop, system administrative tools are accessed from the Applications overview and from GNOME Settings. Here you will find tools to set the time and date, manage users, configure printers, and install software. User Accounts lets you create and modify users. Printing lets you install and reconfigure printers. All tools provide easy-to-use and intuitive desktop interfaces. Tools are identified by simple descriptive terms, whereas their actual names normally begin with terms such as system-config. For example, the printer configuration tool is listed as Printing, but its actual name is **system-config-printer**.

TIP: If you have difficulties with your system configuration, check the http://ubuntuforums.org and the http://askubuntu.org sites for possible solutions. The site offers helpful forums ranging from desktop and installation problems to games, browsers, and multimedia solutions. Also, check the support link at www.ubuntu.com for documentation and mailing lists.

Ubuntu uses the GNOME administrative tools with KDE counterparts, administrative tools adapted from the Fedora distribution supported by Red Hat Linux, and independent tools developed by open source projects. PolicyKit is used for device authorizations, and Ubuntu Software provides software management. Fedora tools have the prefix *system-config*. The Printing administrative tool is Fedora's **system-config-printer**. A Samba desktop tool is still available for Ubuntu, which is the Fedora **system-config-samba** tool. The Fedora **system-config-lvm** tool provides a simple and effective way to manage LVM file systems. In addition, Virus protection is handled by third party application, ClamAV. The Synaptic Package Manager is available, but no longer supported. The older GNOME administrative tools such as Users and Groups are also available, but not installed by default (**gnome-system-tools** package).

Note: Many configuration tasks can also be handled on the command line, invoking programs directly. To use the command line, select the Terminal entry in the Applications overview to open a terminal window with a command line prompt. You will need administrative authorization, so precede the application name with the sudo or the pkexec command.

Controlled Administrative Access

To access administrative tools, you have to log in as a user who has administrative permissions. The user that you created during installation is given administrative permissions automatically. Log in as that user. When you attempt to use an administrative tool, a dialog opens prompting you to enter your user password. This is the password for the user you logged in as. Some tools will open without authorization but remain locked, preventing any modifications. These tools, like "User Accounts" have an Unlock button you can press to gain access. You can use the User Accounts tool to grant or deny particular users administrative access.

To perform system administration operations, you must first have to have access rights enabling you to perform administrative tasks. There are several ways to gain such access: login as a sudo supported user, unlocking an administrative tool for access or using **pkexec** from a terminal window (PolicyKit authorization), and logging in as the root user. PolicyKit is the preferred access method and is used on many administrative tools. The **sudo** granted access method was used in previous Ubuntu releases, and is still used for many tasks including software upgrade and installation. The root user access is still discouraged but provides complete control over the entire system.

PolicyKit: Provides access only to specific applications and only to users with administrative access for that application. Requires that the specific application be configured for use by PolicyKit. Ubuntu 18.04 uses a new version of PolicyKit called policykit-1 (Ubuntu repository). It is not to be confused with the original version, which is named simply policykit (Universe repository). Though the original policykit is still available for use on Ubuntu, it is not supported, whereas policykit-1 is installed by default and fully supported.

sudo and pkexec: Provides access to any application will full administrative authorization. It imposes a time limit to reduce risk. The **pkexec** command is used for graphical administrative tools like the Synaptic Package Manager. You will still need to use **sudo** to perform any command-line Linux commands at the root level, like moving files to an administrative directory or running the **service** command to start or stop servers.

root user access, **su**: Provides complete direct control over the entire system. This is the traditional method for accessing administrative tools. It is disabled by default on Ubuntu, but can be enabled. The **su** command will allow any user to log in as the root user if they know the root user password.

PolicyKit

PolicyKit controls access to certain applications and devices. It is one of the safest ways to grant a user direct access. PolicyKit configuration and support is already set up for you. A new version of PolicyKit, PolicyKit-1, is now used for PolicyKit operations. Configuration files for these operations are held in **/usr/share/polkit-1**. There is, as yet, no desktop tool you can use to configure these settings.

Note: External hard drives, such as USB connected hard drives, are mounted automatically

Difficulties occur if you want to change the authorization setting for certain actions, like mounting internal hard drives. Currently, you can change the settings by manually editing the configuration files in the **/usr/share/polkit-1/actions** directory, but this is risky. To make changes, you first have to know the action to change and the permission to set. The man page for **polkit** will list possible authorizations. The default authorizations are **allow_any** for anyone, **allow_inactive** for a console, and **allow_active** for an active console only (user logged in). These authorizations can be set to the following specific values.

auth_admin	Administrative user only, authorization required always
auth_admin_keep	Administrative user only, authorization kept for a brief period
auth_self	User authorization required
auth_self_keep	User authorization required, authorization kept for a brief period
yes	Always allow access
no	Never allow access

You will need to know the PolicyKit action to modify and the file to edit. The action is listed in the PolicyKit dialog that prompts you to enter the password (expand the Details arrow) when you try to use an application. The filename will be the first segments of the action name with the suffix "policy" attached. For example, the action for mounting drives is:

```
org.freedesktop.udisks2.filesystem-mount-system
```

Its file is:

```
org.freedesktop.udisks2.policy
```

The file is located in the **/usr/share/polkit-1/actions** directory. It's full path name is:

```
/usr/share/polkit-1/actions/org.freedesktop.udisks2.policy
```

Users with administrative access, like your primary user, can mount partitions on your hard drives automatically. However, users without administrative access require authorization using an administrative password before they can mount a partition (see Figure 14-13). Should you want to allow non-administrative users to mount partitions without an authorization request, the

org.freedesktop.udisks2.policy file in the **/usr/share/polkit-1** directory has to be modified to change the **allow_active** default for **filesystem-mount-system** action from **auth_admin_keep** to **yes**. The **auth_admin_keep** option requires administrative authorization.

Enter the following to edit the **org.freedesktop.udisks2.policy** file in the **/usr/share/polkit-1/actions** directory:

```
sudo gedit /usr/share/polkit-1/actions/org.freedesktop.udisks2.policy
```

Locate the **action id** labeled as:

```
<action id ="org.feedesktop.udisks2.filesystem-mount-system">
  <description>Mount a filesystem on a system device</description>
```

This is usually the second action id. At the end of that action section, you will find the following entry. It will be located within a defaults subsection, <defaults>.

```
<allow_active>auth_admin_keep</allow_active>
```

Replace **auth_admin_keep** with **yes**.

```
<allow_active>yes</allow_active>
```

Save the file. Non-administrative users will no longer have to enter a password to mount partitions.

sudo

The sudo service provides administrative access to specific users. You have to be a user on the system with a valid username and password that has been authorized by the sudo service for administrative access. This allows other users to perform specific super user operations without having full administrative level control. You can find more about sudo at **http://www.sudo.ws**.

sudo command

Some administrative operations require access from the command line in the terminal window. For such operations, you would use the **sudo** command. You can open a terminal window from the Applications overview. For easier access, you can pin the Terminal launcher item to the Launcher (right-click and choose "Lock to Launcher").

To use **sudo** to run an administrative command, you would precede the command with the **sudo** command. You are then prompted to enter your password. You will be issued a time-restricted ticket to allow access. The following example sets the system date using the **date** command.

```
sudo date 0406165908
password:
```

You can also use the sudo command to run an application with administrative access. From the terminal window, you would enter the sudo command with the application name as an argument. For example, to use the **nano** editor to edit a system configuration file, you would start **nano** using the **sudo** command in a terminal window, with the **nano** command and the filename as its arguments. This starts up **nano** editor with administrator privileges. The following example will allow you to edit the **/etc/fstab** file to add or edit file system entries. You will be prompted for your user password.

```
sudo nano /etc/fstab
```

sudo configuration

Access for **sudo** is controlled by the **/etc/sudoers** file. This file lists users and the commands they can run, along with the password for access. If the NOPASSWD option is set, then users will not need a password. The ALL option, depending on the context, can refer to all hosts on your network, all root-level commands, or all users. See the Man page for **sudoers** for detailed information on all options.

```
man sudoers
```

To make changes or add entries, you have to edit the file with the special sudo editing command **visudo**. This invokes the nano editor (see Chapter 5) to edit the **/etc/sudoers** file. Unlike a standard editor, **visudo** will lock the **/etc/sudoers** file and check the syntax of your entries. You are not allowed to save changes unless the syntax is correct. If you want to use a different editor, you can assign it to the EDITOR shell variable. Use Ctrl-x to exit and Ctrl-o to save. Be sure to invoke **visudo** with the **sudo** command to gain authorized access.

```
sudo visudo
```

A **sudoers** entry has the following syntax:

```
user    host=command
```

The *host* is a host on your network. You can specify all hosts with the ALL term. The *command* can be a list of commands, some or all qualified by options such as whether a password is required. To specify all commands, you can also use the ALL term. The following gives the user george full root-level access to all commands on all hosts:

```
george  ALL = ALL
```

In addition, you can let a user run as another user on a given host. Such alternate users are placed within parentheses before the commands. For example, if you want to give **george** access to the **beach** host as the user **mydns**, you use the following:

```
george beach = (mydns) ALL
```

To give **robert** access on all hosts to the time tool, you would use

```
robert ALL=/usr/bin/time-admin
```

To specify a group name, you prefix the group with a **%** sign, as in **%mygroup**. This way, you can give the same access to a group of users. By default, **sudo** will grant access to all users in the **admin** group. These are user granted administrative access. The ALL=(ALL) ALL entry allows access by the administrative group users to all hosts as all users to all commands.

```
%admin   ALL=(ALL)   ALL
```

With the NOPASSWD option, you can allow members of a certain group access without a password. A commented **sudo** group is provided in the **/etc/sudoers** file.

```
%sudo   ALL=NOPASSWD:   ALL
```

Though on Ubuntu, sudo is configured to allow **root** user access, Ubuntu does not create a **root** user password. This prevents you from logging in as the **root** user, rendering the sudo root permission useless. The default **/etc/sudoers** file does configure full access for the root user to all commands. The ALL=(ALL) ALL entry allows access by the root to all hosts as all users to all commands. If you were to set up a root password for the root user, the root user could then log in and have full administrative access.

```
root    ALL=(ALL)    ALL
```

If you want to see what commands you can run, you use the **sudo** command with the **-l** option. The **-U** option to specify a particular user. In the following example, the user richard has full administrative access.

```
$ sudo -U richard -l
```

```
User richard may run the following commands on this host:
    (ALL) All
```

pkexec

You can use the **pkexec** command in place of **sudo** to run graphical applications with administrative access. The **pkexec** tool is a policykit alternative to **sudo**, and requires that your application has a corresponding policykit action file. Applications like user accounts, Udisks, and NetworkManager already have action files. Others, like Gedit, do not. To use **pkexec** with Gedit, you have to create a policykit action file for it. This is a simple process, copying most of the entries from the example in the **pkexec** man page. The askubuntu site (**http://askubuntu.com**) also has a detailed explanation on how to do this (search on "pkexec" and open the "How to configure pkexec" entry). The **pkexec** tool will prompt you to enter your password (See Figure 14-1).

Figure 14-1: pkexec prompt for secure access

You can enter the **pkexec** command in a terminal window with the application as an argument, or set up an application launcher with **pkexec** as the command. The following example will start up the Gedit editor with administrative access, allowing you to edit system configuration files directly (see Figure 14-2).

```
pkexec gedit
```

One way to set up a policy file for an application such as Gedit is to copy the example in the **pkexec** man page. Change the example entries to gedit. For the message entry, you only need a simple message. Be sure to add an annotate line at the end for desktop access, setting the **exec.allow_gui** option to true.

```
<annotate key="org.freedesktop.policykit.exec.allow_gui">true</annotate>
```

Alternatively, you could simply copy a simple policy file, change the name, and edit it to replace the program names and the message (for example, making a copy of **com.canonical.xdiagnose.policy** located in the **/usr/share/polkit-1/actions** directory). Be sure to use the **sudo** command with **cp** command in a terminal window to perform the copy.

A sample policy file for Gedit is follows.

org.freedesktop.policykit.pkexec.gedit.policy

```
<?xml version="1.0" encoding="UTF-8"?>
   <!DOCTYPE policyconfig PUBLIC
     "-//freedesktop//DTD PolicyKit Policy Configuration 1.0//EN"
     "http://www.freedesktop.org/standards/PolicyKit/1/policyconfig.dtd">
 <policyconfig>

  <action id="org.freedesktop.policykit.pkexec.gedit">
    <description>Run the Gedit program</description>
    <message>Authentication is required to run gedit</message>
    <icon_name>gedit</icon_name>
    <defaults>
       <allow_any>auth_admin</allow_any>
       <allow_inactive>auth_admin</allow_inactive>
       <allow_active>auth_self_keep</allow_active>
    </defaults>
    <annotate key="org.freedesktop.policykit.exec.path">/usr/bin/gedit</annotate>
    <annotate key="org.freedesktop.policykit.exec.allow_gui">true</annotate>
  </action>

</policyconfig>
```

Figure 14-2: Invoking Gedit with pkexec command

Root User Access: root and su

You can access the root user from any normal terminal window using the **sudo** command on the **su** command. The **su** command is the superuser command. Superuser is another name for the **root** user. A user granted administrative access by **sudo** could then become the **root** user. The following logs into the root user.

```
sudo su
```

Ubuntu is designed never to let anyone directly log in as the root user. The **root** user has total control over the entire system. Instead, certain users are given administrative access with which they can separately access administrative tools, performing specific tasks. Even though a **root** user exists, a password for the root user is not defined, never allowing access to it.

You can activate the root user by using the **passwd** command to create a root user password. Enter the **passwd** command with the **root** username in a **sudo** operation.

```
sudo passwd root
```

You are prompted for your administrative password, and then prompted by the **passwd** command to enter a password for the **root** user. You are then prompted to repeat the password.

```
Enter new UNIX password:
Retype new UNIX password:
passwd: password updated successfully
```

You can then log in with the **su** command as the root user, making you the superuser (you still cannot login as the root user from the display manager login window). Because a superuser has the power to change almost anything on the system, such a password is usually a carefully guarded secret, changed very frequently, and given only to those whose job it is to manage the system. With the correct password, you can log in to the system as a system administrator and configure the system any way you want.

```
su root
```

The **su** command alone will assume the root username.

```
su
```

The **su** command can be used to login to any user, provided you have that user's password.

To exit from an **su** login operation, just enter **exit**.

```
exit
```

/etc/hostname and hostnamectl

The **/etc/hostname** file contains your hostname. You can use the **hostnamectl** command in a terminal window to display your current hostname and all information pertaining to it such as the machine ID, the kernel used, the architecture, chassis (type of computer), and the operating system (you can add the **status** option if you want). Three different kinds of hostnames are supported: static, pretty, and transient. You can set each with the **hostnamectl**'s **set-hostname** command with the corresponding type. The static hostname is used to identify your computer on the network (usually a fully qualified host name). You can use the **--static** option to set it. The pretty hostname is a descriptive hostname made available to users on the computer. This can be set by **set-hostname** with the **--pretty** option. The transient hostname is one allocated by a network service such as DHCP, and can be managed with the **--transient** option. Without options, the **set-hostname** command will apply the name to all the host name types.

```
hostnamectl set-hostname --pretty "my computer"
```

The **set-chassis** command sets the computer type, which can be desktop, laptop, server, tablet, handset, and vm (virtual system). Without a type specified it reverts to the default for the system. The **set-icon-name** command sets the name used by the graphical applications for the host.

User (GNOME Settings | Details | Users)

You can configure and create user accounts using the GNOME Users tool accessible from GNOME Settings as Users. Users does not provide any way to control groups. If you want group control and more configuration options, you can use the GNOME Users and Groups application (system-config-users package).

You can access GNOME Users from the Details | Users tab on GNOME Settings. The Users tab displays and icon bar at the top showing a list of configured users with arrow buttons to the right and left to move through the list. Below the list is information about a selected user (see Figure 14-3). Initially, at the top of the Users tab is an Unlock button. Click on this button to open an authentication dialog, prompting for your password. Once active, you can then change the change the password, account type, icon, or name for the currently selected user. To remove a user, click its Remove User button on the lower right.

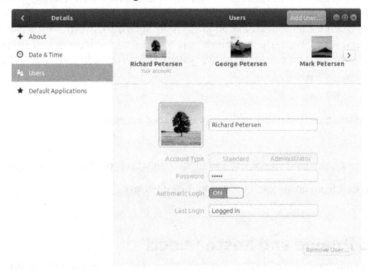

Figure 14-3: GNOME Users

Once authentication is accepted, the Unlock button changes to an Add User button, which you click to add a new user. When you add a new account, the Add User dialog opens, allowing you to set the account type (standard or administrator), the full name of the user, and the username (see Figure 14-4). For the username, you can enter a name or choose from a recommended list of options. You can also choose to set the password at this time. Click the Add button on the upper right to create the user. The new account appears in the icon list of users at the top of the Users tab, showing the name and icon. Selecting the user also shows its account type, language, password, an automatic login option, and the time of the last logon. You can change the account type, language, password, and icon by clicking on their entries.

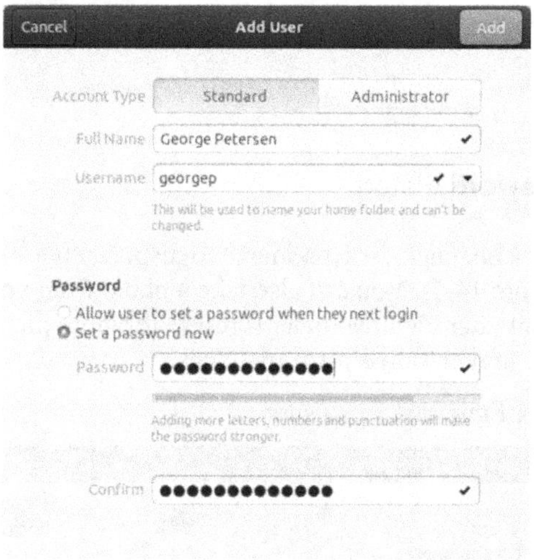

Figure 14-4: Add a new user

The account remains inactive until you specify a password (see Figure 14-5). You can do this when you add the account or later. You can also change the password for an account. Click the password entry to open the "Change Password" dialog in which you can enter the new password (see Figure 14-6). On the right side of an empty Password text box a password generator button is displayed that will generate a password for you when clicked. Once clicked, a generated password is entered the text box and the button disappears, replaced by a checkmark. Deleting the password to show an empty box, once again displays the password generator button. Once the password is selected, the account becomes enabled.

Figure 14-5: Users, inactive user

Figure 14-6: Users, password dialog

To change the user icon, click the icon image to display a pop-up dialog showing available images you can use (see Figure 14-7). You can also take a photo from your web cam (take a photo entry) or select a picture from your Pictures folder (browse for more pictures). Many of the photos used in previous releases are at **/usr/share/pixmaps/faces**.

Currently, group configuration is not supported.

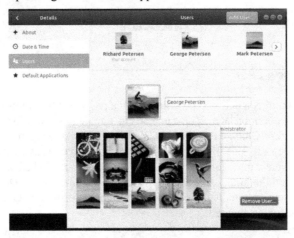

Figure 14-7: **Accounts dialog, User Icon**

Users and Groups

Alternatively, you can install (**gnome-system-tools**) and then use the older "Users and Groups" application (users-admin), accessible from "User and Groups" on the Applications overview (The **gnome-system-tools** package is no longer supported by Ubuntu). This opens a User Settings window, which displays two panes, a left scrollable pane for a list of users, showing their icon and login name, and a right pane showing information about a selected user. Below the left pane are buttons for adding and deleting users. At the bottom of the right pane are buttons for Managing Groups and for a selected user's Advanced Settings.

When you start up the users-admin application, only read access is allowed, letting you scroll through the list of users, but not make any changes or add new ones (see Figure 14-8). Read-only access is provided to all users. Users will be able to see the list of users on your system, but they cannot modify their entries, add new ones, or delete current users. Administrative access is required to perform these operations.

Figure 14-8: Users and Groups

PolicyKit controls administrative access for the users-admin tool. When you first click a task button, such as Add, Delete, or Advanced Settings, an Authenticate dialog will open and prompt you to enter your user password. You will also be prompted to authenticate if you click a Change link to change a user password, account type, or name.

To change settings for a user, select the user in the User Settings window. On the left pane the username, account type and password access are listed with a Change link to the right of each. Clicking on a Change link lets you change that property. When you click a Change link, an authentication dialog will prompt you to enter an administrative user password. To change a username, click the Change link to the right of the username to open the "Change User Name and Login" dialog with a text box for entering the new name.

To change a user password, you would click the Change link to the right of the Password entry to open the "Change User Password" dialog with entries for the current password and the new password (see Figure 14-9). You can also choose to generate a random password.

Figure 14-9: User Settings: Change User Password dialog

An account type can be Administrator, Desktop User, or Custom. When you click the Change link for the Account type, the "Change User Account Type" dialog opens with options for each.

For more detailed configuration, you click the Advanced Settings button to open the "Change Advanced User Settings" dialog, which has tabs for Contact Information, User Privileges, and Advanced (see Figure 14-10). On the Contact tab, you can add basic contact information if you wish, for an office address, as well as work and home phones.

On the User Privileges tab you can control device access and administrative access (see Figure 14-10). You can restrict or allow access to CD-ROMs, scanners, and external storage like USB drives. You can also determine whether the user can perform administrative tasks. The "Administer the system" checkbox is left unchecked by default. If you want to allow the user to perform administration tasks, be sure to check this box.

The Advanced tab lets you select a home directory, the shell to use, a main group, and a user ID. Defaults are already chosen for you. A home directory in the name of the new user is specified and the shell used is the BASH shell. Normally you would not want to change these settings, though you might prefer to use a different shell, like the C-Shell. For the group, the user has a group with its own username (same as the short name).

Figure 14-10: Users and Groups: Change User Privileges

Should to you decide to delete a user, you are prompted to keep or delete the user's home directory along with the user's files.

New Users (Users and Groups)

To create a new user, click the Add button in the Users Settings window to open a "Create New User" dialog, where you can enter the username. A short name is automatically entered for you, using the user's first name and the first letter of the last name. You can change the short name if you wish, but it must be in lowercase. The short name is also the name of the new user main group (see Figure 14-11). The new user is then added to the User Settings window.

The "Change User Password" dialog is then displayed, with entries for the new password and confirmation. You can also choose to use a randomly generated password instead (see Figure 14-12). Click the Generate button generate a password.

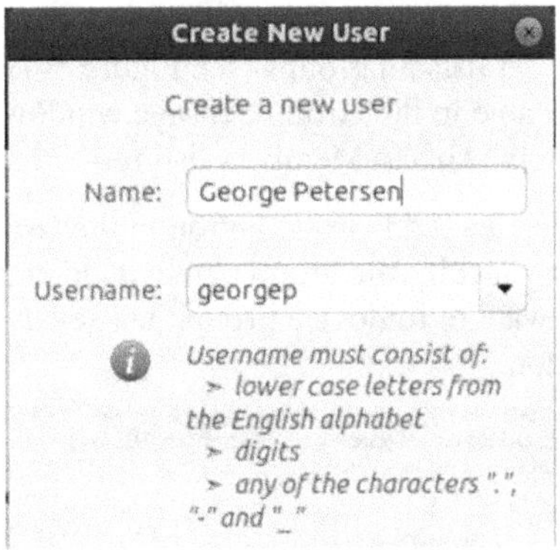

Figure 14-11: Users and Groups: Create New User

Figure 14-12: Users and Groups: new user password

If you decide not to enter a password (click Cancel), the account will remain disabled. To enable it later, click on the Enable Account button to open the "Change User Password" dialog where you can add the password.

The Account type is set initially to Desktop user, restricting access by the new user. Should you want to enable administrative access for this user, click the Change link to the right of the Account type entry to open the "Change User Account Type" dialog, where you can change the account type to Administrator. To set more specific privileges and for key user configuration settings such as the home directory and user id, click the Advanced Settings button to open the "Change Advanced User Settings" dialog with Contact Information, User Privileges, and Advanced tabs.

Alternatively, you can use the **useradd** command in a terminal window or command line to add user accounts and the **userdel** command to remove them. The following example adds the user **dylan** to the system:

```
$ useradd dylan
```

Groups (Users and Groups)

To manage groups, click the Manage Groups button in the Users Settings window. This opens a Group Settings window that lists all groups (see Figure 14-13). To add or remove users to or from a group, click the group name in the Group Settings window and click Properties. You can then check or uncheck users from the Group Members listing.

To add a new group, click the Add Group button in the Group Settings window to open a New Group dialog, where you can specify the group name, its id, and select the users to add to the group (see Figure 14-14). If you want to remove a group, just select its entry in the Groups Settings window and click the Delete button.

Figure 14-13: Users and Groups: Groups settings

Figure 14-14: Group Properties: Group Users panel

Passwords

The easiest way to change your password is to use the User Accounts dialog available from GNOME Settings as User and from the User Switcher menu as User Accounts. Select your username, then click the button to the right of the Password label to open the Change User Password dialog (see Figure 14-7).

Alternatively, you can use the **passwd** command. In a terminal window enter the **passwd** command. The command prompts you for your current password. After entering your current password and pressing ENTER, you are then prompted for your new password. After entering the new password, you are asked to re-enter it. This makes sure you have actually entered the password you intended to enter.

```
$ passwd
Changing password for richard.
(current) UNIX password:
Enter new UNIX password:
Retype new UNIX password:
passwd: password updated successfully
$
```

Managing Services

Many administrative functions operate as services that need to be turned on. They are daemons, constantly running and checking for requests for their services. When you install a service, its daemon is normally turned on automatically. You can start, stop, and restart a service from a terminal window using the **systemctl** command with the service name and the commands: **start**, **stop**, **restart**, and **status**. The **status** command tells you if a service is already running. To restart the Samba file sharing server (**smdb**) you would use the following command. Use the status command to see if it is enabled.

```
sudo systemctl restart smbd
```

To disable a service so that it is note turned on automatically, you would use the disable command. To have it turned on you use the enable command. The enable command starts up the service when you system starts. If you enable before a restart and want to run the service, you would also use the start command.

```
sudo systemctl disable smbd
sudo systemctl enable smbd
sudo systemctl start smbd
```

Ubuntu uses systemd to manage services. The systemd services are managed using **.service** configuration files in the **/lib/systemd/system** and **/etc/systemd/system** directories.

File System Access

Various file systems can be accessed on Ubuntu easily. Any additional internal hard drive partitions on your system, both Linux and Windows NTFS, will be detected automatically, but not mounted. In addition, you can access remote Windows shared folders and make your shared folders accessible.

Access to Internal Linux File Systems

Ubuntu will automatically detect other Linux file systems (partitions) on all your internal hard drives. Entries for these partitions are displayed on a file manager sidebar's Computer section. Initially, they are not mounted. Administrative users can mount internal partitions by clicking on its entry or icon, which mounts the file system and displays its icon on the Launcher. A file manager window opens displaying the top-level contents of the file system. The file system is mounted under the **/media** directory, in a sub-folder with the username, and then in a folder named with the file system (partition) label, or, if unlabeled, with the device UUID name.

Non-administrative users (users you create and do not specify as administrators), cannot mount internal partitions unless the task is authenticated using an administrative user's password. An authorization window will appear, similar to that shown in Figure 14-15. You will be asked to choose a user who has administrative access from a drop-down menu, and then enter that user's password. If there is only one administrative user, that user is selected automatically and you are prompted to enter that user's password. Whenever you start up your system again, you will still have to mount the file system, again providing authorization.

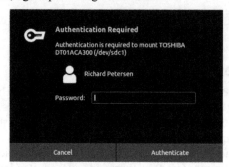

Figure 14-15: Mount authorization request for non-administrative users

Access to Windows NTFS File Systems on Local Drives

If you have installed Ubuntu on a dual-boot system with Windows 7, Vista, or XP, Linux NTFS file system support is installed automatically. Your NTFS partitions are mounted using Filesystem in Userspace (FUSE). The same authentication control used for Linux file systems applies to NTFS file systems. Entries for the NTFS partitions are placed on the file manager sidebar's Devices section with an eject button to mount and unmount the file system. If you are a user with administrative access, the file system is mounted (Eject button on file manager sidebar). If you are a user without administrative access, you will be asked to choose a user that has administrative access from a drop-down menu, and then enter that user's password, providing authorization. The NTFS file system is then mounted with icons displayed on the Launcher. You can access the file system by clicking on its Launcher icon or its entry in a file manager sidebar. The partitions will be mounted under the **/media** directory with their UUID numbers or labels used as folder names. The NTFS partitions are mounted using **ntfs-3g** drivers.

Access to Local Network Shared File Systems (Windows)

Shared Windows folders and printers on any of the computers connected to your local network are automatically accessible from any file manager window sidebar. The DNS discovery service (Avahi) automatically detects hosts on your home or local network. Supporting Samba libraries are already installed and will let you access directly any of their shared folders.

Currently, both Linux and Windows are in the process of transitioning from the older SMBv1 protocol (Secure Message Block) to the more secure SMBv3 protocol. As a result, network browsing through the Linux file manager does not work currently. Instead, you can access Windows shares directly.. You can access Windows shares directly using the Connect to Server entry on the GNOME file manager's Other Locations window. Enter in the **smb://** protocol and the name of the shared folder or that of the remote Windows system you want to access. After being prompted to enter your Samba password (see Figure 14-16), the particular shared folder or the shared folders on that host will be displayed.

Once selected, the shared folders are shown. You can then access a shared folder and it will be mounted automatically on your desktop. The file manager sidebar will show an entry for the folder with an eject button for un-mounting it. Figure 14-18 shows the **myshared-data** shared folder on a Windows system mounted with an eject button on the sidebar.

You can also use these methods to browse all the shared folders on a specific Windows system. Instead of including a shared folder, you simply specify the host preceded by the **smb://** protocol. You can then double-click on a share folder to mount it.

Figure 14-16: Network authorization

Figure 14-17: Network window

Figure 14-18: Mount remote Windows shares

Other local computers cannot access your shared folders until you install a sharing server, Samba for Windows systems and NFS for Linux/Unix systems. Should you attempt to share a directory, a notice is displayed prompting you to install the sharing service (Samba and NFS). Be sure also to allow firewall access for Samba and desktop browsing (see Chapter 15, Firewalls).

Shared Folders for your network

To share a folder on your Ubuntu system, right-click on it and select Local Network Share. This opens a window where you can allow sharing, and choose whether to permit modifying, adding, or deleting files in the folder (see Figure 14-19). You can also use the Share tab on the file's properties dialog (see Figure 14-22). You can allow access to anyone who does not also have an account on your system (guest). Once you have made your selections, click the Create Share button. You can later change the sharing options if you want.

For a user to create a share, they have to have permission to do so. New users are not given this permission by default. On the Users and Groups's Advanced dialog's Privileges tab set the "Share files with the local network" option.

Figure 14-19: Folder Sharing Options

To allow access by other users, permissions on the folder will have to be changed. You will be prompted to allow the file manager to make these changes for you. Just click the "Add the permissions automatically" button (see Figure 14-20).

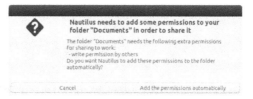

Figure 14-20: Folder Sharing permissions prompt

Note: If you are running a firewall, be sure to configure access for the NFS and Samba services, including browsing support. Otherwise, access to your shared folders by other computers may be blocked (see Chapter 15).

Folders that are shared display a sharing emblem next to their icon on a file manager window.

To allow other computers to access your folders be sure the sharing servers are installed, Samba for Windows systems and NFS (**nfs-kernelserver**) for Linux/Unix systems. The servers are configured automatically for you and run. You will not be able to share folders until these servers are installed. If your sharing servers are not installed, you will be prompted to install them the first time you try to share a folder (see Figure 14-21). Click the Install service button. The Samba servers will be downloaded and installed. You are then prompted to restart your desktop session. Click the Restart session button. You are placed in the GDM login screen. Log in again and then open the folder sharing dialog for the folder you want to share (Sharing Options).

Figure 14-21: Prompt to install sharing service (Samba and NFS)

You can also install the Samba server directly with the Synaptic Package Manager (**samba** package). Two servers are installed and run using the **smbd** and **nmbd** systemd service scripts. The **smbd** server is the Samba server, and the **nmbd** server is the network discovery server.

Should the Samba server fail to start, you can start it manually in a terminal window with the commands:

```
sudo service nmbd start
sudo service smbd start
```

You can check the current status with the **status** option and restart with the **restart** option:

```
sudo service nmbd status
sudo service smbd status
```

When first installed, Samba imports the user accounts already configured on your Ubuntu system. Corresponding Windows users with the same username and password as an Ubuntu account on your Ubuntu system are connected automatically to the Ubuntu shared folders. Should the Windows user have a different password, that user is prompted on Windows to enter a username and password. This is an Ubuntu username and password. In the case of a Windows user with the same username but different password, the user would enter the same username with an Ubuntu user password, not the Windows password.

Access is granted to all shares by any user. Should you want to implement restricted access by specific users and passwords, you have to configure user level access using a Samba configuration tool such as system-config-samba, as discussed in the next section.

To change the sharing permissions for a folder later, open the folder's Properties window and then select the Share tab. When you make a change, a Modify Share button is displayed. Click it to make the changes. In Figure 14-22 share access is added to the Pictures folder.

Figure 14-22: Folder Share panel

Configuring Samba user-level access with system-config-samba

More secure access by Windows systems to your Ubuntu shared folders can be configured using the **system-config-samba** tool. Ubuntu no longer supports **system-config-samba** directly, but it is available on the Ubuntu repository. You can install it with the Synaptic Package Manager. Once installed you have to also create an empty **/etc/libuser.conf** file using the **touch** command in a terminal window.

```
sudo touch /etc/libuser.conf
```

It is also possible to set up a policykit policy file in **/usr/share/polkit-1/actions** folder that will allow you to run system-config-samba directly from the applications dash. The policy file would be the same as a custom policy file that you would set up for gedit, except with system-config-samba in place of gedit. Keep in mind that the location of the program is at **/usr/sbin/system-config-samba** (not /usr/bin).

Samba Server Configuration

With system-config-samba you can set up user level access, requiring Samba user passwords to allow access to shares (see Figure 14-23). You will first have to configure the Samba server, designating users that can have access to shared resources like directories and printers. On the Samba Preferences menu, select Server Settings to open the Server Settings dialog.

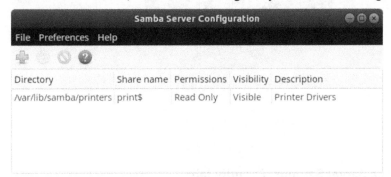

Figure 14-23: Samba server configuration with system-config-samba

On the Basic tab, enter the name of your Windows network workgroup (see Figure 14-24). The default names given by Windows are MSHOME or WORKGROUP. Use the workgroup name already given to your Windows network. For home networks, you can decide this on your own. Just make sure all your computers use the same workgroup name. On a Windows system, the Control Panel's System application will show you the Windows workgroup name. The description is the name you want displayed for your Samba server on your Windows systems. Windows 7 home networks will work with Samba without any special configuration.

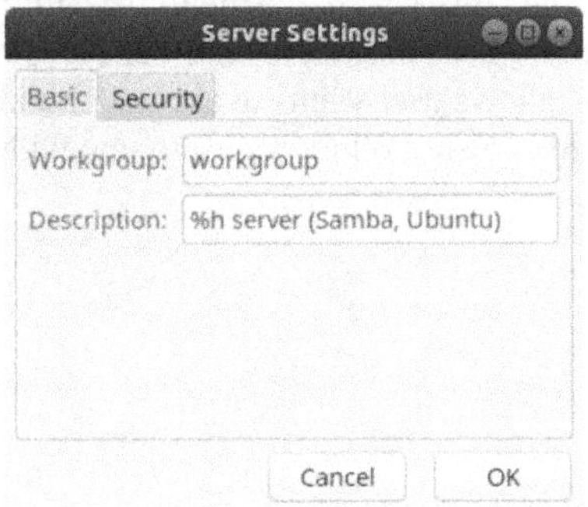

Figure 14-24: Samba Server Settings, Basic tab

On the Security tab, you can select the kind of authentication you want to use. By default, User security is selected (see Figure 14-25). You could also use share or server security. These are more open, but both have been deprecated and may be dropped in later versions.

The authentication mode specifies the access level, which can be user, share, server, ADS, or domain. User-level access restricts access by user password, whereas share access opens access to any guest. Normally, you would elect to encrypt passwords, rather than have them passed over your network in plain text. The Guest user is the name of the account used to allow access to shares or printers that you want open to any user, without having to provide a password. The pop-up menu will list all your current users, with "No Guest Account" as the selected default. Unless you want to provide access by everyone to a share, you would not have a Guest account.

Figure 14-25: Samba Server Settings, Security tab

Samba Users

For user authentication, you need to associate a Windows user with a particular Linux account. Select Samba Users in the Preferences menu to open the Samba Users dialog (see Figure 14-26). Ubuntu users set up on your system when you installed Samba are listed already, using their usernames and password for access by Windows users. If you want to add a new Samba user, click Add User to open the Create New Samba User window where you select the Unix Username from a pop-up menu, and then enter the Windows Username and the Samba password to be used for that user (see Figure 14-27). The Unix Username menu lists all the users on your Samba server. Samba maintains its own set of passwords that users on other computers will need in order to access a Samba share. When a Windows user wants to access a Samba share, they will have to provide their Samba password. If you use a Windows username with spaces, enclose it within quotes.

Figure 14-26: Samba Users

Once you create a Samba user, its name will appear in the list of Samba users on the Samba Users window. To later modify or delete a Samba user, Use the same Samba Users window, select the user from the list, and click the Edit User button to change entries like the password, or, click the Delete User button to remove the Samba user.

Figure 14-27: Create a new samba user

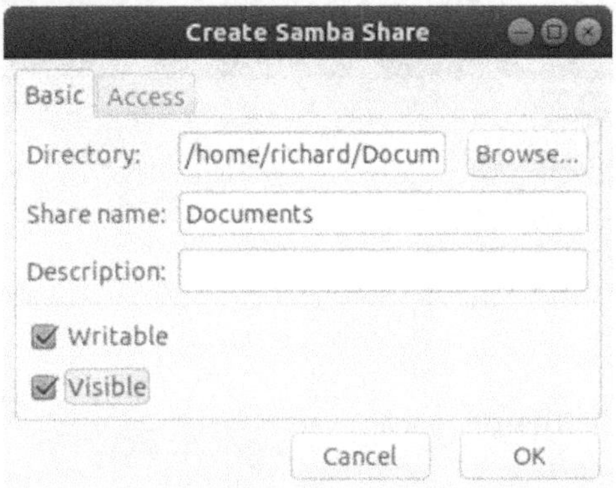

Figure 14-28: New Samba Share, Basic tab

Samba Shares

To set up a simple share, click Add Share in the Samba Server Configuration window, which opens a Create Samba Share window (see Figure 14-28).

Figure 14-29: Samba share, Access tab

On the Basic tab you select the Linux directory to share (click Browse to find it), and then specify whether it will be writable and visible.

On the Access tab, you can choose to open the share to everyone, or just for specific users (see Figure 14-29). All Samba users on your system are listed with checkboxes where you can select those you want to give access.

Your new share is then displayed in the Samba Server Configuration window (see Figure 14-30). The share's directory, share name, its visibility, read/write permissions, and description are shown. To modify a share later, click on its entry and then click on the Properties button (or double-click). This opens an Edit Samba Share window with the same Basic and Access tabs you used to create the share.

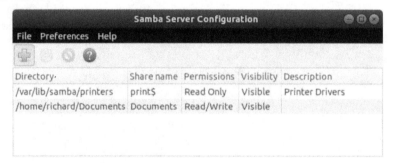

Figure 14-30: Samba with shares

Accessing Samba Shares from Windows

Accessing Samba shares from Windows is an issue for Windows 10. Upgrades to Windows 10 has disabled the SMBv1 network browsing capabilities of Windows, as it transitions to SMBv3 from SMBv1. You could try to manually re-enable SMBv1 browsing, but SMBv1 is being disabled due to security issues. It is not advisable to re-enable it. This means you cannot simply browse a Linux host currently, but you can still easily set up access to each Samba shared folder on that Linux host.

It is still easy to access your Samba Linux shares from Windows 10. You can simply add a new network location for it, that will be accessible from a shortcut you can set up for it on your Windows file manager "This PC" folder. To set up the shortcut, open the Windows file manager to any folder and right-click on the "This PC" entry in the sidebar to display a menu. Click on the "Add a network location" entry to open the "Add Network Location Wizard" and click Next. Click on the "Choose a custom network location" entry and click Next. In the text box labelled "Internet or network address:" enter the host name of your Linux system that holds the shares you want to access, beginning with the two backward slashes and followed by a backward slash (you may have to also enter the name of one of the shared folders on that system).

```
\\richard-laptop\
```

You can then click the Browse button to open a dialog showing a tree of all the shared folders on that host. You can choose a share, or any of a share's subfolders. Their file pathname is automatically added to the address textbox. Alternatively, you could enter the folder path name in the text box directly with the subfolders separated by single backward slashes. If you are sharing your Linux home directories, then the shared folder is the name of the user's Home folder, the user name. Samples are shown here.

```
\\richard-laptop\richard
```

```
\\richard-laptop\richard\Pictures
```

```
\\richard-laptop\mydocs
```

Once the locations for your shared folders are set up in Windows, you can access them again quickly from their shortcuts in the "This PC" folder.

File and Folder Permissions

On the desktop, you can set a directory or file permission using the Permissions tab in its Properties window (see Figure 14-31). For Files, right-click the icon or entry for the file or directory in the file manager window and select Properties. Then select the Permissions tab. Here you will find pop-up menus for read and write permissions, along with rows for Owner, Group, and Others. You can set owner permissions as Read Only or Read And Write. For the group and others, you can also set the None option, denying access. The group name expands to a menu listing different groups; select one to change the file's group. If you want to execute this file as an application (say, a shell script) check the Allow Executing File As Program entry. This has the effect of setting the execute permission

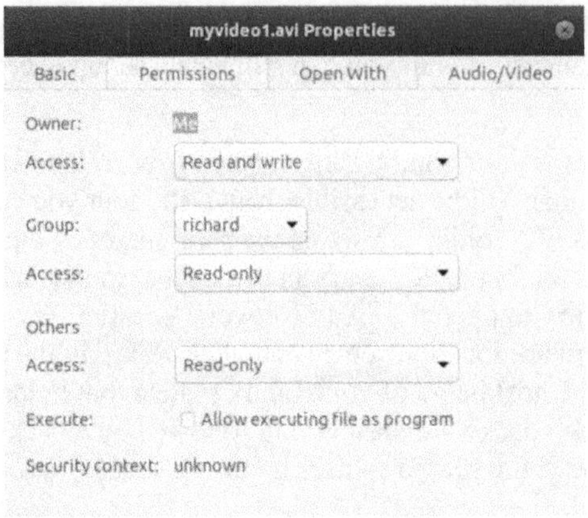

Figure 14-31: File Permissions

The Permissions tab for folders (directories) operates much the same way, with Access menus for Owner, Group, and Others (see Figure 14-32). The Access menu controls access to the folder with options for List Files Only, Access Files, and Create And Delete Files. These correspond to the read, read and execute, and read/write/execute permissions given to directories. To set the permissions for all the files in the directory accordingly (not just the folder), click the "Change Permissions for Enclosed Files" button to open a dialog where you can specify the owner, group, and others permissions for files and folders in the directory (see Figure 14-32). The access options are the same as for files: for the owner, Read or Read and Write. The group and others access menus add a None option to deny access.

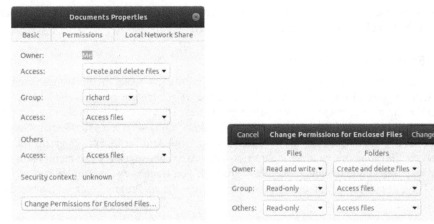

Figure 14-32: Folder Permissions

Automatic file system mounts with /etc/fstab

Though most file systems are automatically mounted for you, there may be instances where you need to have a file system mounted manually. Using the mount command you can do this directly, or you can specify the mount operation in the **/etc/fstab** file to have it mounted automatically. Ubuntu file systems are uniquely identified with their UUID (Universally Unique

IDentifier). These are listed in the **/dev/disk/by-uuid** directory (or with the **sudo blkid** command). In the **/etc/fstab** file, the file system disk partitions are listed as a comment, and then followed by the actual file system mount operation using the UUID. The following example mounts the file system on partition **/dev/sda3** to the **/media/sda3** directory as an **ext4** file system with default options (**defaults**). The UUID for device **/dev/sda3** is b8c526db-cb60-43f6-b0a3-5c0054f6a64a.

```
# /dev/sda3
UUID=b8c526db-cb60-43f6-b0a3-5c0054f6a64a /media/sda3 ext4 defaults 0 2
```

You can also identify your file system by giving it a label. You can use the **ext2label** command to label a file system. In the following **/etc/fstab** file example, the Linux file system labeled **mydata1** is mounted to the **/mydata1** directory as an **ext4** file system type.

To find out the UUID of any device you use the **blkid** command.

```
blkid
```

/etc/fstab

```
# /etc/fstab: static file system information.
#
# <file system> <mount point>   <type>  <options>       <dump>  <pass>
proc            /proc           proc    defaults        0       0
# / was on /dev/sda2 during installation
UUID=a179d6e6-b90c-4cc4-982d-a4cfcedea7df / ext4 defaults,errors=remount-ro 0 1
# /boot/efi was on /dev/sda1 during installation
UUID=7982-2520 /boot/efi vfat defaults 0 1
# /dev/sda1
UUID=b8c526db-cb60-43f6-b0a3-5c0054f6a64a /media/sda3 ext4 defaults 0 2
/swapfile       none    swap    sw      0 0
LABEL=mydata1 /mydata1          ext4            defaults                1 1
```

Should you have to edit your **/etc/fstab** file, you can use the **sudo** command with the **gedit** editor on your desktop. In a terminal window enter the following command. You will first be prompted to enter your password.

```
sudo gedit /etc/fstab
```

To mount a partition manually, use the **mount** command and specify the type with the **-t** option. Use the **-L** option to mount by label. List the file system first, and then the directory name to which it will be mounted. For an NTFS partition, you would use the type **ntfs**. For partitions with the Ext4 file system you would use **ext4**, and for older Linux partitions you would use **ext3**. The mount option has the format:

```
mount -t type  file-system  directory
```

The following example mounts the **mydata1** file system to the **/mydata1** directory

```
mount -t ext4  -L mydata1  /mydata1
```

Bluetooth

Bluetooth is a wireless connection method for locally connected devices such as keyboards, mice, printers, and Bluetooth-capable cell phones. BlueZ is the official Linux Bluetooth protocol and is integrated into the Linux kernel. BlueZ is the official Linux Bluetooth protocol and is integrated into the Linux kernel. The BlueZ protocol was developed originally by Qualcomm and is now an open source project, located at **http://www.bluez.org/**. It is included in the bluez and bluez-libs packages, among others. Check the BlueZ site for a complete list of supported hardware.

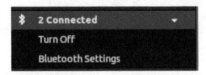

Figure 14-33: Bluetooth Settings (GNOME Settings)

If you have Bluetooth devices attached to your system, a Bluetooth entry is displayed on the system status area menu on the top panel (see Figure 14-33). It will display a message showing the number of connected devices if there are any. Click the entry to display items to turn off Bluetooth and for Bluetooth Settings. Should you turn off Bluetooth, Bluetooth will be disabled and its entry removed from the system status area menu. Use the Bluetooth Settings dialog, accessible from the Settings dialog, to turn it on again.

The Bluetooth Settings item opens Settings to the Bluetooth tab (see Figure 14-34). You can also access Bluetooth tab on GNOME Settings directly. On the Bluetooth settings tab, a Bluetooth switch at the top right lets you turn Bluetooth on or off. Detected devices are listed in the Devices section at the center. Initially, devices are disconnected. Click on a device entry to connect it. A dialog opens with a detected pin number, which you confirm. Then the device configuration dialog is displayed, with a switch to connect or disconnect the device (see Figure 14-35). Pair, type, and address information are also displayed. If the device supports sound, a Sound Setting button is shown, which opens the Sound tab in Settings which displays that device (see Figure 14-36). To remove the device configuration, click the Remove Device button.

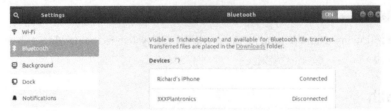

Figure 14-34: Bluetooth Settings (GNOME Settings)

Figure 14-35: Bluetooth Device Configuration

Figure 14-36: Bluetooth Sound

When connecting to a phone (see Figure 14-37), a pin number is detected and displayed. On the configuration dialog, you can choose to connect or disconnect. If you enable a phone to operate as a mobile phone network device (PAN/NAP), then a new entry appears for the device in the system status area menu, which you can expand to list the entries: Use as Internet connection" and "Mobile Broadband Setting." When you click the "Use as Internet connection" entry, it will change to a Turn Off entry, once you have connected.

Figure 14-37: Bluetooth for phones

File sharing for Bluetooth can be set using the file-share keys on the dconf editor, located at org | gnome | desktop | file-sharing. The Bluetooth-enabled key lets you share the Public directory. Share files can be read/write and you can be notified when files are received.

DKMS

DKMS is the Dynamic Kernel Module Support originally developed by DELL. DKMS enabled device drivers can be generated automatically whenever your kernel is updated. This is helpful for proprietary drivers like the Nvidia and AMD proprietary graphics drivers (the X11 open source drivers, Xorg, are automatically included with the kernel package). In the past, whenever you updated your kernel, you also had to download and install a separate proprietary kernel module compiled just for that new kernel. If the module was not ready, then you could not use a proprietary driver. To avoid this problem, DKMS was developed, which uses the original proprietary source code to create new kernel modules as they are needed. When you install a new kernel, DKMS detects the new configuration and compiles a compatible proprietary kernel module for your new kernel. This action is fully automatic and entirely hidden from the user.

On Ubuntu both the Nvidia and AMD proprietary graphics drivers are DKMS enable packages that are managed and generated by the DKMS service. The generated kernel modules are placed in the **/lib/modules/***kernel-version***/kernel/updates** directory. When you install either graphics proprietary package, their source code is downloaded and used to create a graphics driver for use by your kernel. The source code is placed in the **/usr/src** directory. The DKMS configuration files and build locations for different DKMS-enabled software are located in subdirectories in the **/var/lib/dkms** directory. The subdirectories will have the module name like **NVIDIA** for the Nvidia drivers.

DKMS configuration files are located in the **/etc/dkms** directory. The **/etc/dkms/framework.conf** file holds DKMS variable definitions for directories that DKMS uses, like the source code and kernel module directories. The **/etc/init.d/dkms_autoinstaller** is a script the runs the DKMS operations to generate and install a kernel module. DKMS removal and install directives for kernel updates are maintained in the **/etc/kernel** directory.

Should DKMS fail to install and update automatically, you can perform the update manually using the **dkms** command. The **dkms** command with the **build** action creates the kernel module, and then the **dkms** command with the **install** action installs the module to the appropriate kernel module directory. The **-m** option specifies the module you want to build and the **-k** option is the kernel version (use **uname -r** to display your current kernel version). Drivers like Nvidia and AMD release new versions regularly. You use the **-v** option to specify the driver version you want. See the man page for **dkms** for full details.

Editing Configuration Files Directly

Though the administrative tools will handle all configuration settings for you, there may be times when you will need to make changes by editing configuration files directly. Most system configuration files are text files located in the **/etc** directory. To change any of these files, you will need administrative access, requiring you use the **pkexec** or **sudo** commands.

You can use any standard editor, such as nano or Vi, to edit these files, though one of the easiest ways to edit them is to use the Gedit editor on the GNOME desktop. In a terminal window, enter the **sudo** command with the **gedit** command. You will be prompted for the root user password. The Gedit window then opens (see Figures 14-2 and 14-3 near the beginning of this chapter). Click Open to open a file browser where you can move through the file system to locate the file you want to edit.

```
sudo gedit
```

Caution: Be careful when editing your configuration files. Editing mistakes can corrupt your configurations. It is advisable to make a backup of any configuration files you are working on first, before making major changes to the original.

Gedit will let you edit several files at once, opening a tab for each. You can use Gedit to edit any text file, including ones you create yourself. Two commonly edited configuration files are **/etc/default/grub** and **/etc/fstab**. The **/etc/fstab** file lists all your file systems and how they are mounted, and **/etc/default/grub** file is the configuration file for your Grub 2 boot loader.

You also can specify the file to edit when you first start up gedit (the Gedit editor).

```
sudo gedit /etc/default/grub
```

User configuration files, dot files, can be changed by individual users directly without administrative access. An example of a user configuration file is the **.profile** file, which configures your login shell. Dot files like **.profile** have to be chosen from the file manager window, not from the Gedit open operation. First configure the file manager to display dot files by opening the Preferences dialog (select Preferences in the Edit menu of any file manager window), then check the Show Hidden Files entry, and close the dialog. This displays the dot files in your file manager window. Double-click the file to open it in Gedit.

GRUB 2

The Grand Unified Bootloader (GRUB) is a multiboot boot loader used for most Linux distributions. Linux and Unix operating systems are known as multiboot operating systems and take arguments passed to them at boot time. With GRUB, users can select operating systems to run from a menu interface displayed when a system boots up. Use arrow keys to move to an entry and press ENTER. If instead, you need to edit an entry, press **e**, letting you change kernel arguments or specify a different kernel. The **c** command places you in a command line interface. Provided your system BIOS supports very large drives, GRUB can boot from anywhere on them. For detailed information on Grub2 on Ubuntu, check the Ubuntu Grub2 Wiki at:

```
https://wiki.ubuntu.com/Grub2
```

Check the GRUB Man page for GRUB options. GRUB is a GNU project with its home page at **https://www.gnu.org/software/grub/**, the manual at **https://www.gnu.org/software/grub/manual/grub/**. The Ubuntu forums have several helpful threads on using Grub2 on Ubuntu, **http://ubuntuforums.org**. Search on Grub2.

Grub2 detects and generates a menu for you automatically. You do not have to worry about keeping a menu file updated. All your operating systems and Ubuntu kernels are detected when the system starts up, and a menu to display them as boot options is generated at that time.

Figure 14-38: Editing the /etc/default/grub file

With Grub2, configuration is placed in user-modifiable configuration files held in the **/etc/default/grub** file and in the **/etc/grub.d** directory. There is a Grub2 configuration file called **/boot/grub/grub.cfg**, but this file is generated by Grub each time the system starts up, and should never be edited by a user. Instead, you would edit the **/etc/default/grub** file to set parameters like the default operating system to boot. To create your own menu entries, you create entries for them in the **/etc/grub.d/40_custom** file.

Grub options are set by assigning values to Grub options in the **/etc/default/grub** file. You can edit the file directly to change these options (see Figure 14-38). To edit the file with the Gedit editor, open a terminal window and enter the following command. You will be prompted to enter your password. If **sudo** is not already installed, you will have to install it. Alternatively, you can configure Gedit to use policykit and run it with **pkexec**.

```
sudo gedit /etc/default/grub
```

You can then edit the file carefully. The **grub** file used on Ubuntu 18.04 is shown here:

/etc/default/grub

```
# If you change this file, run 'update-grub' afterwards to update
# /boot/grub/grub.cfg.

GRUB_DEFAULT=0
GRUB_HIDDEN_TIMEOUT=0
GRUB_HIDDEN_TIMEOUT_QUIET=true
GRUB_TIMEOUT="10"
GRUB_DISTRIBUTOR=`lsb_release -i -s 2> /dev/null || echo Debian`
GRUB_CMDLINE_LINUX_DEFAULT="quiet splash"
GRUB_CMDLINE_LINUX=""

# Uncomment to enable BadRAM filtering, modify to suit your needs
# This works with Linux (no patch required) and with any kernel that obtains
# the memory map information from GRUB (GNU Mach, kernel of FreeBSD ...)
#GRUB_BADRAM="0x01234567,0xfefefefe,0x89abcdef,0xefefefef"
```

```
# Uncomment to disable graphical terminal (grub-pc only)
#GRUB_TERMINAL=console

# The resolution used on graphical terminal
# note that you can use only modes which your graphic card supports via VBE
# you can see them in real GRUB with the command `vbeinfo'
#GRUB_GFXMODE=640x480

# Uncomment if you don't want GRUB to pass "root=UUID=xxx" parameter to Linux
#GRUB_DISABLE_LINUX_UUID=true

# Uncomment to disable generation of recovery mode menu entrys
#GRUB_DISABLE_RECOVERY="true"

# Uncomment to get a beep at grub start
#GRUB_INIT_TUNE="480 440 1"
```

For dual boot systems (those with both Ubuntu and Windows or Mac), the option that users are likely to change is GRUB_DEFAULT, which sets the operating system or kernel to boot automatically if one is not chosen. The option uses a line number to indicate an entry in the Grub boot menu, with numbering starting from 0 (not 1). First, check your Grub menu when you boot up (press any key on boot to display the Grub menu for a longer time), and then count to where the entry of the operating system you want to make the default is listed. If the Windows entry is at 4th, which would be line 3 (counting from 0), to make it the default you would set the GRUB_DEAULT option to 3.

```
GRUB_DEFAULT=3
```

Should the listing of operating systems and kernels change (adding or removing kernels), you would have to edit the **/etc/default/grub** file again and each time a change occurs. A safer way to set the default is to configure GRUB to use the **grub-set-default** command. First, edit the **/etc/default/grub** file and change the option for GRUB_DEFAULT to **save**.

```
GRUB_DEFAULT=saved
```

Then update GRUB.

```
sudo update-grub
```

The **grub-set-default** command takes as its option the number of the default you want to set (numbering from 0) or the name of the kernel or operating system. The following sets the default to 0, the first kernel entry.

```
sudo grub-set-default 0
```

For a kernel name or operating system, you can use the name as it appears on the GRUB menu (enclosing the name in quotes), such as:

```
sudo grub-set-default  'Windows (loader) (on /dev/sda1)'
```

The GRUB_TIMEOUT option sets the number of seconds Grub will wait to allow a user to access the menu, before booting the default operating system. The default options used for Ubuntu kernels are listed by the GRUB_CMDLINE_LINUX_DEFAULT option. Currently, these include the **splash** and **quiet** options to display the Ubuntu emblem on startup (**splash**), but not the list of startup tasks being performed (**quiet**).

Once you have made your changes, you have to run the **update-grub** command with **sudo**, as noted in the first line of the **/etc/default/grub** file. Otherwise, your changes will not take effect. This command will generate a new **/etc/grub/grub.cfg** file, which determines the actual Grub 2 configuration.

```
sudo update-grub
```

You can add your own Grub2 boot entries by placing them in the **/etc/grub.d/40_custom** file. The file is nearly empty except for an initial **exec tail** command that you must take care not to change. Samples of added entries are shown on the Ubuntu Grub2 Wiki, **https://wiki.ubuntu.com/Grub2**. After you make your additions to the **40_custom** file, you have to run **sudo update-grub** to have the changes take effect.

When the GRUB package is updated by Ubuntu, you will be given the choice to keep your current local version or use the maintainer's version. Keeping the local version is selected by default. However, unless you have extensively customized your configuration, it is always advisable to select the maintainer's version. The maintainer's version is the most up-to-date. If you had made any changes previously to the **/etc/default/grub** file, you will have to edit that file and make the same changes again, such as setting the default operating system to load. Be sure to run **sudo update-grub** to make the changes take effect.

Backup Management: rsync, Deja Dub BackupPC, and Amanda

Backup operations have become an important part of administrative duties. Several backup tools are provided on Linux systems, including Amanda and the traditional dump/restore tools, as well as the **rsync** command used for making individual copies. The Deja Dup is a front end for the duplicity backup tool, which uses rsync to generate backup archives. Deja Dup is the recommended default backup tool, available from the Applications overview as Backup. Amanda provides server-based backups, letting different systems on a network backup to a central server. BackupPC provides network and local backup using configured **rsync** and **tar** tools. The dump tools let you refine your backup process, detecting data changed since the last backup. Table 14-2 lists websites for Linux backup tools.

Website	Tools
`http://rsync.samba.org`	rsync remote copy backup
`https://launchpad.net/deja-dup` `http://www.nongnu.org/duplicity`	Deja Dup frontend for duplicity which uses rsync to perform basic backups
`http://www.amanda.org`	Amanda network backup
`http://dump.sourceforge.net`	dump and restore tools
`http://backuppc.sourceforge.net`	BackupPC network or local backup using configured rsync and tar tools.

Table 14-2: Backup Resources

Deja Dup

Deja Dup is a front end for the duplicity backup tool, which uses rsync to generate backup archives (**http://www.nongnu.org/duplicity/**). Once installed, you can access Deja Dup from Utilities | Backups.

The deja-dup settings dialog show tabs for Overview, Folders to save, Folders to ignore, Storage location, and Scheduling (see Figure 14-39). A switch at the top right of the dialog allows you to turn automatic backups on and off. The Overview tab provides information about your backup configuration with buttons to restore from a backup and to manually perform a backup, as well as the time of the next scheduled backup.

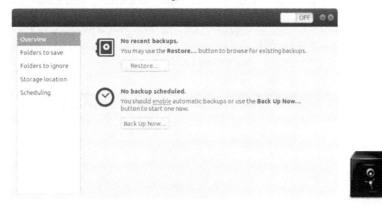

Figure 14-39: Deja Dup settings - overview

The "Folders to save" tab lets you specify folders you want to backup and folders to ignore (see Figure 14-40). Click the plus button (+) at the bottom of the folders list to add a new folder for backup. Do the same to specify folders to ignore. The minus button removes folders from the list. Your home folder has been added already. The "Folders to ignore" tab specifies folders you do not want to back up. The Downloads and Trash folders are selected initially.

Figure 14-40: Deja Dup settings - Folders to save and ignore

The "Storage Location" tab lets you specify a location to store your backups (see Figure 14-41). You can choose different locations, such as an FTP account, a cloud account, SSH server, Samba (Windows) share, or a local folder. Choose the one you want from the "Backup location" menu. With each choice, you are prompted for the appropriate configuration information.

Figure 14-41: Deja Dup settings - storage for Windows share and Local folder

On the Scheduling tab, you can specify the frequency of your backups and how long to keep them (see Figure 14-42). First turn on Automatic backup. Backups can be performed daily, weekly, every two weeks, or monthly. They can be kept for a week, month, several months, a year, or forever.

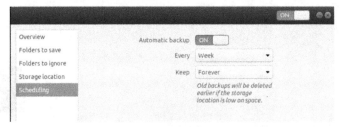

Figure 14-42: Deja Dup settings - backup times

When you perform a backup, you are prompted to backup with or without encryption. For encrypted backups, you are prompted to enter a password, which you will need to restore the files (see Figure 14-43).

Figure 14-43: Deja Dup backup: encryption

When restoring, you are prompted to specify the location you are backing up from, the backup date to restore from, and whether to restore to the original location or a specific folder (see Figure 14-44).

Figure 14-44: Deja Dup restore

Individual Backups: archive and rsync

You can backup and restore particular files and directories with archive tools like **tar**, restoring the archives later. For backups, **tar** is used usually with a tape device. To schedule automatic backups, you can schedule appropriate **tar** commands with the **cron** utility. The archives can be also compressed for storage savings. You can then copy the compressed archives to any medium, such as a DVD disc, a floppy, or tape. On GNOME you can use File Roller (Archive Manager) to create archives easily.

File Roller also supports LZMA compression, a more efficient and faster compression method. On Archive Manager, when creating a new archive, select "Tar compressed with lzma (.tar.lzma)" for the Archive type. When choosing Create Archive from GNOME Files file manager window on selected files, on the Create Archive dialog, choose the **.lzma** file type for just compression, and the **.tar.lzma** type for a compressed archive.

If you want to remote-copy a directory or files from one host to another, making a particular backup, you can use **rsync**, which is designed for network backups of particular directories or files, intelligently copying only those files that have been changed, rather than the contents of an entire directory. In archive mode, it can preserve the original ownership and permissions, providing corresponding users exist on the host system. The following example copies the **/home/george/myproject** directory to the **/backup** directory on the host **rabbit**, creating a corresponding **myproject** subdirectory. The **-t** specifies that this is a transfer. The remote host is referenced with an attached colon, **rabbit:**

```
rsync -t /home/george/myproject   rabbit:/backup
```

If instead, you wanted to preserve the ownership and permissions of the files, you would use the **-a** (archive) option. Adding a **-z** option will compress the file. The **-v** option provides a verbose mode.

```
rsync -avz  /home/george/myproject   rabbit:/backup
```

A trailing slash on the source will copy the contents of the directory, rather than generating a subdirectory of that name. Here the contents of the **myproject** directory are copied to the **george-project** directory.

```
rsync -avz  /home/george/myproject/   rabbit:/backup/george-project
```

The **rsync** command is configured to use Secure Shell (SSH) remote shell by default. You can specify it or an alternate remote shell to use with the **-e** option. For secure transmission, you can encrypt the copy operation with SSH. Either use the **-e ssh** option or set the **RSYNC_RSH** variable to ssh.

```
rsync -avz -e ssh  /home/george/myproject   rabbit:/backup/myproject
```

You can copy from a remote host to the host you are on.

```
rsync -avz  lizard:/home/mark/mypics/  /pic-archive/markpics
```

You can also run rsync as a server daemon. This will allow remote users to synchronize copies of files on your system with versions on their own, transferring only changed files rather than entire directories. Many mirror and software FTP sites operate as rsync servers, letting you update files without have to download the full versions again. Configuration information for rsync as a server is kept in the **/etc/rsyncd.conf** file.

Tip: Though it is designed for copying between hosts, you can also use rsync to make copies within your own system, usually to a directory in another partition or hard drive. Check the rsync Man page for detailed descriptions of each.

BackupPC

BackupPC provides an easily managed local or network backup of your system or hosts, on a system using configured rsync or tar tools. There is no client application to install; just configuration files. BackupPC can backup hosts on a network, including servers, or just a single system. Data can be backed up to local hard disks or to network storage such as shared partitions or storage servers. You can configure BackupPC using your Web page configuration interface. This is the host name of your computer with the **/backuppc** name attached, like **http://richard1/backuppc**. Detailed documentation is installed at **/usr/share/doc/BackupPC**. You can find out more about BackupPC at **http://backuppc.sourceforge.net**. You can install BackupPC using the Synaptic Package Manager and from Ubuntu Software. Canonical provides critical updates.

BackupPC uses both compression and detection of identical files to reduce the size of the backup, allowing several hosts to be backed up in limited space. Once an initial backup is performed, BackupPC will only backup changed files, reducing the time of the backup significantly.

BackupPC has its own service script with which you start the BackupPC service, **/etc/init.d/backuppc**. Configuration files are located at **/etc/BackupPC**. The **config.pl** file holds BackupPC configuration options and the **hosts** file lists hosts to be backed up.

Amanda

To back up hosts connected to a network, you can use the Advanced Maryland Automatic Network Disk Archiver (Amanda) to archive hosts. Amanda uses **tar** tools to back up all hosts to a single host operating as a backup server. Backup data is sent by each host to the host operating as the Amanda server, where they are written out to a backup medium such as tape. With an Amanda server, the backup operations for all hosts become centralized in one server, instead of each host having to perform its backup. Any host that needs to restore data simply requests it from the Amanda server, specifying the file system, date, and filenames. Backup data is copied to the server's holding disk and from there, to tapes. Detailed documentation and updates are provided at **http://www.amanda.org**. For the server, be sure to install the amanda-server package, and for clients you use the amanda-clients package. You can install Amanda using the Synaptic Package

Manager, Utilities (universe) section, and from Ubuntu Software. Canonical does not provide critical updates.

Printing

This section covers the printing-configuration tools: the GNOME 3 Printers tool (GNOME Settings | Devices | Printers) and the older **system-config-printer** tool (Sundry | Print Settings). Most printers are detected for you automatically. You can use the GNOME Settings Printers tool to turn them on or off and access their print queues. As an alternative, you can still use the older **system-config-printer**. Both are front ends for the Common UNIX Printing System (CUPS), which provides printing services (**www.cups.org).**

When you attach a local printer to your system for the first time, the GNOME Printers tool automatically detects the printer and installs the appropriate driver. A message appears briefly in the message tray, indicating that a new printer has been detected. The printer is then listed in both the GNOME Settings Printers tool and in the older **system-config-printer**. If the detection fails, you can use the GNOME Settings Printers tool, accessible from GNOME Settings | Devices, to set up your printer.

Most newer printer models support driverless printing. Instead of installing a driver, the printer supports a driverless driver. You can print to any of these printers without first downloading and installing a driver for them. The printers are automatically detected through DNS Service Discovery (DNS-SD). The CUPS Web configuration interface, system-config-printer, GNOME printers, and **lpadmin** already support driverless printing.

CUPS uses the driverless utility to detect available driverless printers and to generate PPD configuration files for them. The drivers may not be as complete in features as their official drivers, but will print. Currently printers compatible with IPP Anywhere and Apple Raster supported printers can make use of driverless drivers, usually newer printers. GNOME Printer, system-config-printer, and the CUP Web interface all use the driverless tool to detect and configure driverless printers. See the man page for **driverless** for more information.

KDE provides support for adding and configuring CUPS printers through the KDE System Settings | Printer Configuration dialog. Select the Printer Configuration icon under Hardware. USB printers that are automatically detected will be listed in the KDE Printer Configuration dialog.

Printers can be local or remote. Both are referenced using Universal Resource Identifiers (URI). URIs support both network protocols used to communicate with remote printers and device connections used to reference local printers.

Remote printers are referenced by the protocol used to communicate with them, including **ipp** for the Internet Printing Protocol used for UNIX network printers, **smb** for the Samba protocol used for Windows network printers, and **lpd** for the older LPRng UNIX print servers. Their URIs are similar to a web URL, indicating the network addresses of the system the printer is connected to.

```
ipp://mytsuff.com/printers/queue1
smb://guest@lizard/myhp
```

For attached local printers, the URI will use the device connection and the device name. The usb: prefix is used for USB printers; **parallel:** is used for older printers connected to a parallel port; **serial:** is used for printers connected to a serial port; **scsi:** is used for SCSI-connected printers. For a locally attached USB printer, the URI would be something like the following:

```
usb://Canon/S330
```

GNOME Printers: GNOME Settings

The GNOME Printers tool is accessible from the GNOME Settings | Devices | Printers tab. It lists installed printers, letting you configure them and access their job queues (see Figure 14-45). If no printers are detected, an Add button is displayed on the tab, which you can use to detect your printer. To detect additional printers, you can click the Add button. The Printers tab will list entries for detected and configured printers. A printer entry displays the printer name, model, status, a jobs button with the number of jobs, and a configuration button (gear icon). the jobs button to open a dialog listing active jobs for this printer (see Figure 14-46). For each job entry there are buttons to the right to pause or remove the job.

Figure 14-45: GNOME Settings Printers tab

To configure a printer, lick the configure button (gear icon) to display a menu with entries for the printer's options, details, default, and removal (see Figure 14-47). Choosing the "Use Printer by Default", makes it your default printer. The "Remove Printer" entry remove the printer configuration from your system. The "Printer Details" entry opens a dialog with printer's details, such as the name, location, address, and driver. There are buttons for selecting a driver from a search, database, or a PPD file. Clicking on the "Printing Options" entry open the printer's options dialog (see Figure 14-47). You can configure printer features, such as page setup, image quality, and color. The Advanced tab lets you set specialized options, such as contrast, ink type, and saturation.

Figure 14-46: GNOME Printers - Jobs

Figure 14-47: GNOME Printers - Details and Options

On the Settings Printers tab, you can Add button to open the Add Printer dialog, which lists printers attached to your system (see Figure 14-48). They are detected automatically. If you know the address of a printer on your network, you can enter it in the search box at the bottom to have it detected and displayed.

Figure 14-48: GNOME Printers - add printer

Remote Printers

Most newer printers support driverless printing. Available remote printers are detected automatically, and driverless configurations generated by CUPS. To manually search for a remote printer remote printer that is attached to a Windows system or another Linux system running CUPS, you specify its location, using special URL protocols. For another CUPS printer on a remote host, the protocol used is **ipp**, for Internet Printing Protocol, whereas for a Windows printer, it would be **smb**. Older Unix or Linux systems using LPRng would use the **lpd** protocol. Be sure your firewall is configured to allow access to remote printers.

Shared Windows printers on any of the computers connected to your local network are automatically accessible once configured. Supporting Samba libraries are already installed and will let you access directly any of shared Windows printers.

Should you want to share a printer on your Ubuntu computer with users on other computers, you need to install the Samba server (Samba package) and have the Server Message

Block services enabled using the **smbd** and **nmbd** daemons. You would then use system-config-samba to configure the printers as a shared device. You can use the **systemctl** command to restart, stop, and start the services.

```
sudo systemctl restart smbd
sudo systemctl restart nmbd
```

On the GNOME Settings | Devices | Printers tab, click the Add button to open the Add Printer dialog listing Printers attached to your system. Remote printers will be automatically detected and listed. To manually add a remote printer and you know the address of the printer on your network, you can enter it in the search box at the bottom to have it detected and displayed.

Additional Printer Settings: system-config-printer

You can also use the older **system-config-printer** tool to edit a printer configuration or to add a remote printer. You can start **system-config-printer** by clicking the "Additional Printer Settings" button on the Settings | Devices | Printers tab. A printer configuration window is displayed, showing icons for installed printers. As you add printers, icons for them are displayed in the Printer configuration window (see Figure 14-49).

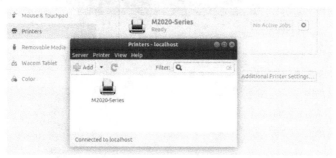

Figure 14-49: system-config-printer

To see the printer settings, such as printer and job options, access controls, and policies, double-click the printer icon or right-click and select Properties. The Printer Properties window opens with six tabs: Settings, Policies, Access Control, Printer Options, Job Options, and Ink/Toner Levels (see Figure 14-50).

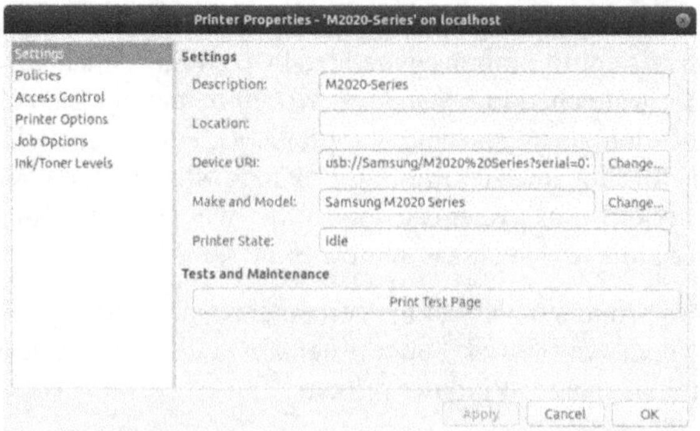

Figure 14-50: Printer Properties window

The Printer configuration window Printer menu lets you rename the printer, enable or disable it, and make it a shared printer. Select the printer icon and then click the Printer menu (see Figure 14-49). The Delete entry will remove a printer configuration. Use the Set As Default entry to make the printer a system-wide or personal default printer. There are also entries for accessing the printer properties and viewing the print queue.

The Printer icon menu is accessed by right-clicking the printer icon. If the printer is already a default, there is no Set As Default entry. The Properties entry opens the printer properties window for that printer.

The View Print Queue entry opens the Document Print Status window, which lists the jobs for that printer. You can change the queue position as well as stop or delete jobs. From the toolbar, you can choose to display printed jobs and reprint them. You will be notified if a job should fail.

To check the server settings, select Settings from the Server menu. This opens a new window showing the CUPS printer server settings. The Common UNIX Printing System (CUPS) is the server that provides printing services (**www.cups.org**).

To select a particular CUPS server, select the Connect entry in the Server menu. This opens a Connect to CUPS Server window with a drop-down menu listing all current CUPS servers from which to choose.

To add, edit, or remove printers requires root-level access. You have to enter your root user password (set up initially during installation) to edit a printer configuration, add a new printer, or remove an old one. For example, when you try to access the printer server settings, you will be prompted to enter the root user password.

Again, when you edit any printer's configuration settings, you will be prompted for authorization. Whenever you try to change a printer setting, such as its driver or URI, you are prompted to enter the root password for device authorization.

To make a printer the default, either right-click the printer icon and select Set As Default or single-click the printer icon and then, from the Printer configuration window's Printer menu, select the Set As Default entry. A Set Default Printer dialog opens with options for setting the system-wide default or setting the personal default. The system-wide default printer is the default for your entire network served by your CUPS server, not just your local system. The system-wide default printer will have a green check mark emblem on its printer icon in the Printer configuration window (see Figure 14-51).

Figure 14-51: Printer Properties window

Should you wish to use a different printer as your default, you can designate it as your personal default. To make a printer your personal default, select the entry Set as My Personal Default Printer in the Set Default Printer dialog. A personal emblem, a heart, will appear on the printer's icon in the Printer configuration window.

If you have more than one printer on your system, you can make one the default by clicking the Make Default Printer button in the printer's properties Settings pane.

The Class entry in the New menu lets you create a printer class. You can access the New menu from the Server menu or from the New button. This feature lets you select a group of printers to print a job, instead of selecting just one. That way, if one printer is busy or down, another printer can be automatically selected to perform the job. Installed printers can be assigned to different classes.

To edit an installed printer, double-click its icon in the Printer configuration window or right-click and select the Properties entry. This opens a Printer Properties window for that printer. A sidebar lists the configuration tabs. Click one to display that tab. There are configuration entries for Settings, Policies, Access Control, Printer Options, Job Options, and Ink/Toner Levels.

To install a new printer, choose the Server | New | Printer menu entry or click the Add button on the toolbar (see Figure 14-52). A New Printer window opens and displays a series of dialog boxes from which you select the connection, model, drivers, and printer name with location.

Figure 14-52: system-config-printer - New Printer

The location is specified using special URI protocols. For another CUPS printer on a remote host, the protocol used is **ipp**, for Internet Printing Protocol, whereas for a Windows printer, it is **smb**. Older UNIX and Linux systems using LPRng use the **lpd** protocol.

Configuring Remote Printers on the Desktop with system-config-printer

You can use system-config-printer to set up a remote printer on Linux, UNIX, or Windows networks. When you add a new printer or edit one, the New Printer dialog will list possible remote connection types under the Network entry. When you select a remote connection entry, a pane will be displayed to the right where you can enter configuration information.

First, you need to install the **smbclient** package, using the Synaptic Package Manager. This package is currently not installed by default.

To find any connected printers on your network automatically, click the Find Network Printer entry. Enter the hostname of the system the remote printer is connected to, then click the Find button. The host is searched and the detected printers are displayed as entries under the Network Printer heading (see Figure 14-53).

Figure 14-53: Finding a network printer

To configure a specific type of printer, choose from the available entries. For a remote Linux or UNIX printer, select either Internet Printing Protocol (ipp), which is used for newer systems, or LPD/LPR Host or Printer, which is used for older systems. Both panes display entries for the Host name and the queue. For the Host name, enter the hostname of the system that controls the printer. For an Apple or HP jet direct printer on your network, select the AppSocket/HP jetDirect entry.

A "Windows printer via Samba" printer is one located on a Windows network. You need to specify the Windows server (hostname or IP address), the name of the share, the name of the printer's workgroup, and the username and password. The format of the printer SMB URL is shown on the SMP Printer pane. The share is the hostname and printer name in the **smb** URI format *//workgroup/hostname/printername.* The workgroup is the windows network workgroup that the printer belongs to. On small networks, there is usually only one. The hostname is the computer where the printer is located. The username and password can be for the printer resource itself, or for access by a particular user. The pane will display a box at the top where you can enter the share host and printer name as an **smb** URI.

Because of the changes from SMB1 to SMB3, the Browse operation accessed by the Browse button does not work.

You also can enter in any needed Samba authentication, if required, like username or password. Check "Authentication required" to allow you to enter the Samba Username and Password. The Connections section to the lower right will list "Windows Printer via Samba" as the connection.

You then continue with install screens for the printer model, driver, and name. Once installed, you can then access the printer properties just as you would any printer.

15. Network Connections

Ubuntu will automatically detect and configure your network connections with Network Manager. Should the automatic configuration either fail or be incomplete for some reason, you can perform a manual configuration using the GNOME Settings Wi-Fi and Network tabs. If you want to make a simple dial-up modem connection, you can use WvDial. Your network will also need a firewall. UFW (with the Gufw interface) or FirewallD is recommended. Table 15-1 lists several network configuration tools.

Network Connections: Dynamic and Static

If you are on a network, you may need to obtain certain information to configure your connection interface. Most networks now support dynamic configuration using either the older Dynamic Host Configuration Protocol (DHCP) or the new IPv6 Protocol and its automatic address configuration. In this case, you need only check the DHCP entry in most network configuration tools. If your network does not support DHCP or IPv6 automatic addressing, or you are using a static connection (DCHP and IPv6 connections are dynamic), you will have to provide detailed information about your connection. For a static connection, you would enter your connection information manually such as your IP address and DNS servers, whereas in a dynamic connection this information is provided automatically to your system by a DHCP server or generated by IPv6 when you connect to the network. For DHCP, a DHCP client on each host will obtain the information from a DHCP server serving that network. IPv6 generates its addresses directly from the device and router information such as the device hardware MAC address.

Network Configuration Tool	Description
Network Manager	Used for all network connections including wired, wireless, mobile broadband, VPN, and DSL. **nmcli** is the command line interface version of Network Manager.
Network (Settings)	GNOME Network connection preferences, allowing quick connection to wired networks and proxies.
Wi-Fi (Settings)	GNOME Wi-Fi connection preferences, allowing quick connection to wireless networks.
ufw	Sets up a network firewall.
Gufw	GNOME interface for UFW firewall
FirewallD	Sets up a network firewall.
wvdial	PPP dial-up modem connection
systemd-networkd	systemd-based network configuration

Table 15-1: Ubuntu Network Configuration Tools

In addition, if you are using a dynamic DSL, ISDN, or a modem connection, you will also have to supply provider, login, and password information, and specify whether your system is dynamic or static. You may also need to supply specialized information such as DSL or modem compression methods or dialup number.

You can obtain most of your static network information from your network administrator, or from your ISP (Internet Service Provider). You would need the following information:

The device name for your network interface   For LAN and wireless connections, this is network device name, which you can find using the **ifconfig** or **ip l** commands. For a modem, DSL, or ISDN connection, this is a PPP device named **ppp0** (**ippp0** for ISDN). Virtual private network (VPN) connections are also supported.

Hostname   Your computer will be identified by this name on the Internet. Do not use localhost; that name is reserved for special use by your system. The name of the host should be a simple word, which can include numbers, but not punctuation such as periods and backslashes. On a small network, the hostname is often a single name. On a large network that could have several domains, the hostname includes both the name of the host and its domain.

Domain name   This is the name of your network.

The Internet Protocol (IP) address assigned to your machine   This is needed only for static Internet connections. Dynamic connections use the DHCP protocol to assign an IP address for you automatically. Every host on the Internet is assigned an IP address. Small and older network addresses might still use the older IPv4 format consisting of a set of four numbers, separated by periods. The IP protocol version 6, IPv6, uses a new format with a complex numbering sequence that is much more automatic.

Your network IP address   Static connections only. This address is similar to the IP address but lacks any reference to a particular host.

The netmask   IPv4 Static connections only. This is usually 255.255.255.0 for most networks. If, however, you are part of a large network, check with your network administrator or ISP.

The broadcast address for your network, if available (optional)   IPv4 Static connections only. Usually, your broadcast address is the same as your IP address with the number 255 added at the end.

The IP address of your network's gateway computer   Static connections only. This is the computer that connects your local network to a larger one like the Internet.

Name servers   The IP address of the name servers your network uses. These enable the use of URLs.

NIS domain and IP address for an NIS server   Necessary if your network uses an NIS server (optional).

User login and password information   Needed for dynamic DSL, ISDN, and modem connections.

Network Manager

Network Manager detects your network connections automatically, both wired and wireless. It uses the automatic device detection capabilities of udev to configure your connections. Should you instead need to configure your network connections manually, you can also use Network Manager to enter the required network connection information. Network Manager operates as a daemon with the name Network Manager. It will automatically scan for both wired and wireless connections. Information provided by Network Manager is made available to other applications. The Network Manager monitors your network connection, indicating its current status on the indicator (status) menu on the top panel.

Network Manager is designed to work in the background, providing status information for your connection and switching from one configured connection to another as needed. For an initial configuration, it detects as much information as possible about a new connection.

Network Manager is also user specific. When a user logs in, wireless connections the user prefers will start up (wired connections are started automatically).

User and System-Wide Network Configuration: Network Manager

Network Manager will automatically detect your network connections, both wired and wireless. It is the default method for managing your network connections. Network Manager makes use of the automatic device detection capabilities of udev to configure your connections. Should you instead have to configure your network connections manually, you would use the GNOME Settings Wi-Fi and Network tabs.

Network Manager is user specific. When a user logs in, it selects the network connection preferred by that user. For wireless connections, the user can choose from a list of current possible connections. For wired connections, a connection can be started automatically, when the system starts up. Initial settings will be supplied from the system-wide configuration.

Configurations can also be applied system-wide to all users. When editing or adding a network connection, the edit or add dialog displays an Available to All Users check box in the lower-left corner. Click this check box and then click the Apply button to make the connection configuration system-wide. A PolicyKit authentication dialog will first prompt you to enter your root password.

Network Manager can configure any network connection. This includes wired, wireless, and all manual connections. Network Interface Connection (NIC cards) hardware is detected using udev. Information provided by Network Manager is made available to other applications over D-Bus.

With multiple wireless access points for Internet connections, a system could have several different network connections to choose from, instead of a single-line connection such as DSL or cable. This is particularly true for notebook computers that access different wireless connections at different locations. Instead of manually configuring a new connection each time one is encountered, the Network Manager tool can automatically configure and select a connection to use.

By default, an Ethernet connection will be preferred, if available. For wireless connections, you will have to choose the one you want.

Network Manager is designed to work in the background, providing status information for your connection and switching from one configured connection to another, as needed. For initial configuration, it detects as much information as possible about the new connection.

Network Manager operates as a daemon with the name NetworkManager. If no Ethernet connection is available, Network Manager will scan for wireless connections, checking for Extended Service Set Identifiers (ESSIDs). If an ESSID identifies a previously used connection, then it is automatically selected. If several are found, then the most recently used one is chosen. If only a new connection is available, the Network Manager waits for the user to choose one. A connection is selected only if the user is logged in. If an Ethernet connection is later made, the Network Manager will switch to it from wireless.

The NetworkManager daemon can be turned on or off, using the **systemctl** command as the root user.

```
sudo systemctl start NetworkManager
sudo systemctl stop NetworkManager
```

Network Manager Manual Configuration using GNOME Network

The GNOME Network configuration is available on GNOME Settings, can be used to configure all your network connections manually. Automatic wireless and wired connections were covered in Chapter 3. On the GNOME Settings dialog there is a Wi-Fi tab for wireless configuration and a Network tab for wired, VPN, and proxy configurations (see Figure 15-1). On the Wi-Fi tab, an Airplane Mode switch and a list of visible wireless connections are listed to the right. The currently active connection will have a checkmark next to its name. On the top right bar is a switch for turning wireless on and off. A menu to the right of the switch list entries for connections to hidden networks, turning your computer's Wi-Fi hotspot capability, and listing previously accessed Wi-Fi Networks.

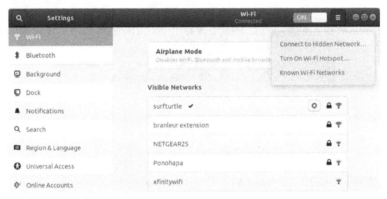

Figure 15-1: Wi-Fi (GNOME Settings)

Selecting an entry in the Visible Networks list will create a gear button for it, which you can click to open the network configuration dialog with tabs for Details, Security, Identity, IPv4, IPv6, and Reset. The Details tab show strength, speed, security methods, IP and hardware addresses, routes, and the DNS server IP address (see Figure 15-2). It also has a "Forget Connection" button for removing this Wi-Fi connection information.

Figure 15-2: Wi-Fi (GNOME Settings) - Details tab

To edit the connection manually, you use the Security, Identity, and IP tabs. The Security tab displays a menu from which you can choose a security method and a password (see Figure 15-3).

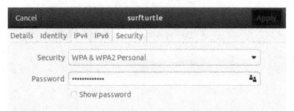

Figure 15-3: Wi-Fi (GNOME Settings) - Security tab

On the Identity tab, you can specify the SSID name, choose a firewall zone, and choose to connect automatically when you log in and whether to make the connection system-wide (available to other users; see Figure 15-4).

Figure 15-4: Wi-Fi (GNOME Settings) - Identity tab

On the IPv4 Settings tab, a switch allows you to turn the IP connection on or off. There are sections for Addresses, the DNS servers, and Routes. An Addresses menu lets you choose the type connection you want. By default, it is set to Automatic. If you change it to Manual, new entries appear for the address, netmask, and gateway (see Figure 15-5). On the IPv6 tab, the netmask is replaced by prefix. You can turn off Automatic switches for the DNS and Routes sections to make them manual. The DNS section has a plus button to let you add more DNS servers.

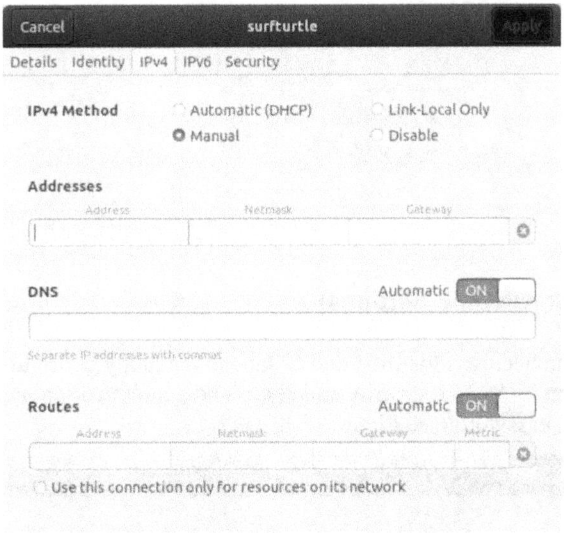

Figure 15-5: Wi-Fi (GNOME Settings) - IPv4 tab, Manual

For a wired connection, click the Network tab on GNOME Settings to display lists for Wired, VPN, and Network Proxy. The Wired list shows your current wired connections with on and off switched for each. A plus button at the top right of the Wired list lets you add more wired connections. Next to a connection's switch a gear button is displayed (see Figure 15-6). Clicking the gear button opens a configuration dialog with tabs for Details, Identity, IPv4, IPv6, and Security (see Figure 15-7).

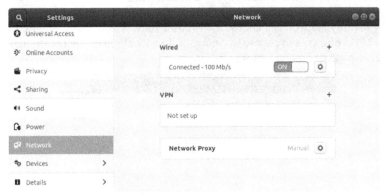

Figure 15-6: Network (GNOME Settings)

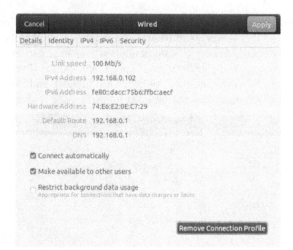

Figure 15-7: Network (GNOME Settings)

You can use the Security, Identity, and IP tabs to manually configure the connection. The Security tab lets you turn on 802.1x security and choose an authentication method, as well as provide a username and password (see Figure 15-8).

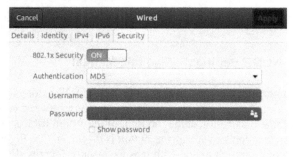

Figure 15-8: Network (GNOME Settings) - Security tab

On the Identity tab, you can choose the firewall zone, set the name, choose the hardware address, set the MTU blocks, and choose to connect automatically and whether to make the connection system-wide (see Figure 15-9).

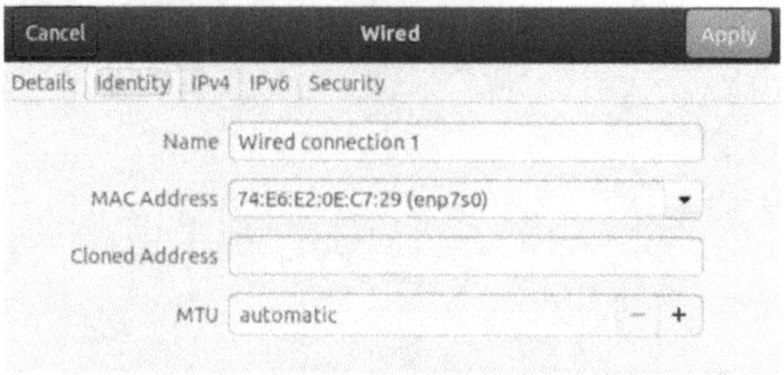

Figure 15-9: Network (GNOME Settings) - Identity tab

On the IP tabs, a switch allows you to turn the connection on or off. The tab has sections for Addresses, DNS servers, and Routes. DNS and Routes have a switch for automatic. Turning the switch off allows you to manually enter a DNS server address or routing information. From the Method set of options at the top, you can also choose to make the connection automatic, manual, link-local, or to disable it. When manual, new entries appear that let you enter the address, netmask, and gateway (see Figure 15-10). On the IPv6 tab, the netmask entry is replaced by a prefix entry.

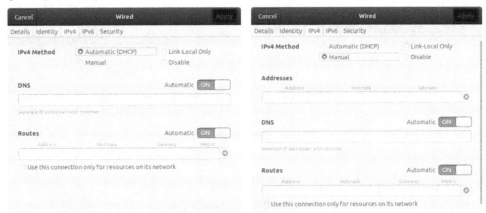

Figure 15-10: Network (GNOME Settings) - IPv4 tab

For VPN connections, click the plus button at the top right of the VPN list to open an Add VPN dialog. The dialog lists supported VPN connection types, such as Point-to-Point or OpenVPN (see Figure 15-11). The Bond, Bridge, and VLAN entries open the Network Connections dialogs for those connections.

Figure 15-11: Network (GNOME Settings), new connections and VPN connections

You can then configure the VPN connections in the "Add VPN" dialog, which shows three tabs: Identity, IPv4, and IPv6 (see Figure 15-12). The IP tabs are the same as for wireless and wired configuration dialogs. On the Identity tab, you can enter the name, gateway, and authentication information. Click the Advanced button for detailed connection configuration.

Several VPN services are available. The PPTP service for Microsoft VPN connections is installed by default. Other popular VPN services include OpenVPN, Cisco Concentrator, and

Openswan (IPSec). Network Manager support is installed using the corresponding Network Manager plugin for these services. The plugin packages begin with the name **network-manager**. To use the **openvpn** service, first install the **openvpn** software along with the **network-manager-openvpn** plugin. For Cisco Concentrator based VPN, us the **network-manager-vpnc** plugin. Strongswan uses the **network-manager-strongswan** plugin.

Figure 15-12: Network (GNOME Settings) OpenVPN connection

Network Manager Manual Configuration Using Network Connections

You can also use the older Network Connections utility (**nm-connection-editor**) to edit any network connection. You may have to run it from a terminal window. Established connections are listed, with at toolbar at the bottom for adding, removing, and editing network connections (see Figure 15-13). Your current network connections should already be listed.

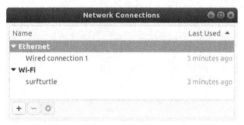

Figure 15-13: Network configuration (nm-connection-editor)

When you add a connection, you can choose its type from a drop-down menu. The menu organizes connection types into three categories: Hardware, Virtual, and VPN. Hardware connections cover both wired (Ethernet, DSL, and InfiniBand) and wireless (Wi-Fi, WiMAX, and Mobile Broadband) connections. VPN lists the supported VPN types, such as OpenVPN, PPTP, and Cisco. You can also import a previously configured connection. Virtual supports VLAN and Bond virtual connections.

Configuration editing dialogs display a General tab from which you can make your configuration available to all users and automatically connect when the network connection is available. You can also choose to use a VPN connection and specify a firewall zone.

Editing an Ethernet connection opens an Editing window. The Create button on the "Choose a Connection Type" dialog is used to add a new connection and opens a similar window, with no settings. The Ethernet tab lists the MAC hardware address and the MTU. The MTU is usually set to automatic. The standard default configuration for a wired Ethernet connection uses DHCP. Connect automatically will set up the connection when the system starts up. There are seven tabs, General, Ethernet, 8.02.1x Security, DCB, Proxy, IPv4 Settings, and IPv6 Settings. The IPv4 Settings tab lets you select the kind of wired connection you have. The manual configuration entries for an IPv4 connection are shown in Figure 15-14. Click the Add button to enter the IP address, network mask, and gateway address. Then enter the address for the DNS servers and your network search domains. The Routes button will open a window in which you can manually enter any network routes.

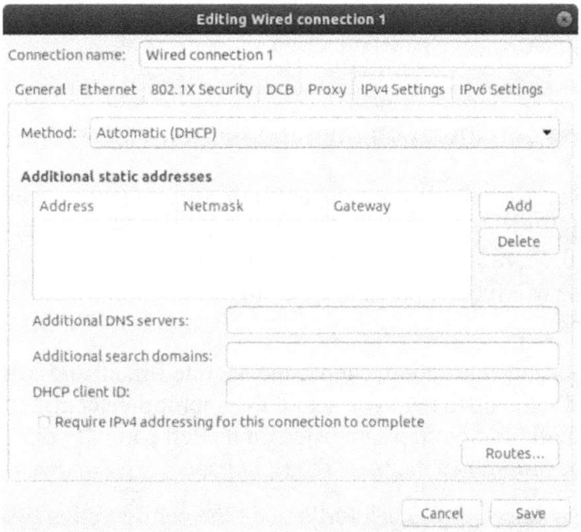

Figure 15-14: IPv4 wired configuration (nm-connection-editor)

For a wireless connection, you enter wireless configuration data, such as your ESSID, password, and encryption method. For wireless connections, you choose Wi-Fi or WiMAX as the connection type. The Editing Wi-Fi connection window opens with tabs for general configuration, your wireless information, security, proxy, and IP settings (see Figure 15-15). On the Wi-Fi tab, you specify your SSID, along with your mode and MAC address.

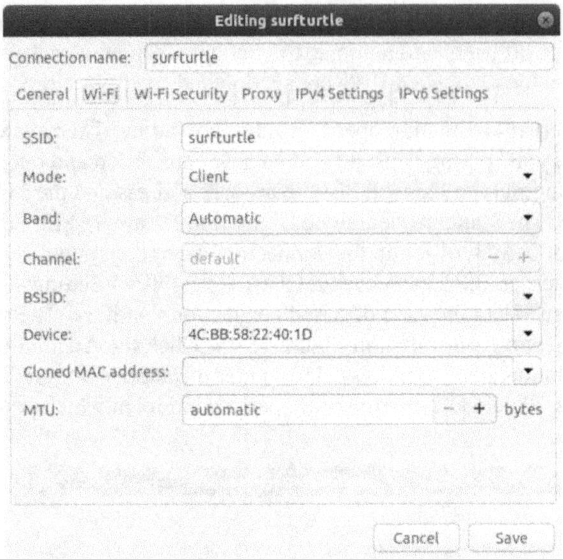

Figure 15-15: Wireless configuration (nm-connection-editor)

On the Wi-Fi Security tab, you enter your wireless connection security method. The commonly used method, WEP, is supported, along with WPA personal. The WPA personal method only requires a password. More secure connections, such as Dynamic WEP and Enterprise WPA, are also supported. These will require much more configuration information, such as authentication methods, certificates, and keys.

For a new broadband connection, choose the Mobile Broadband entry in the connection type menu. A 3G wizard starts up to help you set up the appropriate configuration for your particular 3G service. Configuration steps are listed on the left pane. If your device is connected, you can select it from the drop-down menu on the right pane.

Once a service is selected, you can further edit the configuration by clicking its entry in the Mobile Broadband tab and clicking the Edit button. The Editing window opens with tabs for Mobile Broadband, PPP, IPv4, and IPv6 settings. On the Mobile Broadband tab, you can enter your number, username, and password. Advanced options include the APN, Network, and PIN. The APN should already be entered.

On the Network Manager panel applet menu, the VPN Connection entry submenu will list configured VPN connections for easy access. The Configure VPN entry will open the Network Connections window to the VPN section, from which you can then add, edit, or delete VPN connections. The Disconnect VPN entry will end the current active VPN connection. To add a VPN connection, choose a VPN connection type from the connection type menu.

The Editing VPN Connection dialog opens with two tabs: VPN and IPv4 Settings. On the VPN tab, you enter VPN connection information, such as the gateway address and any additional VPN information that may be required. For an OpenVPN connection, you will have to provide the authentication type, certificates, and keys. Clicking the Advanced button opens the Advanced Options dialog. An OpenVPN connection will have tabs for General, Security, and TLS Authentication. On the Security tab, you can specify the cipher to use.

Network Manager wireless router, using your wireless connection as a Hotspot and for a Hidden Network.

You can set up your wireless connection as a wireless router for your own wireless network. The "Turn On Wi-Fi Hotspot" entry in the Wi-Fi menu opens a dialog letting you set up your computer as a wireless router that other computers can connect to (see Figure 15-16) .

Figure 15-16: Turn on Wi-Fi Hotspot

The wireless network you created will not perform any SSID broadcasting. You access it through the "Connect to Hidden Network" entry on the network menu. This opens the "Connect to Hidden Wi-Fi Network" window (see Figure 15-17).

Figure 15-17: Connect to a Hidden Wi-Fi Network

Managing Network Connections with nmcli

The **nmcli** command is NetworkManager Command Line Interface command. Most network configuration tasks can be performed by **nmcli**. The **nmcli** command manages NetworkManager through a set of objects: general (**g**), networking (**n**), radio (**r**), connection (**c**), device (**d**), and agent (**a**). Each can be referenced using the full name or a unique prefix, such as **con** for connection or **dev** for device. The unique prefix can be as short as a single character, such as **g** for general, **c** for connections, or **d** for device. See Table 15-2 for a list of the objects and commonly used options. The **nmcli** man page provides a complete listing with examples.

The general object shows the current status of NetworkManager and what kind of devices are enabled. You can limit the information displayed using the **-t** (terse) and **-f** (field) options. The STATE field show the connection status, and the CONNECTIVITY field the connection.

Object	Description
general	NetworkManager status and enabled devices. Use the terse (**-t**) and field (**-f**) option to limit the information displayed.
networking	Manage networking, use `on` and `off` to turn networking on or off, and `connectivity` for the connection state.
radio	Turns on or off the wireless networking (on or off). Can turn on or off specific kinds of wireless: `wifi`, `wwan` (mobile broadband), and `wimax`. The `all` option turns on or off all wireless.
connection	Manage network connections.
	`show` List connection profiles. With `--active` show only active connections.
	`up` Activate a connection
	`down` Deactivate a connection
	`add` Add a new connection, specifying `type`, `ifname`, `con-name` (profile).
	`modify` Edit an existing connection, use + and – to add new values to properties
	`edit` Add a new connection or edit an existing one using the interactive editor
	`delete` Delete a configured connection (profile)
	`reload` Reload all connection profiles
	`load` Reload or load a specific
device	Manage network interfaces (devices).
	`status` Display device status
	`show` Display device information
	`connect` Connect the device
	`disconnect` Disconnect the device
	`delete` Delete a software device, such as a bridge.
	`wifi` Display a list of available wifi access points
	`wifi rescan` Rescan for and display access points
	`wifi connect` Connect to a wifi network; specify `password`, `wep-key-type`, `ifname`, `bssid`, and `name` (profile name)
	`wimax` List available WiMAX networks
agent	Run as a Network Manager secret agent or polkit agent.
	`secret` As a secret agent, nmcli listens for secret requests.
	`polkit` As a polkit agent it listens for all authorization requests.

Table 15-2: The nmcli objects

```
$ nmcli general
STATE         CONNECTIVITY  WIFI-HW  WIFI     WWAN-HW  WWAN
connected     full          enabled  enabled  enabled  enabled

$ nmcli -t -f STATE general
connected
```

The **connection** object references the network connection and the **show** option displays that information. The following example displays your current connection.

```
nmcli connection show
```

You can use **c** instead of **connection** and **s** instead of show.

```
$ nmcli c s
NAME        UUID                                   TYPE            DEVICE
enp7s0      f7202f6d-fc66-4b81-8962-69b71202efc0   802-3-ethernet  enp7s0
AT&T LTE 1  65913b39-789a-488c-9559-28ea6341d9e1   gsm             --
```

As with the general object, you can limit the fields displayed using the **-f** option. The following only list the name and type fields.

```
$ nmcli -f name, type c s
NAME        TYPE
enp7s0      802-3-ethernet
AT&T LTE 1  gsm
```

Adding the **--active** option will only show active connections.

```
nmcli c s --active
```

To start and stop a connection (like **ifconfig** does), use the **up** and **down** options.

```
nmcli con up enp7s0.
```

Use the **device** object to manage your network devices. The **show** and **status** options provide information about your devices. To check the status of all your network devices use the **device** object and **status** options:

```
nmcli device status
DEVICE  TYPE      STATE         CONNECTION
enp7s0  ethernet  connected     enp7s0
wlp6s0  wifi      disconnected  --
lo      loopback  unmanaged     --
```

You can abbreviate **device** and **status** to **d** and **s**.

```
nmcli d s
```

You also use the **device** object to connect and disconnect devices. Use the **connect** or **disconnect** options with the interface name (ifname) of the device, in this example, **enp7s0**. With the **delete** option, you can remove a device.

```
nmcli device disconnect enp7s0
nmcli device connect enp7s0
```

To turn networking on or off you use the **networking** object and the **on** and **off** options. Use the **connectivity** option to check network connectivity. The networking object alone tells you if it is enabled or not.

```
$ nmcli networking
enabled

$ nmcli networking on

$ nmcli networking connectivity
full
```

Should you want to just turn on or off the Wifi connection, you would use the **radio** object. Use **wifi**, **wwan**, and **wimax** for a specific type of wifi connection and the **all** option for all of them. The radio object alone shows wifi status of all your wifi connection types.

```
$ nmcli radio
WIFI-HW   WIFI   WWAN-HW   WWAN
enabled   enabled   enabled   enabled

$ nmcli radio wifi on

$ nmcli radio all off
```

nmcli Wired Connections

You can use **nmcli** to add connections, just as you can with the desktop NetworkManager tool. To add a new static connection use the connection object with the **add** option. Specify the connection's profile name with the **con-name** option, the interface name with the **ifname** option, the **type**, such as ethernet. For a static connection you would add the IP address (**ipv4** or **ipv6**), and the gateway address (**gw4** or **gw6**). For a DHCP connection simply do not list the IP address and gateway options. The profile name can be any name. You could have several profile names for the same network device. For example, for your wireless device, you could have several wireless connection profiles, depending on the different networks you want to connect to. Should you connect your Ethernet device to a different network, you would simply use a different connection profile that you have already set up, instead of manually reconfiguring the connection. If you do not specify a connection name, one is generated and assigned for you. The connection name can be the same as the device name as shown here, but keep in mind that the connection name refers to the profile and the device name refers to the actual device.

```
$ nmcli c s
NAME       UUID                                    TYPE            DEVICE
enp7s0     f7202f6d-fc66-4b81-8962-69b71202efc0    802-3-ethernet  enp7s0
```

For a DHCP connection, specify the profile name, connection type, and ifname. The following example creates an Ethernet connection with the profile name "my-wired."

```
nmcli con add con-name my-wired type ethernet ifname enp7s0
```

For a static connection add the IP (**ip4** or **ip6**) and gateway (**gw4** or **gw6**) options with their addresses.

```
nmcli con add con-name my-wired-static ifname enp7s0 type ethernet ip4
192.168.1.0/24 gw4 192.168.1.1
```

In most cases, the type is Ethernet (wired) or wifi (wireless). Check the **nmcli** man page for a list of other types, such as gsm, infiniband, vpn, vlan, wimax, and bridge.

You can also add a connection using the interactive editor. Use the **edit** instead of the **add** option, and specify the **con-name** (profile) and connection type.

```
nmcli con edit type ethernet con-name my-wired
```

To modify an existing connection, use the **modify** option. For an IP connection, the property that is changed is referenced as part of the IP settings, in this example, **ip4**. The IP properties include addresses, gateway, and method (ip4.addresses, ip4.gateway, and ip4.method).

```
nmcli con mod my-wired ip4.gateway 192.168.1.2
```

To add or remove a value for a property use the + and - signs as a prefix. To add a DNS server address you would use **+ip4.dns**. To remove one use **-ip4.dns**.

```
nmcli con mod my-wired +ip4.dns 192.168.1.5
```

You can also modify a connection using the interactive editor. Use the edit instead of the modify option with the connection name.

```
nmcli con edit enp7s0
```

You are then placed in the interactive editor with an **nmcli>** prompt and the settings you can change are listed. The **help** command lists available commands. Use the **describe** command to show property descriptions.

Use **print** to show the current value of a property and **set** to change its value. To see all the properties for a setting, use the print command and the setting name. Once you have made changes, use the **save** command to effect the changes.

```
print ipv4
print ipv4.dns
print connection
set ipv4.address 192.168.0.1
```

The connection edit command can also reference a profile using the **id** option. The Name field in the connection profile information is the same as the ID. Also, each profile is given a unique system UUID, which can also be used to reference the profile.

Once you are finished editing the connection, enter the **quit** command to leave the editor.

nmcli Wireless Connections

To see a list of all the available wifi connections in your area, you use the **wifi** option with the **device** object. You can further qualify it by interface (if you have more than one) by adding the **ifname** option, and by BSSID adding the **bssid** option.

```
nmcli device wifi
```

To connect to a new Wifi network, use the **wifi connect** option and the SSID. You can further specify a password, wep-key-type, key, ifname, bssid, name (profile name), and if it is private. If you do not provide a name (profile name), nmcli will generate one for you.

```
nmcli dev wifi connect surfturtle password mypass wep-key-type wpa ifname wlp6s0
name my-wireless1
```

To reconnect to a Wifi network for which you have previously set up a connection, use the **connection** object with the **up** command and the **id** option to specify the profile name.

```
nmcli connection up id my-wireless1
```

You can also add a new wireless connection using the **connection** object and the **wifi** type with the **ssid** option.

```
nmcli con add con-name my-wireless2 ifname wlp6s0 type wifi ssid ssidname
```

Then, to set the encryption type use the **modify** command to set the **sec.key-mgmt** property, and for the passphrase set the **wifi-sec.psk** property.

```
nmcli con mod my-wirless2 wifi-sec.key-mgmt wpa-psk
nmcli con modify my-wireless2 wifi-sec.psk mypassword
```

Variable	Description
Inherits	Explicitly inherits from the specified section. By default, sections inherit from the [Dialer Defaults] section.
Modem	The device wvdial should use as your modem. The default is **/dev/modem**.
Baud	The speed at which wvdial communicates with your modem. The default is 57,600 baud.
Init1...Init9	Specifies the initialization strings to be used by your modem; wvdial can use up to 9. The default is "ATZ" for Init1.
Phone	The phone number you want wvdial to dial.
Area Code	Specifies the area code, if any.
Dial Prefix	Specifies any needed dialing prefix—for example, 70 to disable call waiting or 9 for an outside line.
Dial Command	Specifies the dial operation. The default is "ATDT".
Login	Specifies the username you use at your ISP.
Login Prompt	If your ISP has an unusual login prompt, you can specify it here.
Password	Specifies the password you use at your ISP.
Password Prompt	If your ISP has an unusual password prompt, you can specify it here.
Force Address	Specifies a static IP address to use (for ISPs that provide static IP addresses to users).
Auto Reconnect	If enabled, wvdial attempts to reestablish a connection automatically if you are randomly disconnected by the other side. This option is on by default.

Table 15-3: Variables for wvdial

Dial-up PPP Modem Access: wvdial

For direct dial-up PPP modem connections, you can use the wvdial dialer, an intelligent dialer that, not only dials up an ISP service but also performs login operations, supplying your username and password. The wvdial tool runs on the command line using the wvdial command, and on the desktop with the GNOME PPP application. The wvdial program first loads its configuration from the **/etc/wvdial.conf** file. In this file, you can place modem and account information, including modem speed, ISP phone number, username, and password.

The **wvdial.conf** file is organized into sections, beginning with a section label enclosed in brackets. A section holds variables for different parameters that are assigned values, such as **username = chris**. The default section holds default values inherited by other sections, so you need not repeat them. Table 15-3 lists the wvdial variables.

You can use the **wvdialconf** utility to create a default **wvdial.conf** file, detecting your modem and setting default values for basic features automatically. You can then edit the **wvdial.conf** file and modify the Phone, Username, and Password entries entering your dial-up information. Remove the preceding semicolon (**;**) to unquote the entry. Any line beginning with a semicolon is ignored as a comment.

You can also create a named dialer. This is helpful if you have different location or services you log in to.

To start wvdial, enter the command **wvdial** in a terminal window, which then reads the connection configuration information from the **/etc/wvdial.conf** file; wvdial dials the location and initiates the PPP connection, providing your username and password when requested.

You can set up connection configurations for any number of connections in the **/etc/wvdial.conf** file. To select one, enter its label as an argument to the **wvdial** command, as shown here:

```
wvdial mylocation
```

Netplan

Netplan is used to configure and set up your network connections. The **/etc/netplan** directory holds network service and interface information for configuring your network device. The actual configuration file is generated when the system starts up and placed in the **/var/run/systemd/network** directory. There is no fixed configuration file in the **/etc** directory. Instead a simple Netplan configuration file in the **/etc/netplan** directory is used to generate the network configuration file. The **/etc/netplan** files are written using YAML (YAML Ain't Markup Language) and have the extension **.yaml**. This method provides a level of abstraction that make configuration of different available network devices much more flexible. The default network service is **networkd**, which is used for the Ubuntu server. But you could use NetworkManager (network-manager) instead if you want. You can find out more about Netplan at:

```
https://netplan.io
```

Use the **networkctl status** command to check on the status of your network connections.

```
networkctl status
```

For information about a specific device add the device name to the status command.

```
networkctl status enp7s0
```

Detailed examples of Netplan configurations files can be found at:

```
/usr/share/doc/netplan.io/examples
```

These include examples for static, wireless, NetworkManager, dhcp, bridge, bonding, and vlans.

Netplan configuration file

The Netplan configuration files are located in the **/etc/netplan** directory. The Ubuntu Desktop version generates a Netplan configuration file for NetworkManager, **01-network-manager-all.yaml**. NetworkManager is the default for the Ubuntu desktop. You can edit this file to add configuration for more devices, or you can add more configuration files, each of which will be read by Netplan and a corresponding runtime configuration file generated in the **/var/run/systemd/network** directory. As NetworkManager is designed to configure multiple devices, you only need the one Netplan configuration file. But for other network managers such as networkd-systemd, you could have files for different types of network devices such as ethernet and Wi-Fi, or a different file for each device. Configuration file names usually begin with number, starting with **1-** for the default, though they can be any name. An easy way to create a new file is to copy the default or an example file from **/usr/share/doc/netplan.io/examples** and then edit it.

A Netplan configuration file is organized into keys consisting of upper level configuration definitions that apply to different types of devices such as ethernets, and lower level IDs that are used to configure devices. The file begins with the top-level **network:** key followed by the Netplan version, in this case, version 2. The **renderer:** ID specifies the network service to use. For the Ubuntu desktop this is **NetworkManager**. Ubuntu uses NetworkManager by default instead of systemd-networkd, which greatly simplifies it default Netplan configuration file. The file holds only the renderer information, as NetworkManager handles all the details. You would use the Settings Network or Network Connections to configure your network.

/etc/netplan/01-network-manager-all.yaml

```
# Let NetworkManager manage all devices on this system
network:
  version: 2
  renderer: NetworkManager
```

For other types of connections such as systemd-networkd, there are additional keys you can use. For a wired connection, the configuration type is **ethernets:** Under **ethernets:** the keys for the available network devices are listed. Under each device are the IDs used to configure it. In the case of a DHCP connection you usually only need one, **dhcp:** Other IDs such as **address:** for a static connection or **gateway:** for a gateway address could also be listed. An sample configuration is shown here.

The run time configuration files for NetworkManager are in the **/run/NetworkManager/system-connections** directory and have the name netplan with the device name, such as **netplan-enp7s0**.

Configure a network with systemd-networkd

The systemd based network manager called **systemd-networkd** can currently be used for basic operations. You would use it as a small, fast, and simple alternative to a larger manager such as NetworkManager. systemd is described in detail in Chapter 5. The service, target, and socket files for systemd-networkd are located in the **/lib/systemd/system**: **systemd-networkd.service**, **systemd-networkd.target**, and **systemd-networkd.socket.** Network resolvconf operations are handled with **systemd-resolved.service**. User configuration files for systemd-networkd are located in **/etc/systemd/network**.

In the **systemd-networkd.service** file several security features are enabled. A capability bounding set (CapabilityBoundingSet) lets you limit kernel capabilities to those specified. The man page for **capabilities** list the available capabilities. The CAP_NET capabilities limit the networkd service to network operations such as interface configuration, firewall administration, multicasting, sockets, broadcasting, and proxies. The CAP_SET capabilities allow for file and process GID and UIDs. The CAP_CHOWN, CAP_DAC_OVERRIDE, and CAP_FOWNER capabilities deal with bypassing permission checks for files. The CAP_SYS capabilities that provide system administrative capabilities are not included. In addition, the ProtectSystem option (**systemd.exec**) prevents the service from making any changes to the system (**/usr**, **/boot**, and **/etc** directories are read only for this service). The ProtectHome option makes the **/home**, **/root**, and **/run/user** directories inaccessible. WatchdogSec sets the watchdog timeout for the service. Check the **systemd.directives** man page for a list of all systemd directives.

systemd-networkd.service

```
[Unit]
Description=Network Service
Documentation=man:systemd-networkd.service(8)
ConditionCapability=CAP_NET_ADMIN
DefaultDependencies=no
# dbus.service can be dropped once on kdbus, and systemd-udevd.service can be
# dropped once tuntap is moved to netlink
After=systemd-udevd.service dbus.service network-pre.target systemd-
sysusers.service systemd-sysctl.service
Before=network.target multi-user.target shutdown.target
Conflicts=shutdown.target
Wants=network.target

# On kdbus systems we pull in the busname explicitly, because it
# carries policy that allows the daemon to acquire its name.
Wants=org.freedesktop.network1.busname
After=org.freedesktop.network1.busname

[Service]
Type=notify
Restart=on-failure
RestartSec=0
ExecStart=/lib/systemd/systemd-networkd
CapabilityBoundingSet=CAP_NET_ADMIN CAP_NET_BIND_SERVICE CAP_NET_BROADCAST
CAP_NET_RAW CAP_SETUID CAP_SETGID CAP_SETPCAP CAP_CHOWN CAP_DAC_OVERRIDE
CAP_FOWNER
ProtectSystem=full
ProtectHome=yes
WatchdogSec=3min

[Install]
WantedBy=multi-user.target
Also=systemd-networkd.socket
```

The **systemd-networkd.socket** file sets **systemd.socket** options for buffer size (ReceiveBuffer), network link (ListenNetlink), passing credentials (PassCredentials). As a condition for starting the service, the CAP_NET_ADMIN capability needs to be set in the capability bounding set (ConditionCapability).

systemd-networkd.socket

```
[Unit]
Description=Network Service Netlink Socket
Documentation=man:systemd-networkd.service(8) man:rtnetlink(7)
ConditionCapability=CAP_NET_ADMIN
DefaultDependencies=no
Before=sockets.target

[Socket]
ReceiveBuffer=8M
ListenNetlink=route 1361
PassCredentials=yes

[Install]
WantedBy=sockets.target
```

The **systemd-resolved.service** provides for the resolvconf operations (DNS server information). It has the same capabilities as **systemd-neworkd.service**, except for the network capabilities.

systemd-resolved.service

```
[Unit]
Description=Network Name Resolution
Documentation=man:systemd-resolved.service(8)
After=systemd-networkd.service network.target

# On kdbus systems we pull in the busname explicitly, because it
# carries policy that allows the daemon to acquire its name.
Wants=org.freedesktop.resolve1.busname
After=org.freedesktop.resolve1.busname

[Service]
Type=notify
Restart=always
RestartSec=0
ExecStart=/lib/systemd/systemd-resolved
CapabilityBoundingSet=CAP_SETUID CAP_SETGID CAP_SETPCAP CAP_CHOWN
CAP_DAC_OVERRIDE CAP_FOWNERs
ProtectSystem=full
ProtectHome=yes
WatchdogSec=3min

[Install]
WantedBy=multi-user.target
```

In addition, the **systemd-networkd-resolvconf-update.service** updates the DNS information. The **systemd-networkd-wait-online.service** delays activation of other services, until **systemd-networkd** service comes online.

The systemd-networkd Netplan configuration file

You have to create a Netplan configuration file for the systemd-networkd service. You could have files for different types of network devices such as ethernet and Wi-Fi, or a different file for each device. Configuration file names usually begin with number, starting with **1-** for the default, though they can be any name.

You would then have to know how networking on your system is configured. For many systems, especially those using DHCP, this is a simple configuration, but for others, such as a static connection, it can be complex. For a system using a standard DHCP connection, as shown in this chapter, you can simply copy the **dhcp.yaml** file from the **/usr/share/doc/netplan.io/examples** directory to the **/etc/netplan** directory. Prefix the file name with a number, such as 2-. You can leave the **01-network-manager.yaml** file in **/etc/netplan** in case you should want to switch back to using NetworkManager

```
cd /usr/share/doc/netplan.io/examples
sudo cp dhcp.yaml /etc/netplan/02-dhcp.yaml
```

If you do not know it already, find out the name of your Ethernet device with **ip link** command. Then use a text editor like **nano** to edit the **02-dhcp.yaml** and replace the name of ethernet device, **enp3s0**, with the name of the one on your system. You can use the **ifconfig** command to find the name or your device. Be sure to use the **sudo** command to start the editor.

```
cd /etc/netplan
sudo nano 02-dhcp.yaml
```

A Netplan configuration file is organized into keys consisting of upper level configuration definitions that apply to different types of devices such as ethernets, and lower level IDs that are used to configure devices. The file begins with the top-level **network:** key followed by the Netplan version, in this case, version 2. The **renderer:** ID specifies the network service to use. For the Ubuntu server this is the netplan default, **networkd**. For a wired connection, the configuration type is **ethernets:**, as shown in this example. Under **ethernets:** the keys for the available network devices are listed. Under each device are the IDs used to configure it. In the case of a DHCP connection you usually only need one, **dhcp:** Other IDs such as **address:** for a static connection or **gateway:** for a gateway address could also be listed. The final would look something like the following.

/etc/netplan/02-dhcp.yaml

```
network:
  version: 2
  renderer: networkd
  ethernets:
    enp7s0:
      dhcp4: true
```

The runtime file generated by Netplan for network configuration will be located in **/var/run/systemd/network** and will have a name that includes "netplan" and the network device name, such as **10-netplan-enp7s0.network**. This file is generated automatically at startup. If you have edited the Netplan configuration file or added a new one, and do not wish to restart your system, you can use the Netplan **generate** command to create the run time configuration file directly, and then use the **apply** command to have Netplan apply that configuration to your network connections.

```
sudo netplan generate
sudo netplan apply
```

You then have to shut down and disable NetworkManager. The service script for managing NetworkManager is **network-manager**.

```
sudo systemctl stop network-manager
sudo systemctl disable network-manager
```

Then enable and start systemd-networkd.

```
sudo systemctl enable systemd-networkd
sudo systemctl start systemd-networkd
```

You can check the status of your network device configuration and activation with the **networkctl** command.

```
networkctl
```

Netplan wireless configuration for systemd-networkd

For systemd-networkd wireless devices you have to edit your Netplan configuration file to add your wireless device name, the wireless network you want to access, and the password for that network. Instead of editing the default file directly, you can copy the **02-dhcp.yaml** file with the 2 changed to 3 and give it a name such as **03-wireless.yaml**. Netplan will read any **yaml** file in the **/etc/netplan** directory. You can find an example of a wireless configuration file at **/usr/share/doc/netplan.io/examples**, but it is for the network that does not support dhcp and is more complicated.

```
cd /etc/netplan
sudo cp 2-dhcp.yaml 03-wireless.yaml
```

Then edit the file to add keys for Wi-Fi, accesspoints, the SSID, and the password.

```
sudo nano 3-wireless.yaml
```

An example of a wireless Netplan configuration is shown below. Instead of the **ethernets:** definition you use the **wifis:** definition. This is followed by a key consisting of the wireless device name, such as **wlp6s0:**. Below that key is the **dhcp4:** ID and the **accesspoints:** ID, used to configure the Wi-Fi device. Under the accesspoints: ID you add an ID consisting of the SSID of the wireless network you want to connect to (the wireless network's name). The SSID must be within quotes. Under this ID you add the **password:** ID and the password for accessing that wireless network. The password must be within quotes.

/etc/netplan/03-wireless.yaml

```
network:
  version: 2
  renderer: networkd
  wifis:
    wlp6s0:
      dhcp4: true
        accesspoints:
          "SSID":
              password: "password"
```

Netplan generates a wireless configuration file at startup in **/run/netplan**. A wireless file will have the name of the device added along with the name of wireless network (SSID), such as **netplan-wlp6s0-surfturtle**.

This file is then use the by **netplan-wpa@service** to submit the SSID and password to **wpa_supplicant**, which then accesses the wireless network. The **netplan-wpa@.service** file is shown here.

netplan-wpa@.service

```
[Unit]
Description=WPA supplicant for netplan %I
Requires=sys-subsystem-net-devices-%i.device
After=sys-subsystem-net-devices-%i.device
Before=network.target
Wants=network.target

[Service]
Type=simple
ExecStart=/sbin/wpa_supplicant -c /run/netplan/wpa-%I.conf -i%I
```

If you reboot, the wireless netplan file will be read and your wireless device configured. To configure your device without rebooting, you can use the Netplan **generate** command to create the run time configuration file directly (**/var/run/systemd/network**), and then use the **apply** command to have Netplan apply that configuration to your network connection.

```
sudo netplan generate
sudo netplan apply
```

Then restart systemd-networkd.

```
sudo systemctl restart systemd-networkd
```

You can use the **networkctl** command to see if your wireless device has been properly configured and is connected. The **networkctl** command works only for systemd-networkd..

```
$ networkctl
IDX LINK          TYPE          OPERATIONAL SETUP
  1 lo            loopback      carrier     unmanaged
  2 enp7s0        ether         routable    configured
  3 wlp6s0        wlan          routable    configured

3 links listed.
```

Switching between systemd-networkd and network-manager

Your original Netplan configuration file for NetworkManager, **01-network-manager-al.yaml**, should still be in your **/etc/netplan** directory.

To change from systemd-networkd back to NetworkManager, first stop and disable systemd-networkd with the **systemctl** command.

```
sudo systemctl stop systemd-networkd
sudo systemctl disable systemd-networkd
```

Then enable and start NetworkManager. Use the service name for NetworkManager, **network-manager**. Also, remove or move the systemd-networkd netplan file in the **/etc/netplan** directory so that it is not read. You could also just rename the extension.

```
sudo systemctl enable network-manager
sudo systemctl start network-manager
sudo mv /etc/netplan/netplan/02-dhcp.yaml /home
```

You can use the status command for systemctl to see if your network device is active or inactive.

```
systemctl status systemd-networkd
systemctl status network-manager
```

To change back to systemd-networkd, disable NetworkManager and enable systemd-networkd. Also add your systemd-networkd netplan file back to the **/etc/netplan** directory.

```
sudo systemctl stop network-manager
sudo systemctl disable network-manager
sudo systemctl enable systemd-networkd
sudo systemctl start systemd-networkd
```

If your NetworkManager file is, for some reason, missing from the /etc/netplan directory, you can just copy the **network_manager.yaml** file from the netplan.io doc directory, **/usr/share/doc/netplan.io/examples**.

```
cd /usr/share/doc/netplan.io/examples
sudo cp network_manager.yaml  /etc/netplan/1-network-manager.yaml
```

Then use the netplan command with the apply option to generate a new network configuration file.

```
sudo netplan generate
sudo netplan apply
```

Firewalls

You can choose from several different popular firewall management tools. Ubuntu provides a firewall management tool called the Uncomplicated Firewall (ufw), which is based on IPtables. You can also choose to use other popular management tools like FirewallD or Fwbuilder. FirewallD does not use IPtables but uses a firewall daemon instead. Both ufw and FirewallD are covered in this chapter. Search Synaptic Package Manager for "firewall" to see a complete listing.

Important Firewall Ports

Commonly used services like Linux and Windows file sharing, FTP servers, BitTorrent, and Secure SHell remote access, use certain network connection ports on your system (see Table 15-4). A default firewall configuration will block these ports. You have to configure your firewall to allow access to the ports these services use before the services will work.

Port number	Service
135,137,138,and 445	Samba ports and Microsoft discovery service (445): 135 and 445 use the TCP Protocol, and 137 and 138 use the UDP protocol.
139	Netbios-ssn
22	Secure SHell, ssh
2049	NFS, Linux and Unix shares
631	IPP, Internet Printing Protocol, access to remote Linux/Unix printers
21	FTP
25	SMTP, forward mail
110	POP3, receive mail
143	IMAP, receive mail

Table 15-4: Service ports

For example, to access a Windows share, you not only have to have the Samba service running, but also have to configure your firewall to allow access on ports 135, 137, 138 (the ports Samba services use to connect to Windows systems), and port 445 used for Microsoft network discovery. In particular, to allow direct access to the detected shares on your system (Avahi), you have to allow access on port 139. Most can be selected easily as preconfigured items in firewall configuration tools, like Gufw and FirewallD. Some, though, may not be listed.

Setting up a firewall with ufw

The Uncomplicated Firewall, ufw, is the supported firewall application for Ubuntu. It provides a simple firewall that can be managed with the Gufw desktop interface or with **ufw** commands. Like all firewall applications, ufw uses IPtables to define rules and run the firewall. The ufw application is just a management interface for IPtables. The IPtables rule files are held in the **/etc/ufw** directory. Default IPtables rules are kept in **before** and **after** files, with added rules in user files. Firewall configuration for certain packages will be placed in the **/usr/share/ufw.d** directory. The ufw firewall is started up using the Upstart script **/etc/init/ufs.conf** script. You can find out more about ufw at the Ubuntu Firewall site at **https://wiki.ubuntu.com/UncomplicatedFirewall** and at the Ubuntu firewall section in the Ubuntu Server Guide at **http://doc.ubuntu.com**. The Server Guide also shows information on how to implement IP Masquerading on ufw.

Gufw

Gufw provides an easy to use GNOME interface for managing your ufw firewall. A simple interface lets you add rules, both custom and standard. You can install Gufw from Ubuntu Software or from the Synaptic Package Manager (Universe repository, **gufw** package). On the Applications overview, search on firewall and choose Firewall Configuration. If Gufw does not start, you may also have to install the **python-gobject** package.

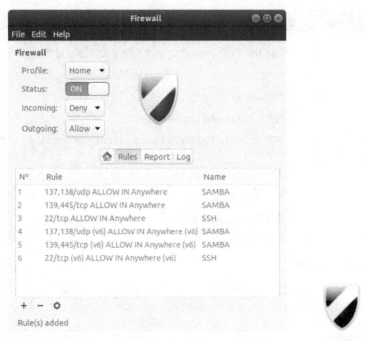

Figure 15-18: Gufw

```
sudo apt-get install python-gobject
```

Gufw will initially open with the firewall disabled, with no ports configured. The application is locked initially. The Status button is set to off, and the shield image will be gray. To enable the firewall, just click the left side of the Status button, setting the status to on. The shield image will be colored and the firewall rules will be listed. Figure 15-18 shows the firewall enabled and several rules listed Samba ports. Rules for both IPv4 and IPv6 (**v6**) network protocols are listed.

The Gufw dialog has a Firewall section and three tabs: Rules, Report, and Log. The Firewall section has a Status button for turning the firewall on or off. There is a Profile menu for Home, Office, and Public configurations. The Incoming and Outgoing drop down menus for setting the default firewall rules. Options are Deny, Reject, or Allow, and are applied to incoming and outgoing traffic respectively. By default, incoming traffic is denied (Deny), and outgoing traffic is allowed (Allow). Rules you specified in the Rules tab will make exceptions, allowing only certain traffic in or out. Should you select the Allow option, the firewall accepts all incoming traffic. In this case you should set up rules to deny access to some traffic, otherwise, the firewall becomes ineffective, allowing access to all traffic. The Report tab lists active services and ports such as the Samba server (smbd) on port 139. The Log tab list firewall notices. You can copy notices, as well as delete a log. The Home tab provides basic help on how to use Gufw.

To add a rule, click the Rules tab, and then click the plus button (**+**) on the lower left corner of the Rules tab to open the "Add rule" dialog, which has three tabs for managing rules: Preconfigured, Simple, and Advanced. The Preconfigured tab provides five menus: the first for the policy (Allow, Deny, Reject, and Limit), the second for the traffic direction (In or Out), the third for the category of the application and the fourth for a subcategory, and the fifth for the particular application or service for the rule. The main categories are Audio video, Games, Network, Office, and System. The Network category lists most network services like SSH, Samba, and FTP. Should there be a security issue with the rule, a warning is displayed.

Figure 15-19: Gufw Preconfigured rules

Should you need to modify the default rule for an application, you can click on the arrow button to open the Advanced tab for that rule.

Click the Add button to add the rule. Once added a port entry for the rule appears in the Rules section. In Figure 15-19 the Samba service has been selected and then added, showing up in the Rules section as "137,138/udp ALLOW IN Anywhere."

Applications and services can also be blocked. To prevent access by the FTP service, you would first select Deny, then Service, and then the FTP entry.

Besides Allow and Deny, you can also choose a Limit option. The Limit option will enable connection rate limiting, restricting connections to no more than 6 every 30 seconds for a given port. This is meant to protect against brute force attacks.

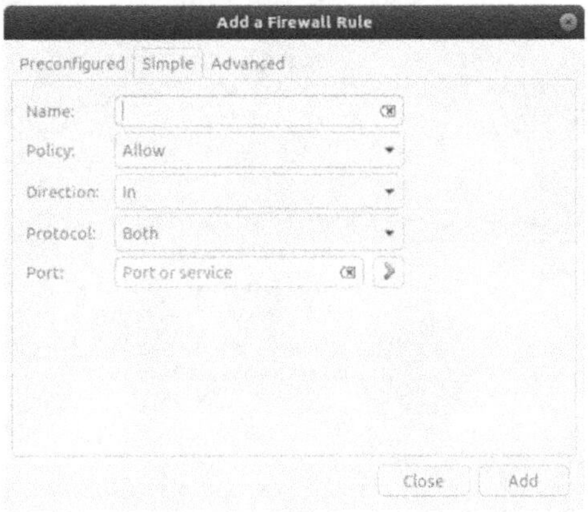

Figure 15-20: Gufw Simple rules

Should there be no preconfigured entry, you can use the Simple tab to allow access to a port (see Figure 15-20). The first menu is for the rule (Allow, Deny, Reject, and Limit), and the second for the protocol (TCP, UDP, or both). In the Port text box, you enter the port number.

On the Advanced tab, you can enter more complex rules. You can set up allow or deny rules for tcp or udp protocols, and specify the incoming and outgoing host (ip) and port (see Figure 15-21).

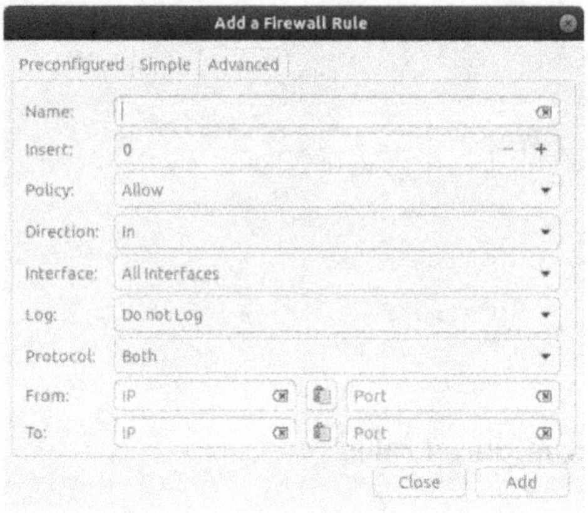

Figure 15-21: Gufw Advanced rules

If you decide to remove a rule, select it in the Rules section and then click the minus button on the lower left corner (–). To remove several rules, click and press Shift-click or use Ctrl-click to select a collection of rules, and then click the minus button.

You can edit any rule by selecting it and clicking the edit button (gear image) to open an "Update a Firewall Rule" dialog (see Figure 15-22). For a default or simple rule, you can only change a few options, but you can turn on logging.

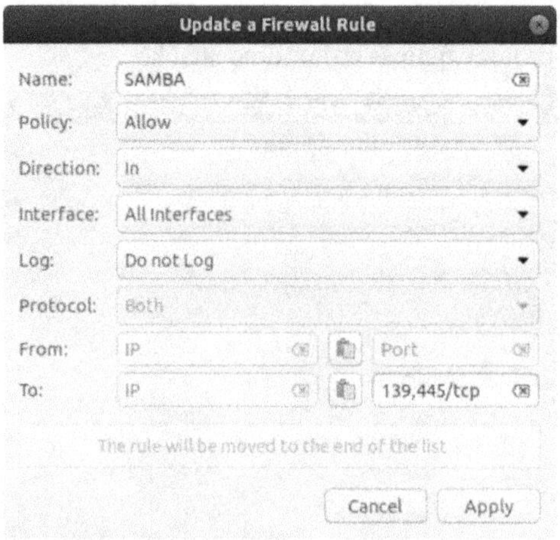

Figure 15-22: Gufw edit a rule

You can also create rules for detected active ports. Click the Report tab and then select a port and click on the plus button at the bottom of the tab. An "Add a Firewall Rule" dialog opens to the Advanced tab with the name of the service active on that port and the port number (see Figure 15-23). You can change any of the options. The port number is already entered.

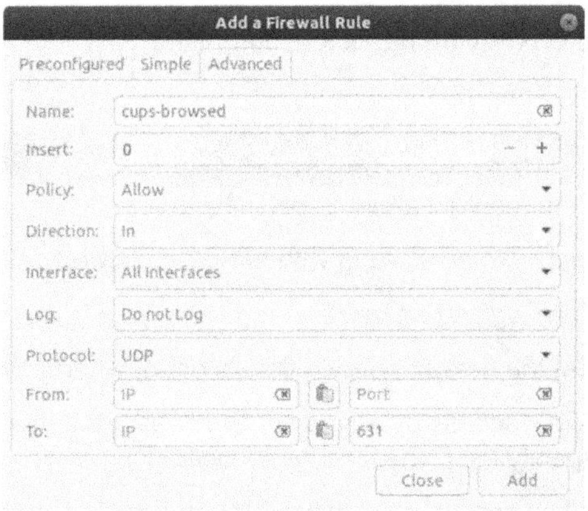

Figure 15-23: Gufw create a rule for an active port

ufw commands

You can also manage your ufw firewall using **ufw** commands entered on a command line in a Terminal window. A **ufw** command requires administrative access and must be run with the **sudo** command. To check the current firewall status, listing those services allowed or blocked, use the **status** command.

```
sudo ufw status
```

If the firewall is not enabled, you first will have to enable it with the **enable** command.

```
sudo ufw enable
```

You can restart the firewall, reloading your rules, using the **service** command with the **restart** option.

```
sudo service ufw restart
```

You can add rules using allow and deny rules and their options as listed in Table 15-5. To allow a service, specify the allow rule and the service name. This is the name for the service listed in the **/etc/services** file. For connection rate limiting, use the **limit** option in place of **allow**. The following allows the ftp service.

```
sudo ufw allow ftp
```

If the service you want is not listed in **/etc/services**, and you know the port and protocol it uses, you can specify the port and protocol directly. For example, the Samba service uses port 445 and protocol tcp (among others, see Table 15-4).

```
sudo ufw allow 445/tcp
```

The status operation shows what services the firewall rules allow currently.

```
sudo ufw status
To                  Action          From
21:tcp              ALLOW           Anywhere
21:udp              ALLOW           Anywhere
445:tcp             ALLOW           Anywhere
```

To remove a rule, prefix it with the **delete** command.

```
sudo ufw delete allow 445/tcp
```

Commands	Description
enable | disable	Turn the firewall on or off
status	Display status along with services allowed or denied.
logging on | off	Turn logging on or off
default allow | deny	Set the default policy, allow is open, whereas deny is restrictive
allow *service*	Allow access by a service. Services are defined in **/etc/services**, which specify the ports for that service.
allow *port /protocol*	Allow access on a particular port using specified protocol.
deny *service*	Deny access by a service
delete *rule*	Delete an installed rule, use allow, deny, or limit and include rule specifics.
proto *protocol*	Specify protocol in allow, deny, or limit rule
from *address*	Specify source address in allow, deny, or limit rule
to *address*	Specify destination address in allow, deny, or limit rule
port *port*	Specify port in allow, deny, or limit rule for from and to address

Table 15-5: UFW firewall operations

More detailed rules can be specified using address, port, and protocol commands. These are very similar to the actual IPtables commands. Packets to and from particular networks, hosts, and ports can be controlled. The following denies ssh access (port 22) from host 192.168.03.

```
sudo ufw deny proto tcp from 192.168.03 to any port 22
```

ufw rule files

The rules you add are placed in the **/lib/ufw/user.rules** file as IPtables rules. The ufw program is just a front end for **iptables-restore**, which will read this file and set up the firewall using **iptables** commands. **ufw** will also have **iptables-restore** read the **before.rules** and **after.rules** files in the **/etc/ufw** directory. These files are considered administrative files that include needed supporting rules for your IPtables firewall. Administrators can add their own IPtables rules to these files for system specific features like IP Masquerading. The **before.rules** file will specify a table with the * symbol, as in ***filter** for the netfilter table. For the NAT table, you would use ***nat**. At the end of each table segment, a COMMIT command is needed to instruct ufw to apply the rules. Rules use **-A** for allow and **-D** for deny, assuming the **iptables** command.

Default settings for ufw are placed in **/etc/default/ufw**. Here you will find the default INPUT, OUTPUT, and FORWARD policies specified by setting associated variables, like DEFAULT_INPUT_POLICY for INPUT and DEFAULT_OUTPUT_POLICY for OUTPUT. The DEFAULT_INPUT_POLICY variable is set to DROP, making DROP the default policy for the INPUT rule. The DEFAULT_OUTPUT_POLICY variable is set to ACCEPT, and the DEFAULT_FORWARD_POLICY variable is set to DROP. To allow IP Masquerading, DEFAULT_FORWARD_POLICY would have to be set to ACCEPT. These entries set default policies only. Any user rules you have set up would take precedence.

FirewallD and firewall-config

Though not supported by Ubuntu directly, you can use the new FirewallD dynamic firewall daemon to set up a firewall. To configure FirewallD you use the **firewalld-config** graphical interface. You can also use **firewalld-cmd** command from the command line. To set up your firewall, run firewall-config (System | Firewall) (see Figure 15-24). You can install firewalld-config as Firewall Configuration on Ubuntu Software . Both the FirewallD daemon and the firewalld-config packages are installed.

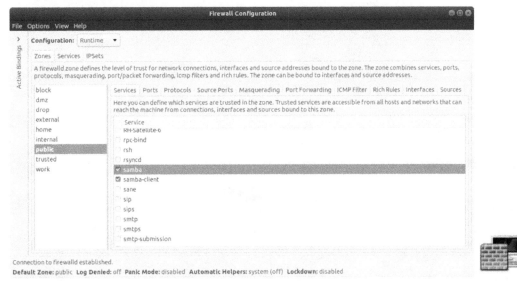

Figure 15-24: firewall-config: Runtime Configuration

You will have to start the FirewallD daemon in a terminal window with the following command.

```
sudo service firewalld start
```

You can stop it with a stop command.

```
sudo service firewalld stop
```

With **firewall-config,** you can configure either a Runtime or Permanent configuration. Select one from the Configuration menu. The Runtime configuration shows your current runtime set up, whereas a Permanent configuration does not take effect until you reload or restart. If you wish to edit your zones and services, you need to choose the Permanent Configuration (see Figure 15-25). This view displays a zone toolbar for editing zone at the bottom of the zone scroll box, and an Edit Services button on the Services tab for editing service protocols, ports, and destination addresses.

Additional tabs can be displayed from the View menu for configuring ICMP types, and for adding firewall rules directly (Direct Configuration).

From the Options menu, you can reload your saved firewall.

Figure 15-25: firewall-config: Permanent Configuration

Figure 15-26: Default Zone

A firewall configuration is set up for a given zone, such as a home, work, internal, external, or public zone. Zones provide an added level of protection by the firewall. They divide the network protected by the Firewall into separate segments, which can only communicate as permitted by the firewall. In effect, zones separate one part of your network from another. Each zone has its own configuration. Zones are listed in the Zone scroll box on the left side of the firewall-config window. Select the one you want to configure. The firewall-config window opens to the default, Public. You can choose the default zone from the System Default Zone dialog (see Figure 15-26), which you open from the Options menu as "Change Default Zone."

To the left of the Zones tab is the Active Bindings section, which list the network connections, interfaces, and sources on your system. For each active connection the zone bound to it is listed, such as the public zone bound to the wired connection in Figure 10-37. To change the zone bound to an connection you select the entry and click the Change Zone button at the bottom of the Active Binding section. This open a Select zone dialog where you can choose a different zone to be bound to connection. You can choose from any of the zones in the zones tab. You can also change connection binding from the Options menu by choosing "Change Zones of Connections."

If you choose Permanent Configuration from the Current View Menu, a toolbar for zones is displayed below the Zone scroll box, as shown here. The plus button lets you add a zone, minus removes a zone. The pencil button lets you edit a zone. The add and edit buttons open the Base Zone Settings dialog, where you enter or edit the zone name, version, description, and the target (see Figure 15-27. The default target is ACCEPT. Other options are REJECT and DROP. The Load Zone Defaults button (yellow arrow) loads default settings, removing any you have made.

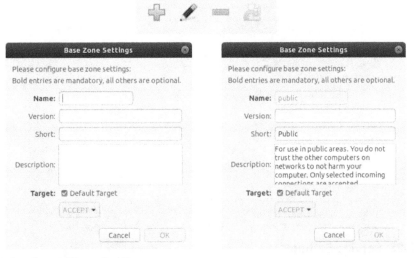

Figure 15-27: Base Zone Settings

Each zone, in turn, can have one or more network connections. From the Options menu choose "Change Zones of Connections" to open the Network Connections dialog where you can add a network connection.

For a given zone you can configure services, ports, masquerading, port forwarding, and ICMP filter. A Linux system is often used to run servers for a network. If you are creating a strong firewall but still want to run a service such as a Web server, an FTP server, Samba desktop browsing, or SSH encrypted connections, you must specify them in the Services tab. Samba desktop browsing lets you access your Samba shares, like remote Windows file systems, from your GNOME or KDE desktops.

For a selected service, you can specify service settings such as ports and protocols it uses, any modules, and specific network addresses. Default settings are already set up for you such as port 139 for Samba, using the TCP protocol. To modify the settings for service, click the Services tab on the Firewall Configuration window to list your services (see Figure 15-28). Choose the service you want to edit from the Service scroll box at the left. For a given service you can then use the Ports, Protocols, Modules, and Destination tabs to specify ports, protocols, modules, and addresses. On the Ports tab, click the Add button to open the Port and Protocol dialog where you can add a port or port range, and choose a protocol from the Protocol menu (see Figure 15-29). On the Destination tab, you can enter an IPv4 or IPv6 destination address for the service.

Your system is already configured to check for updates automatically on a daily basis. You can opt not to check for updates by choosing never from the "Automatically check for updates" menu. You also have options for how updates are handled. You can install any security updates automatically, without confirmation. You can download updates in the background. Or you can just be notified of available updates, and then choose to install them when you want. The options are exclusive.

Figure 15-28: Service Settings

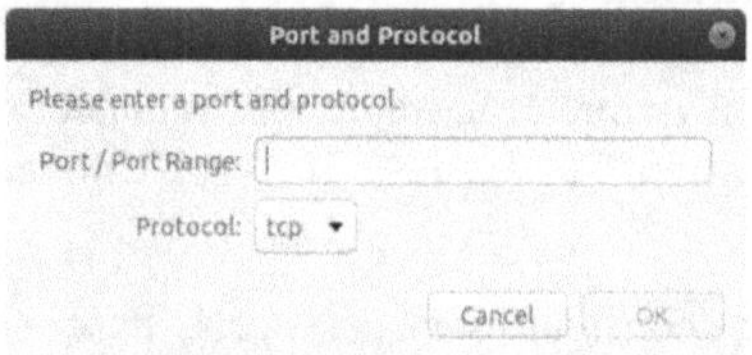

Figure 15-29: Service Protocols and Ports

On the Zones tab, the Ports tab lets you specify ports that you may want opened for certain services, like BitTorrent. Click the Add button to open a dialog where you can select the port number along with the protocol to control (tcp or udp), or enter a specific port number or range.

If your system is being used as a gateway to the Internet for your local network, you can implement masquerading to hide your local hosts from outside access from the Internet. This, though, also requires IP forwarding which is automatically enabled when you choose masquerading. Local hosts will still be able to access the Internet, but they will masquerade as your gateway system. You would select for masquerading the interface that is connected to the Internet. Masquerading is available only for IPv4 networks, not IPv6 networks.

The Port Forwarding tab lets you set up port forwarding, channeling transmissions from one port to another, or to a different port on another system. Click the Add button to add a port, specifying its protocol and destination (see Figure 15-30).

Figure 15-30: Port Forwarding

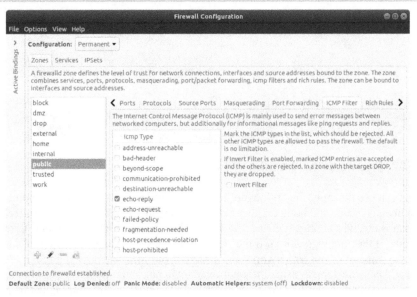

Figure 15-31: ICMP Filters

The ICMP Filters tab allows you to block ICMP messages. By default, all ICMP messages are allowed. Blocking ICMP messages makes for a more secure system. Certain types of ICMP messages are often blocked as they can be used to infiltrate or overload a system, such as the ping and pong ICMP messages (see Figure 15-31).

If you have specific firewall rules to add, use the Direct Configuration tab (displayed from the View | Direct Configuration menu).

GNOME Nettool

The GNOME Nettool utility (**gnome-nettool**) provides a GNOME interface for network information tools like the ping and traceroute operations as well as Finger, Whois, and Lookup for querying users and hosts on the network (see Figure 15-32). You can install it from the Ubuntu Software Center as Network Tools. Nettool is installed by default and is accessible from the Applications overview as Network Tools. The first tab, Devices, describes your connected network devices, including configuration and transmission information about each device, such as the hardware address and bytes transmitted. Both IPv4 and IPv6 host IP addresses are listed.

Figure 15-32: Gnome network tool

You can use the ping, finger, lookup, whois, and traceroute operations to find out status information about systems and users on your network. The ping operation is used to check if a remote system is up and running. You use finger to find out information about other users on your network, seeing if they are logged in or if they have received mail. The traceroute tool can be used to track the sequence of computer networks and systems your message passed through on its way to you. Whois will provide domain name information about a particular domain, and Lookup will provide both domain name and IP addresses. Netstat shows your network routing (addresses used) and active service (open ports and the protocols they use). Port Scan lists the ports and services they use on a given connection (address).

Predictable and unpredictable network device names

Network devices now use a predictable naming method that differs from the older naming method. Names are generated based on the specific device referencing the network device type, its hardware connection and slot, and even its function. The traditional network device names used the **eth** prefix with the number of the device for an Ethernet network device. The name **eth0** referred to the first Ethernet connection on your computer. This naming method was considered unpredictable as it did not accurately reference the actual Ethernet device. The old system relied on probing the network driver at boot, and if you're your system had several Ethernet connections, the names could end up being switched, depending you how the startup proceeded. With systemd udev version 197, the naming changed to a predictable method that specifies a particular device. The predictable method references the actual hardware connection on your system.

The name used to reference predictable device names connection has a prefix for the type of device followed by several qualifiers such as the type of hardware, the slot used, and the function number. Instead of the older unpredictable name like **eth0**, the first Ethernet device is referenced by a name like **enp7s0**. The interface name **enp7s0** references an Ethernet (en) connection, at pci slot 7 (p7) with the hotplug slot index number 0 (s0). **wlp6s0** is a wireless (wl) connection, at pci slot 6 (p6) with the hotplug slot index number 0 (s0). **virvb0** is a virtual (vir) bridge (vb) network interface. Table 15-6 lists predictable naming prefixes.

Name	Description
sen	Ethernet
sl	serial line IP (slip)
wl	wlan, wireless local area network
ww	wwan, wireless wide area network (mobile broadband)
p	pci geographical location (pci-e slot)
s	hotplug slot index number
o	onboard cards
f	function (used for cards with more than one port)
u	USB port
i	USB port interface

Table 15-6: Network Interface Device Naming

Unlike the older unpredictable name, the predictable name will most likely be different for each computer. Predictable network names, along with alternatives, are discussed at:

https://www.freedesktop.org/wiki/Software/systemd/PredictableNetworkInterfaceName
s/

The naming is carried out by the kernel and is describe in the comment section of the kernel source's **systemd/src/udev/udev-bultin-net_id.c** file.

Network device path names

The directory /sys/devices lists all your devices in subdirectories, including your network devices. The path to the devices progresses through subdirectories named for the busses connecting the device. To quickly find the full path name, you can us the /sys/class directory instead. For network devices use /sys/class/net. Then use the ls -l command to list the network devices with their links to the full pathname in the /sys/devices directory (the **../..** path references a cd change up two directories (class/net) to the /sys directory).

```
$ cd /sys/class/net
$ ls
enp7s0  lo  wlp6s0
$ ls -l
total 0
lrwxrwxrwx 1 root root 0 Feb 19 12:27 enp7s0 ->
../../devices/pci0000:00/0000:00:1c.3/0000:07:00.0/net/enp7s0
lrwxrwxrwx 1 root root 0 Feb 19 12:27 lo -> ../../devices/virtual/net/lo
lrwxrwxrwx 1 root root 0 Feb 19 12:28 wlp6s0 ->
../../devices/pci0000:00/0000:00:1c.2/0000:06:00.0/net/wlp6s0
```

So the full path name in the /sys/devices directory for enp7s0 is:

```
/sys/devices/pci0000:00/0000:00:1c.3/0000:07:00.0/net/enp7s0
```

You can find the pci bus slot used with the lspci command. This command lists all your pci connected devices. In this example, the pci bus slot used 7, which is why the pci part of the name enp7s0 is p7. The s part refers to a hotplug slot, in this example s0.

```
$ lspci
06:00.0 Network controller: Qualcomm Atheros QCA9565 / AR9565 Wireless Network
Adapter (rev 01)
07:00.0 Ethernet controller: Realtek Semiconductor Co., Ltd. RTL8101/2/6E PCI
Express Fast/Gigabit Ethernet controller (rev 07)
```

Devices have certain properties defined by udev, which manages all devices. Some operations, such as systemd link files, make use these properties. The ID_PATH, ID_NET_NAME_MAC, and INTERFACE properties can be used to identify a device to udev. To display these properties, you use the **udevadm** command to query the udev database. With the **info** and **-e** options, properties of all active devices are displayed. You can pipe (|) this output to a **grep** command to display only those properties for a given device. In the following example, the properties for the **enp7s0** device are listed. Preceding the properties for a given device is a line, beginning (^) with a "P" and ending with the device name. The **.*** matching characters match all other intervening characters on that line, **^P.*enp7s0**. The **-A** option displays the specified number of additional lines after that match, **-A 22**.

```
$ udevadm info -e | grep -A 22 ^P.*enp7s0
P: /devices/pci0000:00/0000:00:1c.3/0000:07:00.0/net/enp7s0
E: DEVPATH=/devices/pci0000:00/0000:00:1c.3/0000:07:00.0/net/enp7s0
E: ID_BUS=pci
E: ID_MM_CANDIDATE=1
E: ID_MODEL_FROM_DATABASE=RTL8101/2/6E PCI Express Fast/Gigabit Ethernet
controller
E: ID_MODEL_ID=0x8136
E: ID_NET_DRIVER=r8169
```

```
E:  ID_NET_LINK_FILE=/lib/systemd/network/99-default.link
E:  ID_NET_NAME_MAC=enx74e6e20ec729
E:  ID_NET_NAME_PATH=enp7s0
E:  ID_OUI_FROM_DATABASE=Dell Inc.
E:  ID_PATH=pci-0000:07:00.0
E:  ID_PATH_TAG=pci-0000_07_00_0
E:  ID_PCI_CLASS_FROM_DATABASE=Network controller
E:  ID_PCI_SUBCLASS_FROM_DATABASE=Ethernet controller
E:  ID_VENDOR_FROM_DATABASE=Realtek Semiconductor Co., Ltd.
E:  ID_VENDOR_ID=0x10ec
E:  IFINDEX=2
E:  INTERFACE=enp7s0
E:  SUBSYSTEM=net
E:  SYSTEMD_ALIAS=/sys/subsystem/net/devices/enp7s0
E:  TAGS=:systemd:
E:  USEC_INITIALIZED=1080179
```

For certain tasks, such as renaming, you many need to know the MAC address. You can find this with the ip link command, which you can abbreviate to ip l. The MAC address is before the brd string. In this example, the MAC address for enp7s0 is 74:e6:e2:0e:c7:29. The ip link command also provides the MTU (Maximum Transmission Unit) and the current state of the connection.

```
$ ip link
1: lo: <LOOPBACK,UP,LOWER_UP> mtu 65536 qdisc noqueue state UNKNOWN mode DEFAULT
group default qlen 1 link/loopback 00:00:00:00:00:00 brd 00:00:00:00:00:00
2: enp7s0: <BROADCAST,MULTICAST,UP,LOWER_UP> mtu 1500 qdisc fq_codel state UP
mode DEFAULT group default qlen 1000 link/ether 74:e6:e2:0e:c7:29 brd
ff:ff:ff:ff:ff:ff
3: wlp6s0: <BROADCAST,MULTICAST> mtu 1500 qdisc noop state DOWN mode DEFAULT
group default qlen 1000 link/ether 4c:bb:58:22:40:1d brd ff:ff:ff:ff:ff:ff
```

Renaming network device names with udev rules

If you should change your hardware, like your motherboard with its Ethernet connection, or, if you use an Ethernet card and simply change the slot it is connected to, then the name will change. For firewall rules referencing a particular Ethernet connection, this could be a problem. You can, if you wish, change the name to one of your own choosing, even using the older unpredictable names. This way you would only have to update the name change, rather than all your rules and any other code that reference the network device by name.

You can change device name by adding a user udev rule for network device names. Changes made with udev rules work for both NetworkManager and systemd-networkd. In the **/etc/udev/rules.d** directory, create a file with the .rules extension and prefixed by a number less than 80, such as **70-my-net-names.rules**.The .rules files in **/etc/udev/rules.d** take precedence over those in the udev system directory, **/lib/udev/rules.d**.

In the udev rule, identify the subsystem as net (SUBSYSTEM=="net"), the action to take as add (ACTION=="add")), then the MAC address (ATTR[address}, the address attribute). Use ip link to obtain the mac address. The MAC address is also listed as the ID_NET_NAME_MAC entry in the **udevadm info** output (be sure to remove the prefix and add intervening colons). Use the NAME field to specify the new name for the device. Use the single = operator to make the name assignment.

/etc/udev/rules.d/70-my-net-names.rules

```
SUBSYSTEM=="net", ACTION=="add", ATTR{address}=="74:e6:e2:0e:c7:29", NAME="eth0"
```

To further specify the device you can add the kernel name (KERNEL) of the device. The kernel name is the INTERFACE entry.

```
SUBSYSTEM=="net", ACTION=="add", ATTR{address}=="74:e6:e2:0e:c7:29",
KERNEL=="enp7s0", NAME="eth0"
```

Renaming network device names for systemd-networkd with systemd.link

The systemd-networkd manager provides an alternate way to change network device names (keep in mind that an udev rule will also work for systemd-networkd). To change the name you would set up a systemd link file in the /etc/systemd/network directory. The systemd.link man page shows how to do this. A systemd link file consists of Match and Link sections. In the Match section you specify the network device, and in the Link section to specify the name you want to give it. The network device can be referenced by its predictable name (Path) or MAC address (MACAddress).

The default systemd link file is /lib/systemd/network/99-default.link. The file had only a Link section which lists policies to use in determining the name. The NamePolicy key lists the policies to be checked, starting with the kernel, then the udev database, udev firmware onboard information, udev hot-plug slot information, and the device path. In most cases, the slot policy is used. The MACAddressPolicy is set to persistent, for devices that have or need fixed MAC addresses.

99-default.link

```
[Link]
NamePolicy=kernel database onboard slot path
MACAddressPolicy=persistent
```

To rename a device, you would set up a systemd link file in the /etc/systemd/network directory. The /etc/systemd directory takes precedence over the /lib/systemd directory. A link file consists of a priority number, any name, and the .link extension. Lower numbers have a higher priority. In this example, the network device enp7s0 has its named changed to eth0. The Match section uses the Path key to match on the device path, using the ID_PATH property for the device provided by udev.

You can query the udev database for information on your network device using the udevadm info command and match on the device. An added **grep** operation for ID_PATH= will display only the ID_PATH property.

```
$ udevadm info -e | grep -A 22 ^P.*enp7s0 | grep ID_PATH=
E: ID_PATH=pci-0000:07:00.0
```

For the Path key, use the udev ID_PATH value and a * glob matching character for the rest of the path. The Link section uses the Name key to specify the new name. The MacAddressPolicy should be set to persistent, indicating a fixed connection. Start the name of the link file with a number less than 99, so as to take precedence over the 99-default.link file.

10-my-netname.link

```
[Match]
Path=pci-0000:07:00.0-*

[Link]
Name=eth0
MacAddressPolicy=persistent
```

Instead of the Path key, you could use the MACAddress key to match on the hardware address of the network device. The MAC address is udev ID_NET_NAME_MAC property without the prefix and with colons separation. The MAC address in this example is 74:e6:e2:0e:c7:29. You can also use **ip link** to find the MAC address (the numbers before **brd**).

10-my-netname.link

```
[Match]
MACAddress=74:e6:e2:0e:c7:29

[Link]
Name=eth0
MacAddressPolicy=persistent
```

Alternatively, you could use the OriginalName key in the Match section instead of the Path. The original name is the udev INTERFACE property, which also the name of the device as displayed by **ifconfig**.

10-my-netname.link

```
[Match]
OriginalName=enp7s0*

[Link]
Name=eth0
MacAddressPolicy=persistent
```

Table Listing

Figure Listing

Index